Shojo Beat

Tail of the Moon™

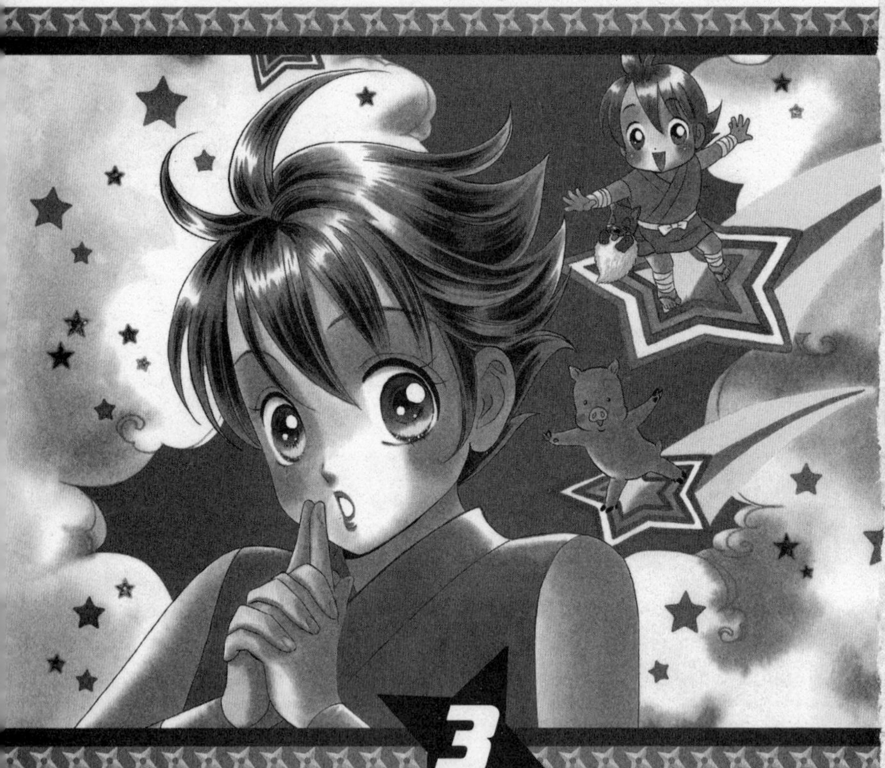

3

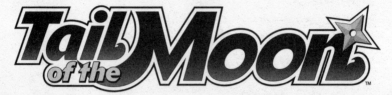

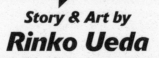

Story & Art by

Rinko Ueda

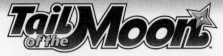

Volume 3

CONTENTS

Story Thus Far...

It is the Era of the Warring States. Usagi is a failure as a ninja, but she is a skilled herbalist. At the age of 15, she is still unable to qualify as a ninja, so she is suddenly ordered to get married!

The man who has been selected for her is Hattori Hanzo (aka "Shimo no Hanzo"), the most handsome man in all of Iga. But after rushing over to meet Hanzo, she is told by Hanzo himself that he has no intention of getting married. Usagi begins to train hard so that Hanzo will accept her.

Usagi and her friends journey to Hamamatsu to help the lovers Kami no Hanzou and Sara, but Usagi is captured and thrown into the castle dungeon! Luckily, with the help of Tokugawa Ieyasu, Hanzou and Sara are permitted to be together, but in exchange Usagi must remain in Hamamatsu as Ieyasu's herbalist.

Usagi starts her new life working with the senior herbalist Yukimaru. Yukimaru looks and sounds like a beautiful girl, but Usagi discovers that Yukimaru is really a boy…?!

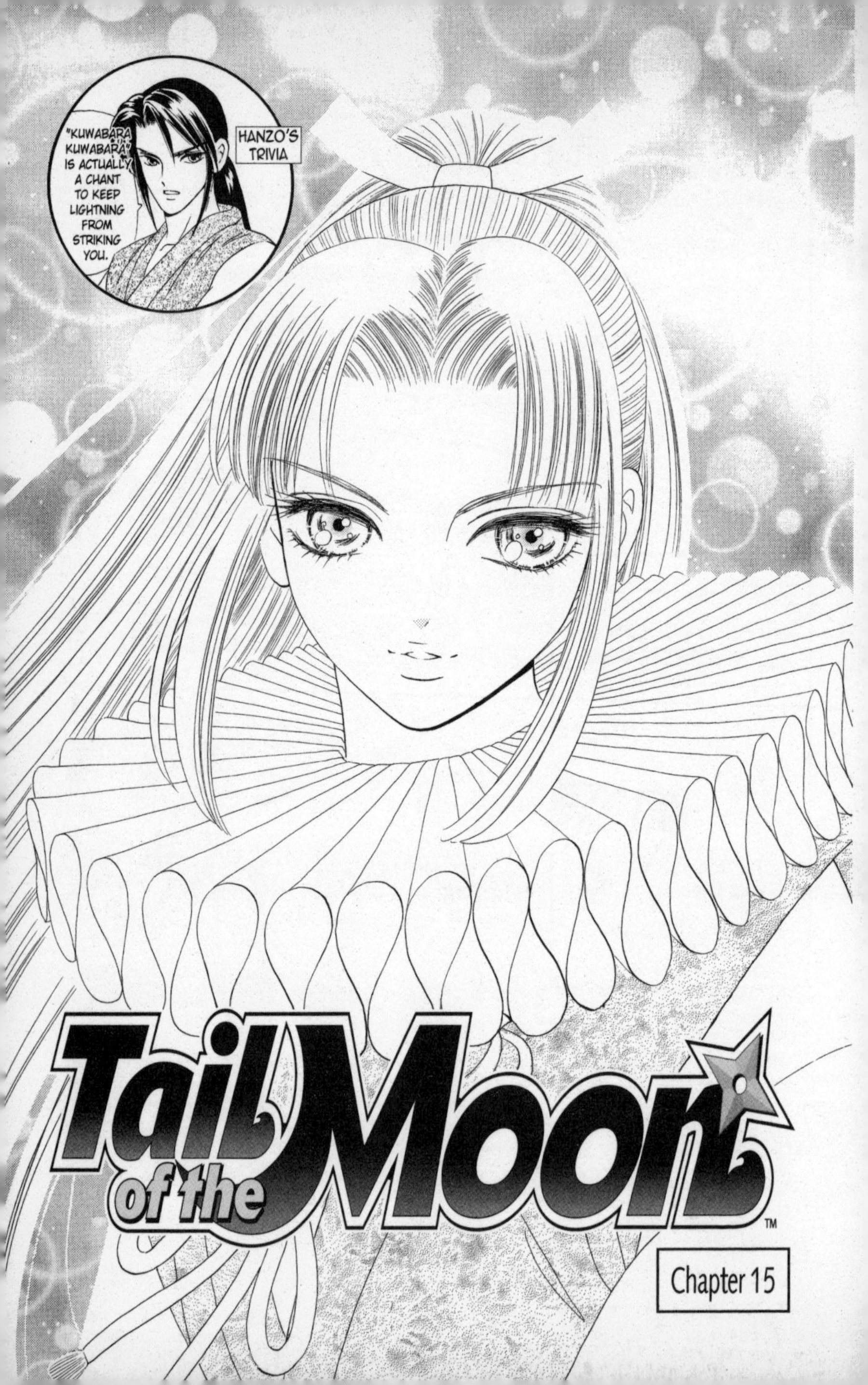
HANZO'S TRIVIA
"KUWABARA KUWABARA" IS ACTUALLY A CHANT TO KEEP LIGHTNING FROM STRIKING YOU.
Tail of the Moon™
Chapter 15

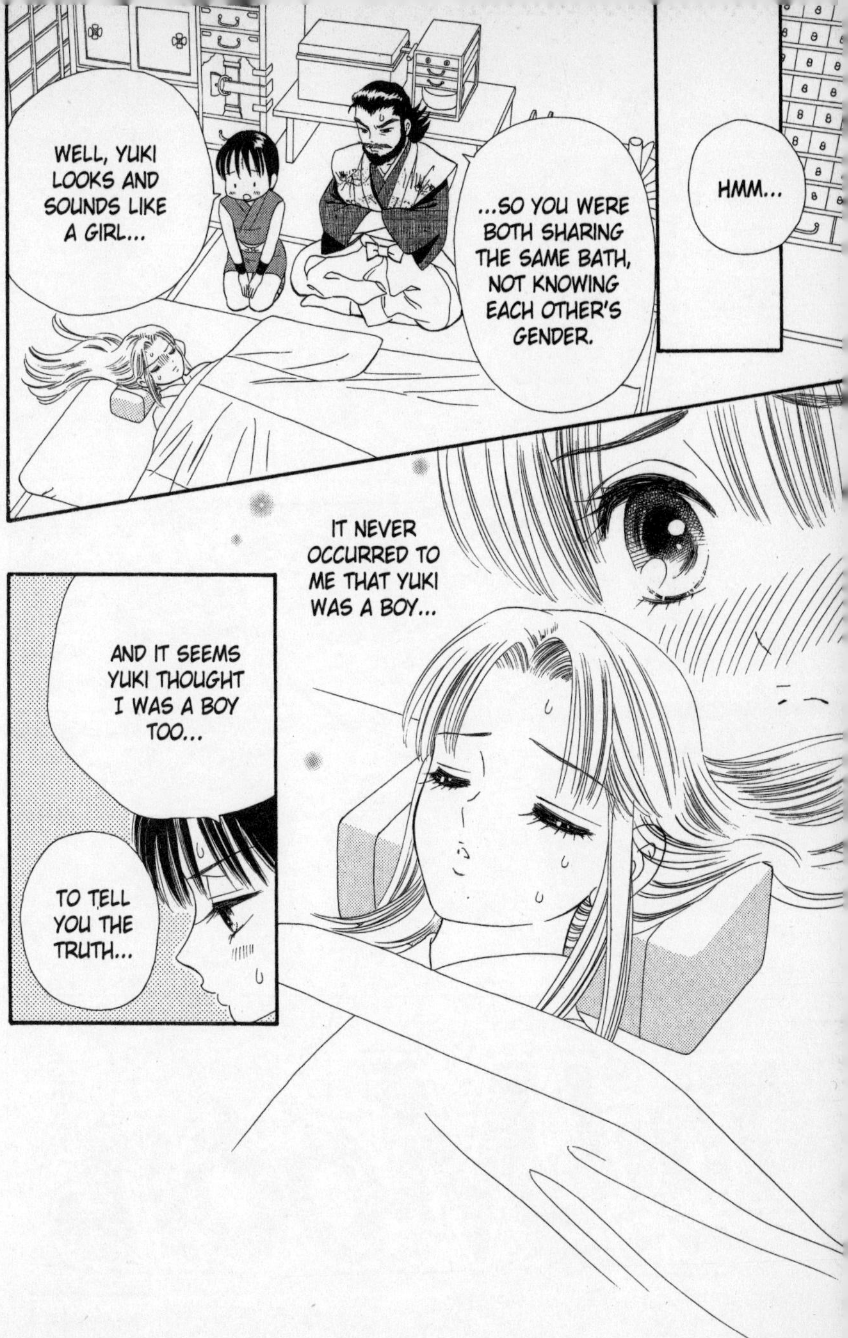
HMM...
...SO YOU WERE BOTH SHARING THE SAME BATH, NOT KNOWING EACH OTHER'S GENDER.
WELL, YUKI LOOKS AND SOUNDS LIKE A GIRL...
IT NEVER OCCURRED TO ME THAT YUKI WAS A BOY...
AND IT SEEMS YUKI THOUGHT I WAS A BOY TOO...
TO TELL YOU THE TRUTH...

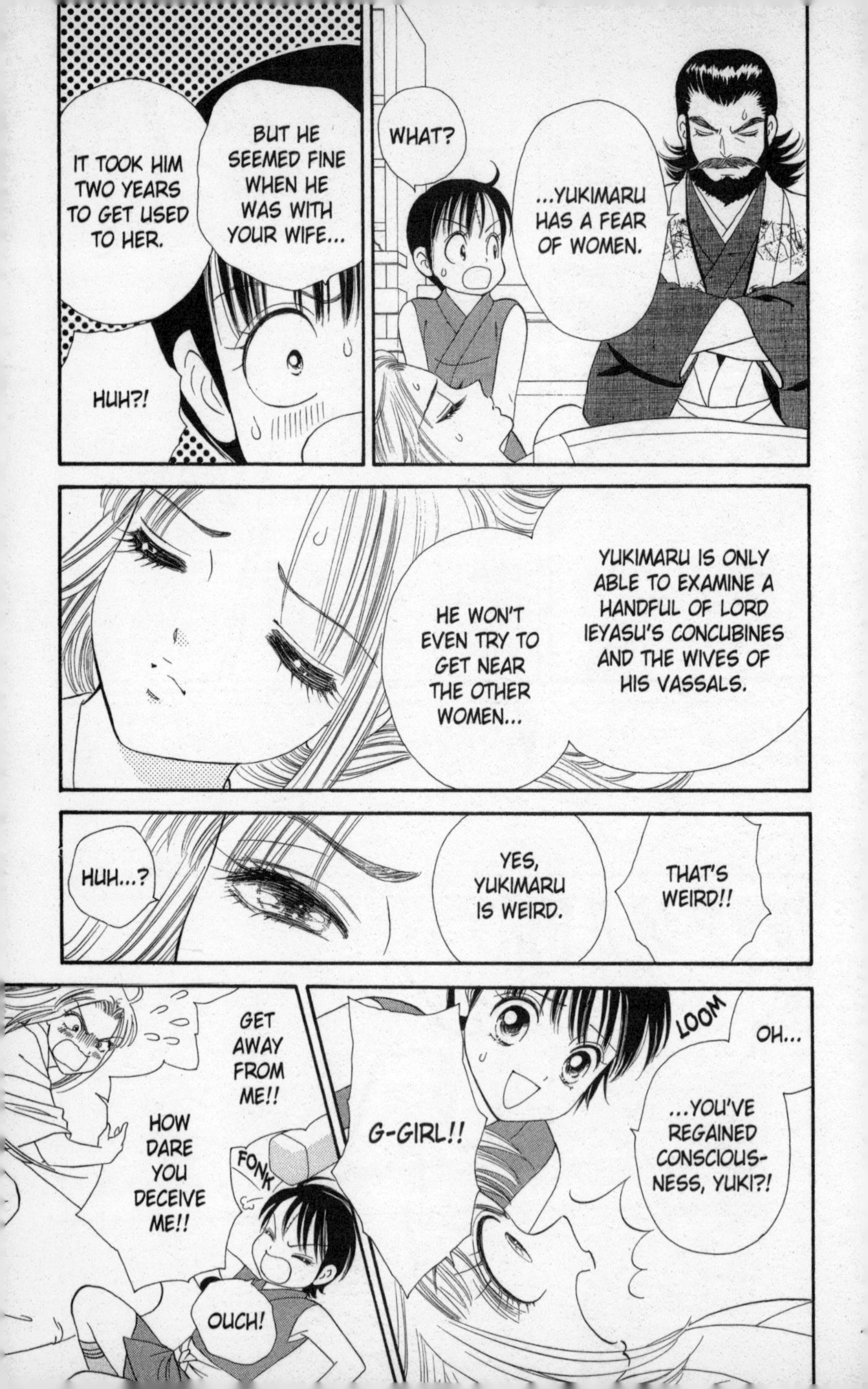
...YUKIMARU HAS A FEAR OF WOMEN.
WHAT?
BUT HE SEEMED FINE WHEN HE WAS WITH YOUR WIFE...
IT TOOK HIM TWO YEARS TO GET USED TO HER.
HUH?!
YUKIMARU IS ONLY ABLE TO EXAMINE A HANDFUL OF LORD IEYASU'S CONCUBINES AND THE WIVES OF HIS VASSALS.
HE WON'T EVEN TRY TO GET NEAR THE OTHER WOMEN...
THAT'S WEIRD!!
YES, YUKIMARU IS WEIRD.
HUH...?
OH...
LOOM
...YOU'VE REGAINED CONSCIOUS-NESS, YUKI?!
G-GIRL!!
GET AWAY FROM ME!!
HOW DARE YOU DECEIVE ME!!
FONK
OUCH!

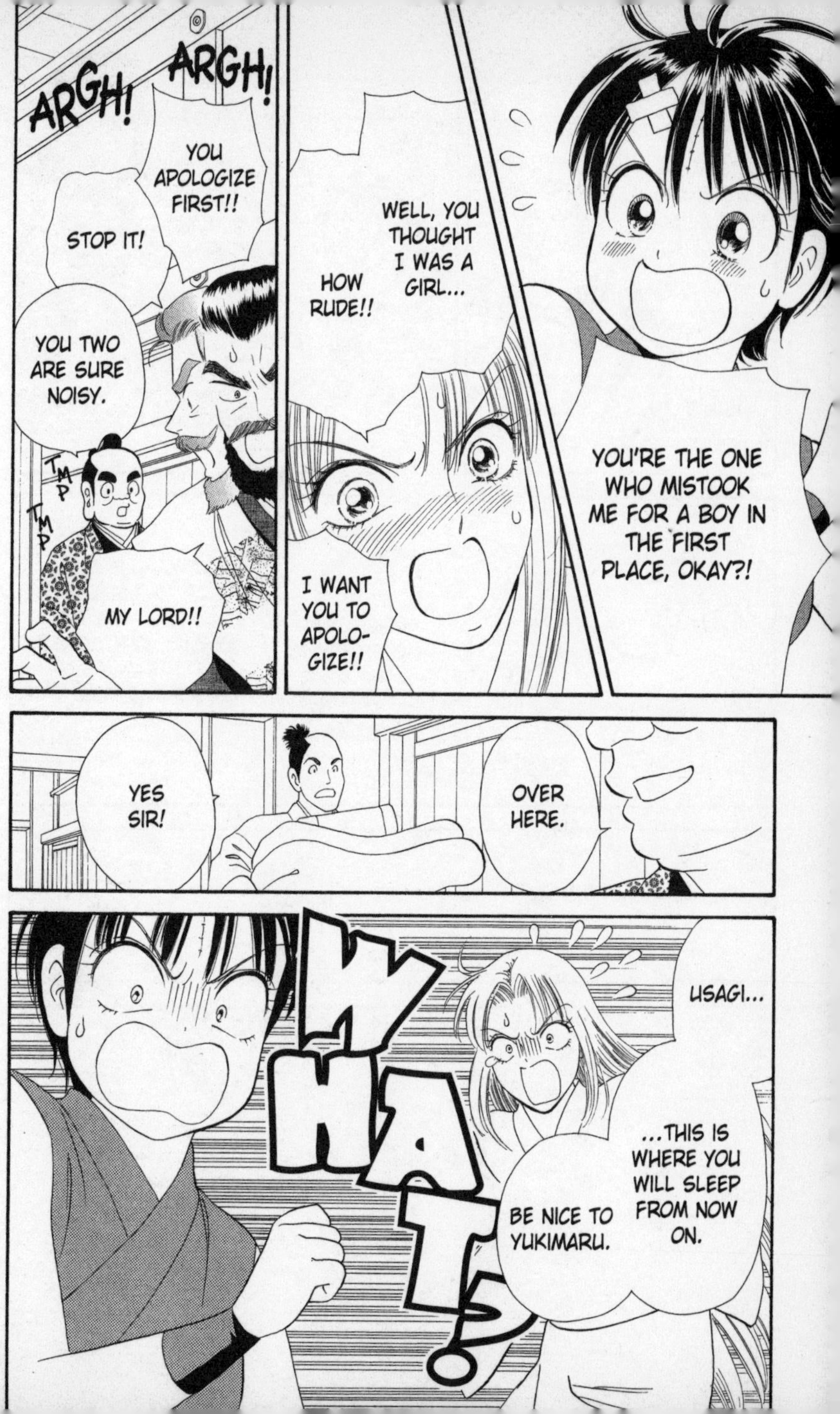
YOU'RE THE ONE WHO MISTOOK ME FOR A BOY IN THE FIRST PLACE, OKAY?!
WELL, YOU THOUGHT I WAS A GIRL...
HOW RUDE!!
I WANT YOU TO APOLOGIZE!!
ARGH!
ARGH!
YOU APOLOGIZE FIRST!!
STOP IT!
YOU TWO ARE SURE NOISY.
TMP
TMP
MY LORD!!
OVER HERE.
YES SIR!
USAGI...
...THIS IS WHERE YOU WILL SLEEP FROM NOW ON.
BE NICE TO YUKIMARU.
WHAT?!

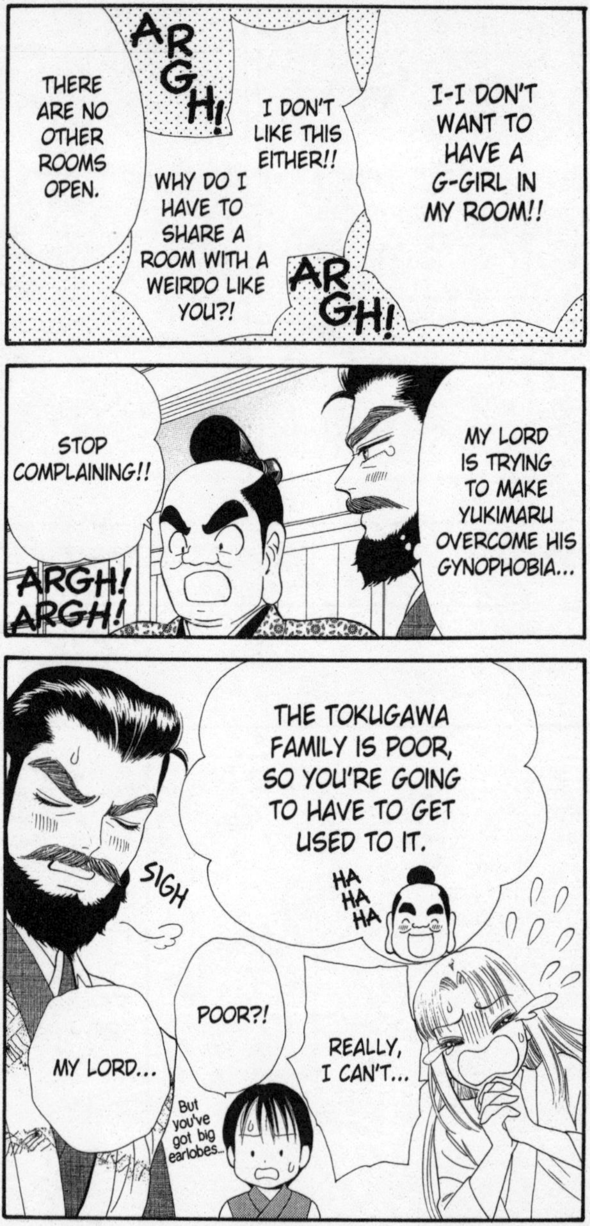
I-I DON'T WANT TO HAVE A G-GIRL IN MY ROOM!!
ARGH!
I DON'T LIKE THIS EITHER!!
WHY DO I HAVE TO SHARE A ROOM WITH A WEIRDO LIKE YOU?!
ARGH!
THERE ARE NO OTHER ROOMS OPEN.
MY LORD IS TRYING TO MAKE YUKIMARU OVERCOME HIS GYNOPHOBIA...
STOP COMPLAINING!!
ARGH! ARGH!
THE TOKUGAWA FAMILY IS POOR, SO YOU'RE GOING TO HAVE TO GET USED TO IT.
HA HA HA
SIGH
REALLY, I CAN'T...
POOR?!
But you've got big earlobes...
MY LORD...

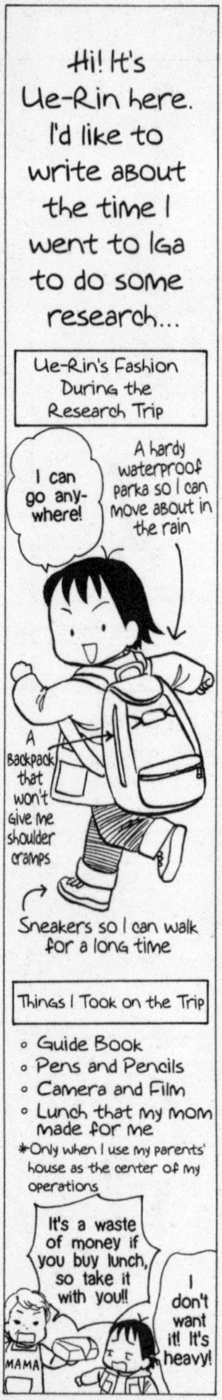
Hi! It's Ue-Rin here. I'd like to write about the time I went to Iga to do some research...
Ue-Rin's Fashion During the Research Trip
A hardy waterproof parka so I can move about in the rain
I can go anywhere!
A backpack that won't give me shoulder cramps
Sneakers so I can walk for a long time
Things I Took on the Trip
∘ Guide Book
∘ Pens and Pencils
∘ Camera and Film
∘ Lunch that my mom made for me
*Only when I use my parents' house as the center of my operations
It's a waste of money if you buy lunch, so take it with you!!
I don't want it! It's heavy!
MAMA

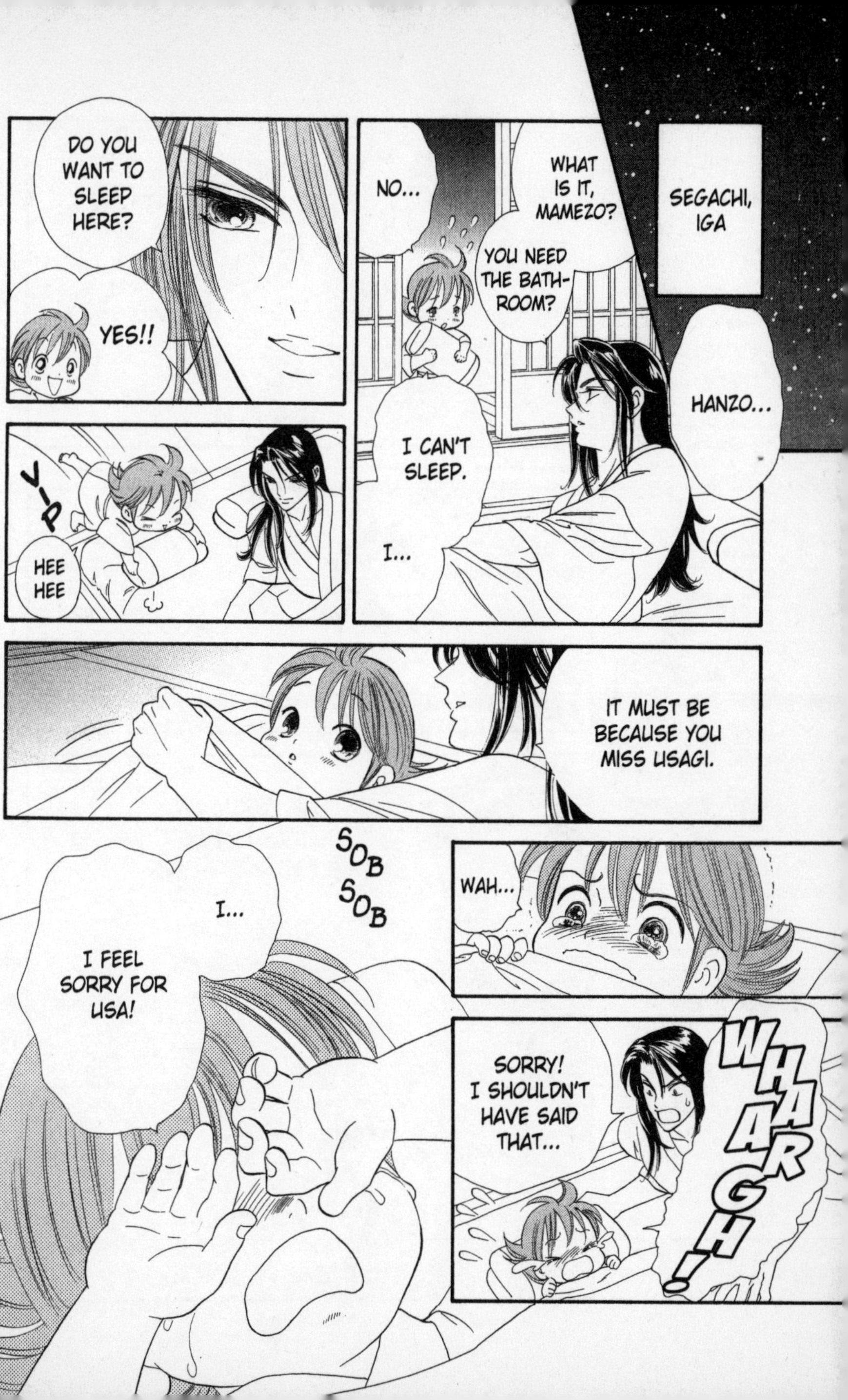
SEGACHI, IGA
HANZO...
WHAT IS IT, MAMEZO?
YOU NEED THE BATH-ROOM?
NO...
I CAN'T SLEEP.
I...
DO YOU WANT TO SLEEP HERE?
YES!!
V-P
HEE HEE
IT MUST BE BECAUSE YOU MISS USAGI.
WAH...
WHAARGH!
SORRY! I SHOULDN'T HAVE SAID THAT...
SOB SOB
I...
I FEEL SORRY FOR USA!

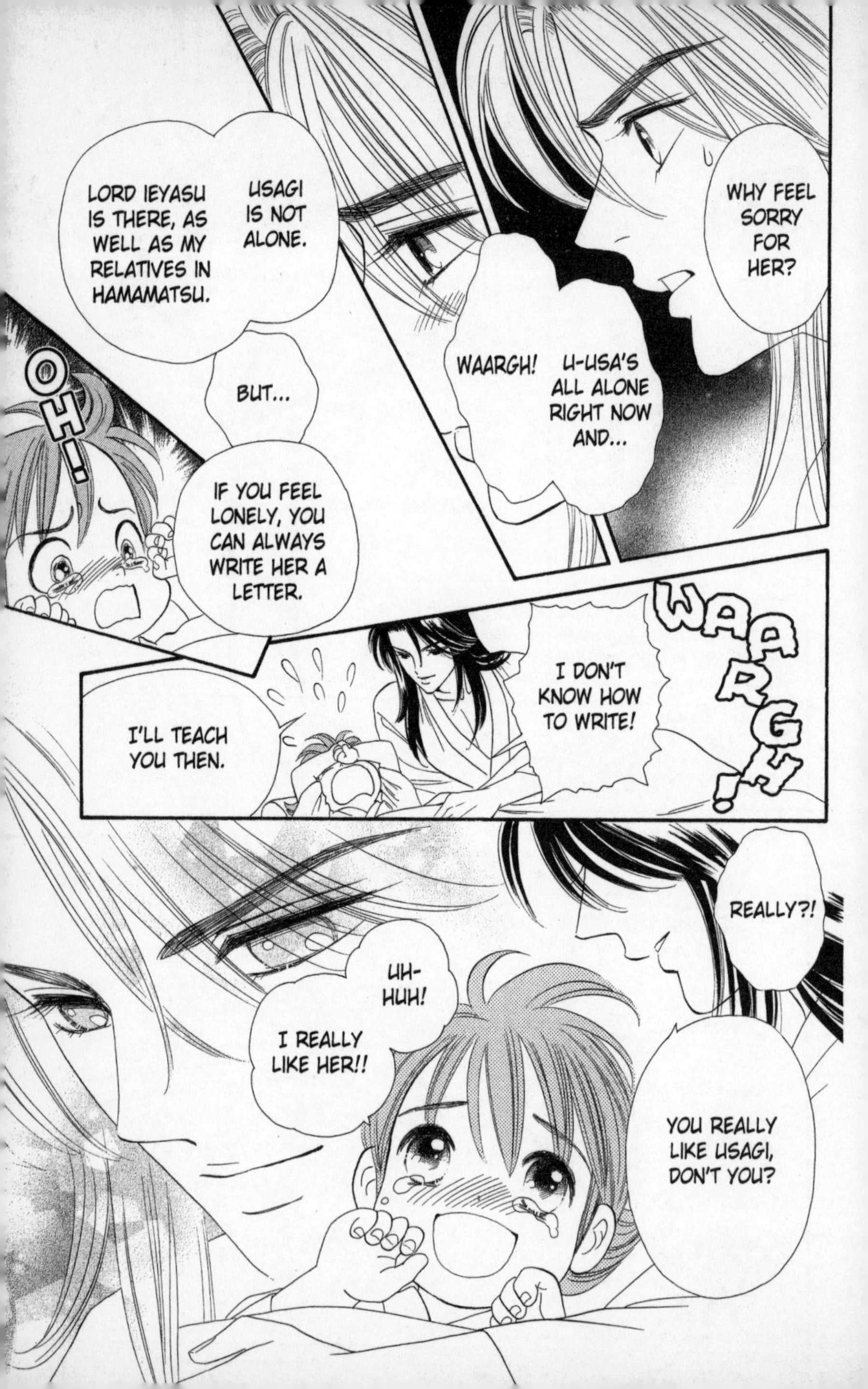
WHY FEEL SORRY FOR HER?
WAARGH! U-USA'S ALL ALONE RIGHT NOW AND...
USAGI IS NOT ALONE.
LORD IEYASU IS THERE, AS WELL AS MY RELATIVES IN HAMAMATSU.
BUT...
OH!
IF YOU FEEL LONELY, YOU CAN ALWAYS WRITE HER A LETTER.
WAARGH!
I DON'T KNOW HOW TO WRITE!
I'LL TEACH YOU THEN.
REALLY?!
YOU REALLY LIKE USAGI, DON'T YOU?
UH-HUH!
I REALLY LIKE HER!!

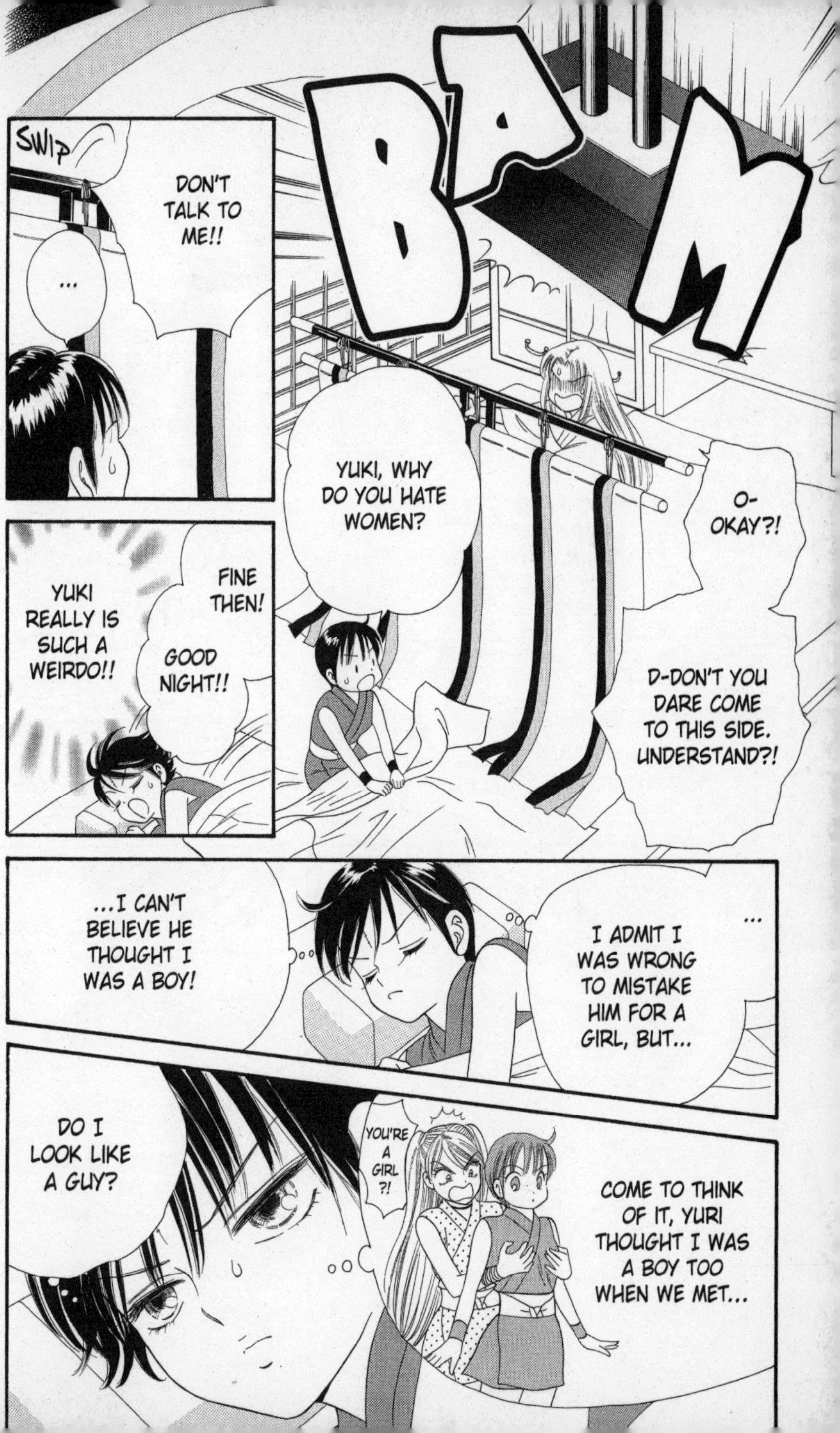
BAM
O-OKAY?!
YUKI, WHY DO YOU HATE WOMEN?
D-DON'T YOU DARE COME TO THIS SIDE. UNDERSTAND?!
SWIP
DON'T TALK TO ME!!
...
FINE THEN!
GOOD NIGHT!!
YUKI REALLY IS SUCH A WEIRDO!!
...
I ADMIT I WAS WRONG TO MISTAKE HIM FOR A GIRL, BUT...
...I CAN'T BELIEVE HE THOUGHT I WAS A BOY!
COME TO THINK OF IT, YURI THOUGHT I WAS A BOY TOO WHEN WE MET...
YOU'RE A GIRL?!
DO I LOOK LIKE A GUY?

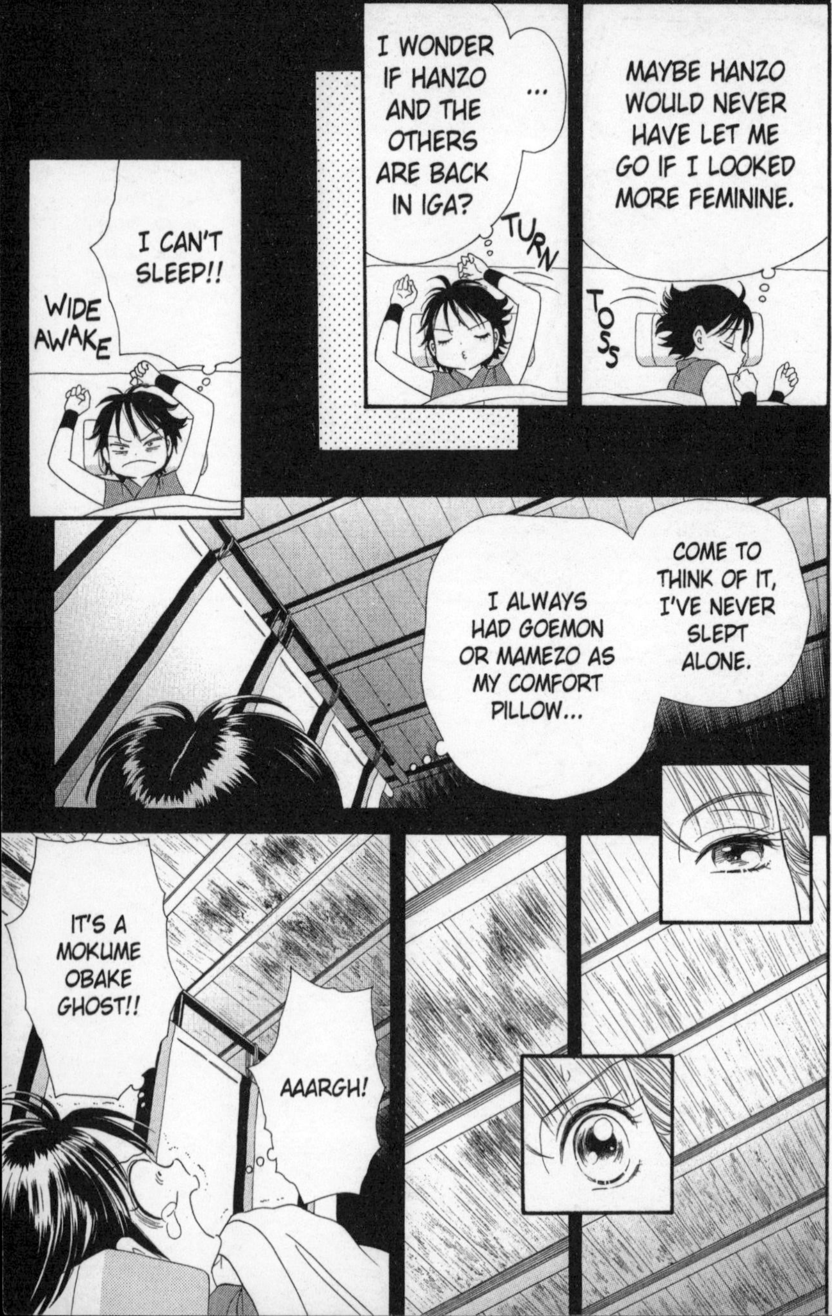
MAYBE HANZO WOULD NEVER HAVE LET ME GO IF I LOOKED MORE FEMININE.
TOSS
I WONDER IF HANZO AND THE OTHERS ARE BACK IN IGA?
...
TURN
I CAN'T SLEEP!!
WIDE AWAKE
COME TO THINK OF IT, I'VE NEVER SLEPT ALONE.
I ALWAYS HAD GOEMON OR MAMEZO AS MY COMFORT PILLOW...
IT'S A MOKUME OBAKE GHOST!!
AAARGH!

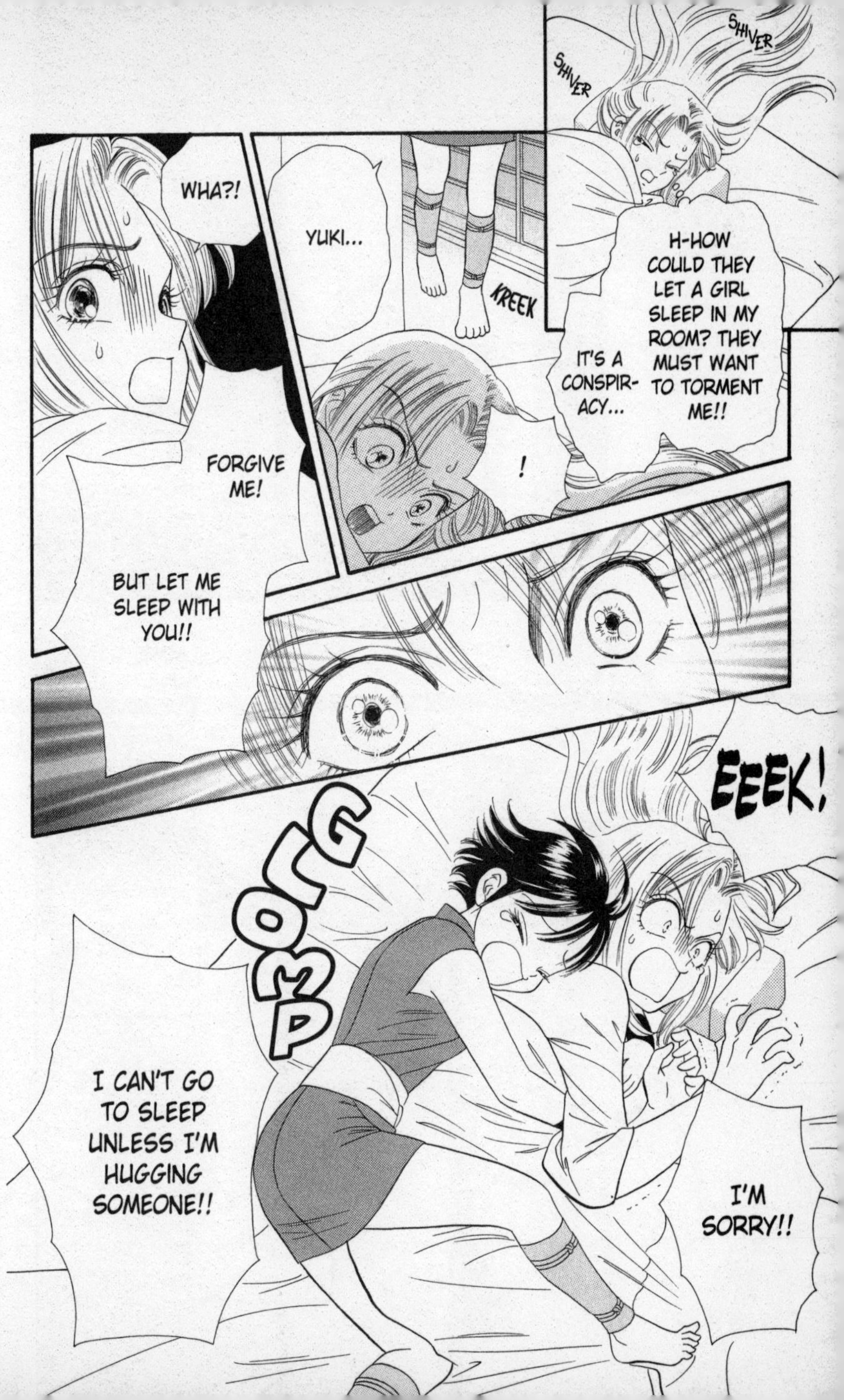
SHIVER
SHIVER
H-HOW COULD THEY LET A GIRL SLEEP IN MY ROOM? THEY MUST WANT TO TORMENT ME!!
IT'S A CONSPIRACY...
KREEK
YUKI...
!
WHA?!
FORGIVE ME!
BUT LET ME SLEEP WITH YOU!!
EEEK!
GLOMP
I'M SORRY!!
I CAN'T GO TO SLEEP UNLESS I'M HUGGING SOMEONE!!

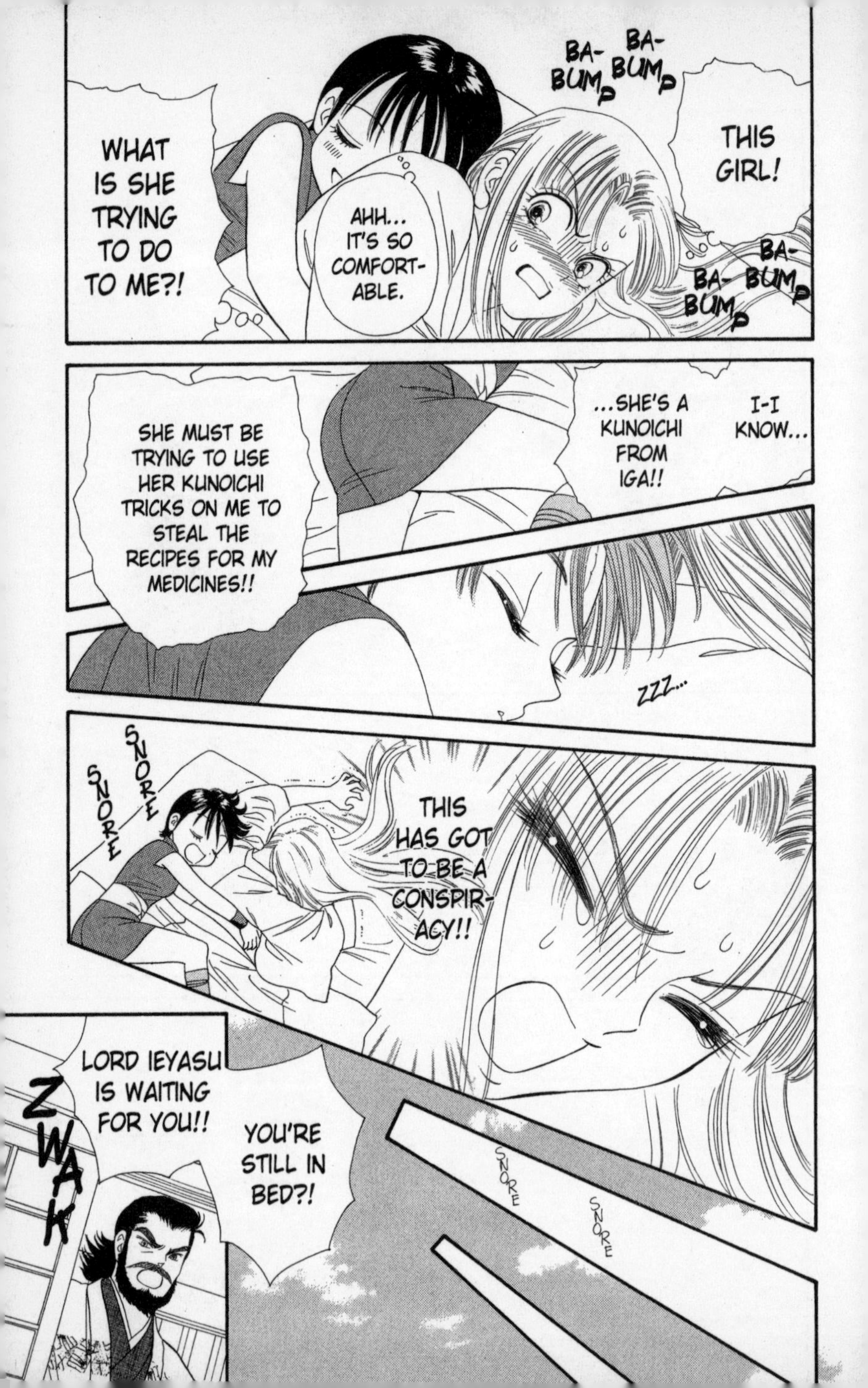
BA-BUMP BA-BUMP
THIS GIRL!
BA-BUMP BA-BUMP
AHH... IT'S SO COMFORTABLE.
WHAT IS SHE TRYING TO DO TO ME?!
I-I KNOW...
...SHE'S A KUNOICHI FROM IGA!!
SHE MUST BE TRYING TO USE HER KUNOICHI TRICKS ON ME TO STEAL THE RECIPES FOR MY MEDICINES!!
ZZZ...
THIS HAS GOT TO BE A CONSPIRACY!!
SNORE SNORE
SNORE SNORE
YOU'RE STILL IN BED?!
LORD IEYASU IS WAITING FOR YOU!!
ZWAK

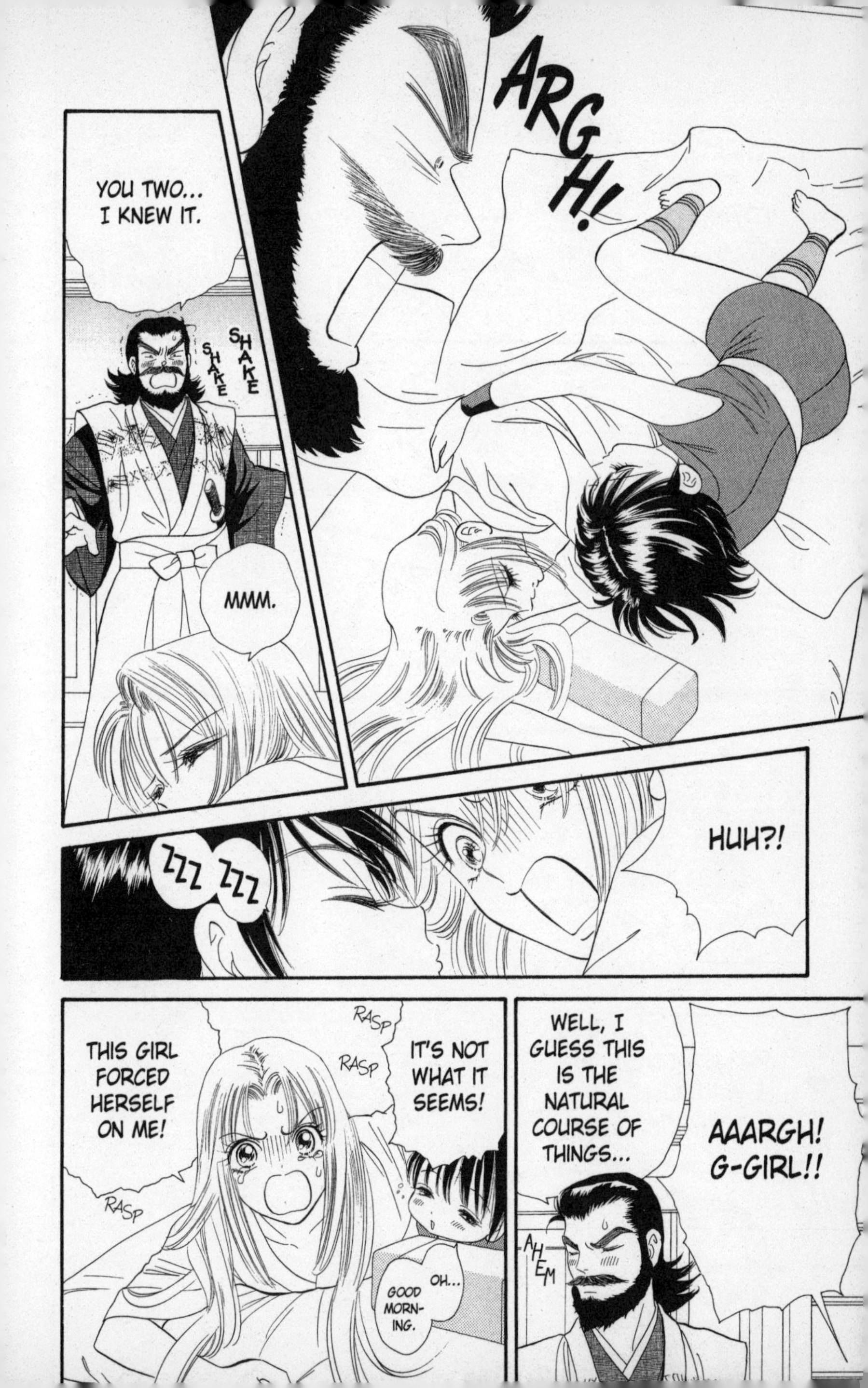
ARGH!
YOU TWO... I KNEW IT.
SHAKE SHAKE
MMM.
HUH?!
ZZZ ZZZ
AAARGH! G-GIRL!!
WELL, I GUESS THIS IS THE NATURAL COURSE OF THINGS...
AHEM
IT'S NOT WHAT IT SEEMS!
RASP RASP
THIS GIRL FORCED HERSELF ON ME!
RASP
OH... GOOD MORNING.

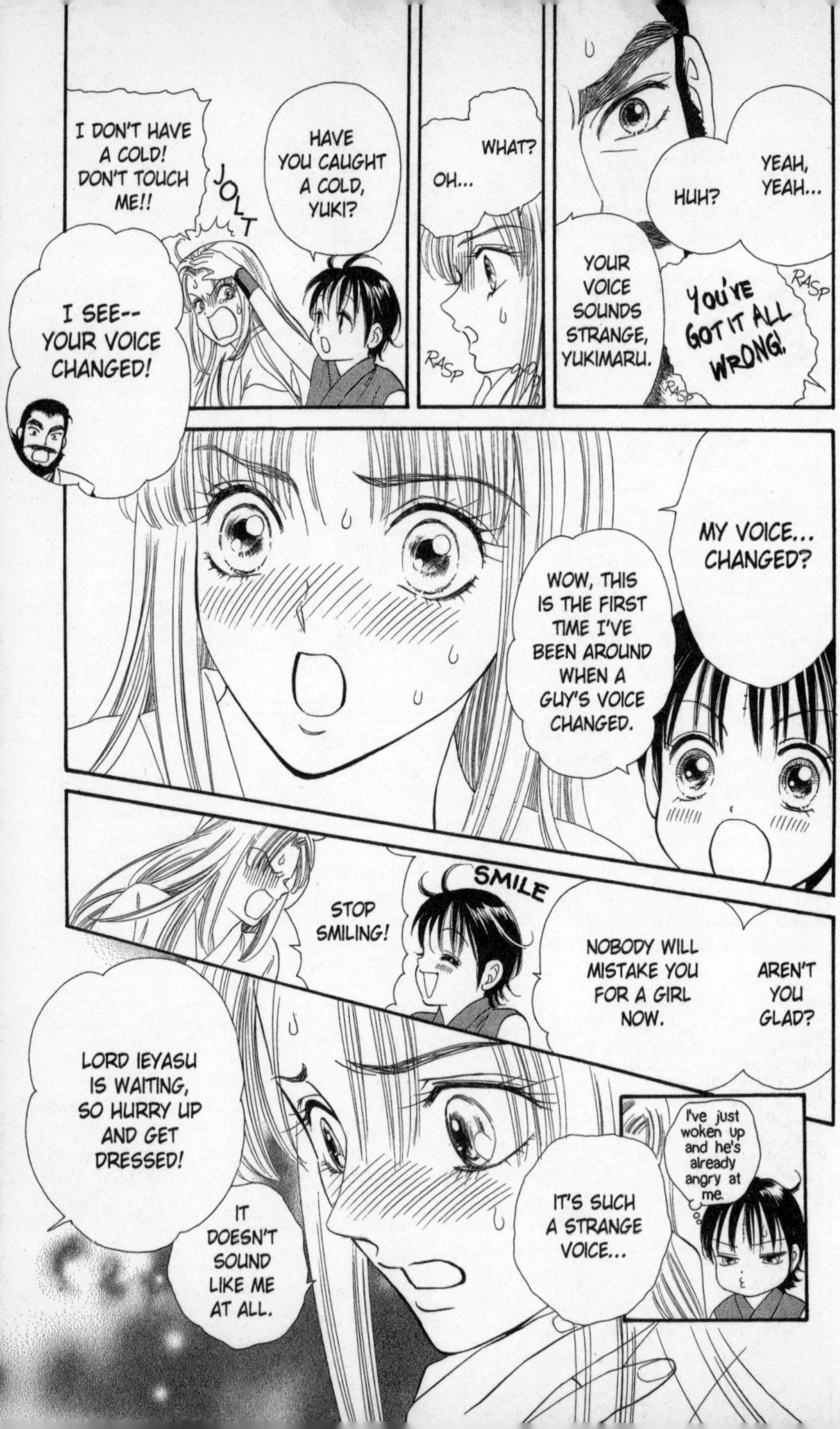
YEAH, YEAH...
HUH?
YOUR VOICE SOUNDS STRANGE, YUKIMARU.
YOU'VE GOT IT ALL WRONG!
RASP
RASP
WHAT?
OH...
RASP
HAVE YOU CAUGHT A COLD, YUKI?
I DON'T HAVE A COLD! DON'T TOUCH ME!!
JOLT
I SEE-- YOUR VOICE CHANGED!
MY VOICE... CHANGED?
WOW, THIS IS THE FIRST TIME I'VE BEEN AROUND WHEN A GUY'S VOICE CHANGED.
SMILE
AREN'T YOU GLAD?
NOBODY WILL MISTAKE YOU FOR A GIRL NOW.
STOP SMILING!
I've just woken up and he's already angry at me.
IT'S SUCH A STRANGE VOICE...
IT DOESN'T SOUND LIKE ME AT ALL.
LORD IEYASU IS WAITING, SO HURRY UP AND GET DRESSED!

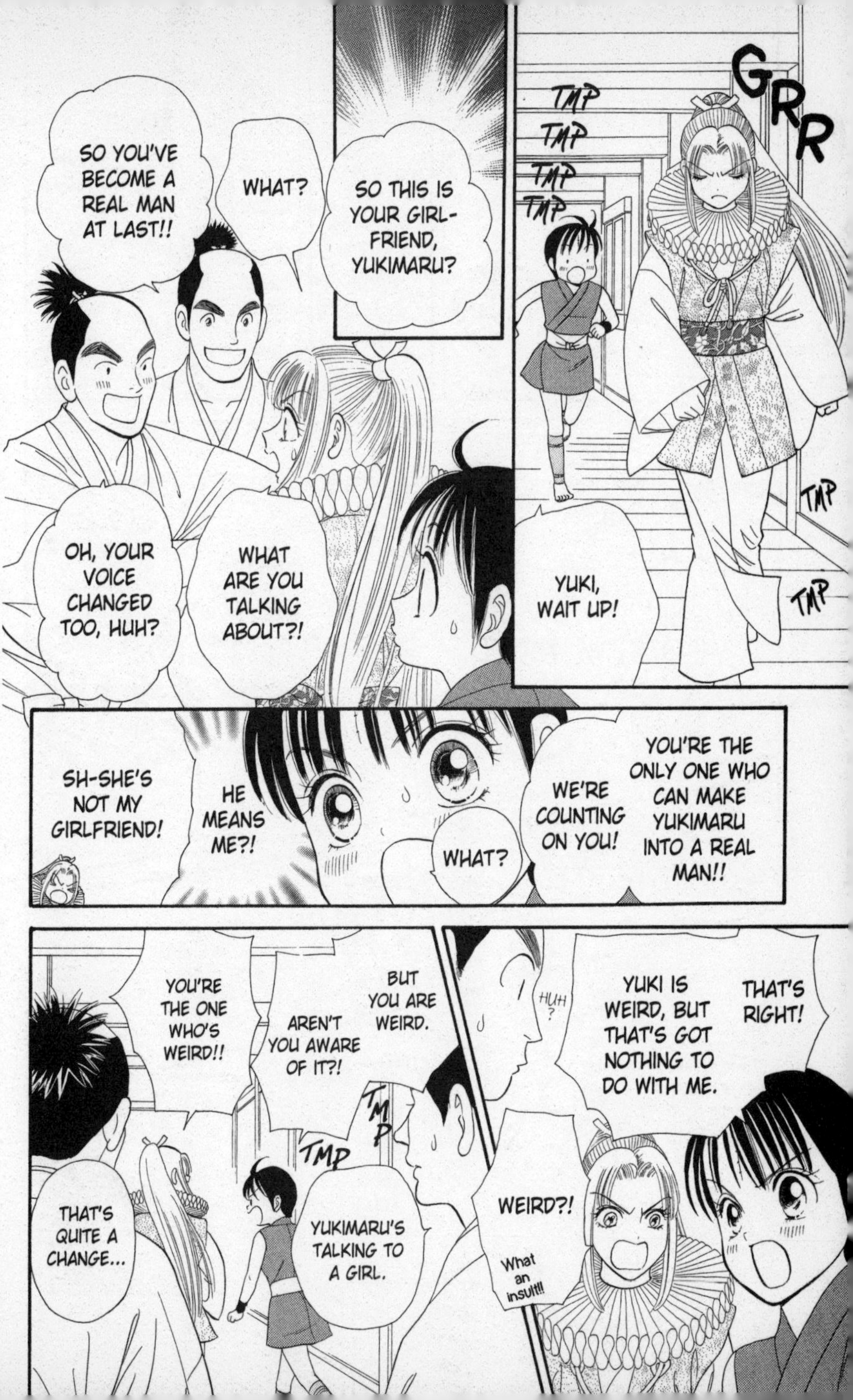
GRR
TMP TMP TMP TMP
TMP
TMP
YUKI, WAIT UP!
SO THIS IS YOUR GIRL-FRIEND, YUKIMARU?
WHAT?
SO YOU'VE BECOME A REAL MAN AT LAST!!
WHAT ARE YOU TALKING ABOUT?!
OH, YOUR VOICE CHANGED TOO, HUH?
YOU'RE THE ONLY ONE WHO CAN MAKE YUKIMARU INTO A REAL MAN!!
WE'RE COUNTING ON YOU!
WHAT?
HE MEANS ME?!
SH-SHE'S NOT MY GIRLFRIEND!
THAT'S RIGHT!
YUKI IS WEIRD, BUT THAT'S GOT NOTHING TO DO WITH ME.
HUH?
WEIRD?!
What an insult!!
BUT YOU ARE WEIRD.
YOU'RE THE ONE WHO'S WEIRD!!
AREN'T YOU AWARE OF IT?!
TMP
TMP
YUKIMARU'S TALKING TO A GIRL.
THAT'S QUITE A CHANGE...

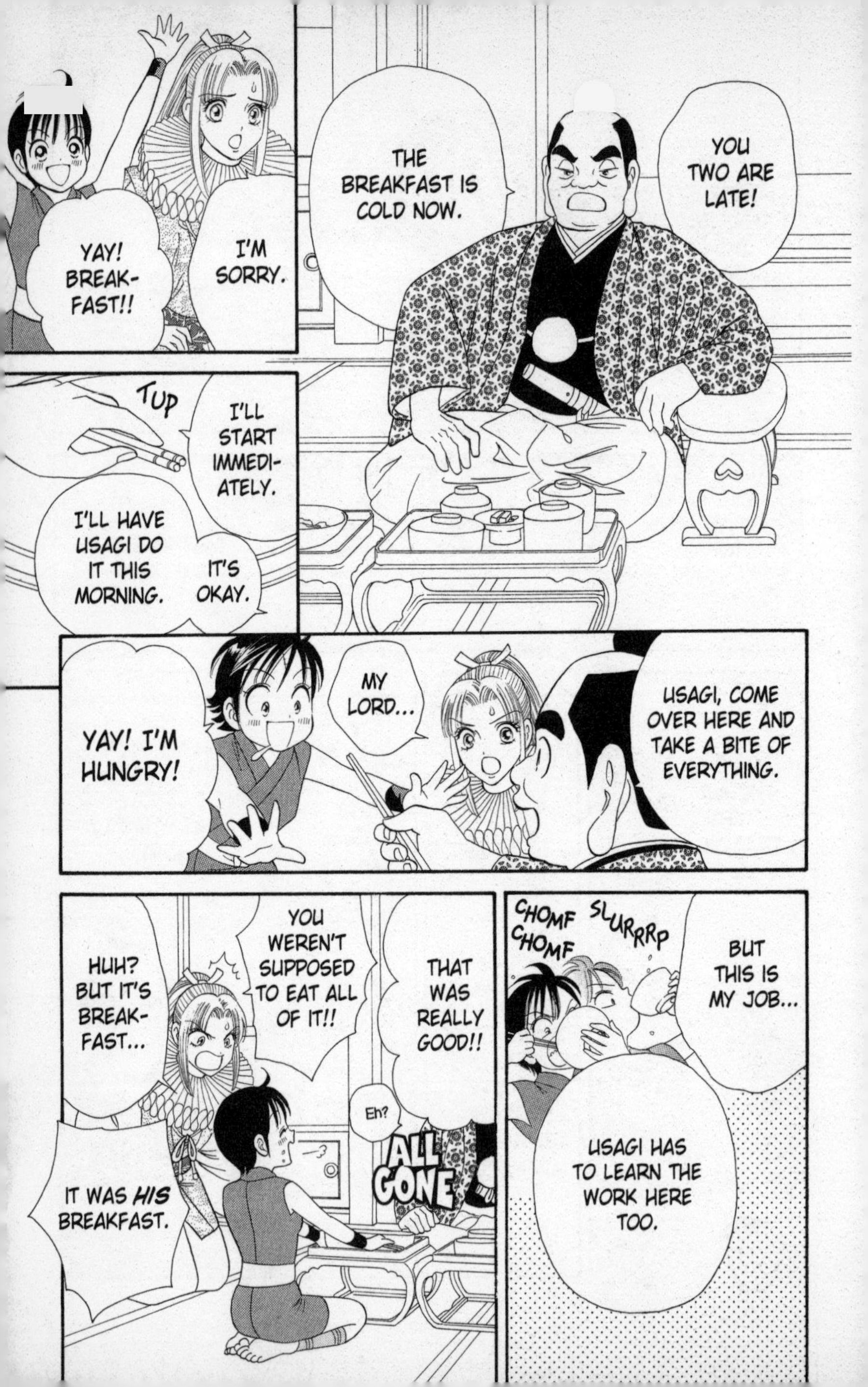
YOU TWO ARE LATE!
THE BREAKFAST IS COLD NOW.
I'M SORRY.
YAY! BREAKFAST!!
I'LL START IMMEDIATELY.
TUP
IT'S OKAY.
I'LL HAVE USAGI DO IT THIS MORNING.
USAGI, COME OVER HERE AND TAKE A BITE OF EVERYTHING.
MY LORD...
YAY! I'M HUNGRY!
CHOMF CHOMF
SLURRRP
BUT THIS IS MY JOB...
USAGI HAS TO LEARN THE WORK HERE TOO.
THAT WAS REALLY GOOD!!
YOU WEREN'T SUPPOSED TO EAT ALL OF IT!!
HUH? BUT IT'S BREAKFAST...
Eh?
ALL GONE
IT WAS *HIS* BREAKFAST.

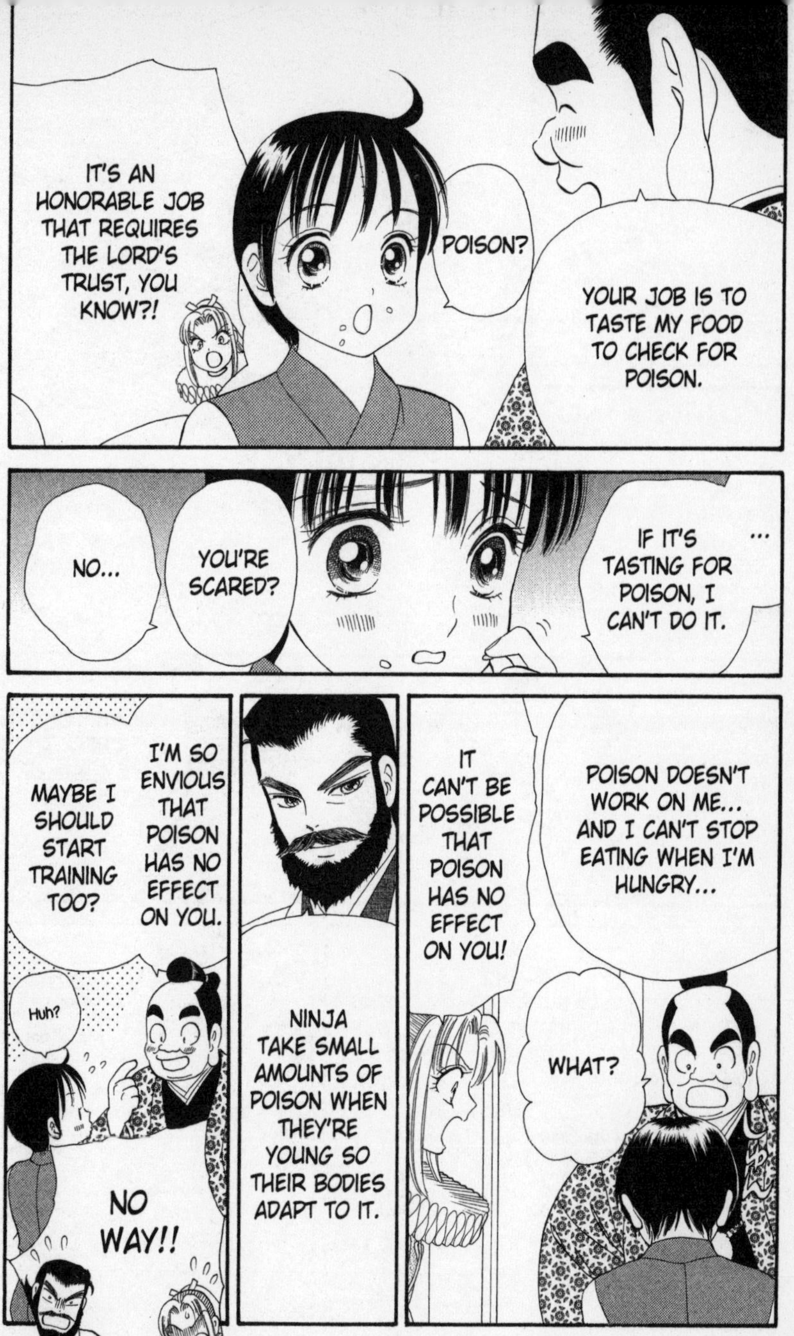
YOUR JOB IS TO TASTE MY FOOD TO CHECK FOR POISON.
POISON?
IT'S AN HONORABLE JOB THAT REQUIRES THE LORD'S TRUST, YOU KNOW?!
...
IF IT'S TASTING FOR POISON, I CAN'T DO IT.
YOU'RE SCARED?
NO...
POISON DOESN'T WORK ON ME... AND I CAN'T STOP EATING WHEN I'M HUNGRY...
IT CAN'T BE POSSIBLE THAT POISON HAS NO EFFECT ON YOU!
WHAT?
NINJA TAKE SMALL AMOUNTS OF POISON WHEN THEY'RE YOUNG SO THEIR BODIES ADAPT TO IT.
I'M SO ENVIOUS THAT POISON HAS NO EFFECT ON YOU.
MAYBE I SHOULD START TRAINING TOO?
Huh?
NO WAY!!

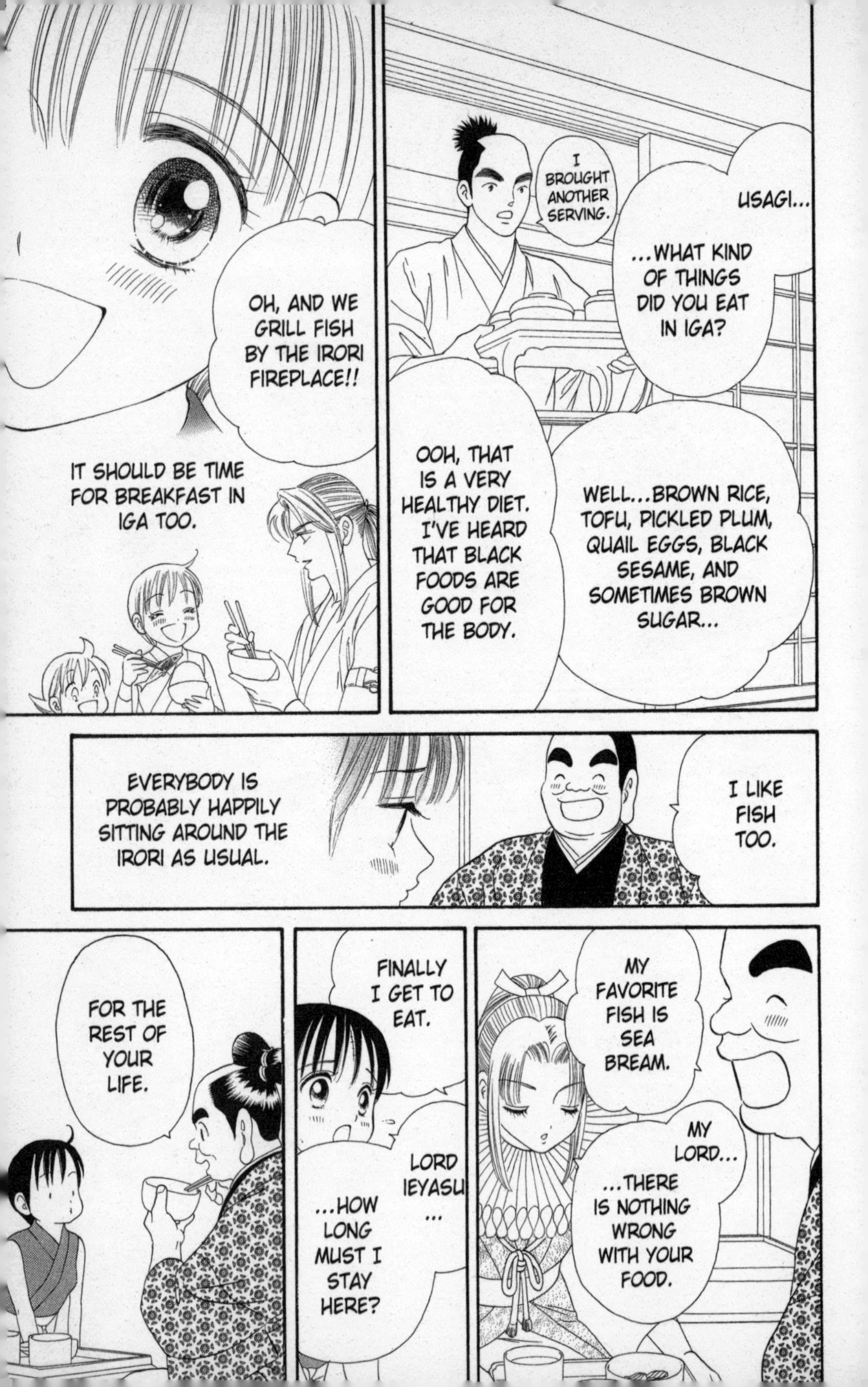
USAGI...
...WHAT KIND OF THINGS DID YOU EAT IN IGA?
I BROUGHT ANOTHER SERVING.
WELL...BROWN RICE, TOFU, PICKLED PLUM, QUAIL EGGS, BLACK SESAME, AND SOMETIMES BROWN SUGAR...
OOH, THAT IS A VERY HEALTHY DIET. I'VE HEARD THAT BLACK FOODS ARE GOOD FOR THE BODY.
OH, AND WE GRILL FISH BY THE IRORI FIREPLACE!!
IT SHOULD BE TIME FOR BREAKFAST IN IGA TOO.
I LIKE FISH TOO.
EVERYBODY IS PROBABLY HAPPILY SITTING AROUND THE IRORI AS USUAL.
MY FAVORITE FISH IS SEA BREAM.
MY LORD...
...THERE IS NOTHING WRONG WITH YOUR FOOD.
FINALLY I GET TO EAT.
LORD IEYASU...
...HOW LONG MUST I STAY HERE?
FOR THE REST OF YOUR LIFE.

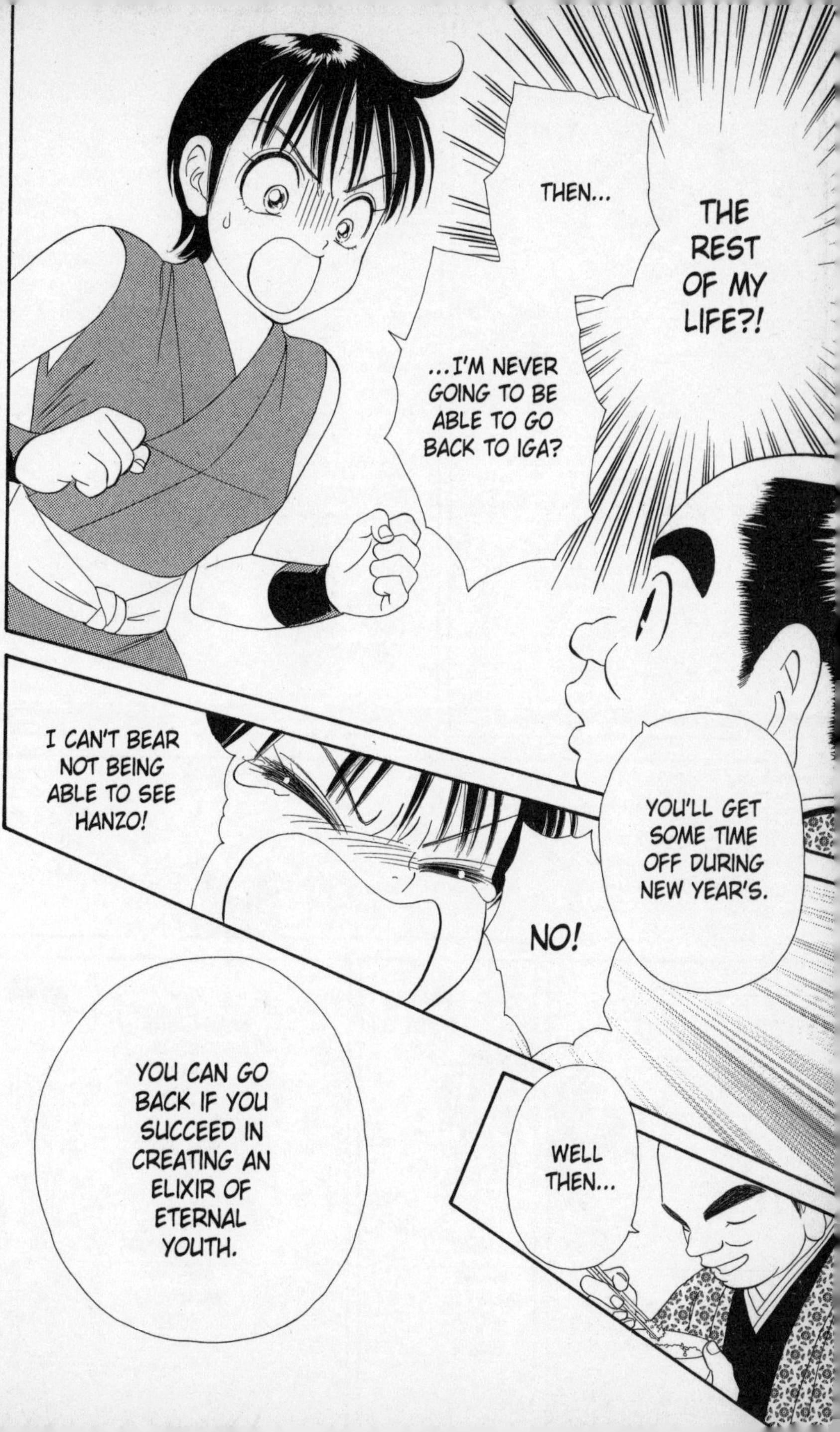
THE REST OF MY LIFE?!
THEN...
...I'M NEVER GOING TO BE ABLE TO GO BACK TO IGA?
YOU'LL GET SOME TIME OFF DURING NEW YEAR'S.
NO!
I CAN'T BEAR NOT BEING ABLE TO SEE HANZO!
WELL THEN...
YOU CAN GO BACK IF YOU SUCCEED IN CREATING AN ELIXIR OF ETERNAL YOUTH.

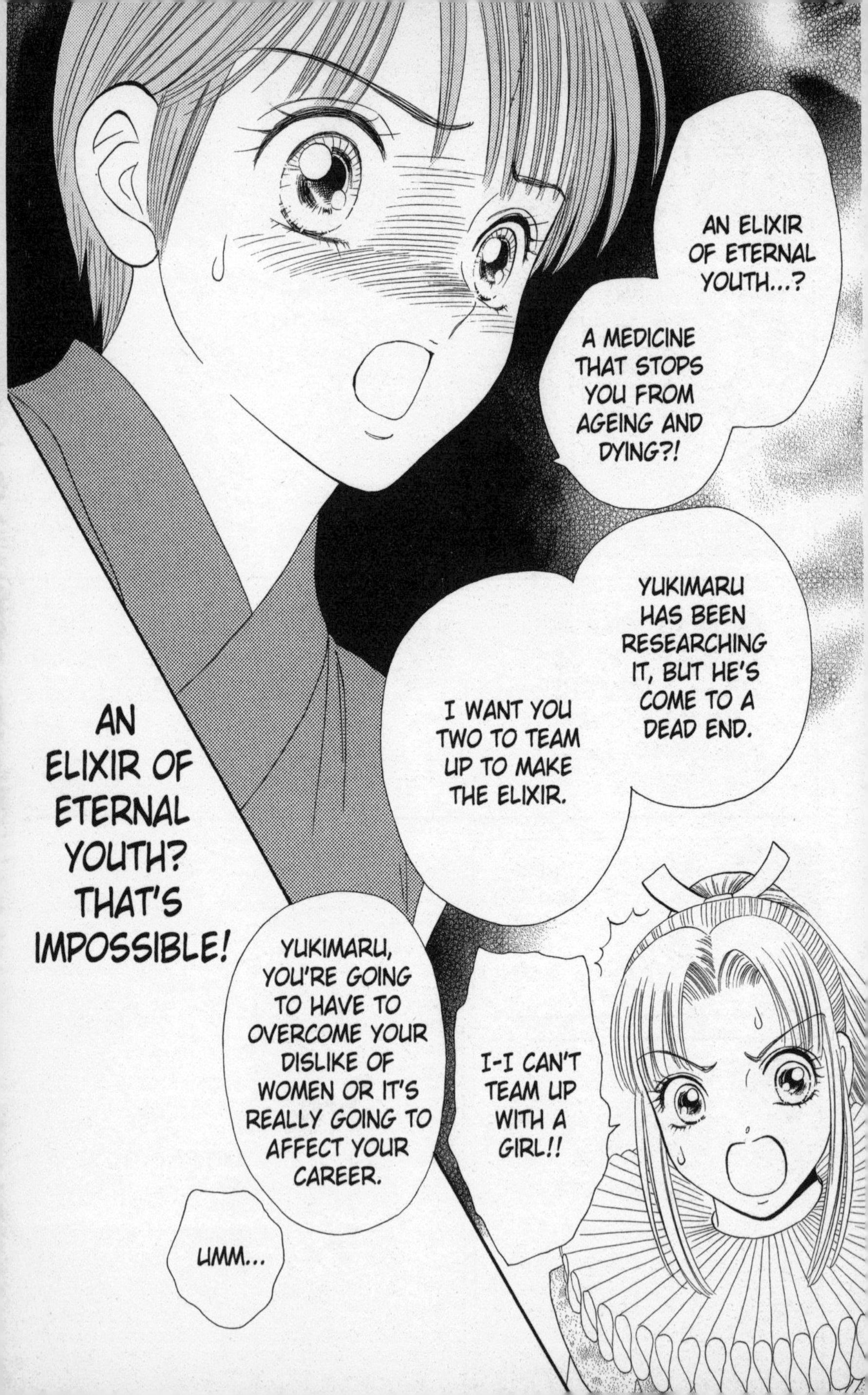
AN ELIXIR OF ETERNAL YOUTH...?
A MEDICINE THAT STOPS YOU FROM AGEING AND DYING?!
YUKIMARU HAS BEEN RESEARCHING IT, BUT HE'S COME TO A DEAD END.
I WANT YOU TWO TO TEAM UP TO MAKE THE ELIXIR.
AN ELIXIR OF ETERNAL YOUTH? THAT'S IMPOSSIBLE!
I-I CAN'T TEAM UP WITH A GIRL!!
YUKIMARU, YOU'RE GOING TO HAVE TO OVERCOME YOUR DISLIKE OF WOMEN OR IT'S REALLY GOING TO AFFECT YOUR CAREER.
UMM...

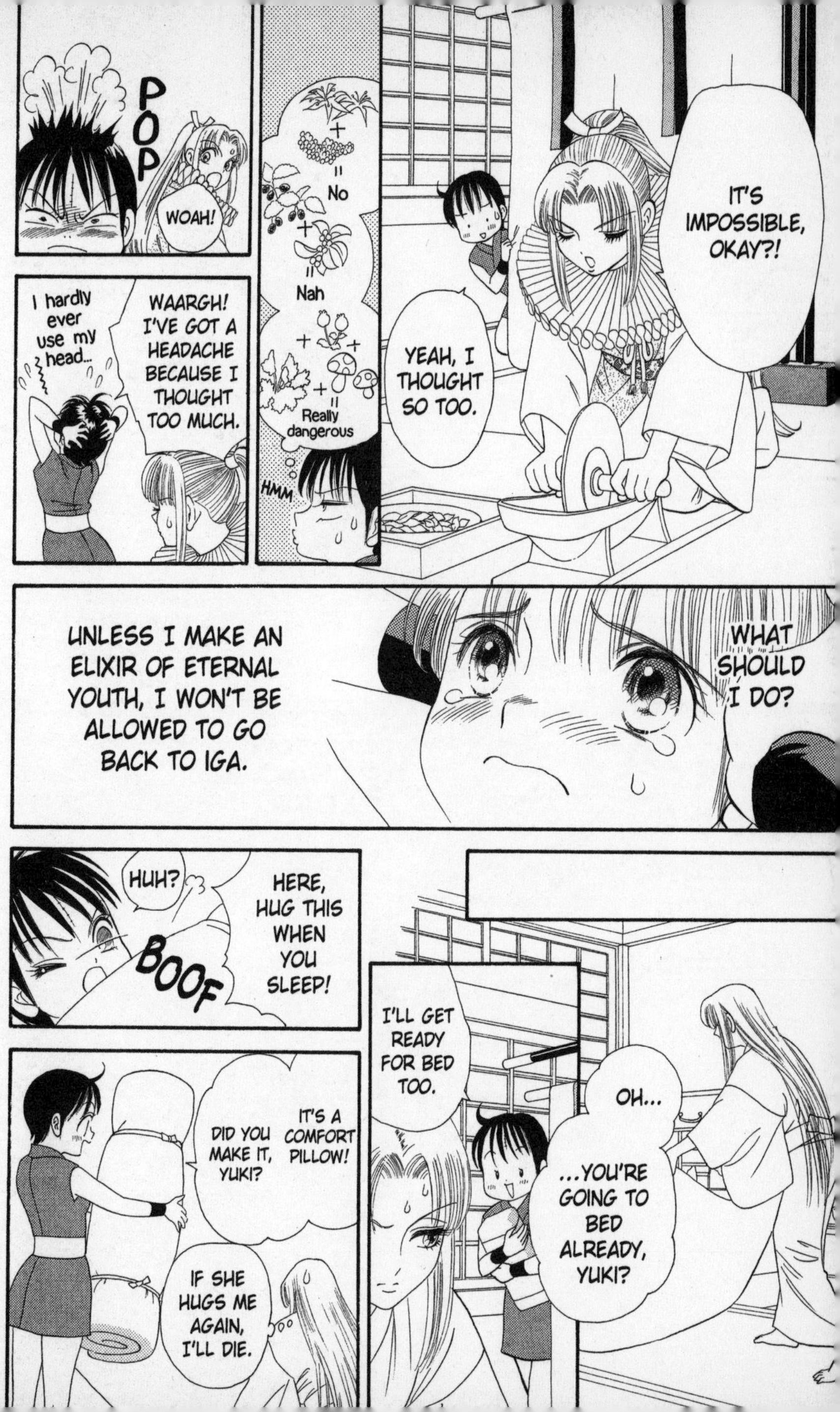
IT'S IMPOSSIBLE, OKAY?!
YEAH, I THOUGHT SO TOO.
+
=
No
+
=
Nah
+
+
+
=
Really dangerous
HMM
POP
WOAH!
WAARGH! I'VE GOT A HEADACHE BECAUSE I THOUGHT TOO MUCH.
I hardly ever use my head...
WHAT SHOULD I DO?
UNLESS I MAKE AN ELIXIR OF ETERNAL YOUTH, I WON'T BE ALLOWED TO GO BACK TO IGA.
OH...
...YOU'RE GOING TO BED ALREADY, YUKI?
I'LL GET READY FOR BED TOO.
HERE, HUG THIS WHEN YOU SLEEP!
HUH?
BOOF
IT'S A COMFORT PILLOW!
DID YOU MAKE IT, YUKI?
IF SHE HUGS ME AGAIN, I'LL DIE.

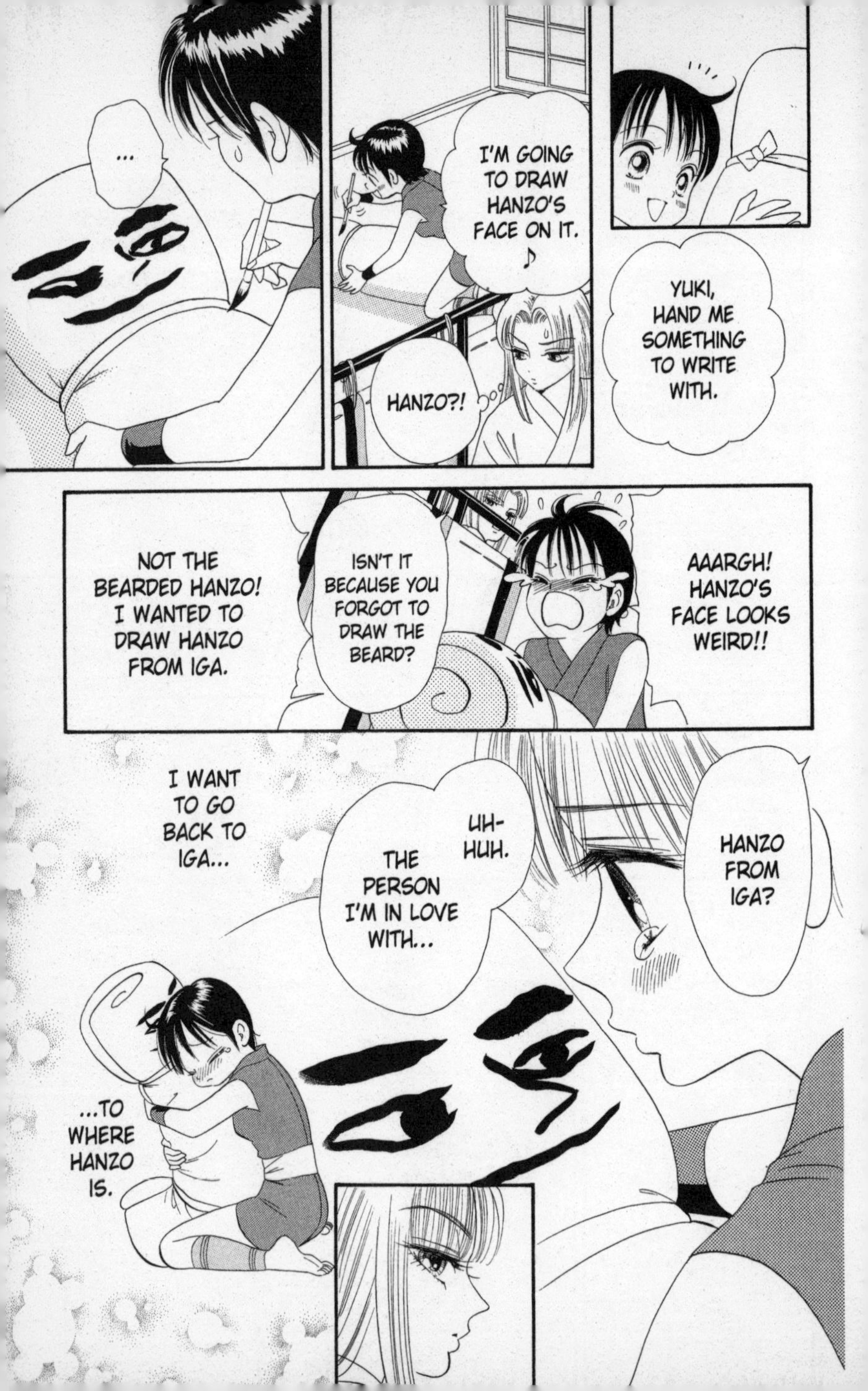
YUKI, HAND ME SOMETHING TO WRITE WITH.
I'M GOING TO DRAW HANZO'S FACE ON IT. ♪
HANZO?!
...
AAARGH! HANZO'S FACE LOOKS WEIRD!!
ISN'T IT BECAUSE YOU FORGOT TO DRAW THE BEARD?
NOT THE BEARDED HANZO! I WANTED TO DRAW HANZO FROM IGA.
HANZO FROM IGA?
UH-HUH.
THE PERSON I'M IN LOVE WITH...
I WANT TO GO BACK TO IGA...
...TO WHERE HANZO IS.

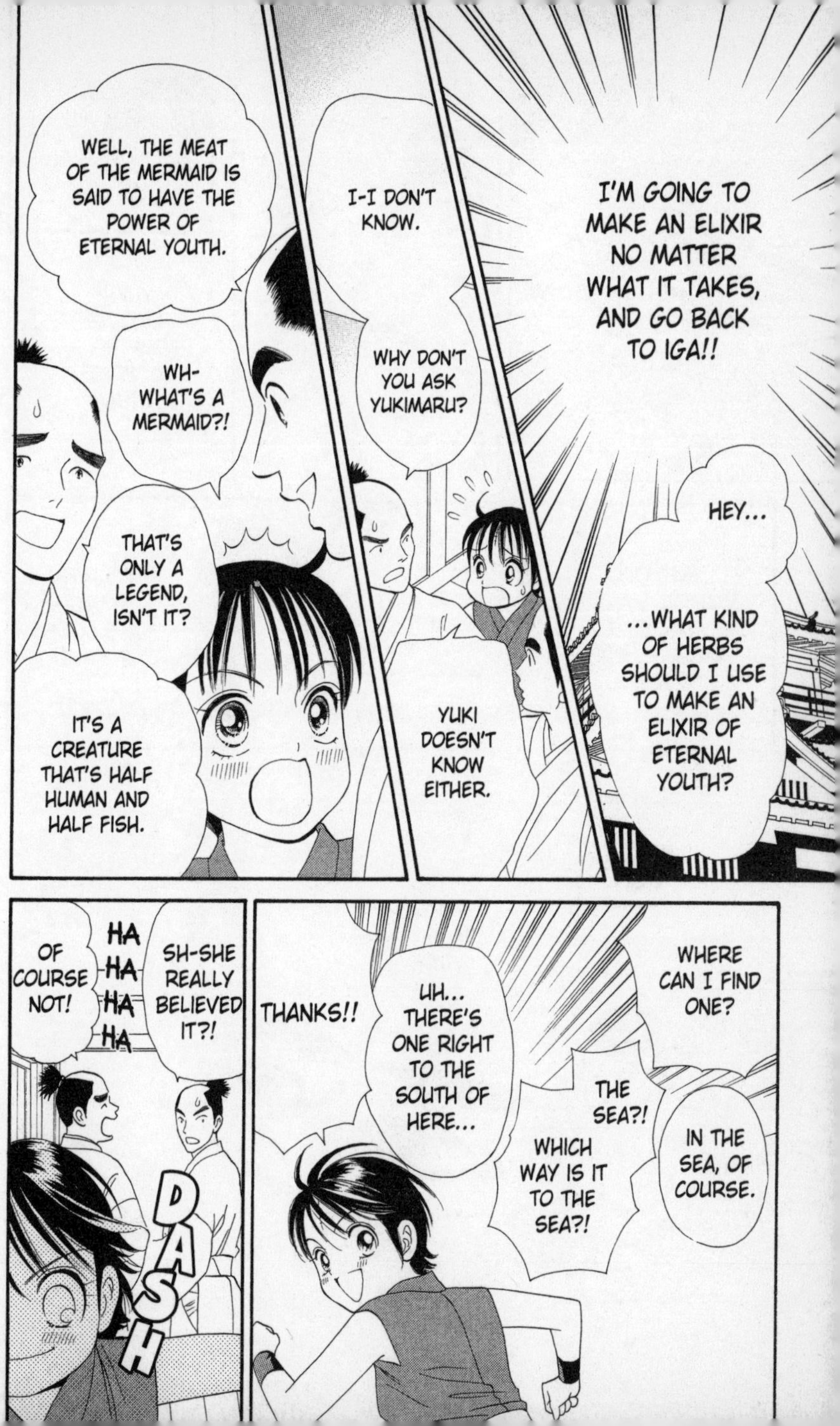
I'M GOING TO MAKE AN ELIXIR NO MATTER WHAT IT TAKES, AND GO BACK TO IGA!!
HEY...
...WHAT KIND OF HERBS SHOULD I USE TO MAKE AN ELIXIR OF ETERNAL YOUTH?
I-I DON'T KNOW.
WHY DON'T YOU ASK YUKIMARU?
YUKI DOESN'T KNOW EITHER.
WELL, THE MEAT OF THE MERMAID IS SAID TO HAVE THE POWER OF ETERNAL YOUTH.
WH- WHAT'S A MERMAID?!
IT'S A CREATURE THAT'S HALF HUMAN AND HALF FISH.
THAT'S ONLY A LEGEND, ISN'T IT?
WHERE CAN I FIND ONE?
IN THE SEA, OF COURSE.
THE SEA?!
WHICH WAY IS IT TO THE SEA?!
UH... THERE'S ONE RIGHT TO THE SOUTH OF HERE...
THANKS!!
DASH
SH-SHE REALLY BELIEVED IT?!
HA HA HA HA
OF COURSE NOT!

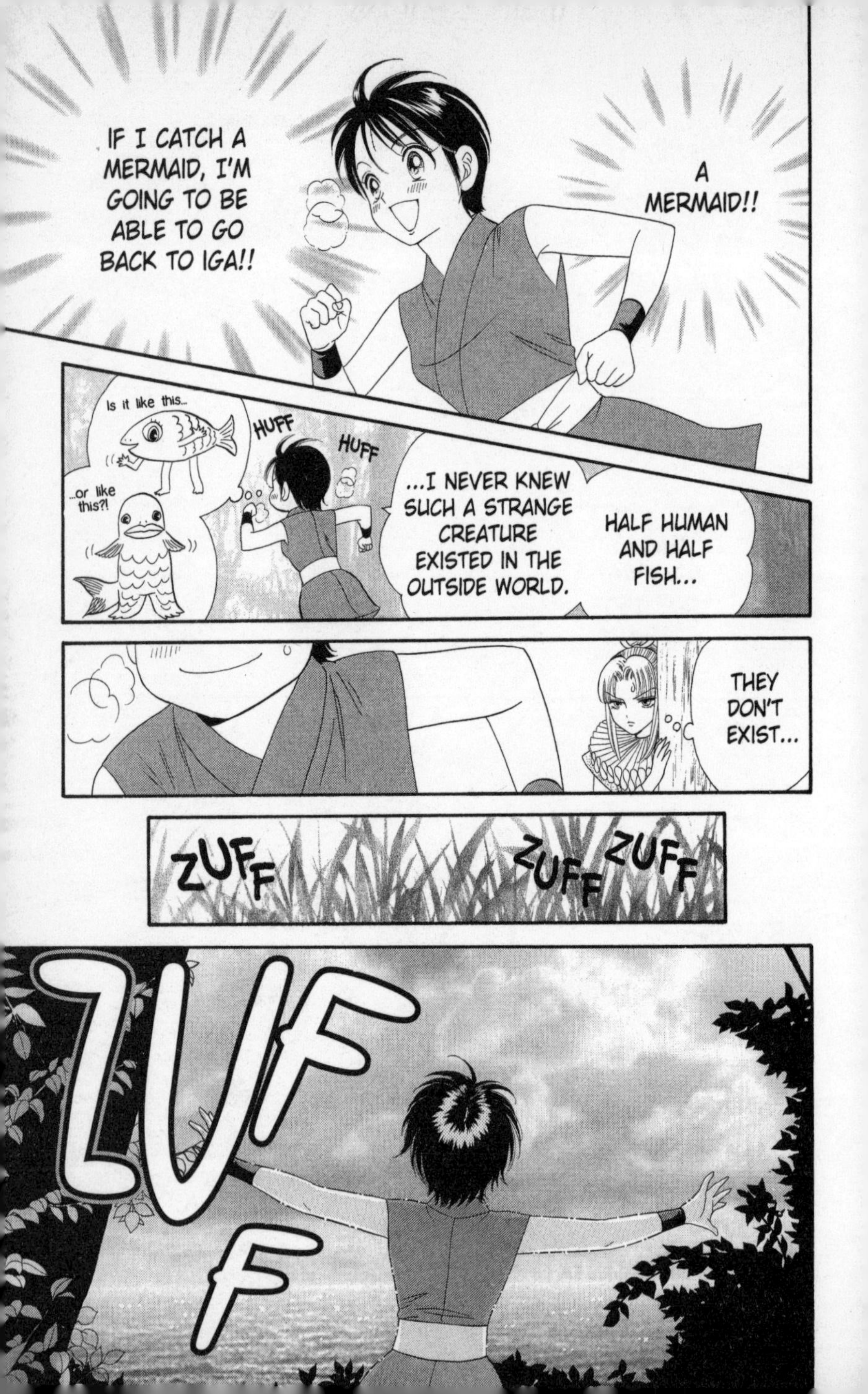
A MERMAID!!
IF I CATCH A MERMAID, I'M GOING TO BE ABLE TO GO BACK TO IGA!!
HALF HUMAN AND HALF FISH...
...I NEVER KNEW SUCH A STRANGE CREATURE EXISTED IN THE OUTSIDE WORLD.
HUFF
HUFF
Is it like this...
...or like this?!
THEY DON'T EXIST...
ZUFF
ZUFF
ZUFF
ZUFF

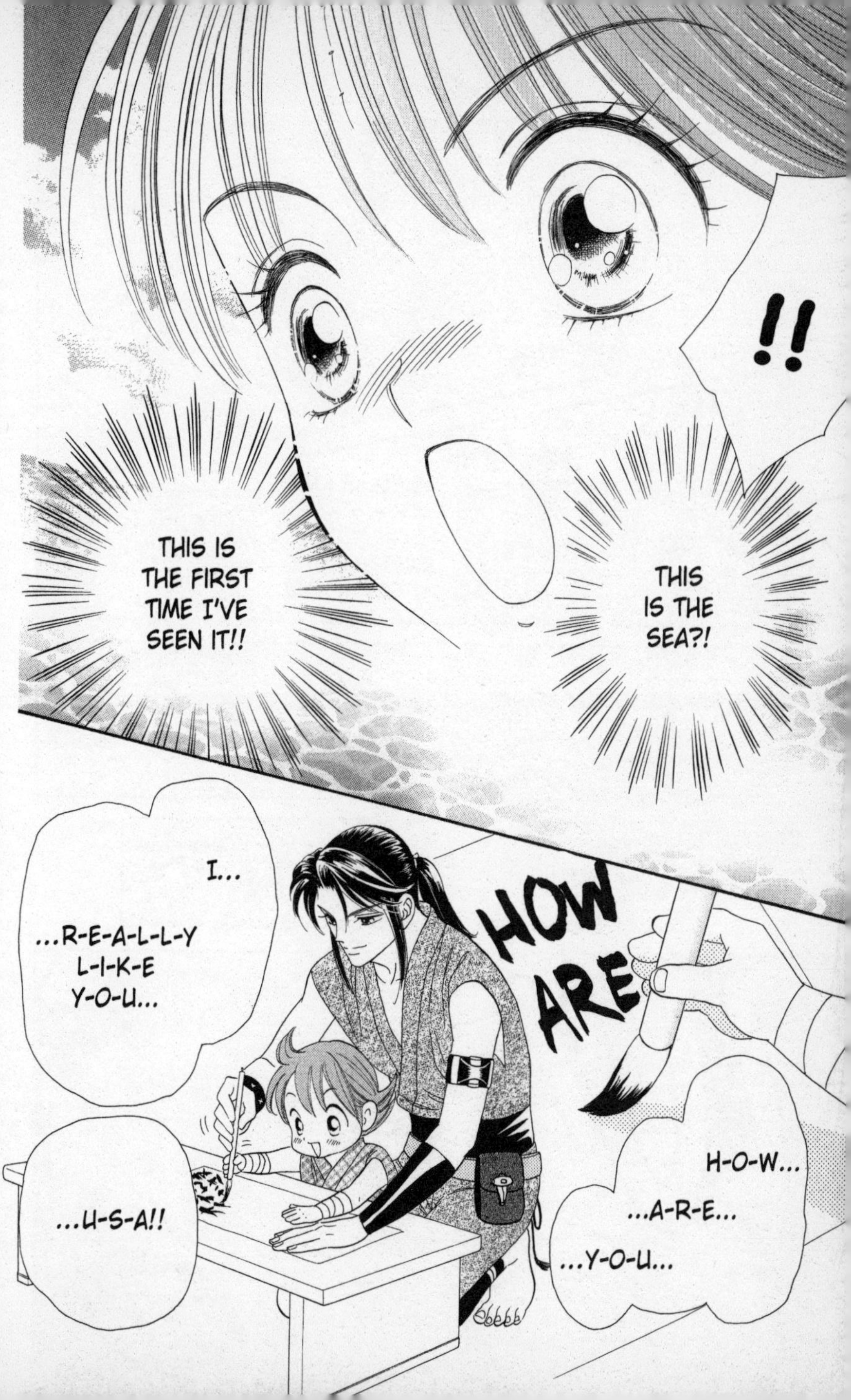
!!
THIS IS THE SEA?!
THIS IS THE FIRST TIME I'VE SEEN IT!!
HOW ARE
H-O-W...
...A-R-E...
...Y-O-U...
I...
...R-E-A-L-L-Y L-I-K-E Y-O-U...
...U-S-A!!

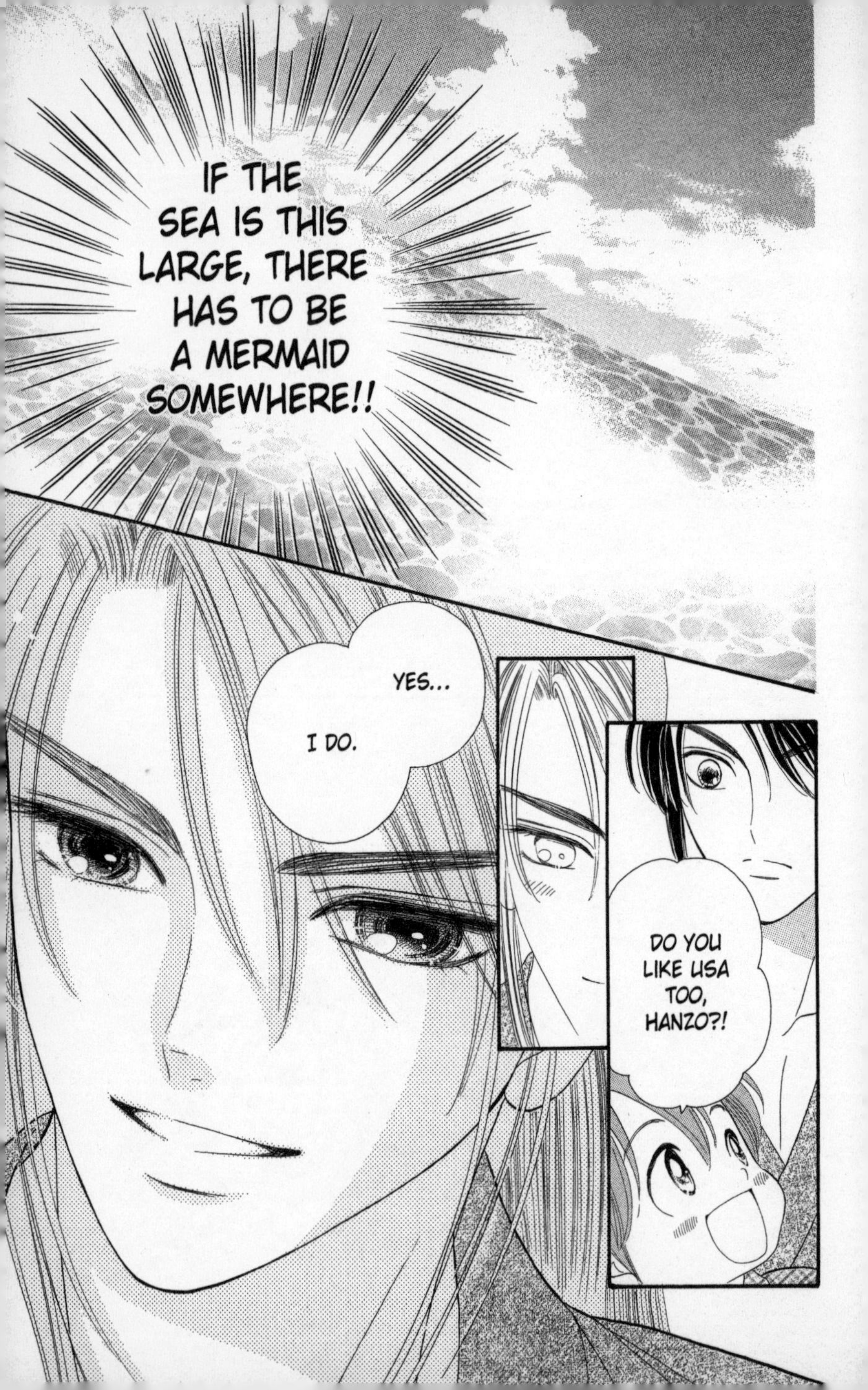
IF THE SEA IS THIS LARGE, THERE HAS TO BE A MERMAID SOMEWHERE!!
DO YOU LIKE USA TOO, HANZO?!
YES...
I DO.

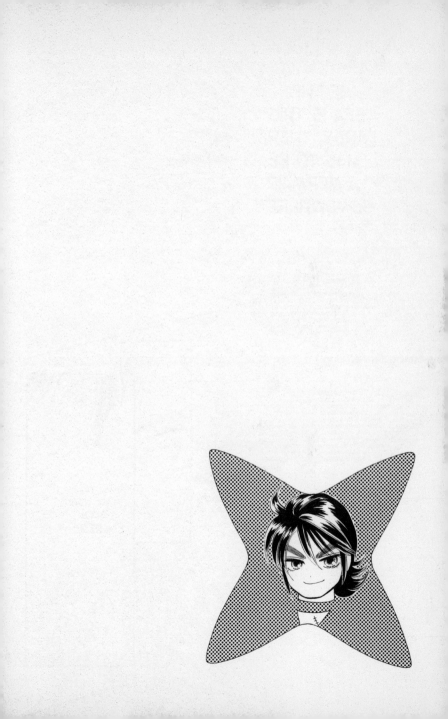

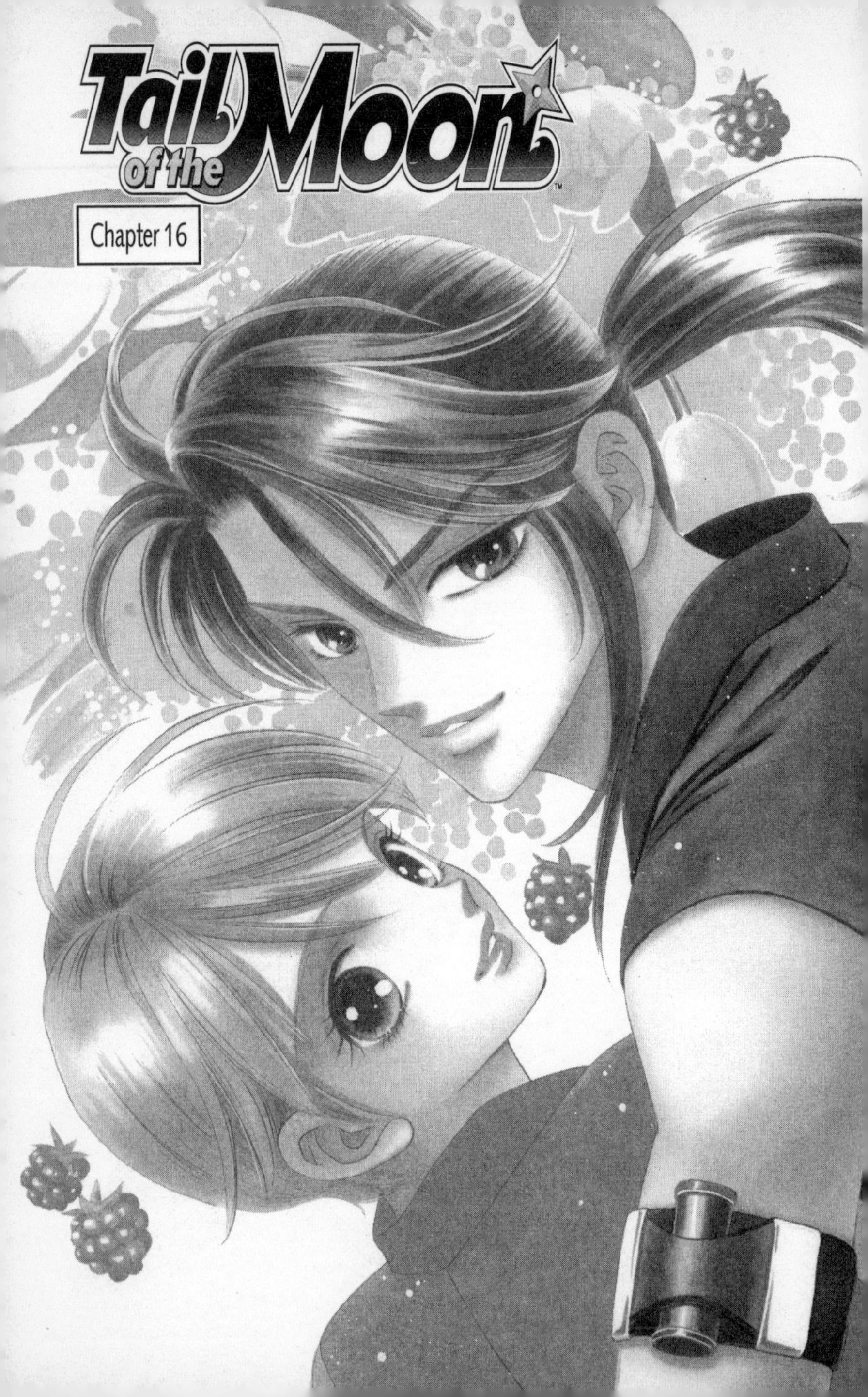
Tail of the Moon™
Chapter 16

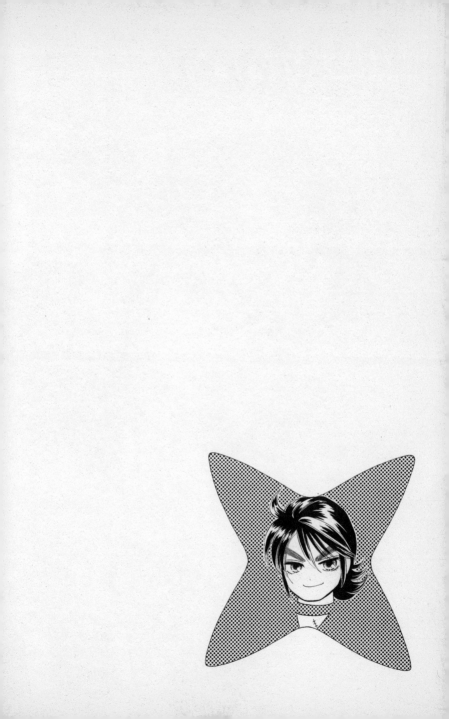

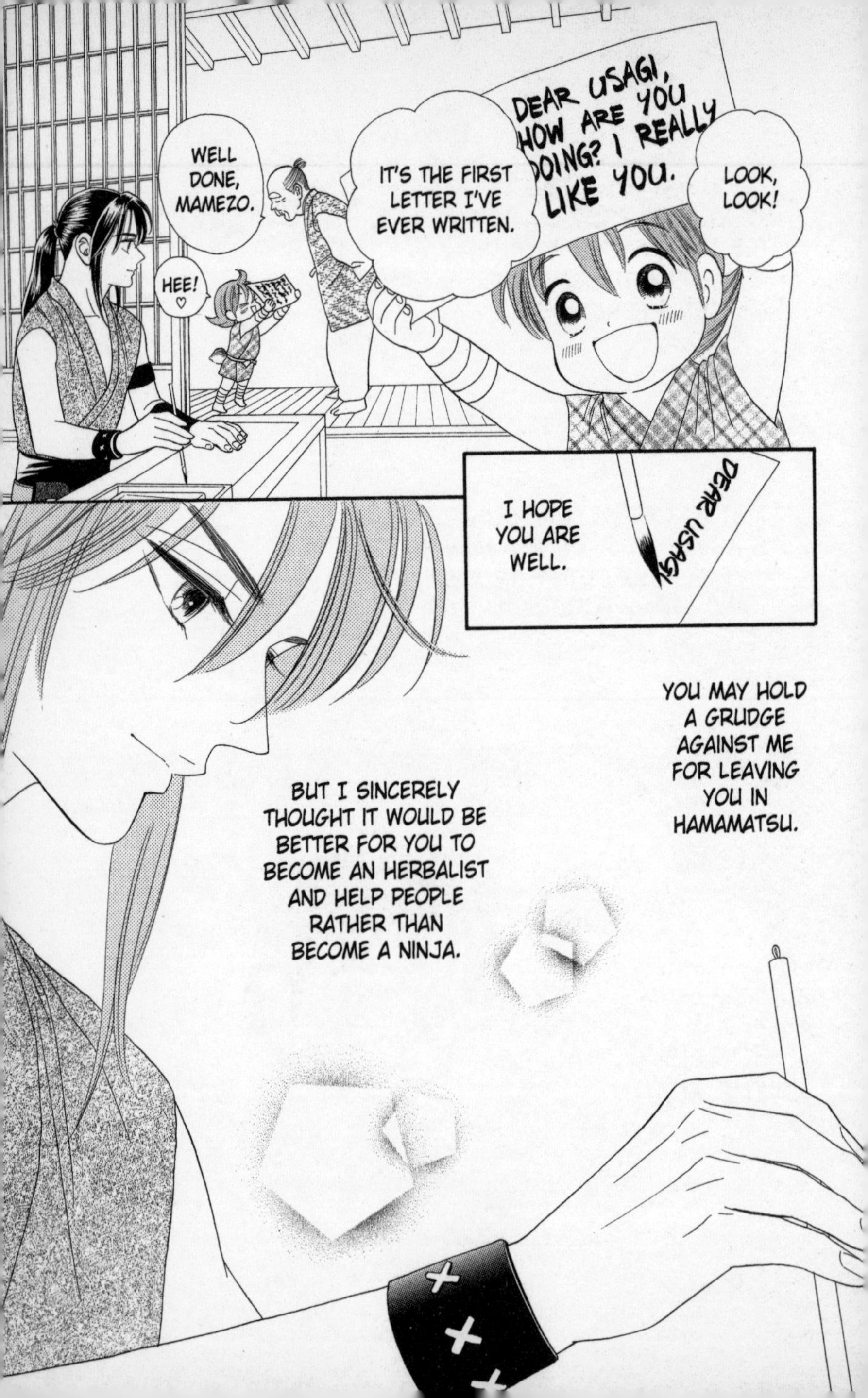
LOOK, LOOK!
DEAR USAGI, HOW ARE YOU DOING? I REALLY LIKE YOU.
IT'S THE FIRST LETTER I'VE EVER WRITTEN.
WELL DONE, MAMEZO.
HEE! ♡
DEAR USAGI
I HOPE YOU ARE WELL.
YOU MAY HOLD A GRUDGE AGAINST ME FOR LEAVING YOU IN HAMAMATSU.
BUT I SINCERELY THOUGHT IT WOULD BE BETTER FOR YOU TO BECOME AN HERBALIST AND HELP PEOPLE RATHER THAN BECOME A NINJA.

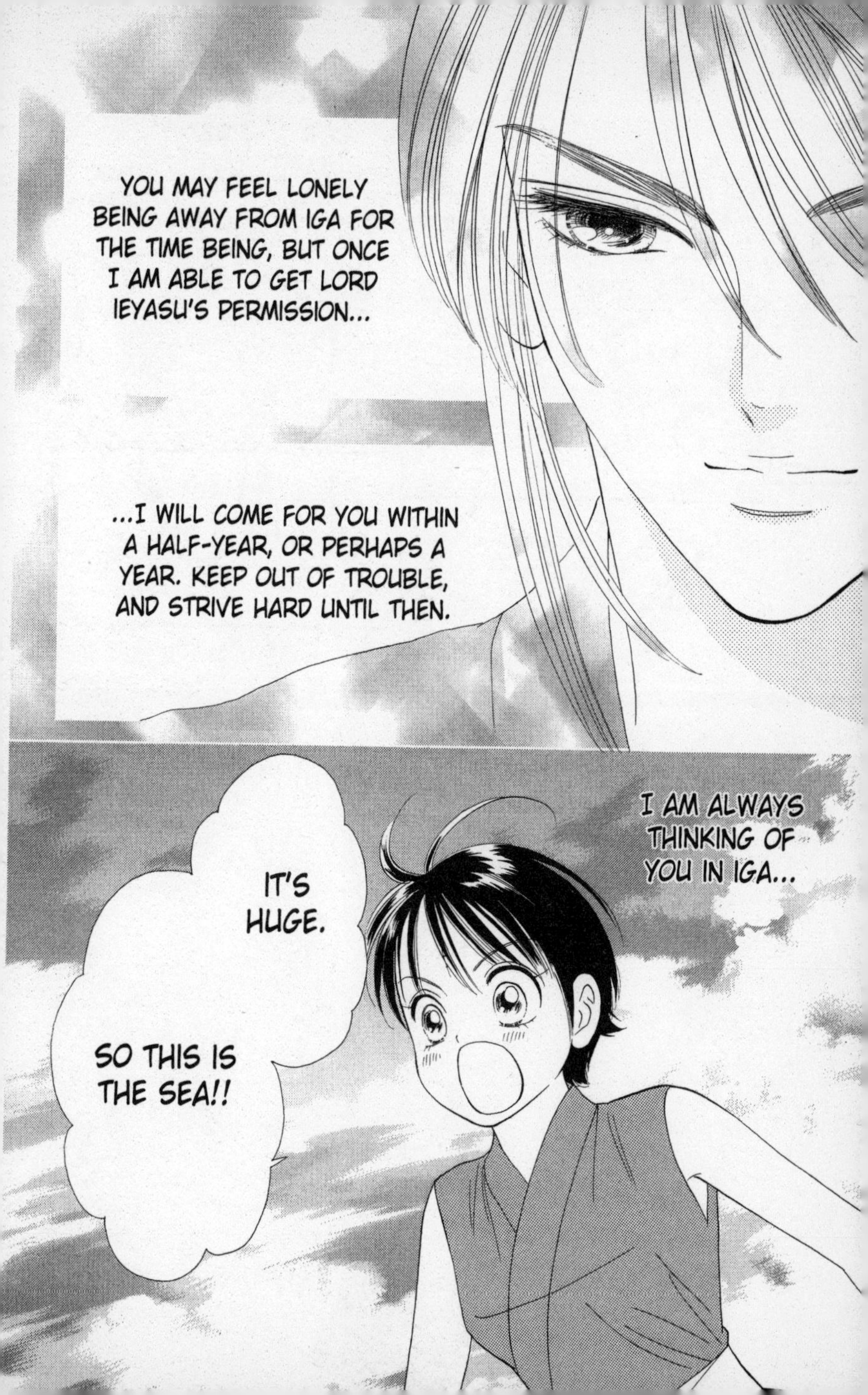
YOU MAY FEEL LONELY BEING AWAY FROM IGA FOR THE TIME BEING, BUT ONCE I AM ABLE TO GET LORD IEYASU'S PERMISSION...
...I WILL COME FOR YOU WITHIN A HALF-YEAR, OR PERHAPS A YEAR. KEEP OUT OF TROUBLE, AND STRIVE HARD UNTIL THEN.
I AM ALWAYS THINKING OF YOU IN IGA...
IT'S HUGE.
SO THIS IS THE SEA!!

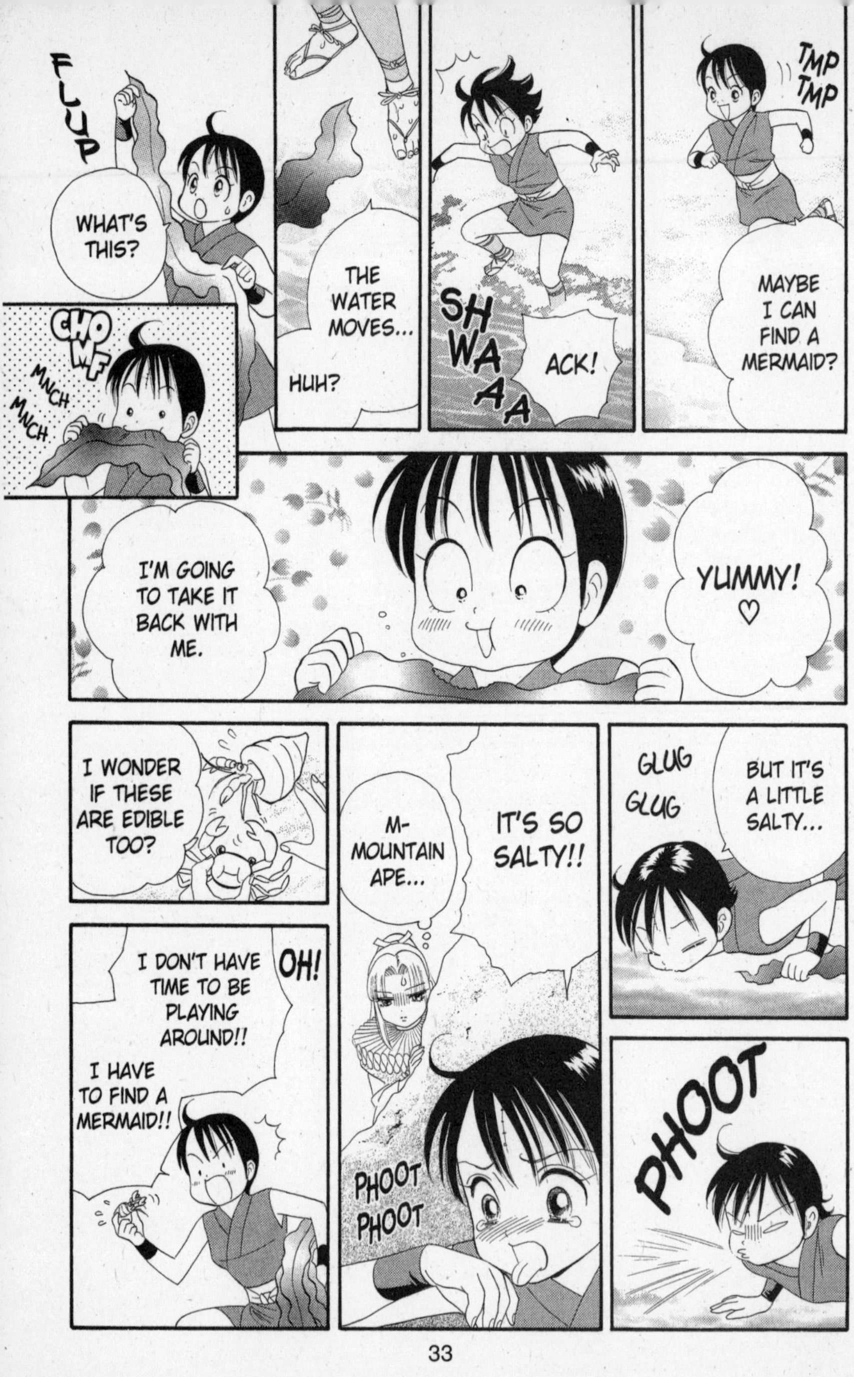
TMP TMP
MAYBE I CAN FIND A MERMAID?
SHWAAA
ACK!
THE WATER MOVES...
HUH?
FLUP
WHAT'S THIS?
CHOMF
MNCH MNCH
YUMMY! ♡
I'M GOING TO TAKE IT BACK WITH ME.
BUT IT'S A LITTLE SALTY...
GLUG GLUG
PHOOT
IT'S SO SALTY!!
M-MOUNTAIN APE...
PHOOT PHOOT
I WONDER IF THESE ARE EDIBLE TOO?
OH!
I DON'T HAVE TIME TO BE PLAYING AROUND!!
I HAVE TO FIND A MERMAID!!

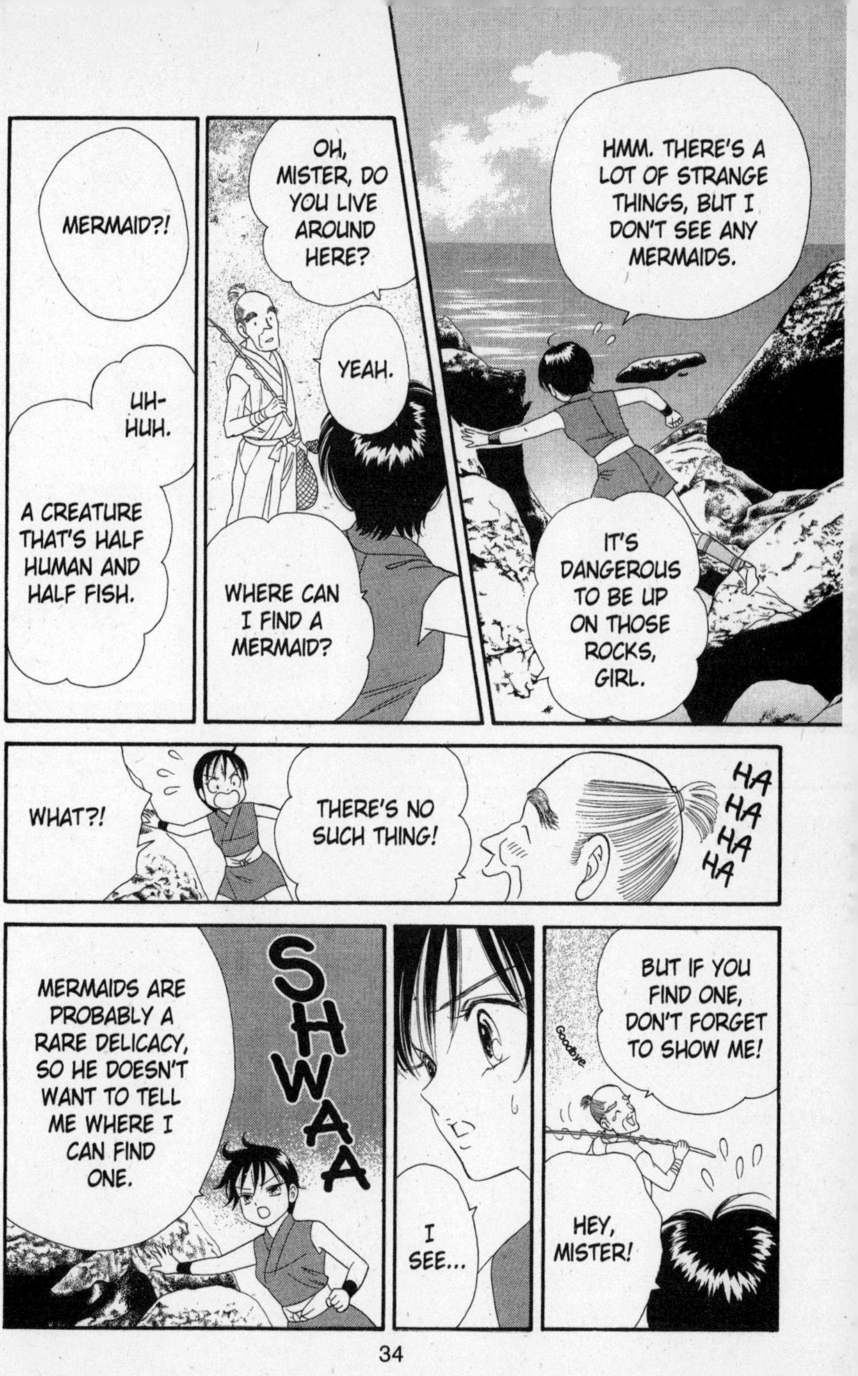
HMM. THERE'S A LOT OF STRANGE THINGS, BUT I DON'T SEE ANY MERMAIDS.
IT'S DANGEROUS TO BE UP ON THOSE ROCKS, GIRL.
OH, MISTER, DO YOU LIVE AROUND HERE?
YEAH.
WHERE CAN I FIND A MERMAID?
MERMAID?!
UH-HUH.
A CREATURE THAT'S HALF HUMAN AND HALF FISH.
HA HA HA HA
THERE'S NO SUCH THING!
WHAT?!
BUT IF YOU FIND ONE, DON'T FORGET TO SHOW ME!
Goodbye
HEY, MISTER!
I SEE...
SHWAA
MERMAIDS ARE PROBABLY A RARE DELICACY, SO HE DOESN'T WANT TO TELL ME WHERE I CAN FIND ONE.

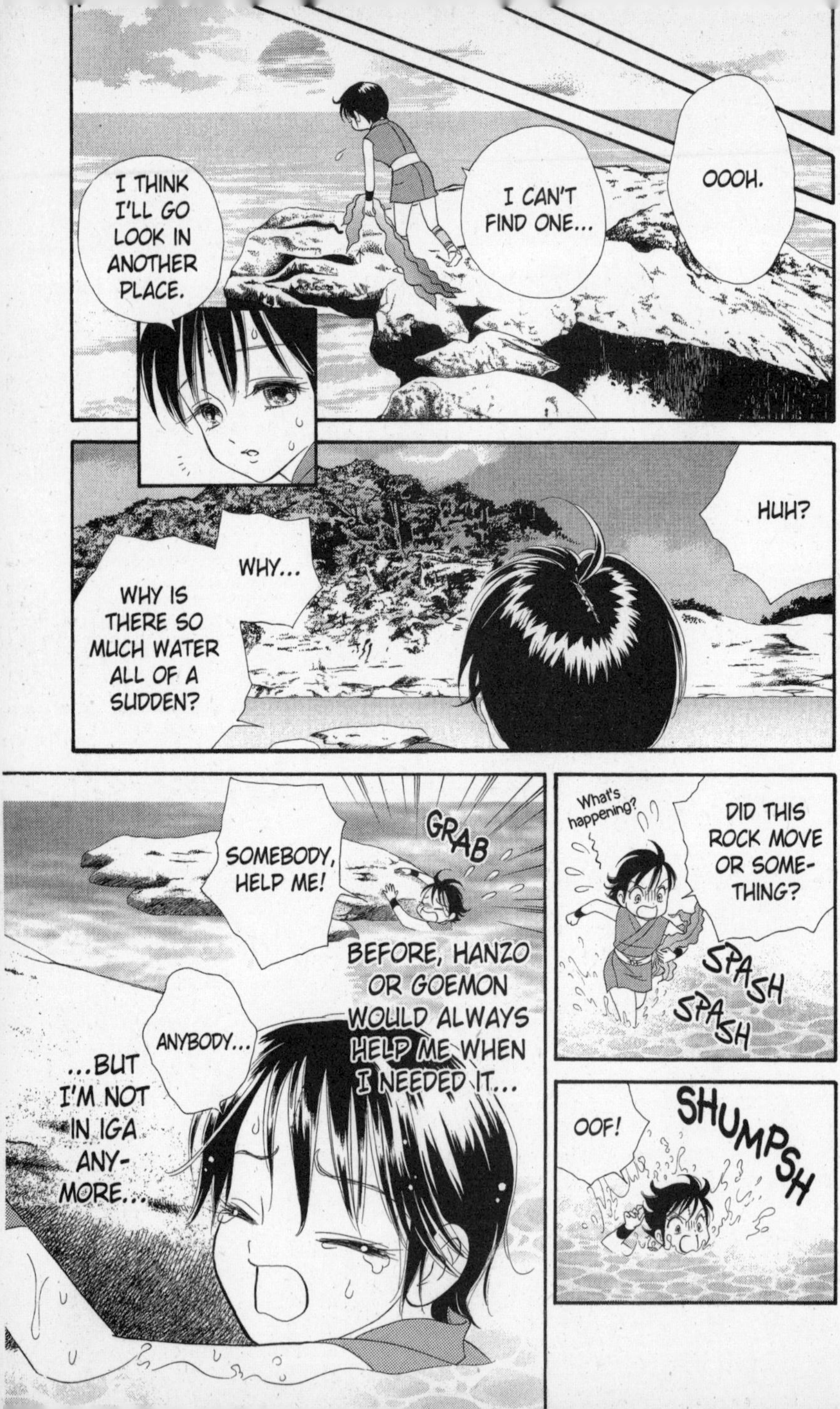
OOOH.
I CAN'T FIND ONE...
I THINK I'LL GO LOOK IN ANOTHER PLACE.
HUH?
WHY...
WHY IS THERE SO MUCH WATER ALL OF A SUDDEN?
DID THIS ROCK MOVE OR SOME-THING?
What's happening?
SPASH
SPASH
SHUMPSH
OOF!
GRAB
SOMEBODY, HELP ME!
BEFORE, HANZO OR GOEMON WOULD ALWAYS HELP ME WHEN I NEEDED IT...
ANYBODY...
...BUT I'M NOT IN IGA ANY-MORE...

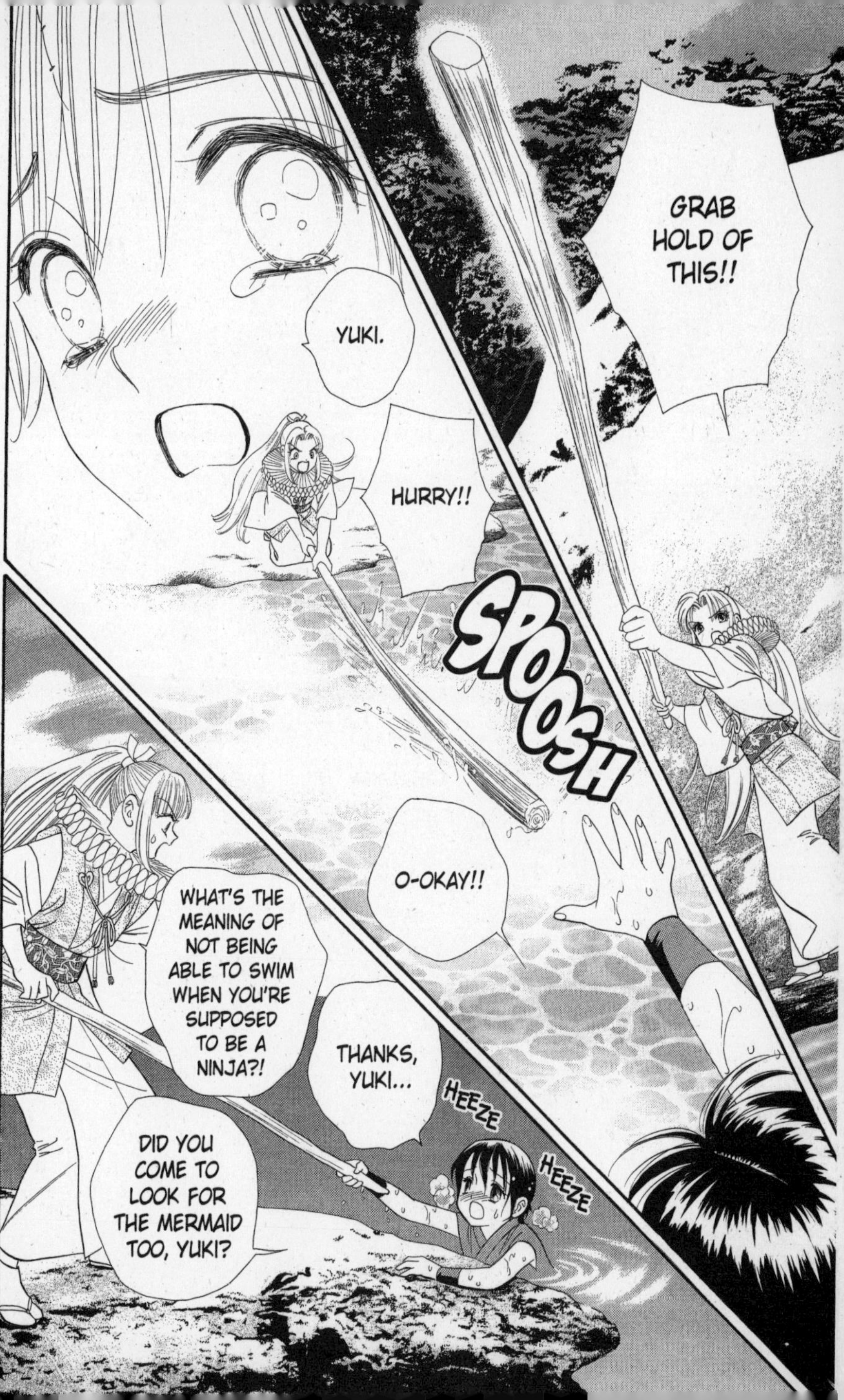
GRAB HOLD OF THIS!!
YUKI.
HURRY!!
SPOOSH
O-OKAY!!
THANKS, YUKI...
HEEZE
HEEZE
WHAT'S THE MEANING OF NOT BEING ABLE TO SWIM WHEN YOU'RE SUPPOSED TO BE A NINJA?!
DID YOU COME TO LOOK FOR THE MERMAID TOO, YUKI?

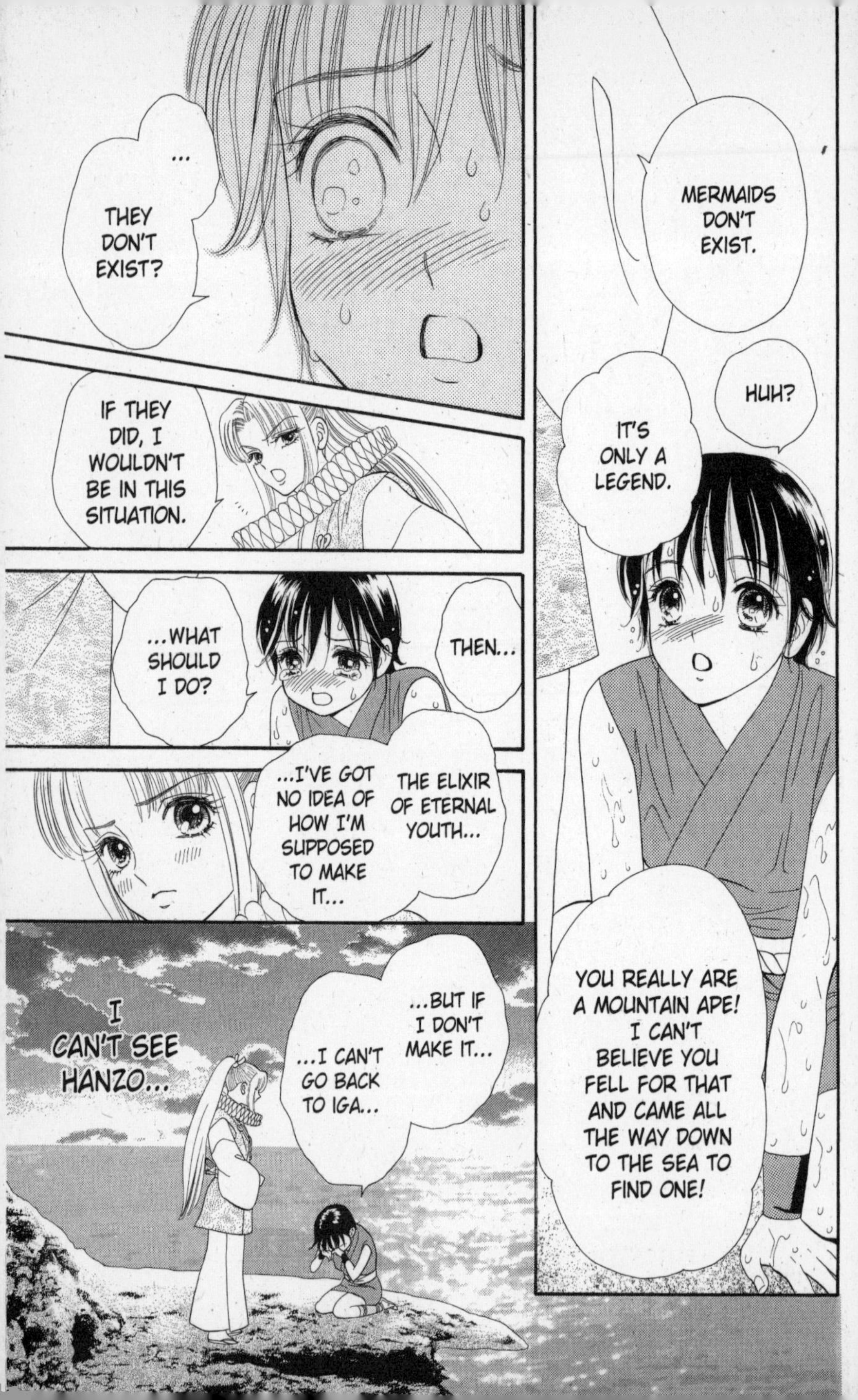
MERMAIDS DON'T EXIST.
HUH?
IT'S ONLY A LEGEND.
YOU REALLY ARE A MOUNTAIN APE! I CAN'T BELIEVE YOU FELL FOR THAT AND CAME ALL THE WAY DOWN TO THE SEA TO FIND ONE!
...
THEY DON'T EXIST?
IF THEY DID, I WOULDN'T BE IN THIS SITUATION.
THEN...
...WHAT SHOULD I DO?
THE ELIXIR OF ETERNAL YOUTH...
...I'VE GOT NO IDEA OF HOW I'M SUPPOSED TO MAKE IT...
...BUT IF I DON'T MAKE IT...
...I CAN'T GO BACK TO IGA...
I CAN'T SEE HANZO...

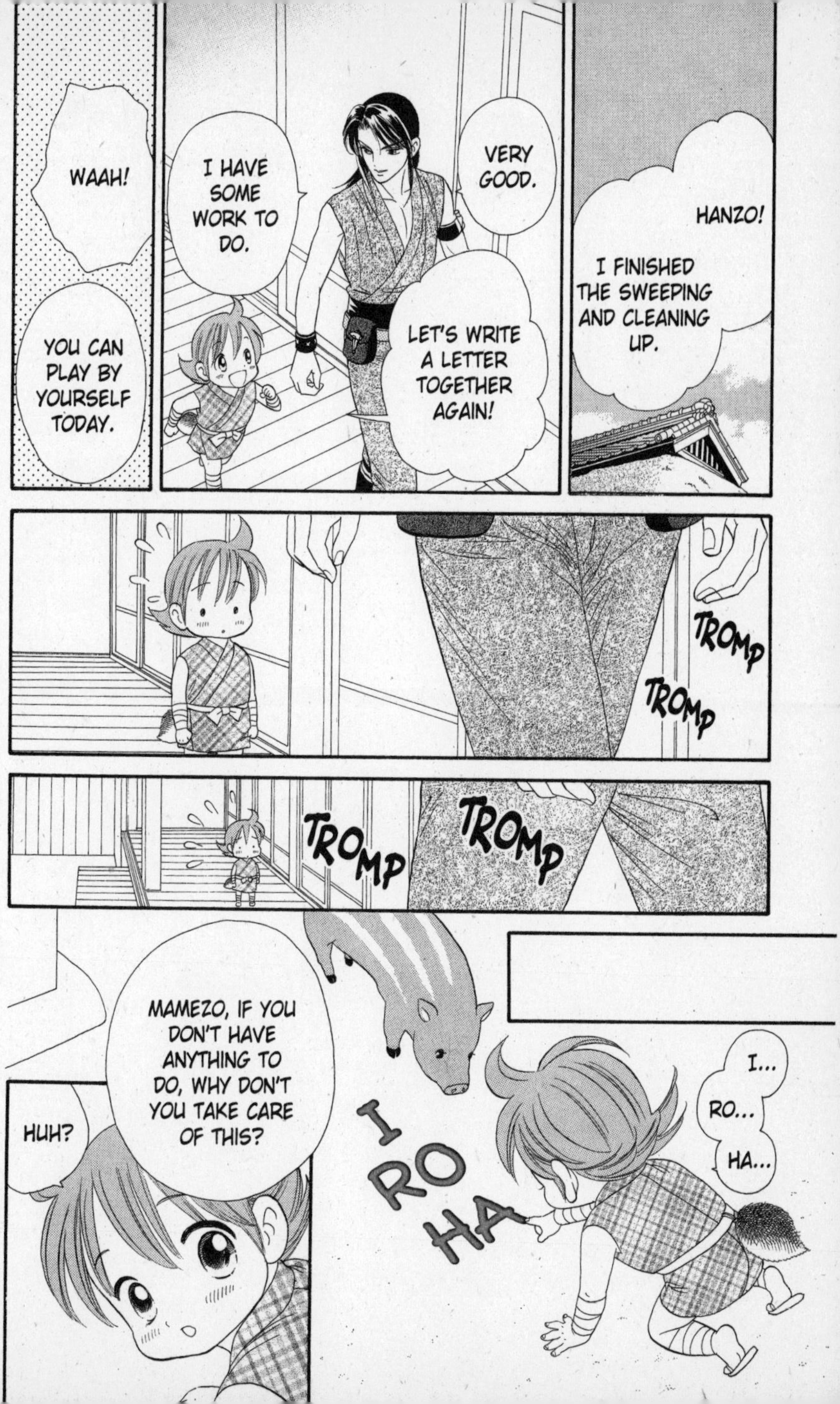
HANZO!
I FINISHED THE SWEEPING AND CLEANING UP.
VERY GOOD.
LET'S WRITE A LETTER TOGETHER AGAIN!
I HAVE SOME WORK TO DO.
WAAH!
YOU CAN PLAY BY YOURSELF TODAY.
TROMP
TROMP
TROMP
TROMP
I... RO... HA...
I RO HA
MAMEZO, IF YOU DON'T HAVE ANYTHING TO DO, WHY DON'T YOU TAKE CARE OF THIS?
HUH?

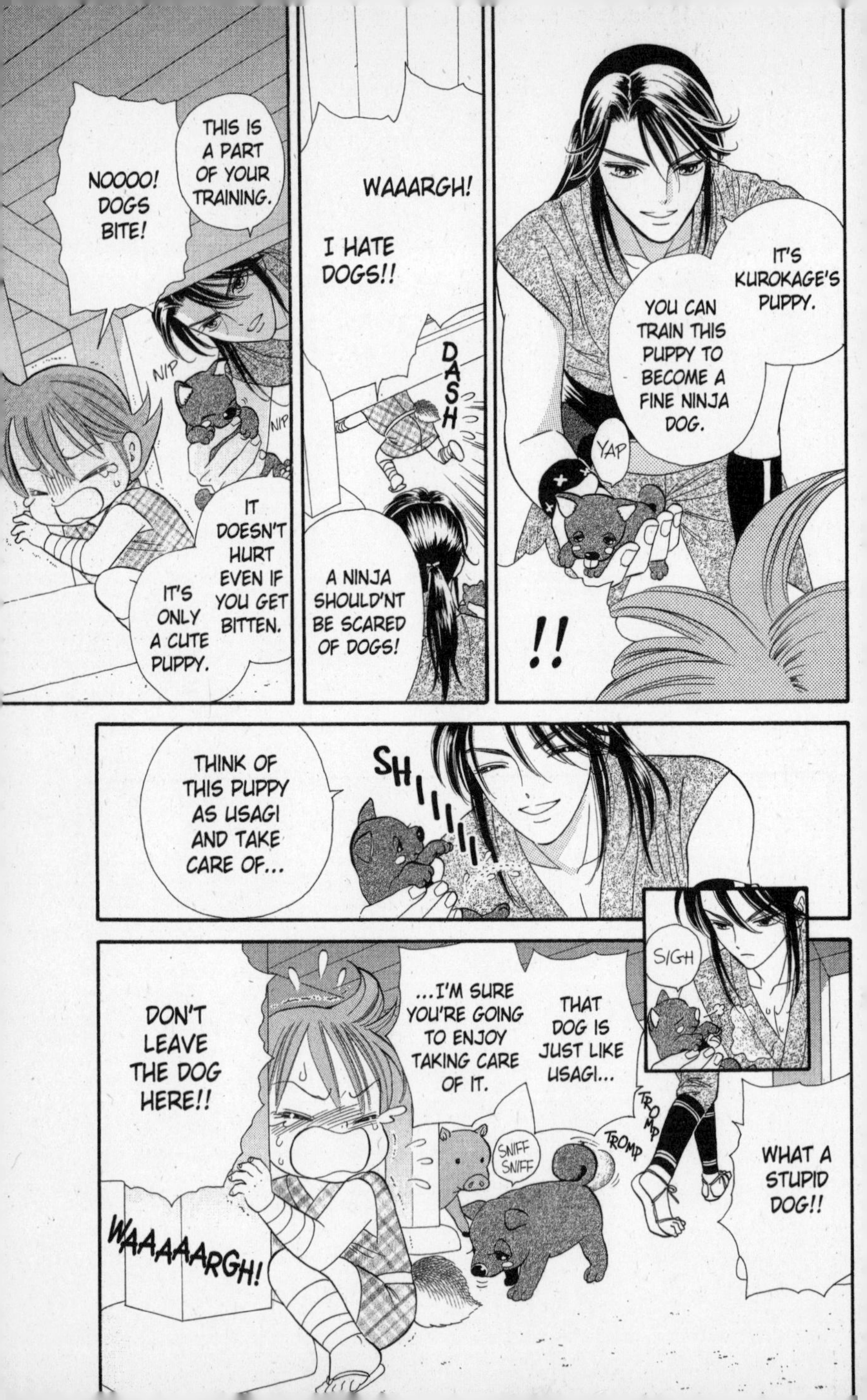
IT'S KUROKAGE'S PUPPY.
YOU CAN TRAIN THIS PUPPY TO BECOME A FINE NINJA DOG.
YAP
!!
WAAARGH!
I HATE DOGS!!
DASH
A NINJA SHOULD'NT BE SCARED OF DOGS!
THIS IS A PART OF YOUR TRAINING.
NOOOO! DOGS BITE!
NIP
NIP
IT DOESN'T HURT EVEN IF YOU GET BITTEN.
IT'S ONLY A CUTE PUPPY.
THINK OF THIS PUPPY AS USAGI AND TAKE CARE OF...
SHIIIII
SIGH
WHAT A STUPID DOG!!
TROMP
TROMP
THAT DOG IS JUST LIKE USAGI...
...I'M SURE YOU'RE GOING TO ENJOY TAKING CARE OF IT.
SNIFF SNIFF
DON'T LEAVE THE DOG HERE!!
WAAAAARGH!

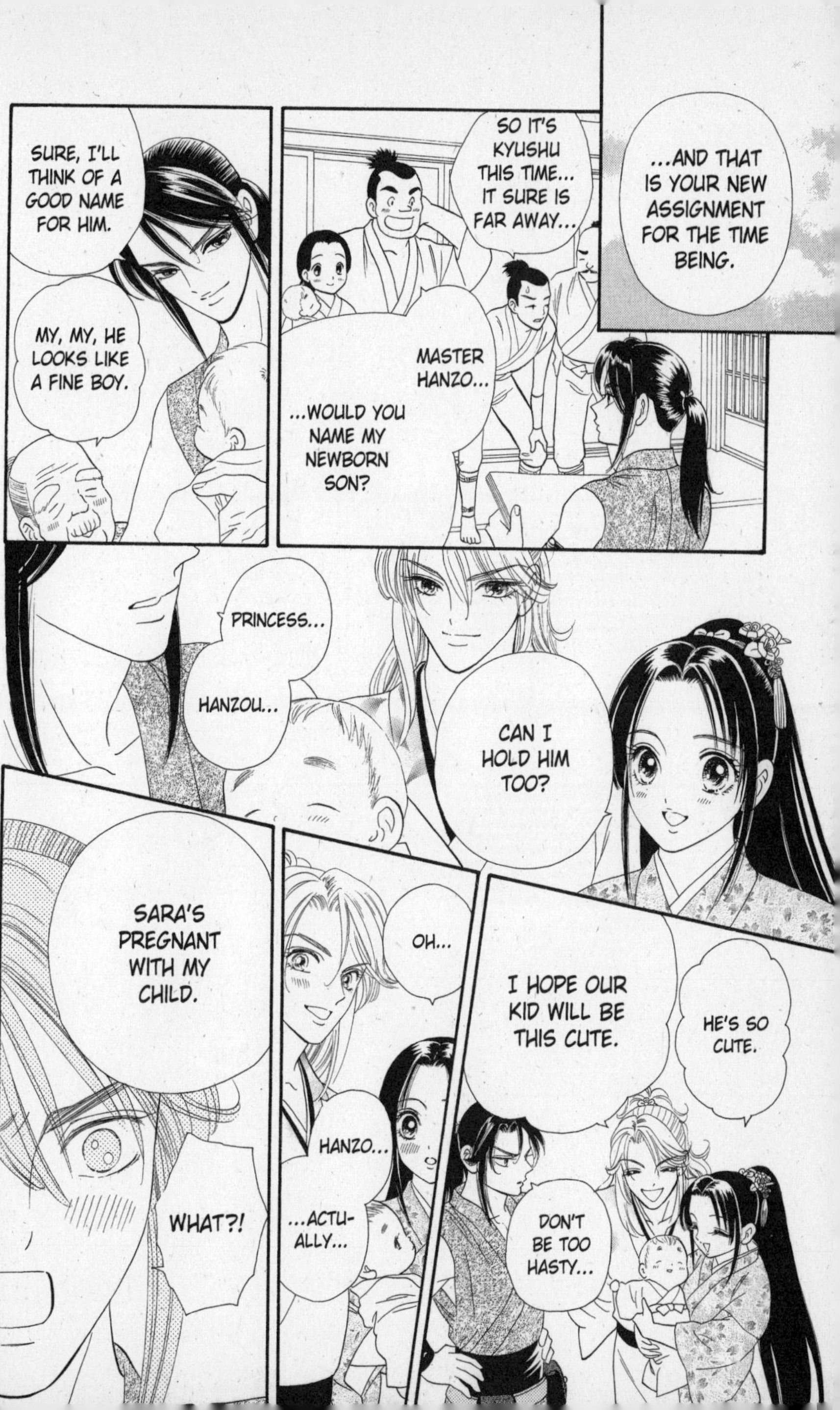
...AND THAT IS YOUR NEW ASSIGNMENT FOR THE TIME BEING.
SO IT'S KYUSHU THIS TIME... IT SURE IS FAR AWAY...
MASTER HANZO...
...WOULD YOU NAME MY NEWBORN SON?
SURE, I'LL THINK OF A GOOD NAME FOR HIM.
MY, MY, HE LOOKS LIKE A FINE BOY.
CAN I HOLD HIM TOO?
PRINCESS...
HANZOU...
HE'S SO CUTE.
I HOPE OUR KID WILL BE THIS CUTE.
DON'T BE TOO HASTY...
OH...
HANZO...
...ACTU-ALLY...
SARA'S PREGNANT WITH MY CHILD.
WHAT?!

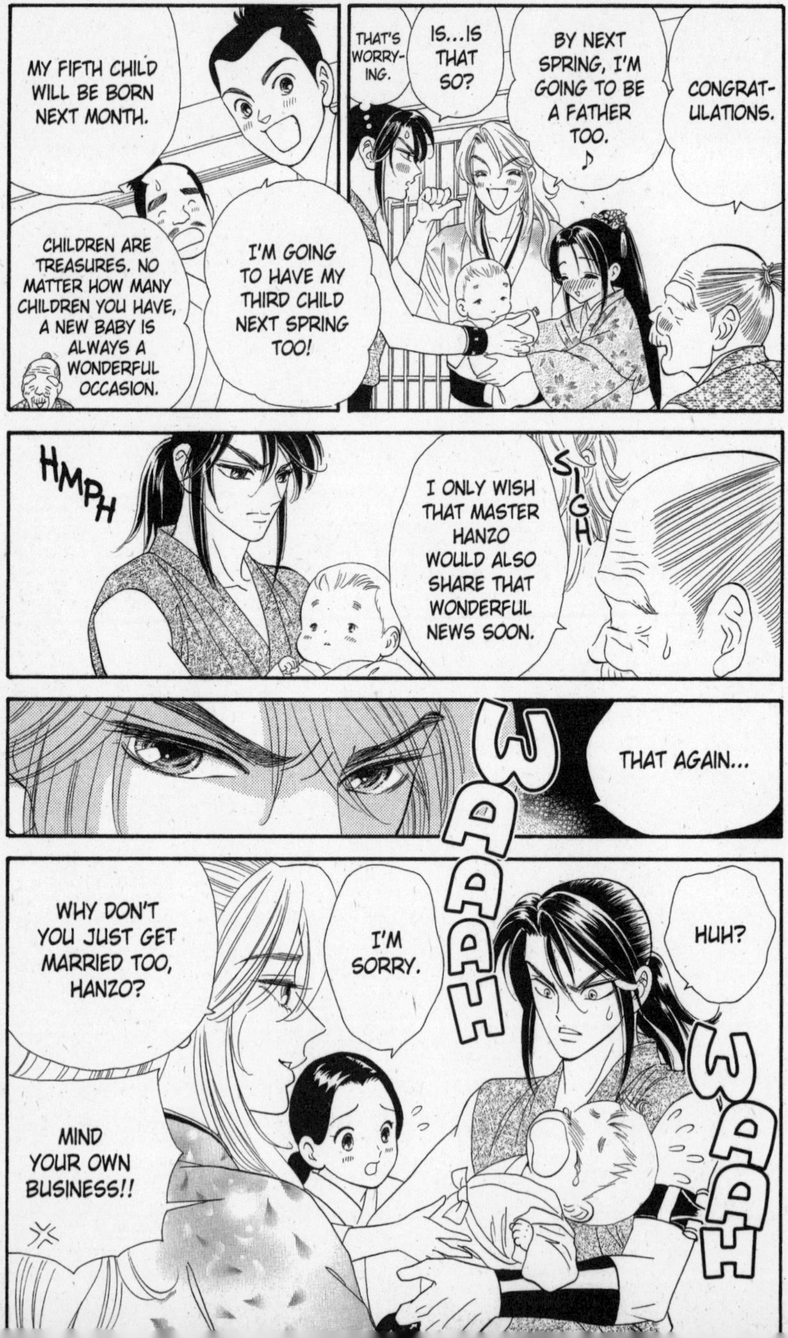
CONGRATULATIONS.
BY NEXT SPRING, I'M GOING TO BE A FATHER TOO. ♪
IS...IS THAT SO?
THAT'S WORRYING.
MY FIFTH CHILD WILL BE BORN NEXT MONTH.
I'M GOING TO HAVE MY THIRD CHILD NEXT SPRING TOO!
CHILDREN ARE TREASURES. NO MATTER HOW MANY CHILDREN YOU HAVE, A NEW BABY IS ALWAYS A WONDERFUL OCCASION.
SIGH
I ONLY WISH THAT MASTER HANZO WOULD ALSO SHARE THAT WONDERFUL NEWS SOON.
HMPH
THAT AGAIN...
WAAAAH
WAAAH
HUH?
I'M SORRY.
WHY DON'T YOU JUST GET MARRIED TOO, HANZO?
MIND YOUR OWN BUSINESS!!

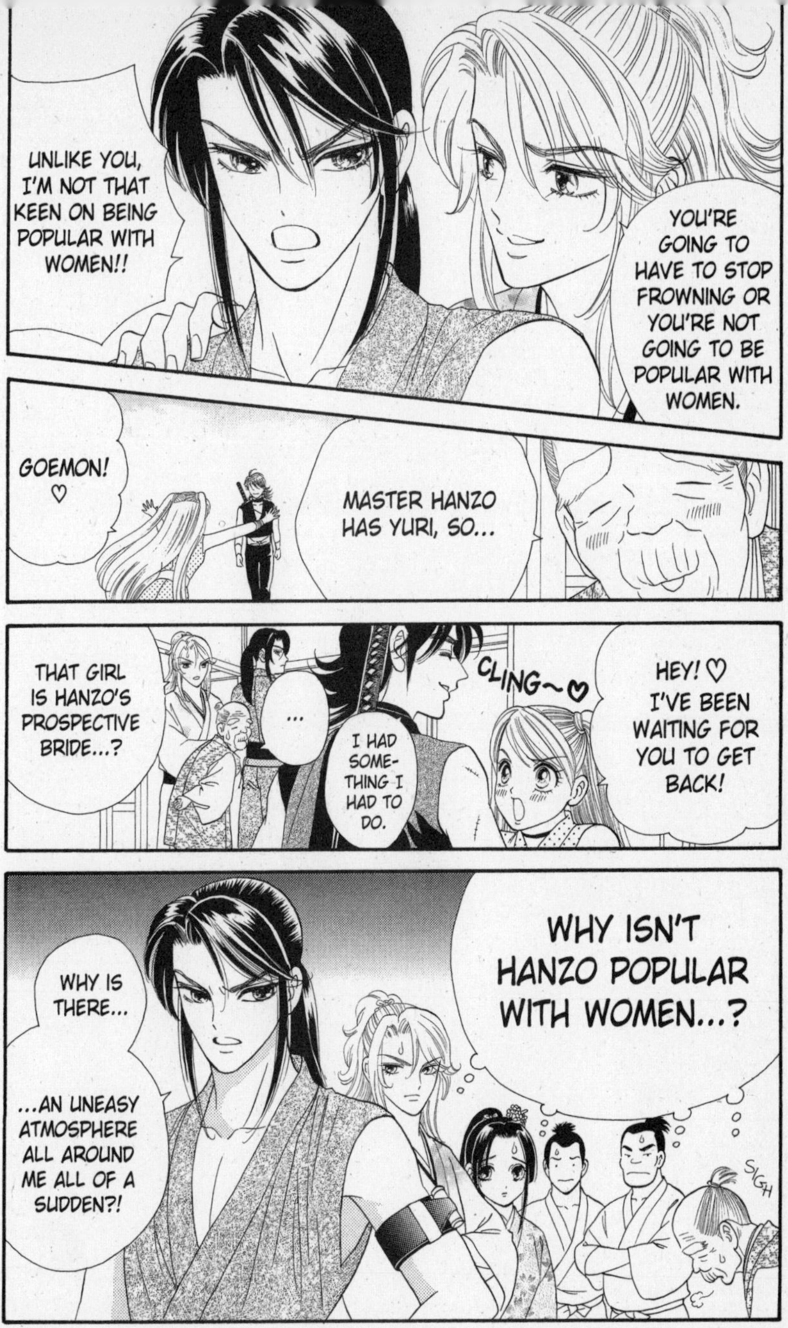
YOU'RE GOING TO HAVE TO STOP FROWNING OR YOU'RE NOT GOING TO BE POPULAR WITH WOMEN.
UNLIKE YOU, I'M NOT THAT KEEN ON BEING POPULAR WITH WOMEN!!
MASTER HANZO HAS YURI, SO...
GOEMON! ♡
HEY! ♡ I'VE BEEN WAITING FOR YOU TO GET BACK!
CLING~♡
I HAD SOME-THING I HAD TO DO.
...
THAT GIRL IS HANZO'S PROSPECTIVE BRIDE...?
WHY ISN'T HANZO POPULAR WITH WOMEN...?
SIGH
WHY IS THERE...
...AN UNEASY ATMOSPHERE ALL AROUND ME ALL OF A SUDDEN?!

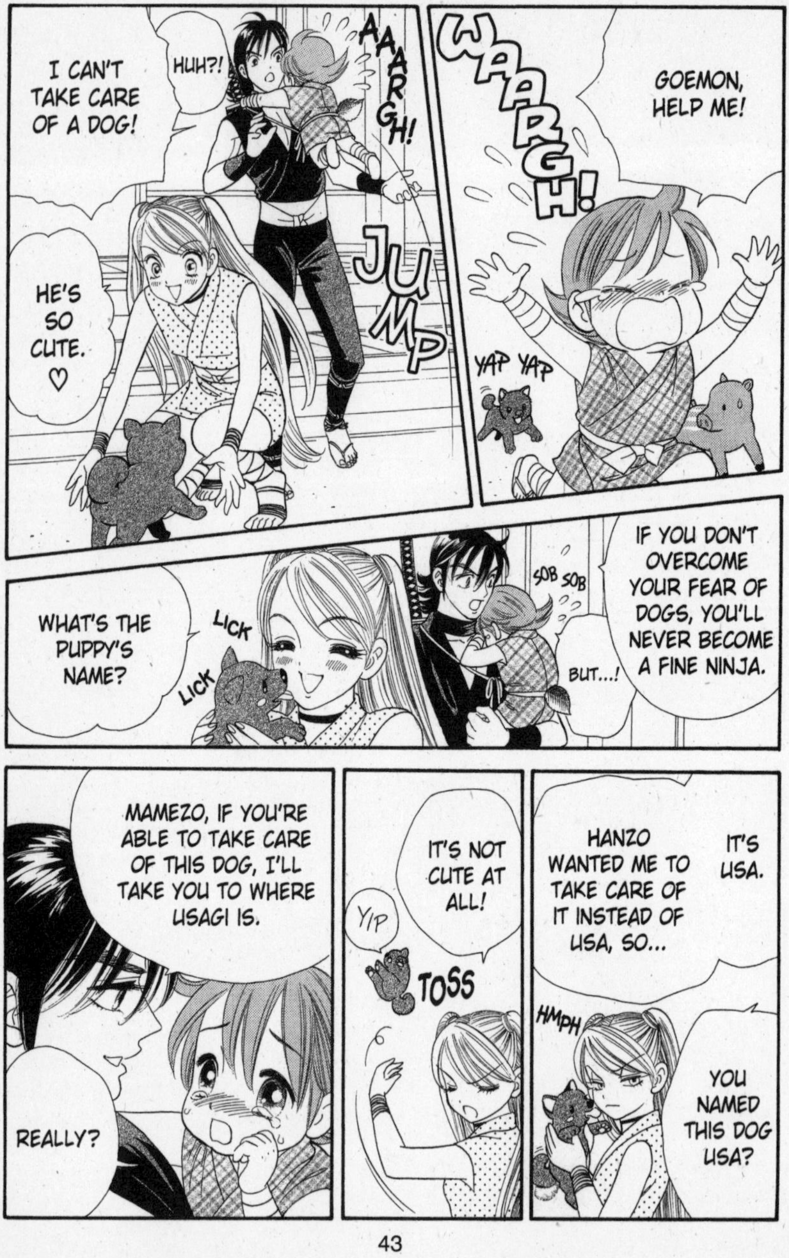
GOEMON, HELP ME!
WAARGH!
YAP YAP
AAARGH!
HUH?!
I CAN'T TAKE CARE OF A DOG!
JUMP
HE'S SO CUTE. ♡
IF YOU DON'T OVERCOME YOUR FEAR OF DOGS, YOU'LL NEVER BECOME A FINE NINJA.
SOB SOB
BUT...!
WHAT'S THE PUPPY'S NAME?
LICK
LICK
IT'S USA.
HANZO WANTED ME TO TAKE CARE OF IT INSTEAD OF USA, SO...
YOU NAMED THIS DOG USA?
HMPH
IT'S NOT CUTE AT ALL!
YIP
TOSS
MAMEZO, IF YOU'RE ABLE TO TAKE CARE OF THIS DOG, I'LL TAKE YOU TO WHERE USAGI IS.
REALLY?

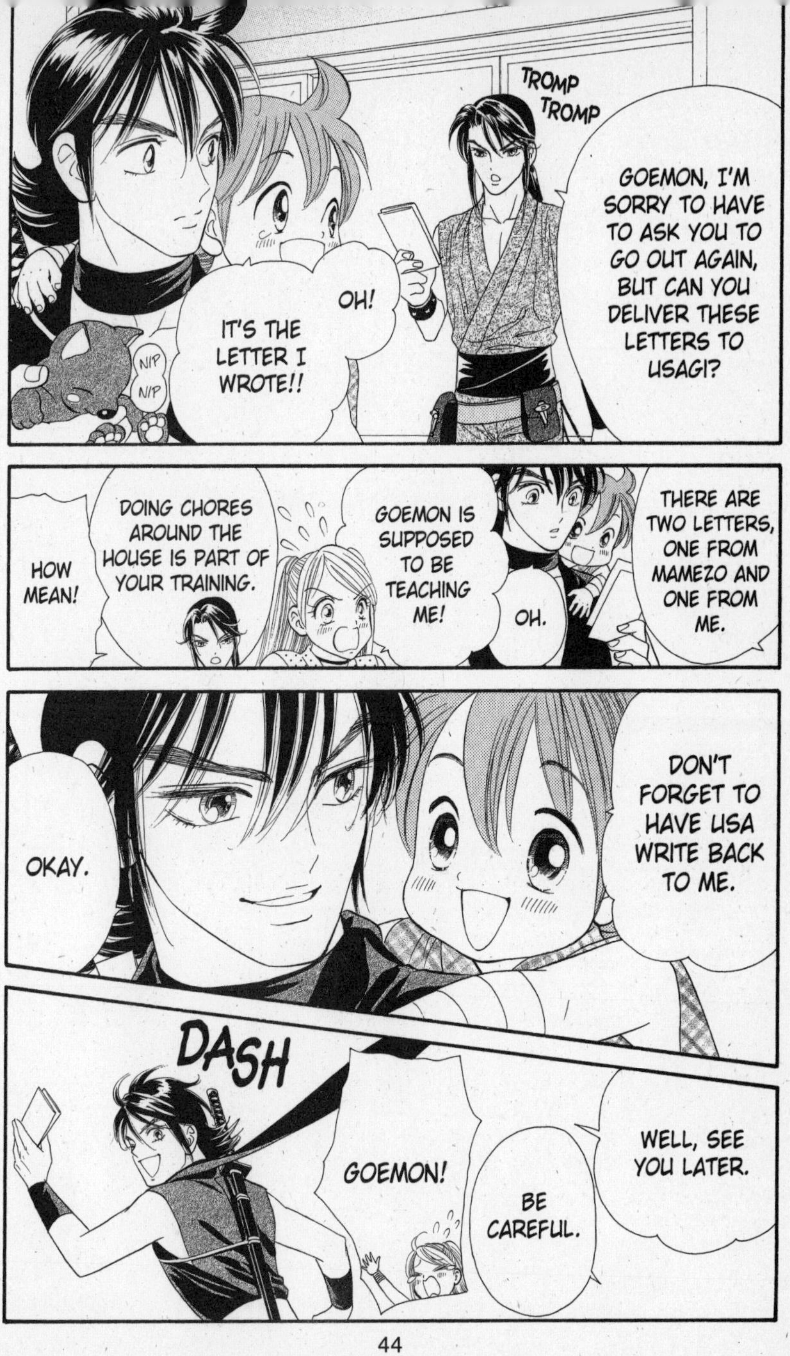
TROMP TROMP
GOEMON, I'M SORRY TO HAVE TO ASK YOU TO GO OUT AGAIN, BUT CAN YOU DELIVER THESE LETTERS TO USAGI?
OH!
IT'S THE LETTER I WROTE!!
NIP NIP
THERE ARE TWO LETTERS, ONE FROM MAMEZO AND ONE FROM ME.
OH.
GOEMON IS SUPPOSED TO BE TEACHING ME!
DOING CHORES AROUND THE HOUSE IS PART OF YOUR TRAINING.
HOW MEAN!
DON'T FORGET TO HAVE USA WRITE BACK TO ME.
OKAY.
WELL, SEE YOU LATER.
BE CAREFUL.
GOEMON!
DASH

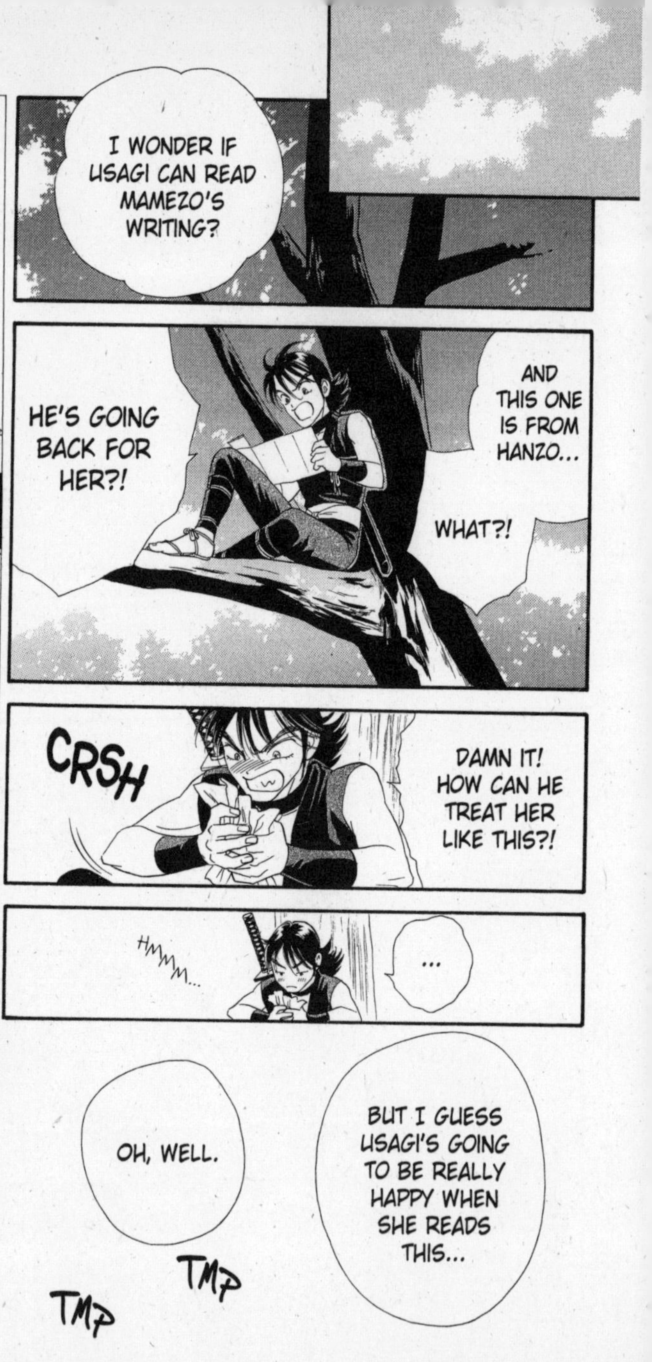

I WONDER IF USAGI CAN READ MAMEZO'S WRITING?
AND THIS ONE IS FROM HANZO...
WHAT?!
HE'S GOING BACK FOR HER?!
DAMN IT! HOW CAN HE TREAT HER LIKE THIS?!
CRSH
...
HMMM...
BUT I GUESS USAGI'S GOING TO BE REALLY HAPPY WHEN SHE READS THIS...
OH, WELL.
TMP
TMP

Stories About My Research Trip #1

I left my parent's house in Nara and rode the Kintetsu Line to Iga Ueno Station!! I was immediately greeted there by a Ninja Train.

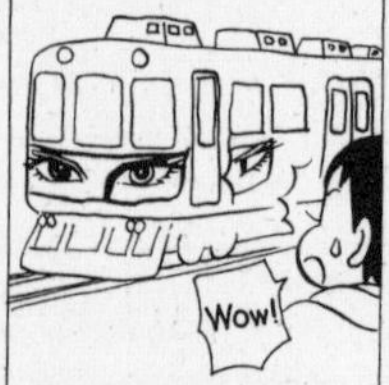

Wow!

The pink train had a huge kunoichi drawn on it, and the green train had a huge ninja on it. How nice! ♪ So, without hesitation, I took a photograph of the Ninja Train as a souvenir. I learned about the major tourist spots at the tourist information center located right next to the station, and even got hold of a map and a book on ninja history.

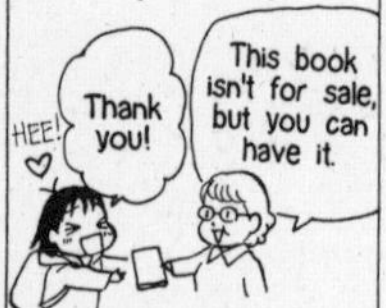

This book isn't for sale, but you can have it.
Thank you!
HEE! ♡

My first destination is the Iga-ryu Ninja Museum. Let's go!!

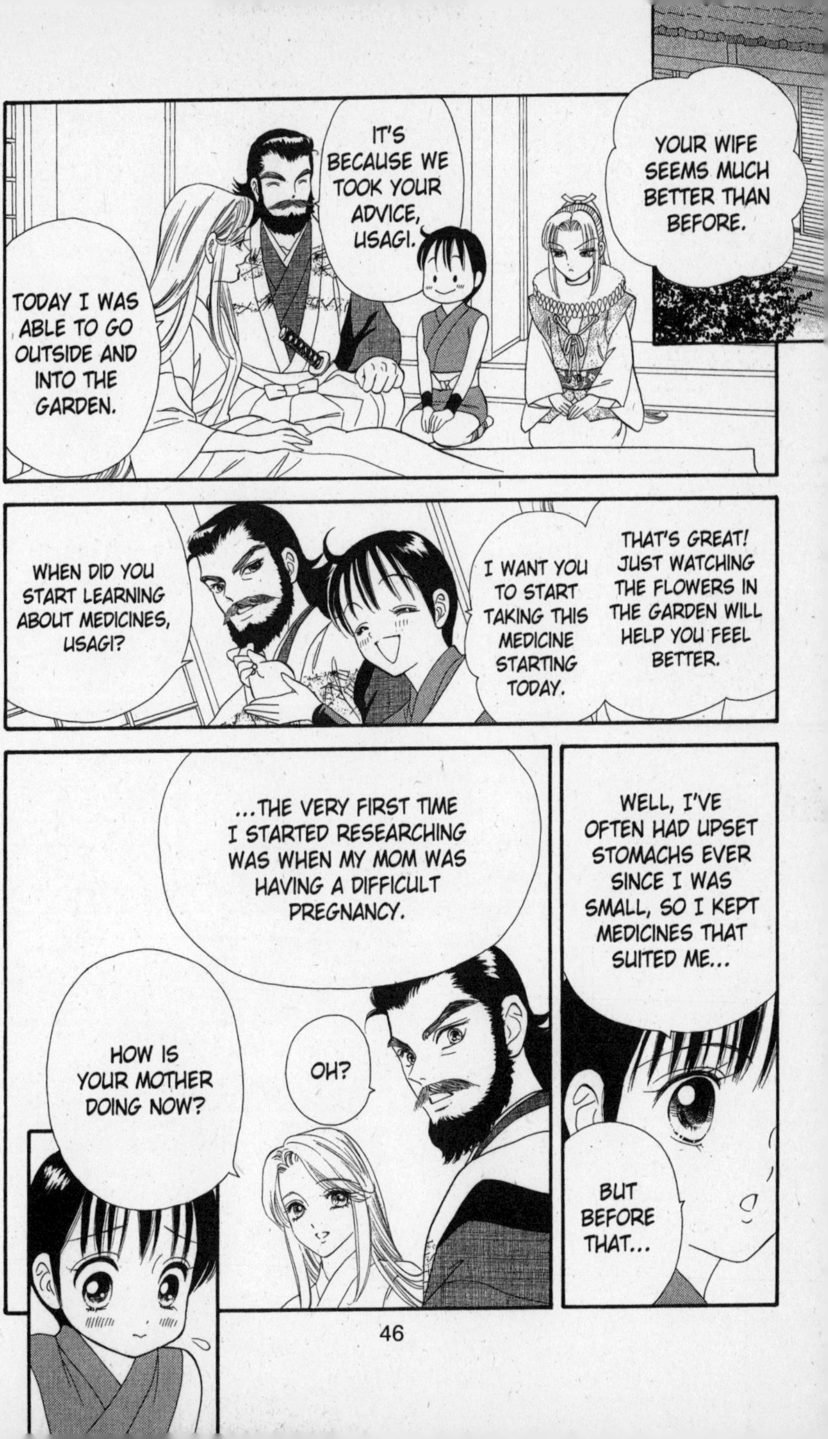

YOUR WIFE SEEMS MUCH BETTER THAN BEFORE.
IT'S BECAUSE WE TOOK YOUR ADVICE, USAGI.
TODAY I WAS ABLE TO GO OUTSIDE AND INTO THE GARDEN.
THAT'S GREAT! JUST WATCHING THE FLOWERS IN THE GARDEN WILL HELP YOU FEEL BETTER.
I WANT YOU TO START TAKING THIS MEDICINE STARTING TODAY.
WHEN DID YOU START LEARNING ABOUT MEDICINES, USAGI?
WELL, I'VE OFTEN HAD UPSET STOMACHS EVER SINCE I WAS SMALL, SO I KEPT MEDICINES THAT SUITED ME...
BUT BEFORE THAT...
...THE VERY FIRST TIME I STARTED RESEARCHING WAS WHEN MY MOM WAS HAVING A DIFFICULT PREGNANCY.
OH?
HOW IS YOUR MOTHER DOING NOW?

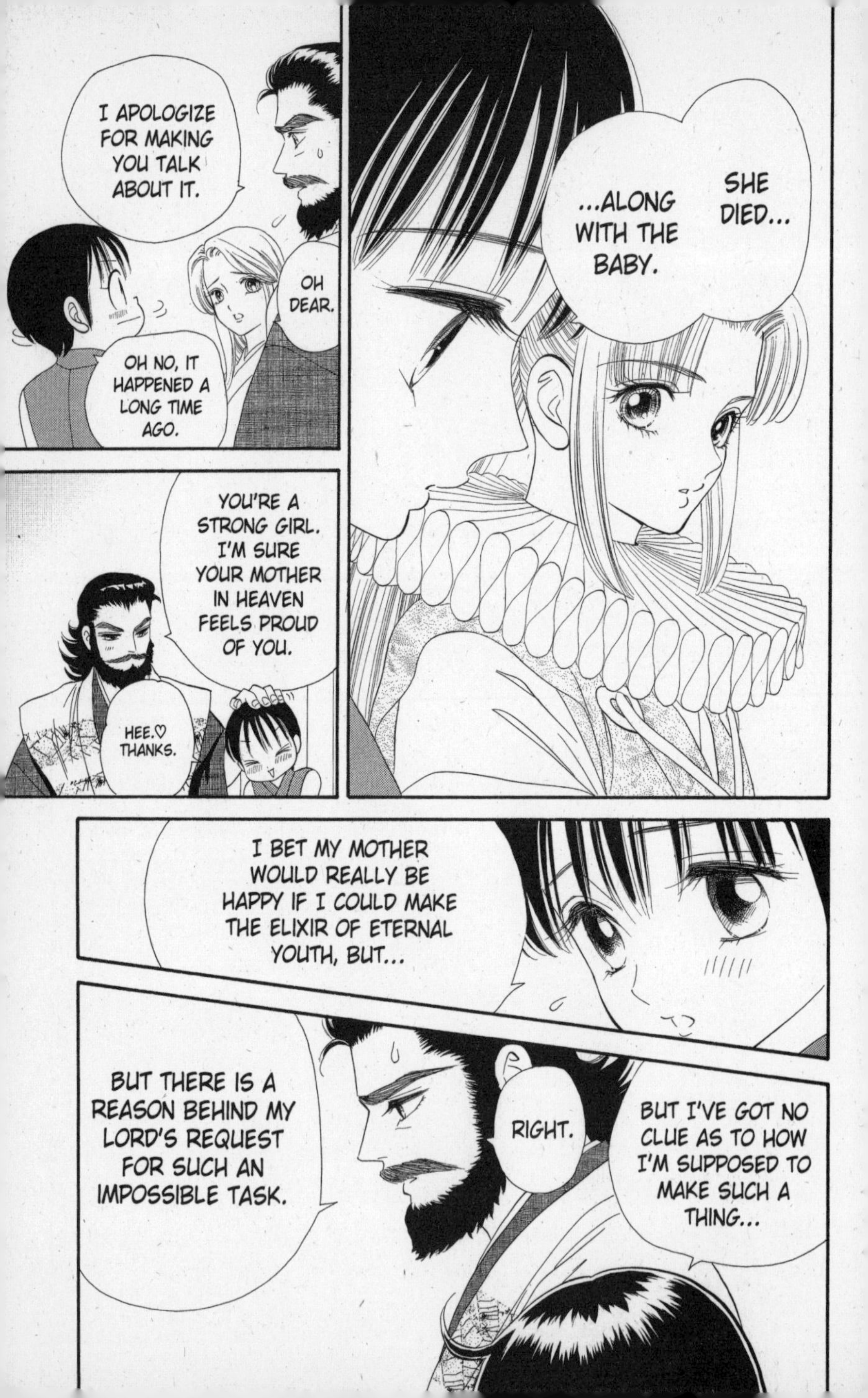
SHE DIED...
...ALONG WITH THE BABY.
I APOLOGIZE FOR MAKING YOU TALK ABOUT IT.
OH DEAR.
OH NO, IT HAPPENED A LONG TIME AGO.
YOU'RE A STRONG GIRL. I'M SURE YOUR MOTHER IN HEAVEN FEELS PROUD OF YOU.
HEE.♡ THANKS.
I BET MY MOTHER WOULD REALLY BE HAPPY IF I COULD MAKE THE ELIXIR OF ETERNAL YOUTH, BUT...
BUT I'VE GOT NO CLUE AS TO HOW I'M SUPPOSED TO MAKE SUCH A THING...
RIGHT.
BUT THERE IS A REASON BEHIND MY LORD'S REQUEST FOR SUCH AN IMPOSSIBLE TASK.

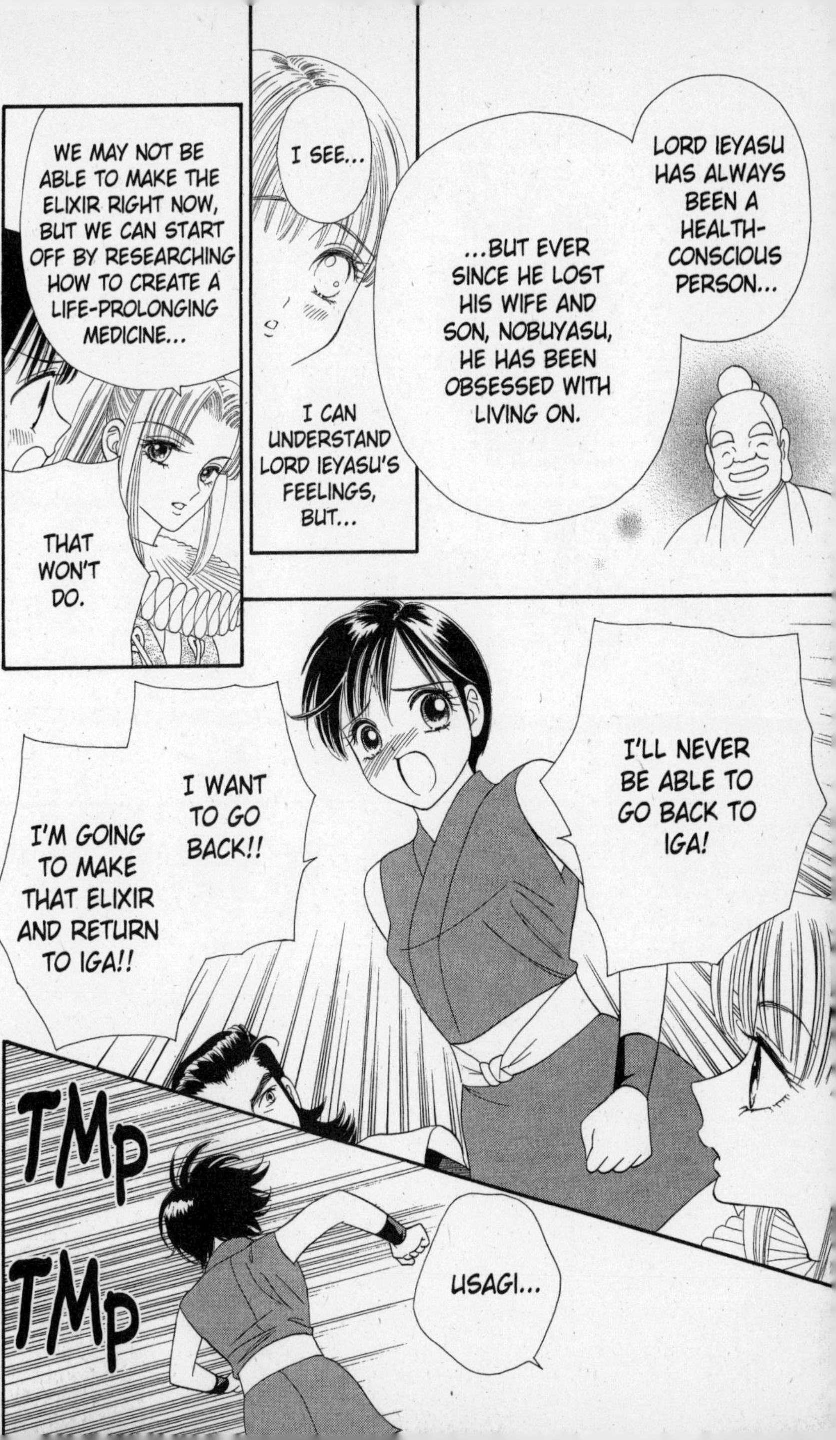
LORD IEYASU HAS ALWAYS BEEN A HEALTH-CONSCIOUS PERSON...
...BUT EVER SINCE HE LOST HIS WIFE AND SON, NOBUYASU, HE HAS BEEN OBSESSED WITH LIVING ON.
I SEE...
I CAN UNDERSTAND LORD IEYASU'S FEELINGS, BUT...
WE MAY NOT BE ABLE TO MAKE THE ELIXIR RIGHT NOW, BUT WE CAN START OFF BY RESEARCHING HOW TO CREATE A LIFE-PROLONGING MEDICINE...
THAT WON'T DO.
I'LL NEVER BE ABLE TO GO BACK TO IGA!
I WANT TO GO BACK!!
I'M GOING TO MAKE THAT ELIXIR AND RETURN TO IGA!!
USAGI...
TMp
TMp

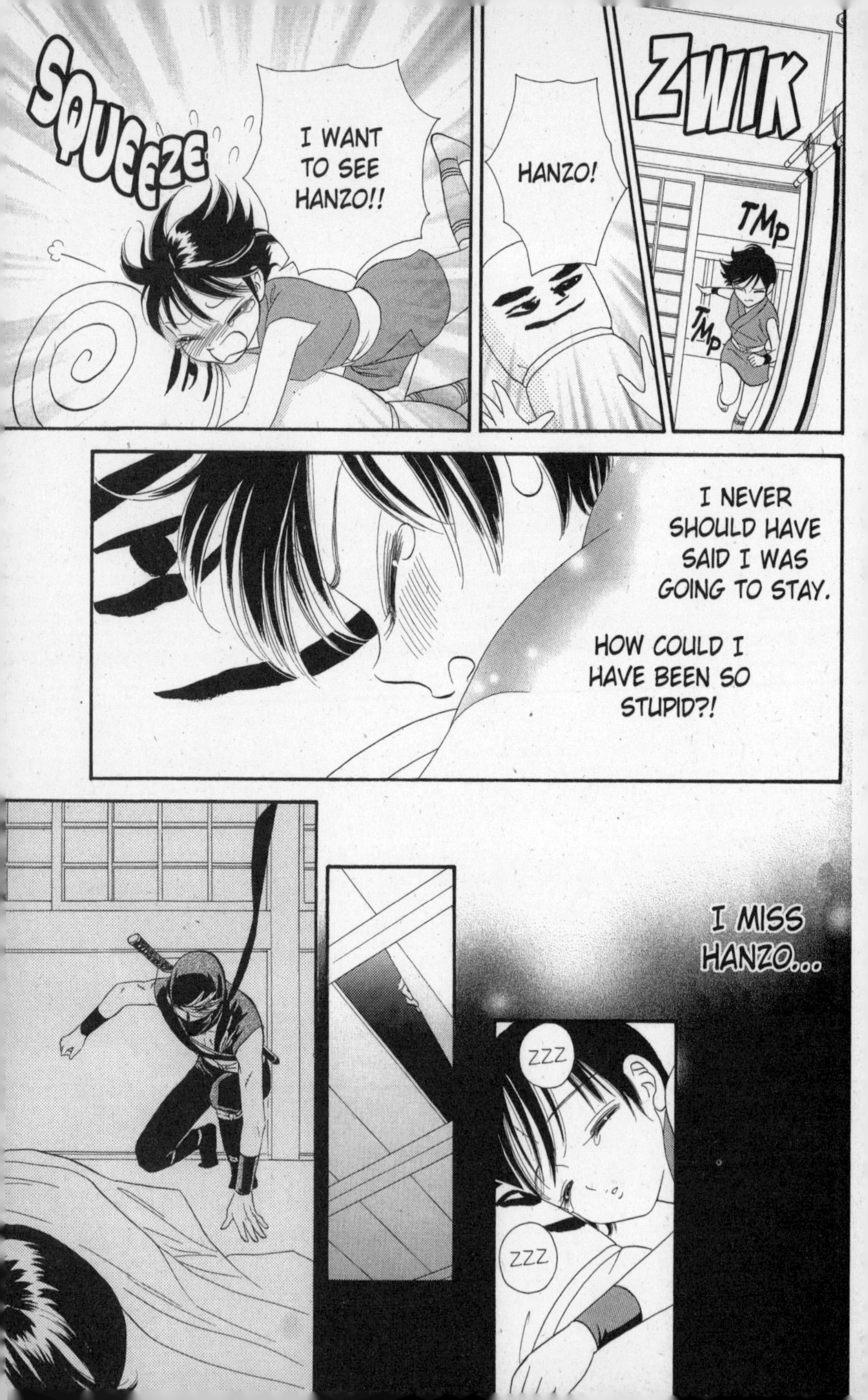
ZWIK
TMp
TMp
HANZO!
SQUEEZE
I WANT TO SEE HANZO!!
I NEVER SHOULD HAVE SAID I WAS GOING TO STAY.
HOW COULD I HAVE BEEN SO STUPID?!
I MISS HANZO...
ZZZ
ZZZ

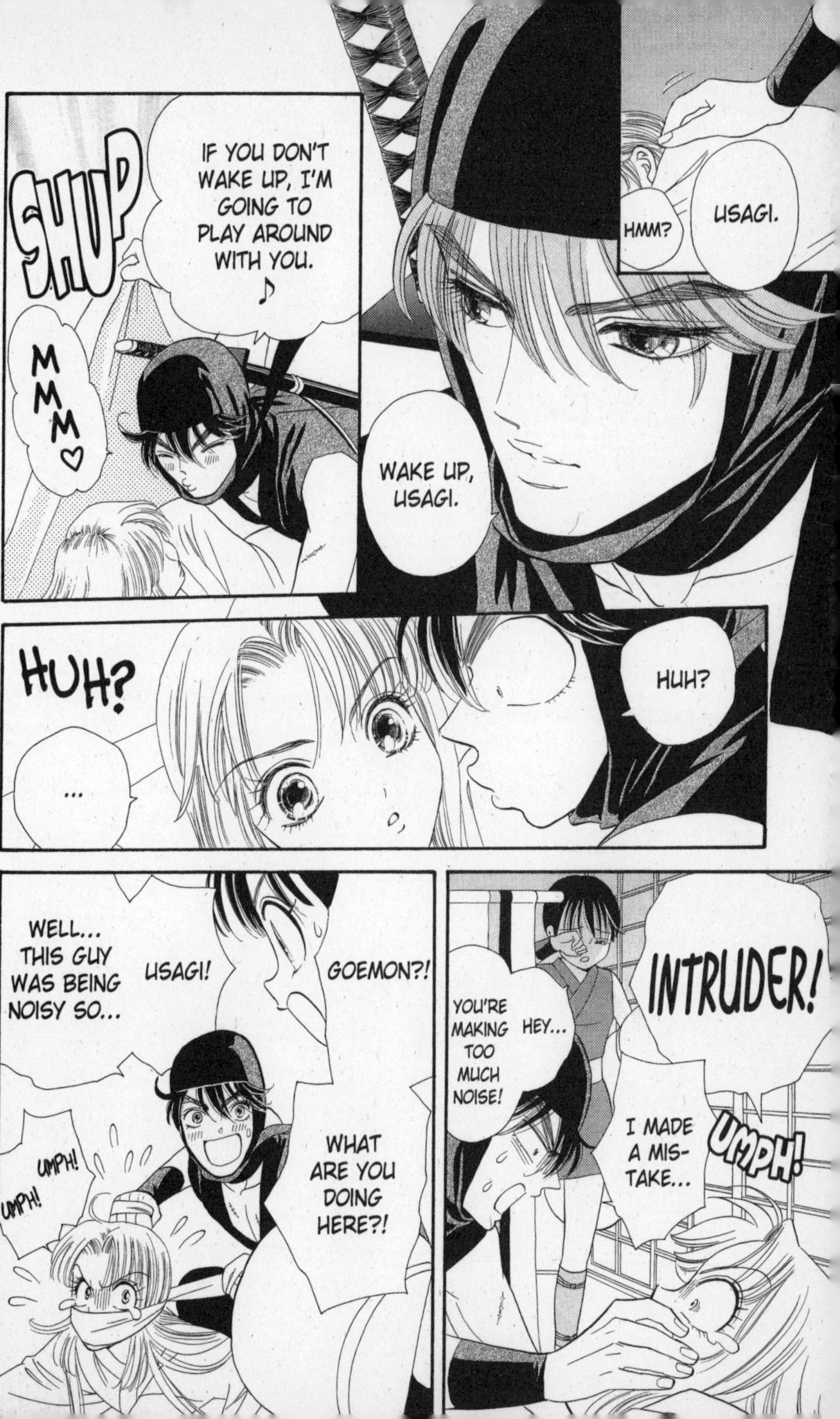

USAGI.
HMM?
WAKE UP, USAGI.
SHUP
IF YOU DON'T WAKE UP, I'M GOING TO PLAY AROUND WITH YOU. ♪
MMM♡
HUH?
HUH?
...
INTRUDER!
HEY...
YOU'RE MAKING TOO MUCH NOISE!
I MADE A MIS-TAKE...
UMPH!
GOEMON?!
USAGI!
WELL... THIS GUY WAS BEING NOISY SO...
WHAT ARE YOU DOING HERE?!
UMPH!
UMPH!

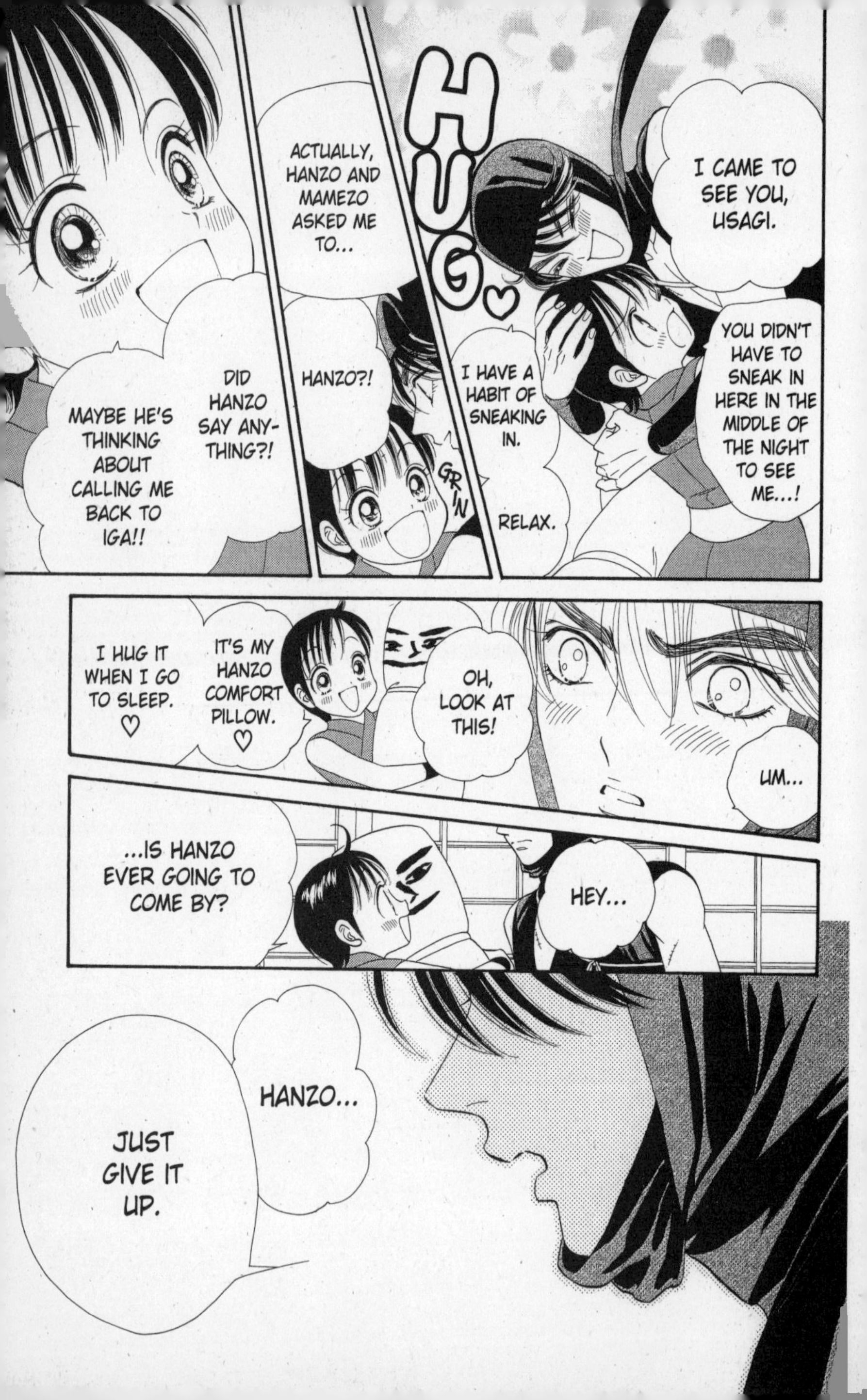
HUG ♡
I CAME TO SEE YOU, USAGI.
YOU DIDN'T HAVE TO SNEAK IN HERE IN THE MIDDLE OF THE NIGHT TO SEE ME...!
I HAVE A HABIT OF SNEAKING IN.
RELAX.
ACTUALLY, HANZO AND MAMEZO ASKED ME TO...
GRIN
HANZO?!
DID HANZO SAY ANY-THING?!
MAYBE HE'S THINKING ABOUT CALLING ME BACK TO IGA!!
UM...
OH, LOOK AT THIS!
IT'S MY HANZO COMFORT PILLOW. ♡
I HUG IT WHEN I GO TO SLEEP. ♡
HEY...
...IS HANZO EVER GOING TO COME BY?
HANZO...
JUST GIVE IT UP.

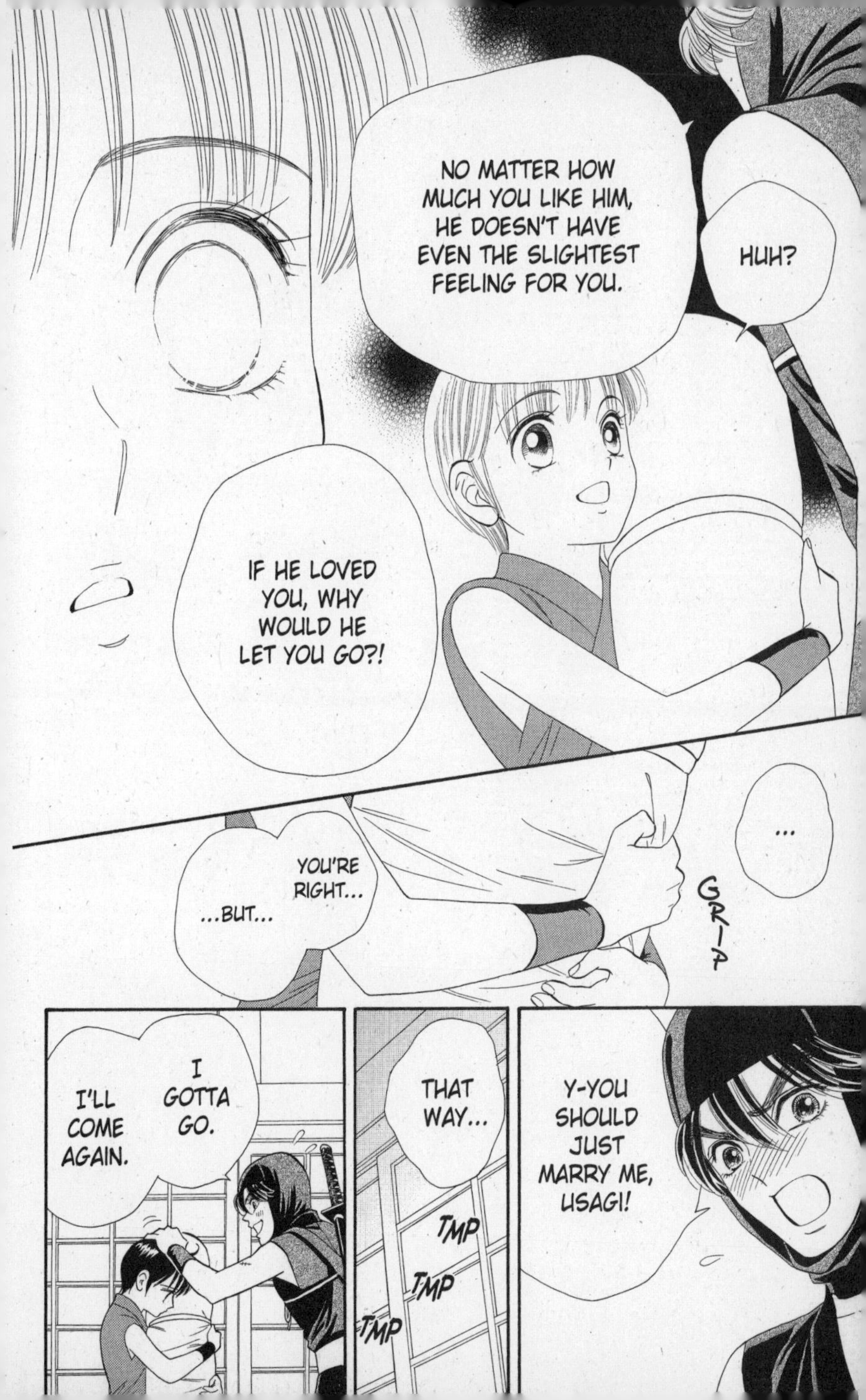
NO MATTER HOW MUCH YOU LIKE HIM, HE DOESN'T HAVE EVEN THE SLIGHTEST FEELING FOR YOU.
HUH?
IF HE LOVED YOU, WHY WOULD HE LET YOU GO?!
...
GRIP
YOU'RE RIGHT...
...BUT...
Y-YOU SHOULD JUST MARRY ME, USAGI!
THAT WAY...
TMP
TMP
TMP
I GOTTA GO.
I'LL COME AGAIN.

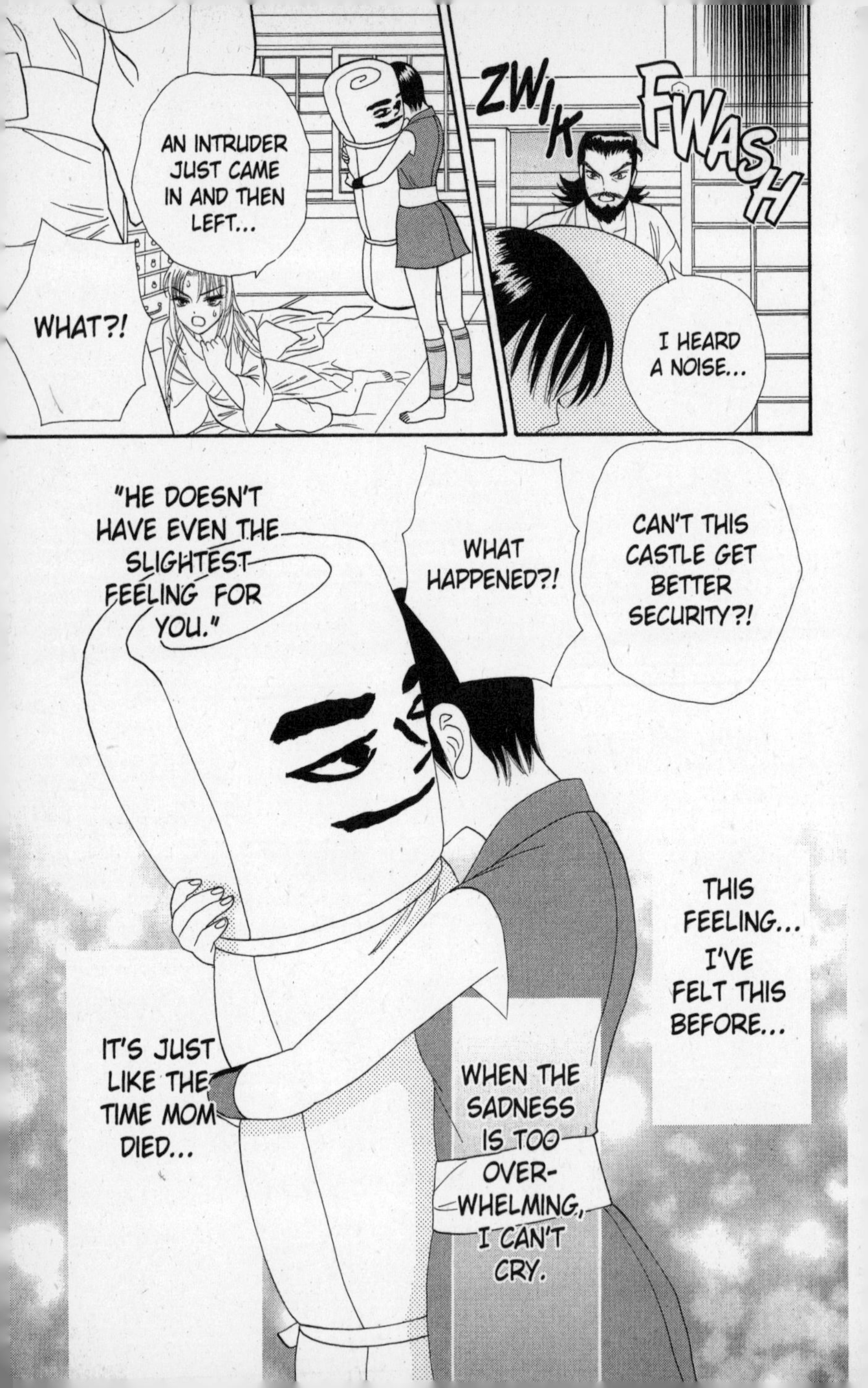
ZWIK
FWASH
I HEARD A NOISE...
AN INTRUDER JUST CAME IN AND THEN LEFT...
WHAT?!
CAN'T THIS CASTLE GET BETTER SECURITY?!
WHAT HAPPENED?!
"HE DOESN'T HAVE EVEN THE SLIGHTEST FEELING FOR YOU."
THIS FEELING... I'VE FELT THIS BEFORE...
WHEN THE SADNESS IS TOO OVER-WHELMING, I CAN'T CRY.
IT'S JUST LIKE THE TIME MOM DIED...

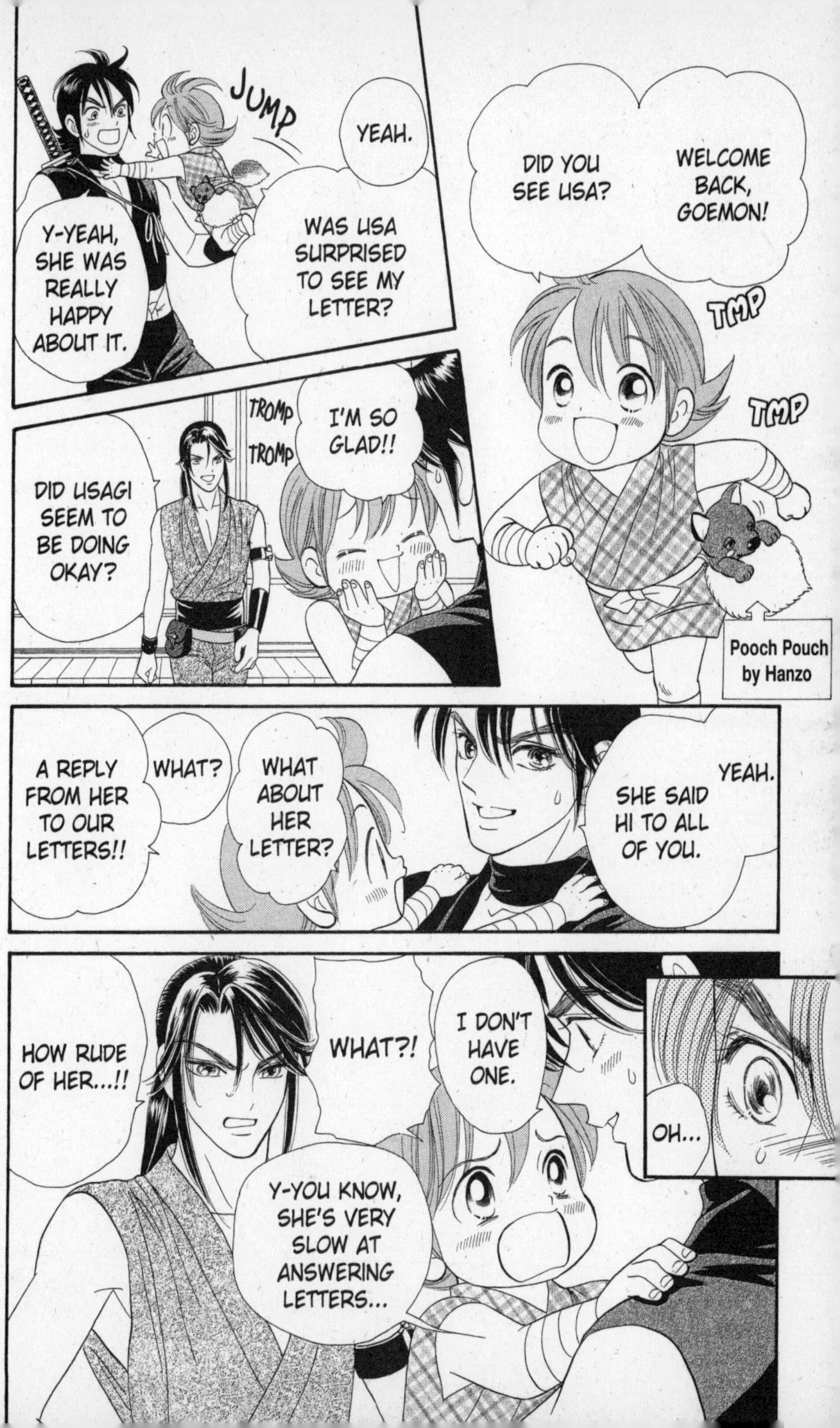
WELCOME BACK, GOEMON!
DID YOU SEE USA?
TMP
TMP
Pooch Pouch by Hanzo
JUMP
YEAH.
WAS USA SURPRISED TO SEE MY LETTER?
Y-YEAH, SHE WAS REALLY HAPPY ABOUT IT.
I'M SO GLAD!!
TROMP
TROMP
DID USAGI SEEM TO BE DOING OKAY?
YEAH.
SHE SAID HI TO ALL OF YOU.
WHAT ABOUT HER LETTER?
WHAT?
A REPLY FROM HER TO OUR LETTERS!!
OH...
I DON'T HAVE ONE.
WHAT?!
HOW RUDE OF HER...!!
Y-YOU KNOW, SHE'S VERY SLOW AT ANSWERING LETTERS...

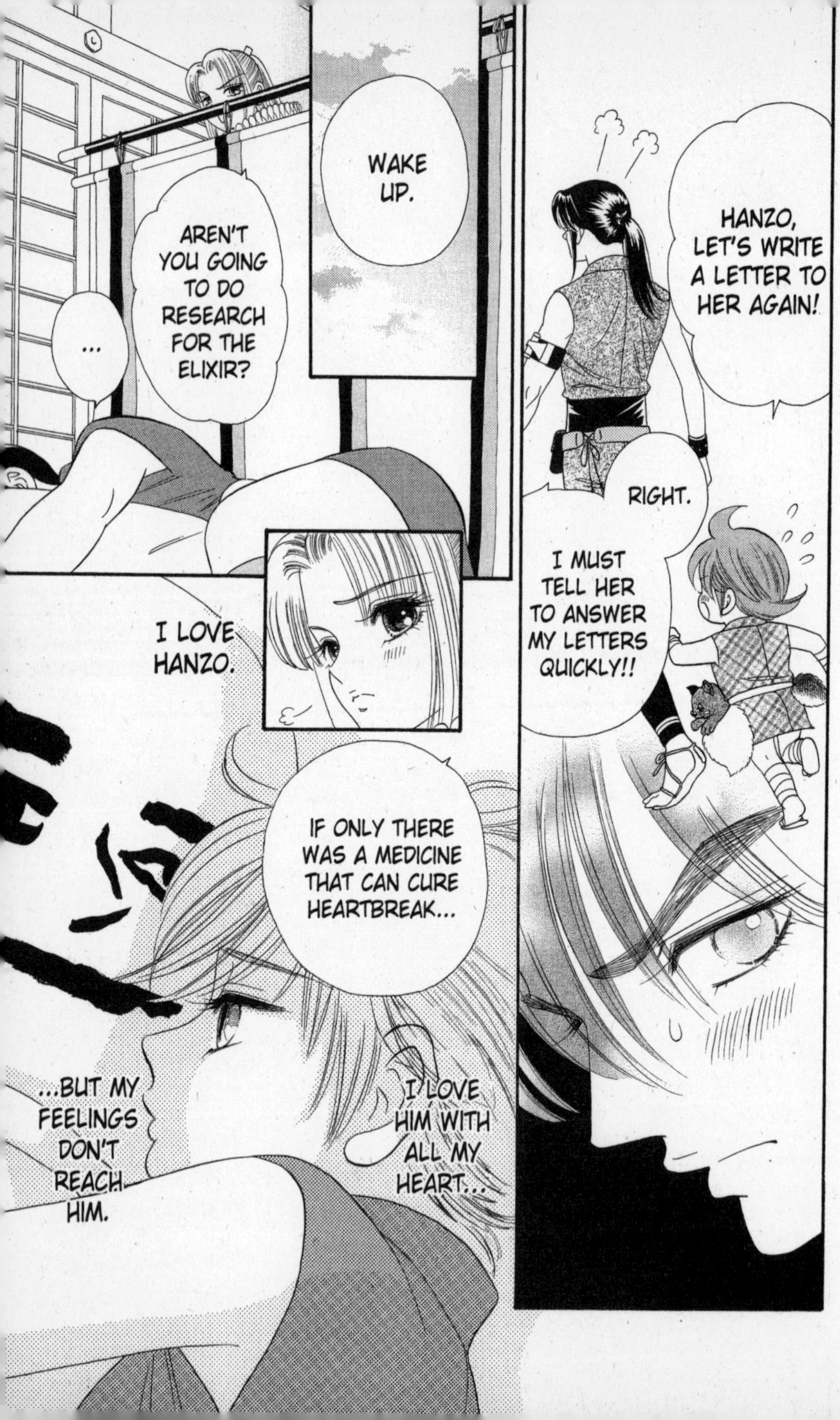
HANZO, LET'S WRITE A LETTER TO HER AGAIN!
RIGHT.
I MUST TELL HER TO ANSWER MY LETTERS QUICKLY!!
WAKE UP.
AREN'T YOU GOING TO DO RESEARCH FOR THE ELIXIR?
...
I LOVE HANZO.
IF ONLY THERE WAS A MEDICINE THAT CAN CURE HEARTBREAK...
I LOVE HIM WITH ALL MY HEART...
...BUT MY FEELINGS DON'T REACH HIM.

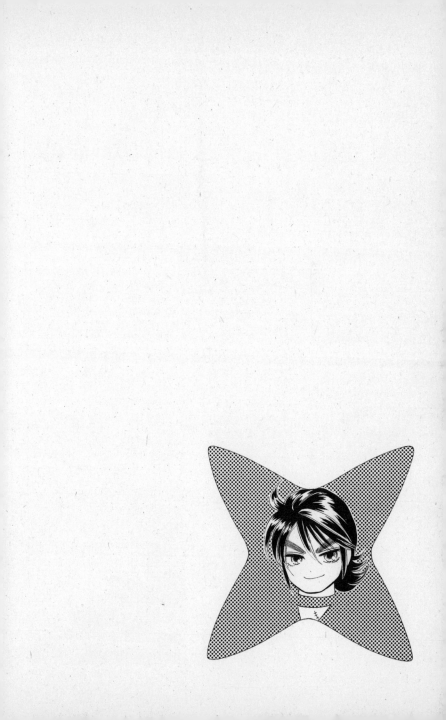

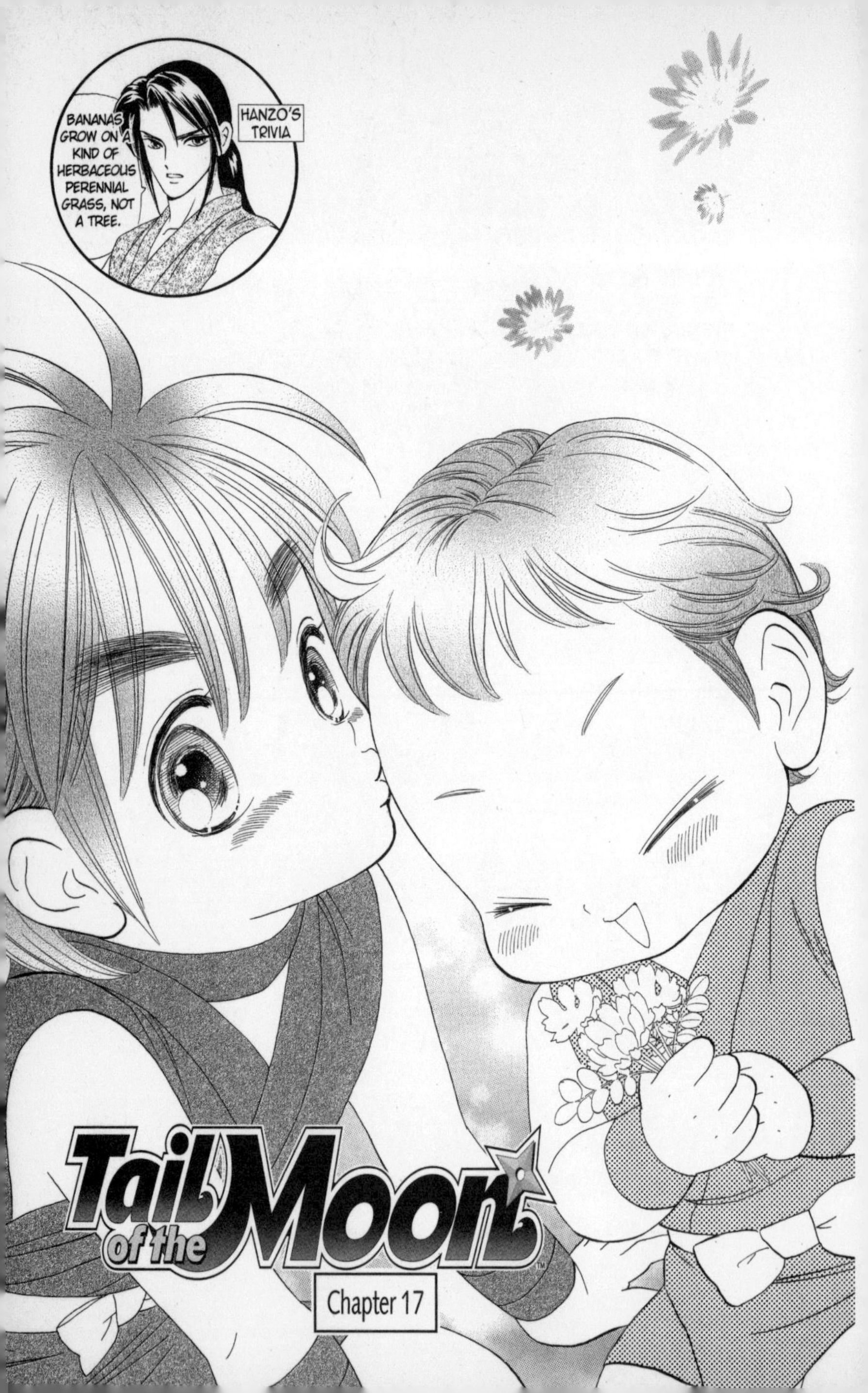
HANZO'S TRIVIA
BANANAS GROW ON A KIND OF HERBACEOUS PERENNIAL GRASS, NOT A TREE.
Tail of the Moon
Chapter 17

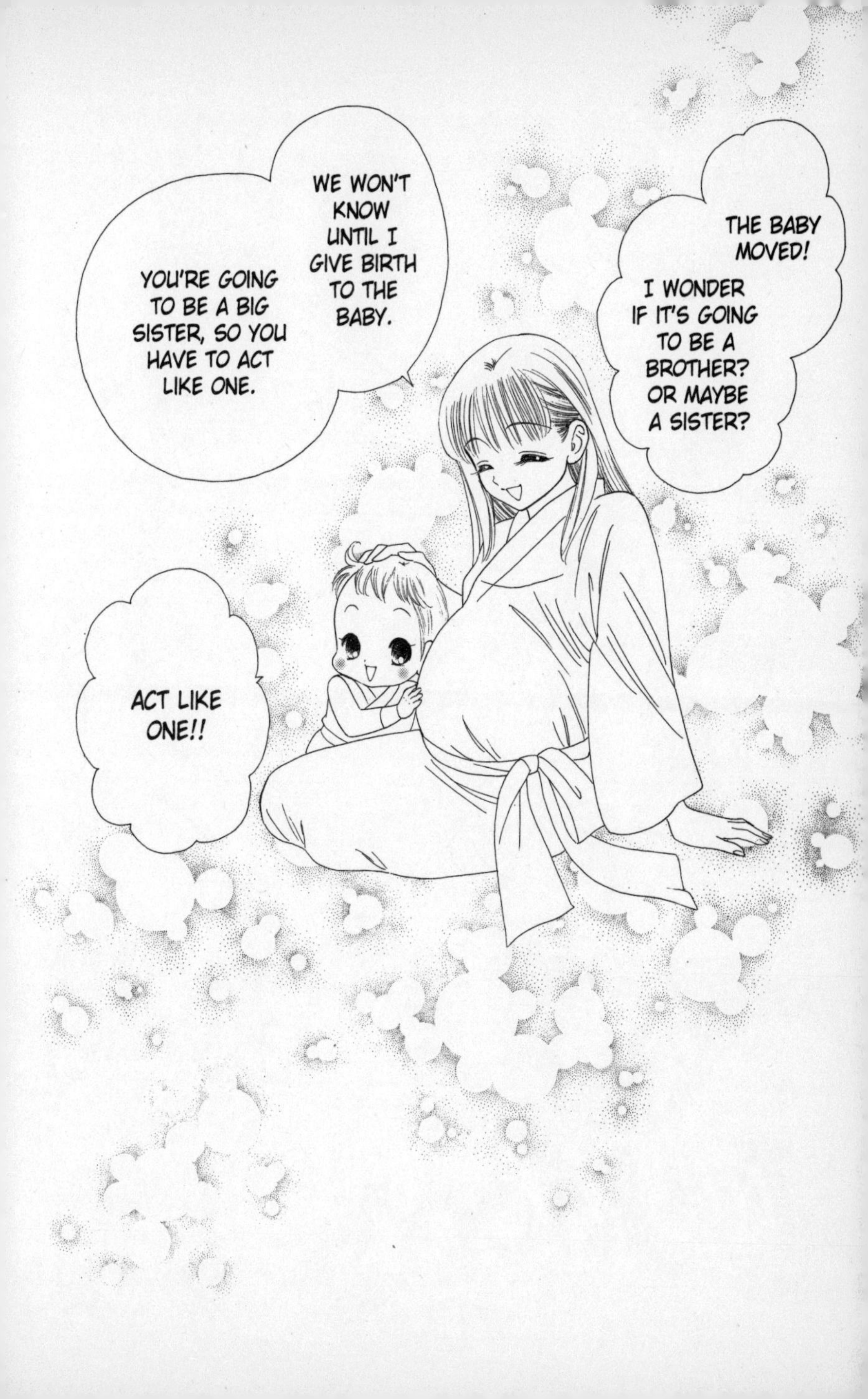
THE BABY MOVED!
I WONDER IF IT'S GOING TO BE A BROTHER? OR MAYBE A SISTER?
WE WON'T KNOW UNTIL I GIVE BIRTH TO THE BABY.
YOU'RE GOING TO BE A BIG SISTER, SO YOU HAVE TO ACT LIKE ONE.
ACT LIKE ONE!!

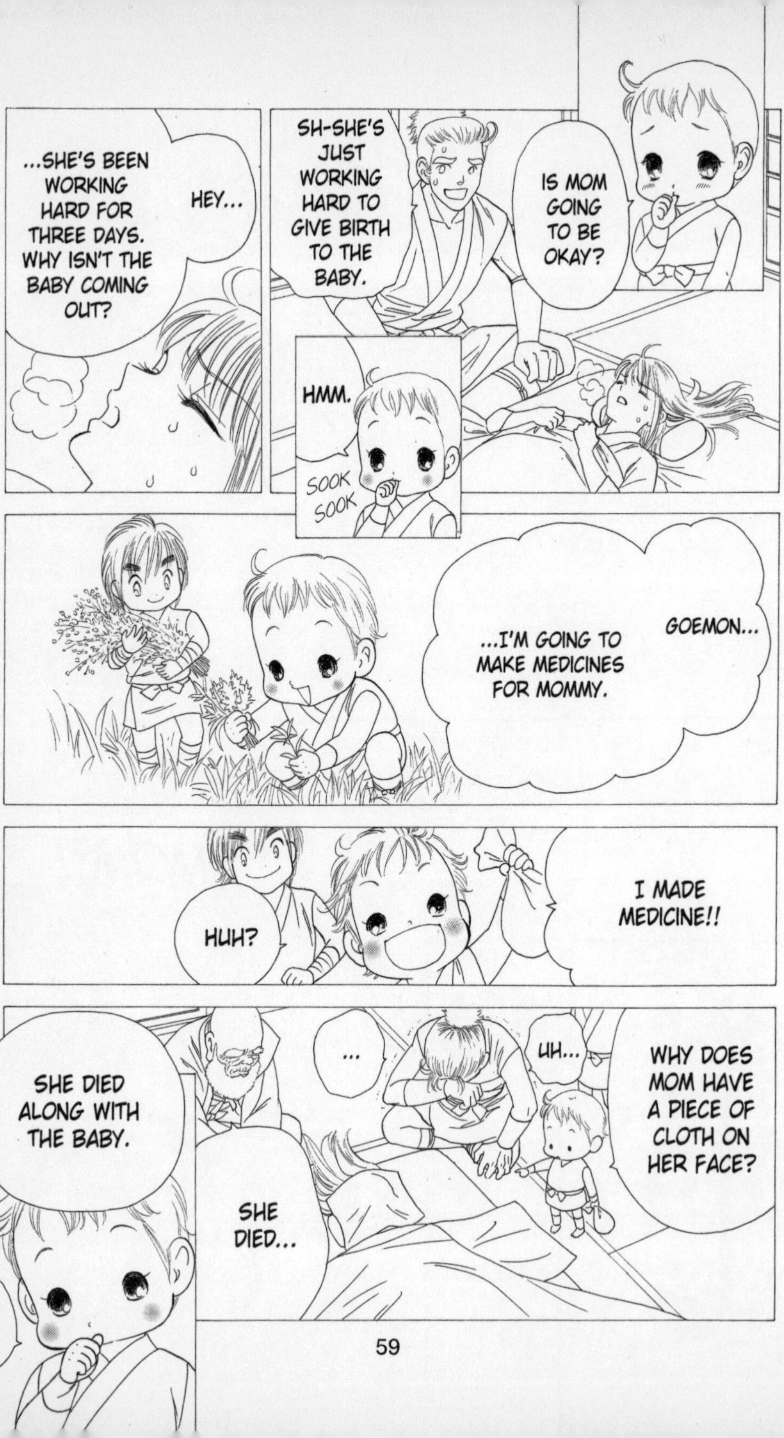
IS MOM GOING TO BE OKAY?
SH-SHE'S JUST WORKING HARD TO GIVE BIRTH TO THE BABY.
HMM.
SOOK SOOK
HEY...
...SHE'S BEEN WORKING HARD FOR THREE DAYS. WHY ISN'T THE BABY COMING OUT?
GOEMON...
...I'M GOING TO MAKE MEDICINES FOR MOMMY.
I MADE MEDICINE!!
HUH?
WHY DOES MOM HAVE A PIECE OF CLOTH ON HER FACE?
UH...
...
SHE DIED...
SHE DIED ALONG WITH THE BABY.
...

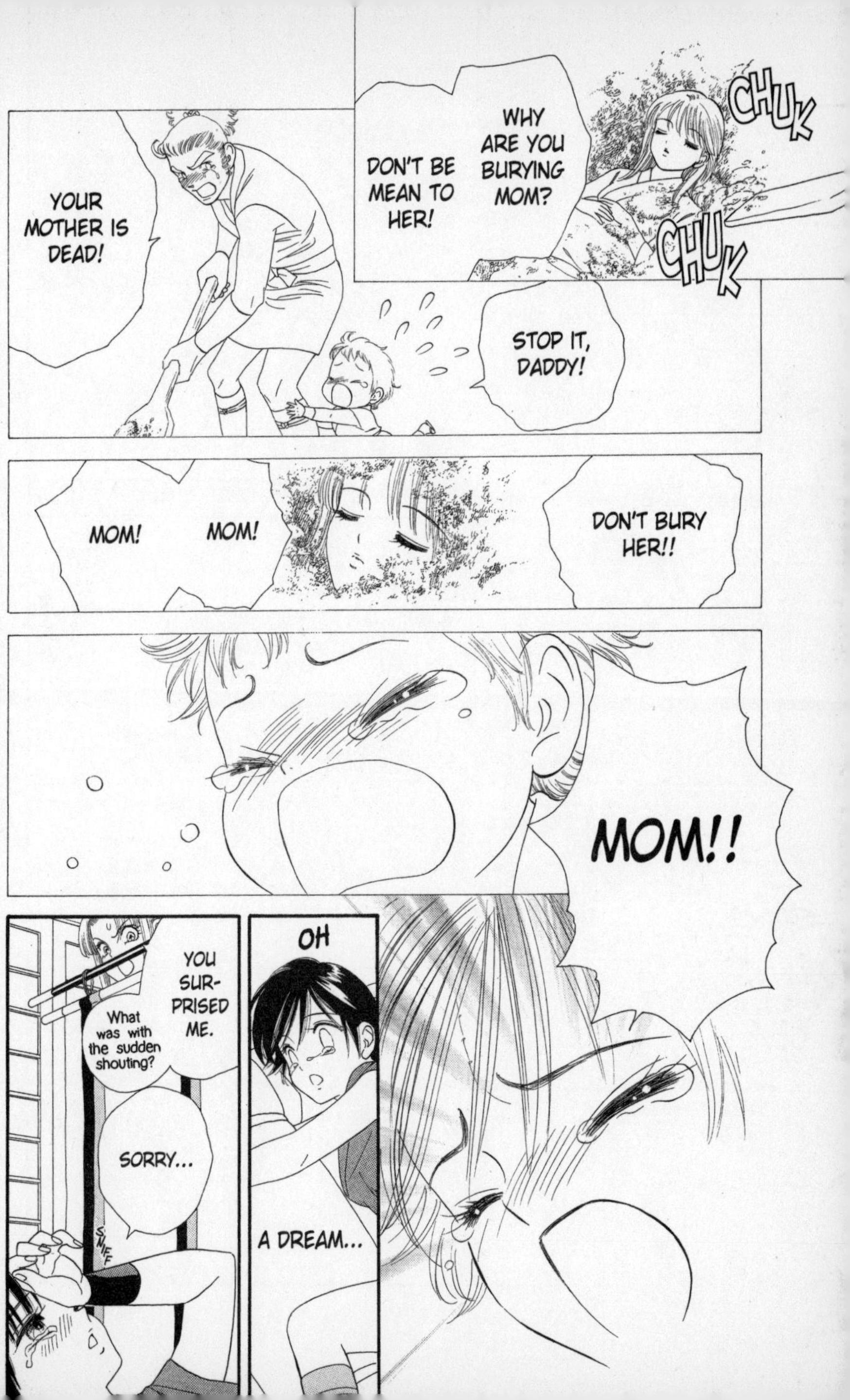
CHUK
WHY ARE YOU BURYING MOM?
DON'T BE MEAN TO HER!
CHUK
STOP IT, DADDY!
YOUR MOTHER IS DEAD!
DON'T BURY HER!!
MOM!
MOM!
MOM!!
OH
A DREAM...
YOU SUR-PRISED ME.
What was with the sudden shouting?
SORRY...
SNIFF

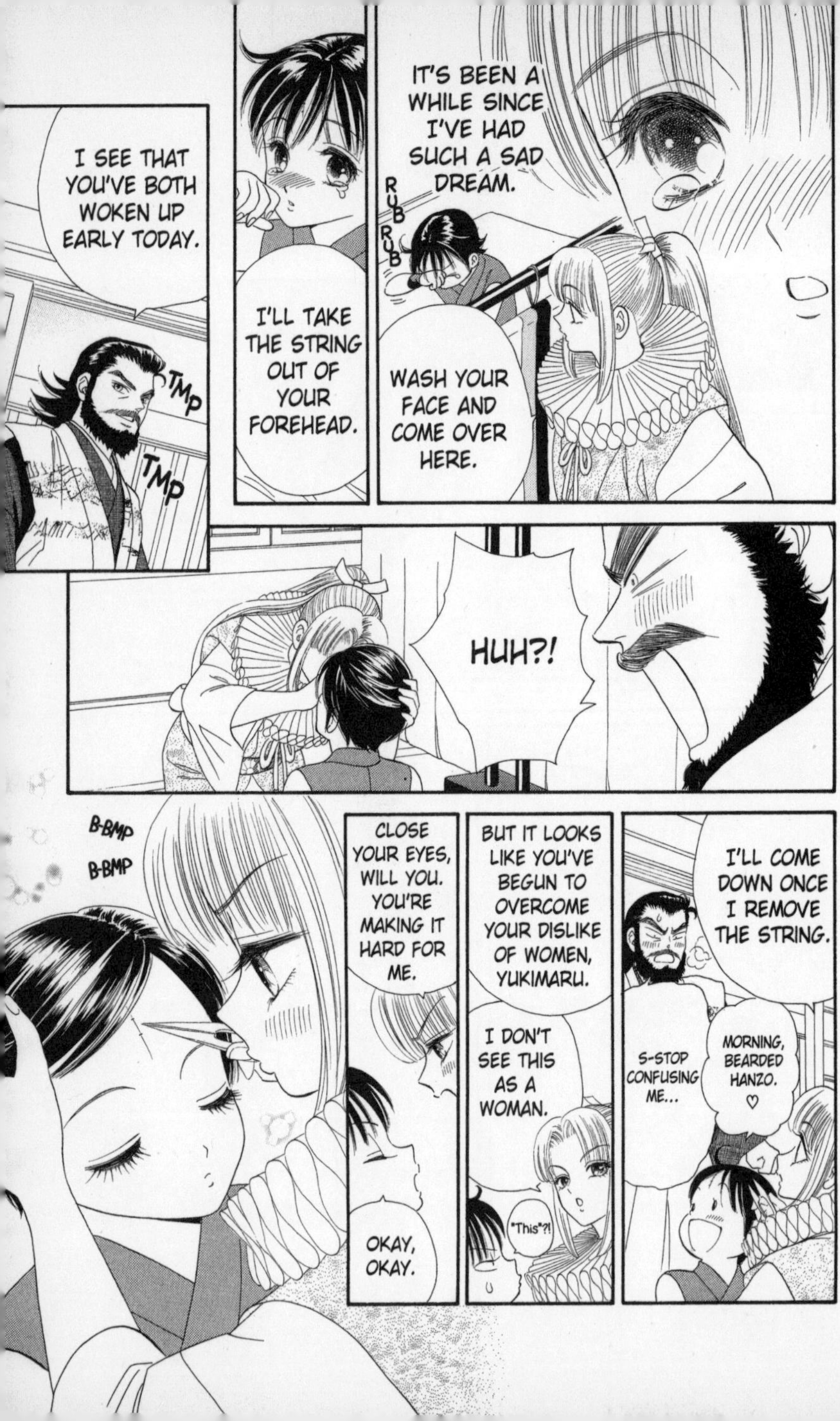
IT'S BEEN A WHILE SINCE I'VE HAD SUCH A SAD DREAM.
RUB RUB
WASH YOUR FACE AND COME OVER HERE.
I'LL TAKE THE STRING OUT OF YOUR FOREHEAD.
I SEE THAT YOU'VE BOTH WOKEN UP EARLY TODAY.
TMP
TMP
HUH?!
I'LL COME DOWN ONCE I REMOVE THE STRING.
MORNING, BEARDED HANZO. ♡
S-STOP CONFUSING ME...
BUT IT LOOKS LIKE YOU'VE BEGUN TO OVERCOME YOUR DISLIKE OF WOMEN, YUKIMARU.
I DON'T SEE THIS AS A WOMAN.
"This"?!
CLOSE YOUR EYES, WILL YOU. YOU'RE MAKING IT HARD FOR ME.
OKAY, OKAY.
B-BMP
B-BMP

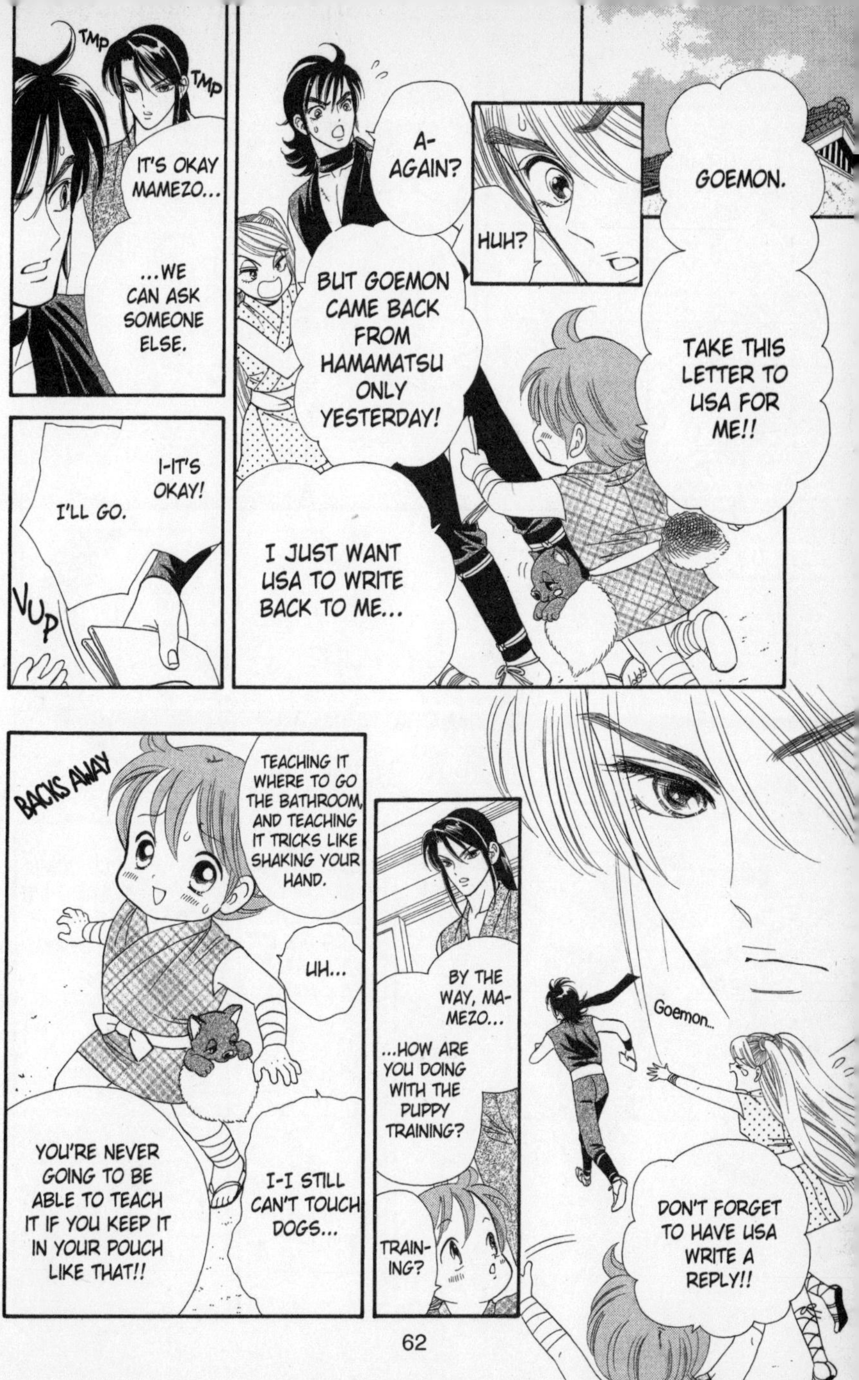
GOEMON.
TAKE THIS LETTER TO USA FOR ME!!
HUH?
A- AGAIN?
BUT GOEMON CAME BACK FROM HAMAMATSU ONLY YESTERDAY!
I JUST WANT USA TO WRITE BACK TO ME...
TMP
TMP
IT'S OKAY MAMEZO...
...WE CAN ASK SOMEONE ELSE.
I-IT'S OKAY!
I'LL GO.
VUP
Goemon...
DON'T FORGET TO HAVE USA WRITE A REPLY!!
BY THE WAY, MA-MEZO...
...HOW ARE YOU DOING WITH THE PUPPY TRAINING?
TRAIN-ING?
TEACHING IT WHERE TO GO THE BATHROOM, AND TEACHING IT TRICKS LIKE SHAKING YOUR HAND.
BACKS AWAY
UH...
I-I STILL CAN'T TOUCH DOGS...
YOU'RE NEVER GOING TO BE ABLE TO TEACH IT IF YOU KEEP IT IN YOUR POUCH LIKE THAT!!

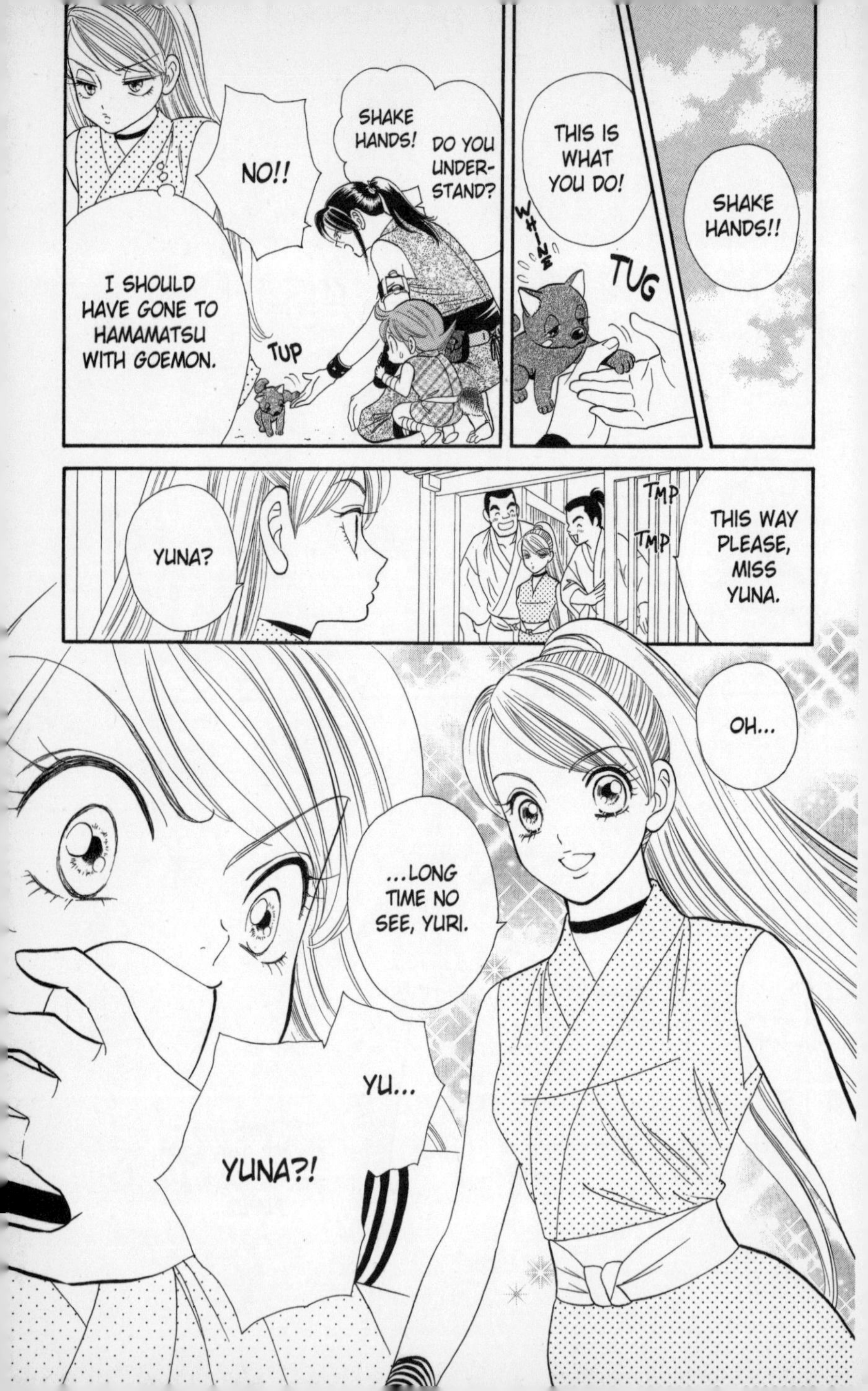
SHAKE HANDS!!
THIS IS WHAT YOU DO!
TUG
WHINE
DO YOU UNDERSTAND?
SHAKE HANDS!
NO!!
TUP
I SHOULD HAVE GONE TO HAMAMATSU WITH GOEMON.
THIS WAY PLEASE, MISS YUNA.
TMP
TMP
YUNA?
OH...
...LONG TIME NO SEE, YURI.
YU...
YUNA?!

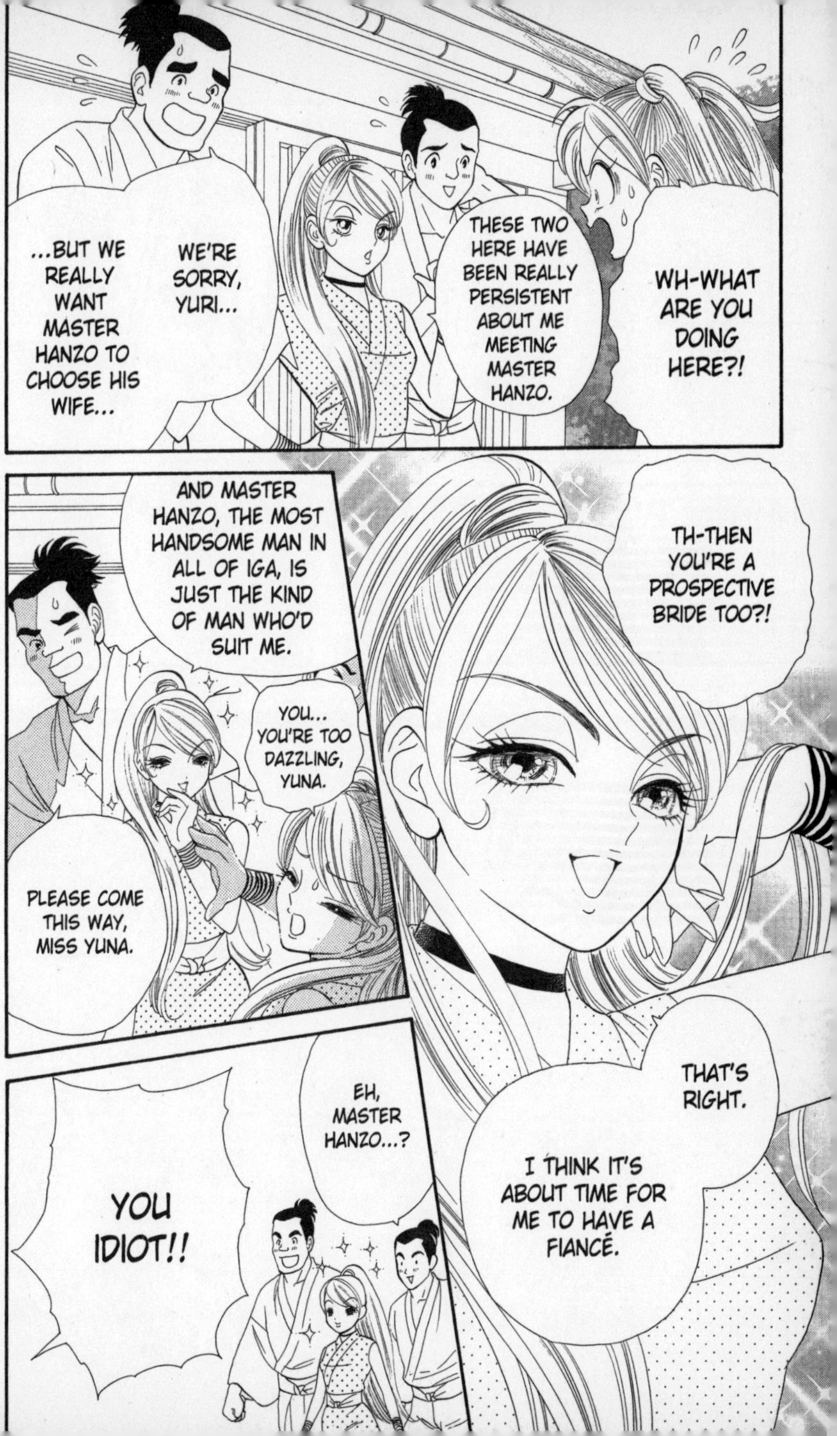
WH-WHAT ARE YOU DOING HERE?!
THESE TWO HERE HAVE BEEN REALLY PERSISTENT ABOUT ME MEETING MASTER HANZO.
WE'RE SORRY, YURI...
...BUT WE REALLY WANT MASTER HANZO TO CHOOSE HIS WIFE...
TH-THEN YOU'RE A PROSPECTIVE BRIDE TOO?!
THAT'S RIGHT.
I THINK IT'S ABOUT TIME FOR ME TO HAVE A FIANCÉ.
AND MASTER HANZO, THE MOST HANDSOME MAN IN ALL OF IGA, IS JUST THE KIND OF MAN WHO'D SUIT ME.
YOU... YOU'RE TOO DAZZLING, YUNA.
PLEASE COME THIS WAY, MISS YUNA.
EH, MASTER HANZO...?
YOU IDIOT!!

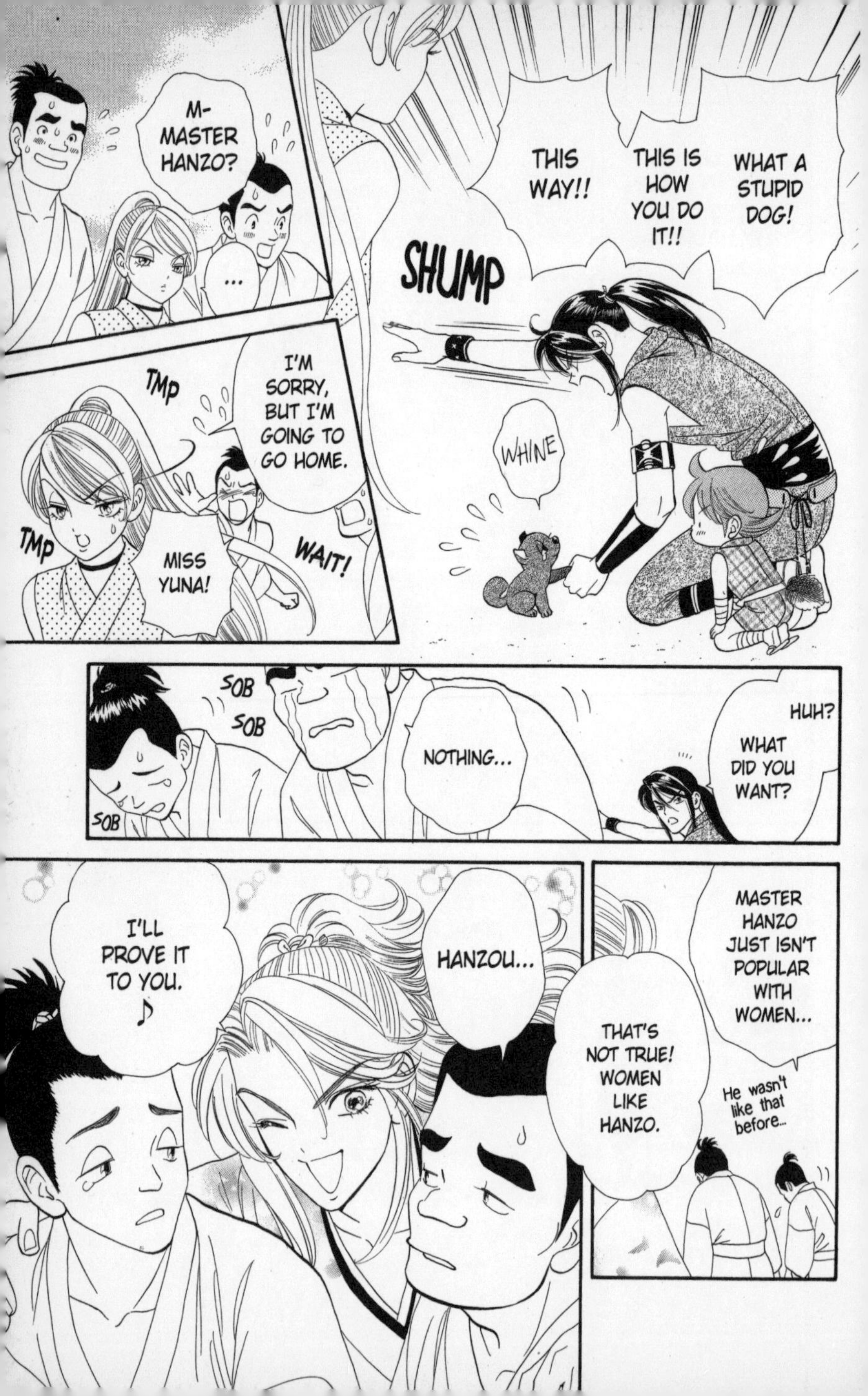
WHAT A STUPID DOG!
THIS IS HOW YOU DO IT!!
THIS WAY!!
SHUMP
WHINE
M-MASTER HANZO?
...
I'M SORRY, BUT I'M GOING TO GO HOME.
TMP
TMP
WAIT!
MISS YUNA!
HUH?
WHAT DID YOU WANT?
NOTHING...
SOB
SOB
SOB
MASTER HANZO JUST ISN'T POPULAR WITH WOMEN...
He wasn't like that before...
THAT'S NOT TRUE! WOMEN LIKE HANZO.
HANZOU...
I'LL PROVE IT TO YOU. ♪

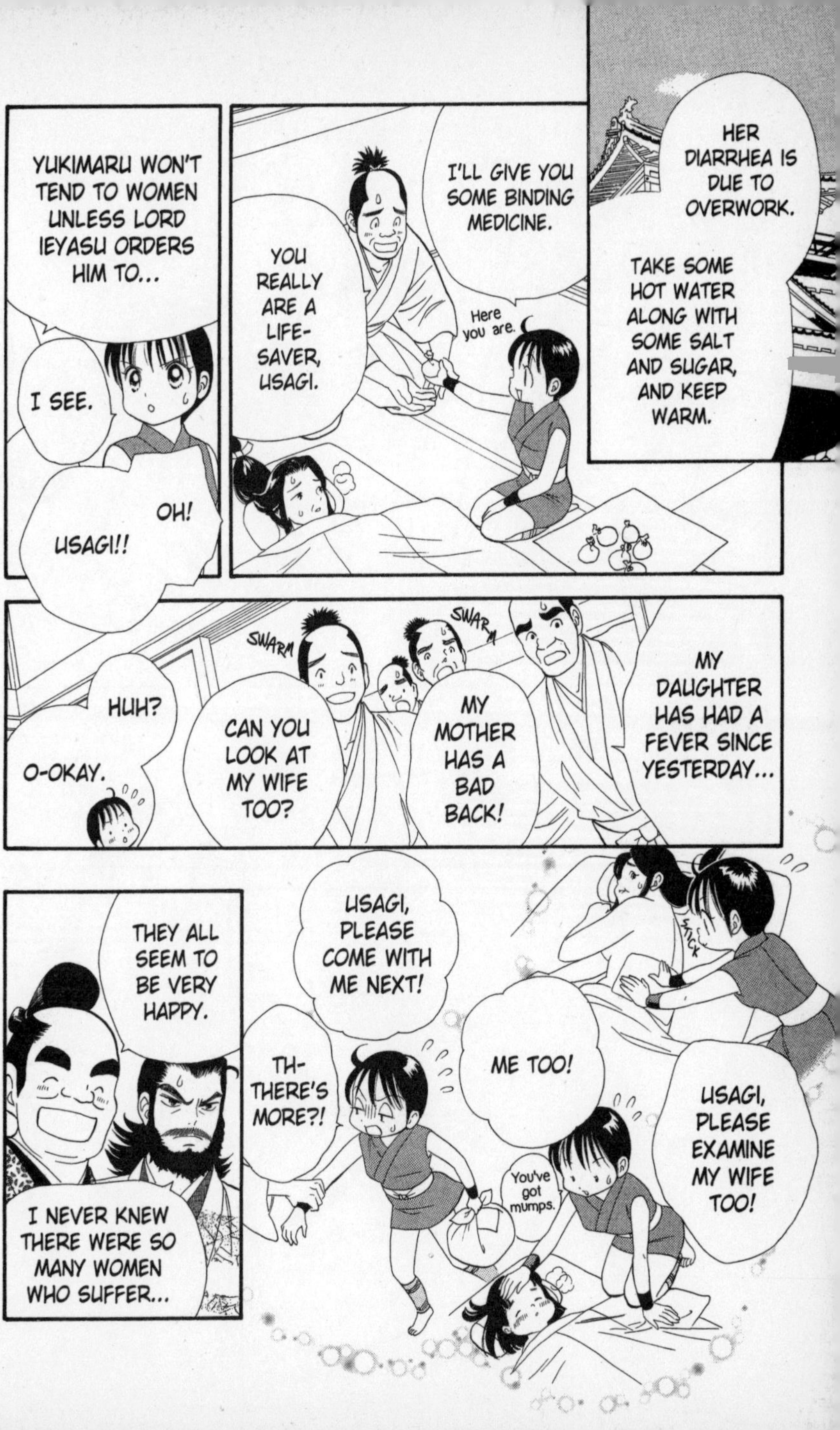
HER DIARRHEA IS DUE TO OVERWORK.
TAKE SOME HOT WATER ALONG WITH SOME SALT AND SUGAR, AND KEEP WARM.
I'LL GIVE YOU SOME BINDING MEDICINE.
Here you are.
YOU REALLY ARE A LIFE-SAVER, USAGI.
YUKIMARU WON'T TEND TO WOMEN UNLESS LORD IEYASU ORDERS HIM TO...
I SEE.
OH!
USAGI!!
MY DAUGHTER HAS HAD A FEVER SINCE YESTERDAY...
SWARM
MY MOTHER HAS A BAD BACK!
SWARM
CAN YOU LOOK AT MY WIFE TOO?
HUH?
O-OKAY.
USAGI, PLEASE EXAMINE MY WIFE TOO!
ME TOO!
You've got mumps.
USAGI, PLEASE COME WITH ME NEXT!
TH-THERE'S MORE?!
THEY ALL SEEM TO BE VERY HAPPY.
I NEVER KNEW THERE WERE SO MANY WOMEN WHO SUFFER...

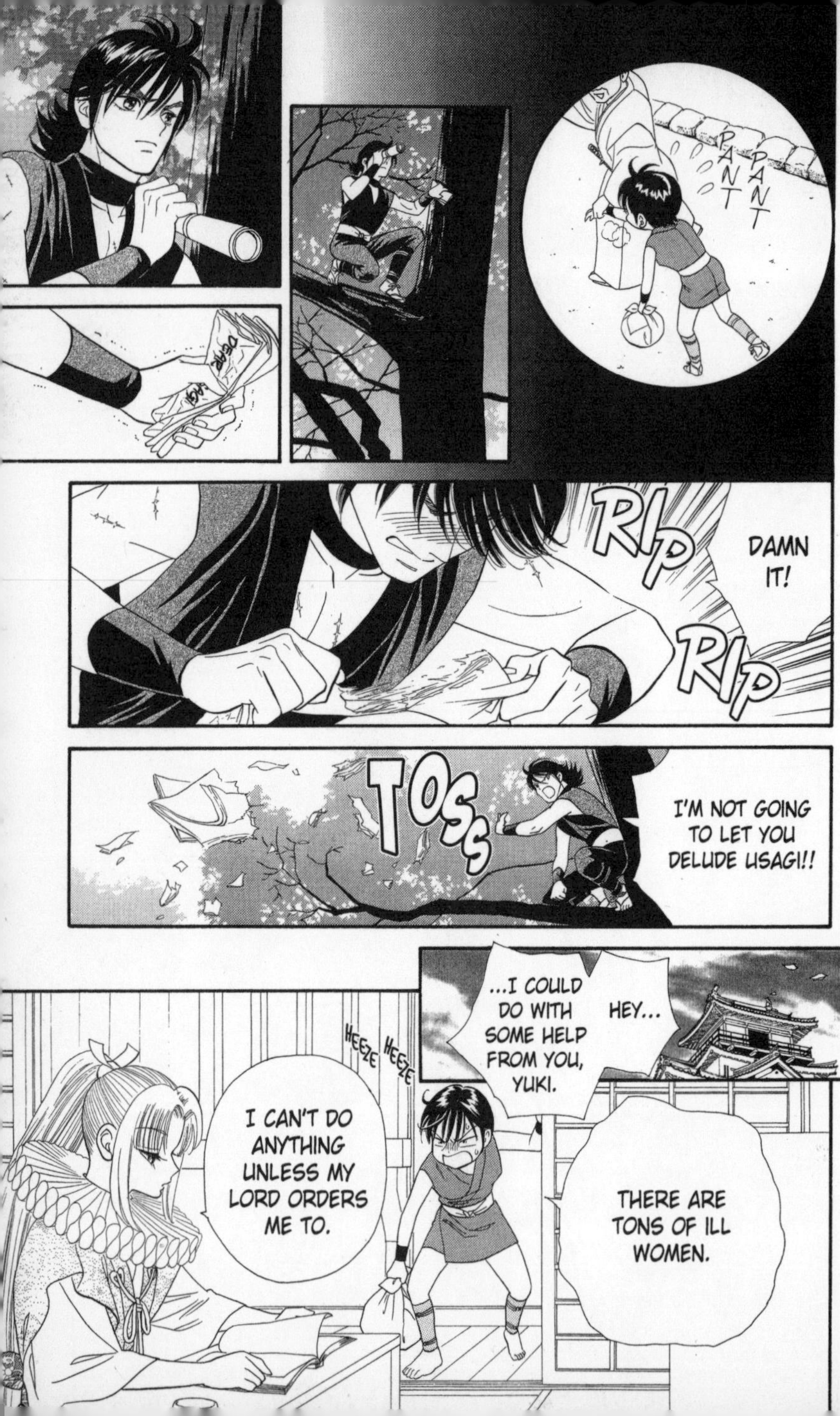
PANT PANT
DEAR
RIP
DAMN IT!
RIP
TOSS
I'M NOT GOING TO LET YOU DELUDE USAGI!!
HEY...
...I COULD DO WITH SOME HELP FROM YOU, YUKI.
THERE ARE TONS OF ILL WOMEN.
HEEZE HEEZE
I CAN'T DO ANYTHING UNLESS MY LORD ORDERS ME TO.

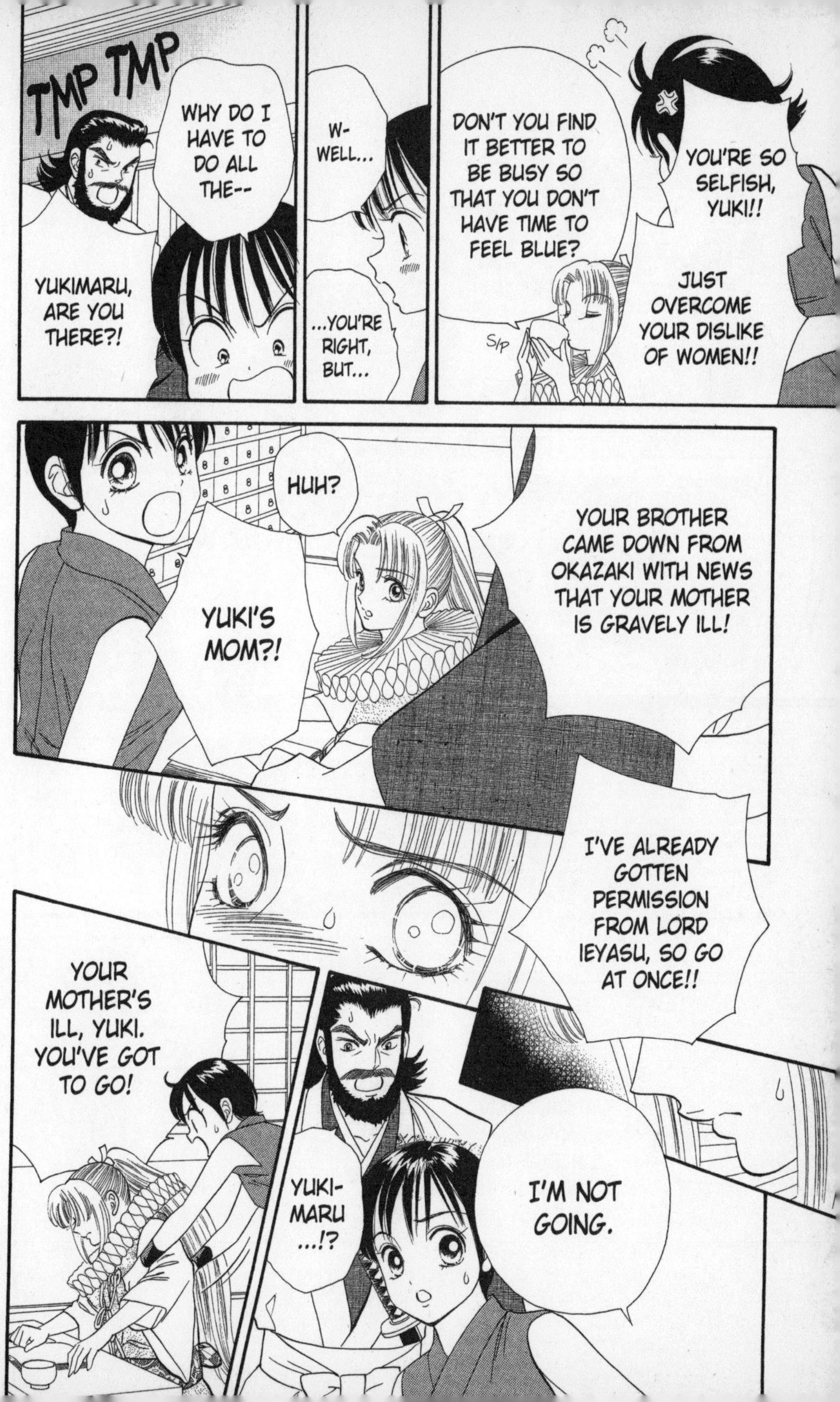
YOU'RE SO SELFISH, YUKI!!
JUST OVERCOME YOUR DISLIKE OF WOMEN!!
DON'T YOU FIND IT BETTER TO BE BUSY SO THAT YOU DON'T HAVE TIME TO FEEL BLUE?
SIP
W-WELL...
...YOU'RE RIGHT, BUT...
WHY DO I HAVE TO DO ALL THE--
TMP TMP
YUKIMARU, ARE YOU THERE?!
YOUR BROTHER CAME DOWN FROM OKAZAKI WITH NEWS THAT YOUR MOTHER IS GRAVELY ILL!
HUH?
YUKI'S MOM?!
I'VE ALREADY GOTTEN PERMISSION FROM LORD IEYASU, SO GO AT ONCE!!
I'M NOT GOING.
YUKI-MARU ...!?
YOUR MOTHER'S ILL, YUKI. YOU'VE GOT TO GO!

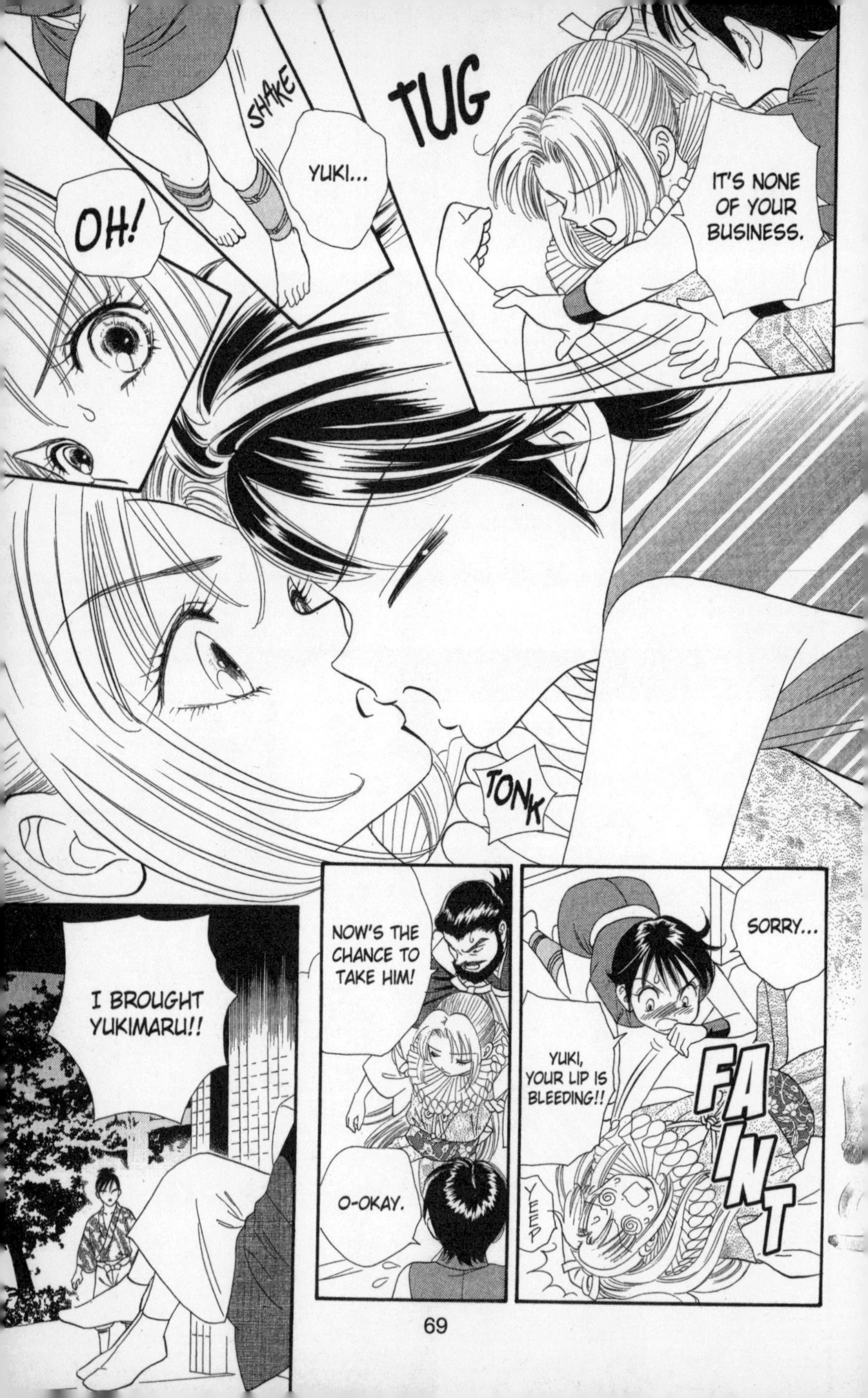
TUG
IT'S NONE OF YOUR BUSINESS.
SHAKE
YUKI...
OH!
TONK
SORRY...
FAINT
YUKI, YOUR LIP IS BLEEDING!!
YEEP
NOW'S THE CHANCE TO TAKE HIM!
O-OKAY.
I BROUGHT YUKIMARU!!

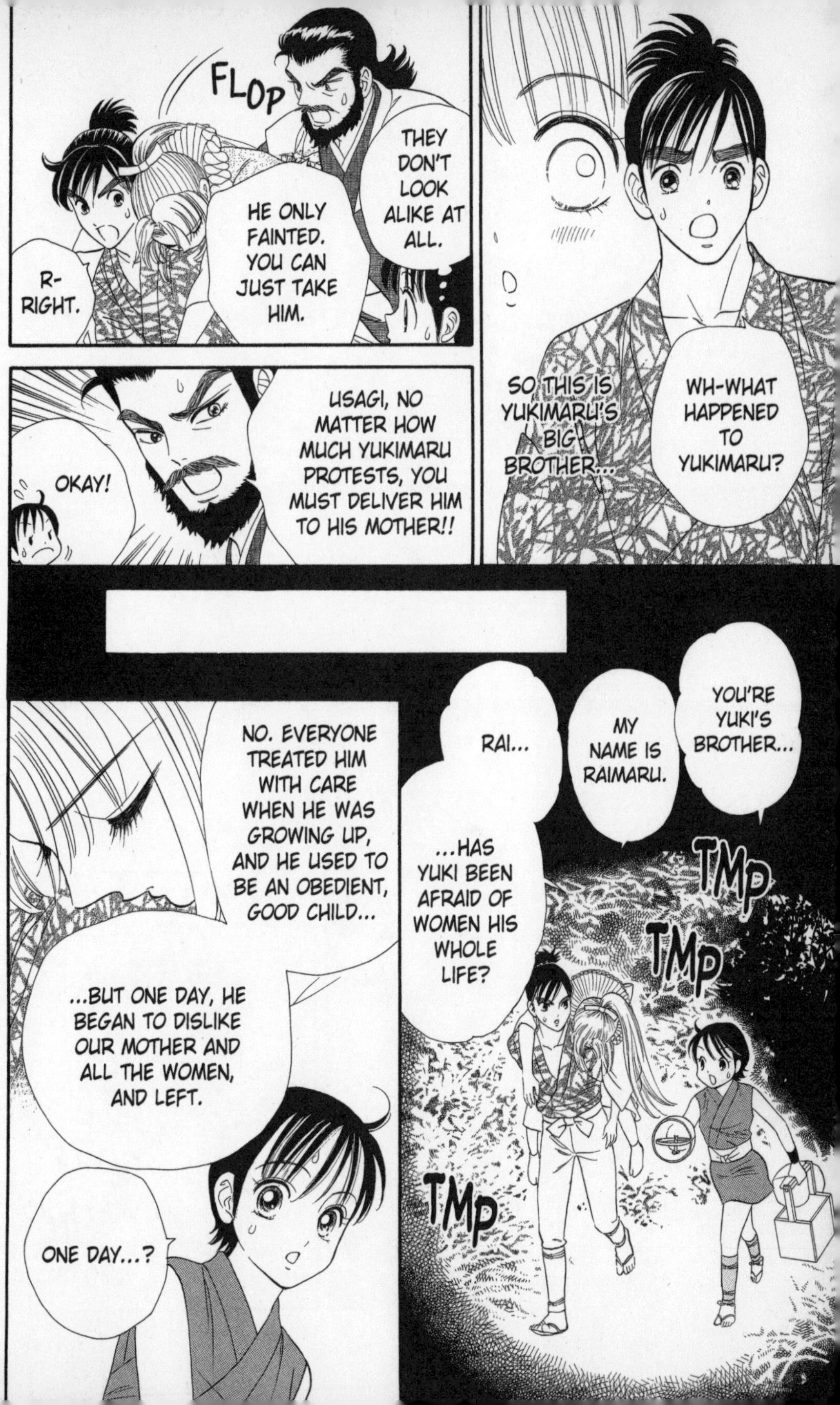
WH-WHAT HAPPENED TO YUKIMARU?
SO THIS IS YUKIMARU'S BIG BROTHER...
FLOP
THEY DON'T LOOK ALIKE AT ALL.
HE ONLY FAINTED. YOU CAN JUST TAKE HIM.
R-RIGHT.
USAGI, NO MATTER HOW MUCH YUKIMARU PROTESTS, YOU MUST DELIVER HIM TO HIS MOTHER!!
OKAY!
YOU'RE YUKI'S BROTHER...
MY NAME IS RAIMARU.
RAI...
...HAS YUKI BEEN AFRAID OF WOMEN HIS WHOLE LIFE?
TMP
TMP
TMP
NO. EVERYONE TREATED HIM WITH CARE WHEN HE WAS GROWING UP, AND HE USED TO BE AN OBEDIENT, GOOD CHILD...
...BUT ONE DAY, HE BEGAN TO DISLIKE OUR MOTHER AND ALL THE WOMEN, AND LEFT.
ONE DAY...?

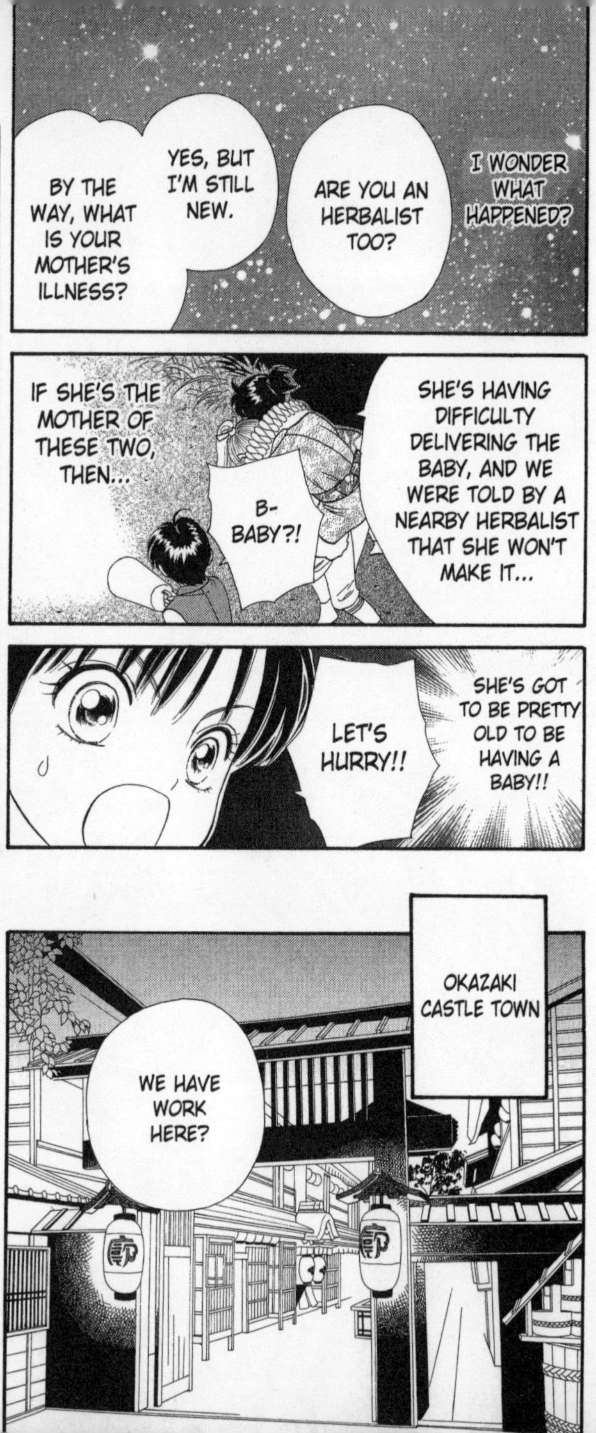
I WONDER WHAT HAPPENED?
ARE YOU AN HERBALIST TOO?
YES, BUT I'M STILL NEW.
BY THE WAY, WHAT IS YOUR MOTHER'S ILLNESS?
SHE'S HAVING DIFFICULTY DELIVERING THE BABY, AND WE WERE TOLD BY A NEARBY HERBALIST THAT SHE WON'T MAKE IT...
B-BABY?!
IF SHE'S THE MOTHER OF THESE TWO, THEN...
SHE'S GOT TO BE PRETTY OLD TO BE HAVING A BABY!!
LET'S HURRY!!
OKAZAKI CASTLE TOWN
WE HAVE WORK HERE?

Stories About My Research Trip #2

When I got to the Iga-ryu Ninja Museum, located in Ueno-Castle Park, I was greeted by a pretty kunoichi and a handsome ninja!! At first sight, the house looked like a thatched-roof farmhouse, but that was the ninja house!!

I went inside with about 10 other tourists, and watched the pretty kunoichi demonstrate secret revolving doors, secret rooms, rope ladders, secret passages, and so forth.

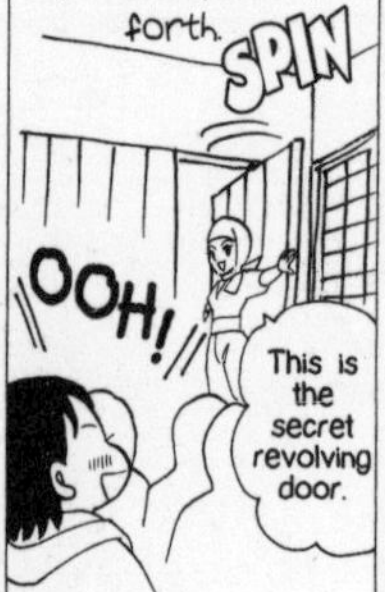
SPIN
OOH!
This is the secret revolving door.

The ninja house was built extremely rationally and skillfully, and I was able to come up with many ideas just by looking around.

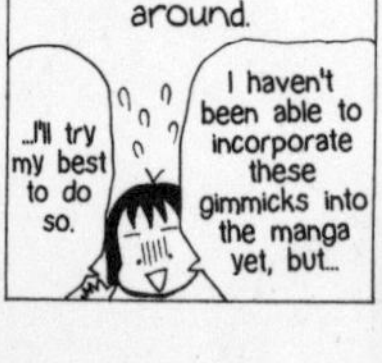
I haven't been able to incorporate these gimmicks into the manga yet, but...
...I'll try my best to do so.

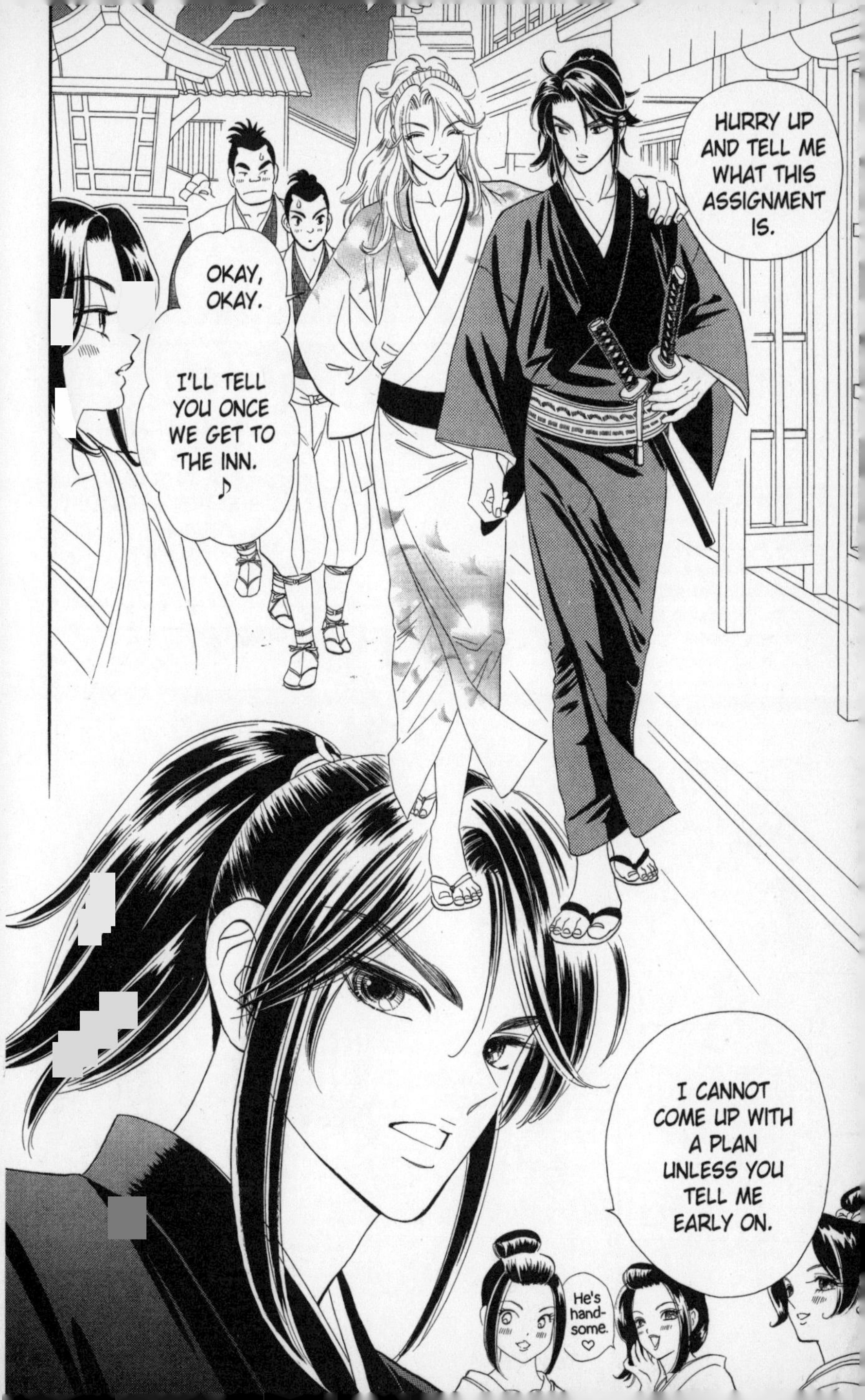
HURRY UP AND TELL ME WHAT THIS ASSIGNMENT IS.
OKAY, OKAY.
I'LL TELL YOU ONCE WE GET TO THE INN. ♪
I CANNOT COME UP WITH A PLAN UNLESS YOU TELL ME EARLY ON.
He's hand-some. ♡

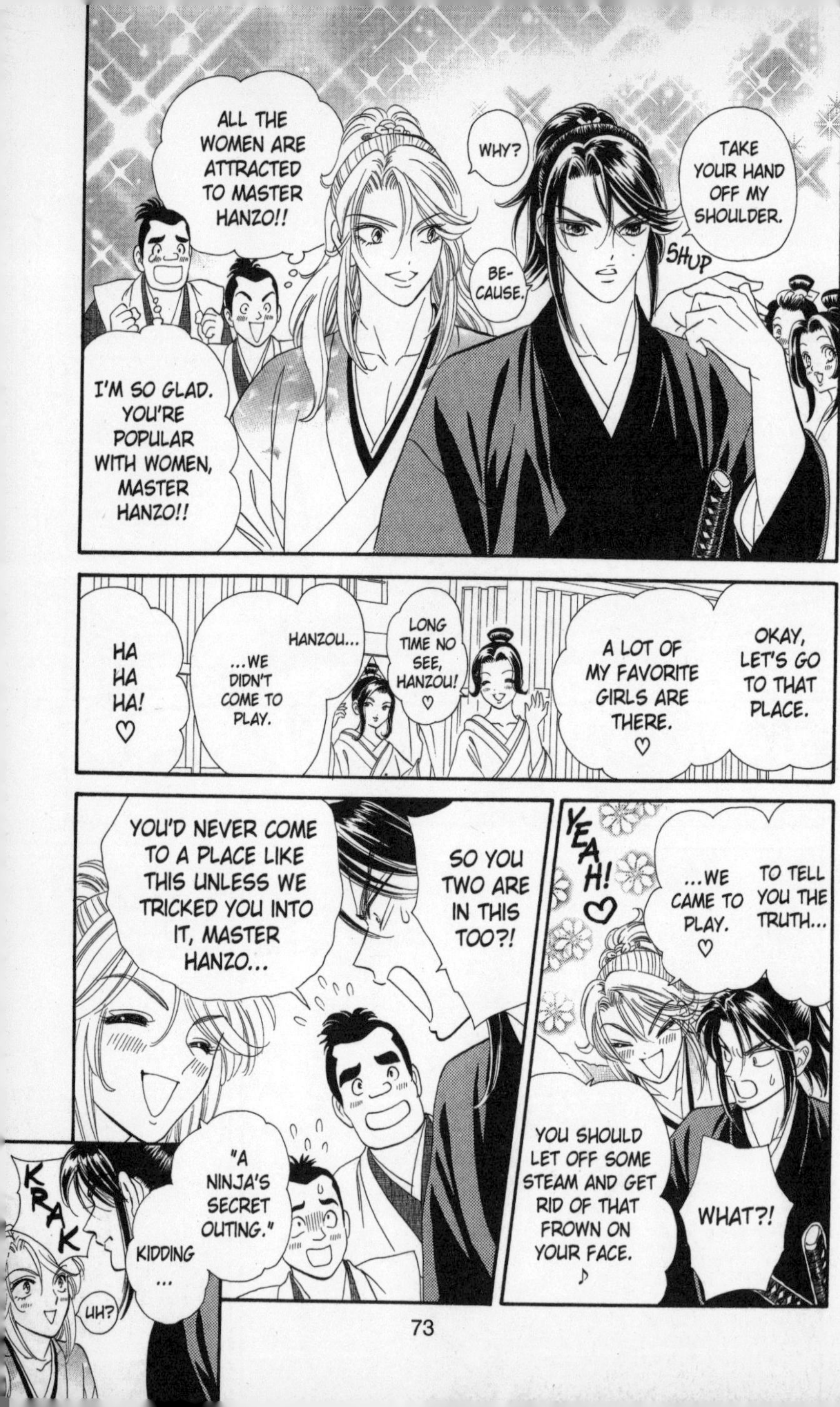
TAKE YOUR HAND OFF MY SHOULDER.
SHUP
WHY?
BE-CAUSE.
ALL THE WOMEN ARE ATTRACTED TO MASTER HANZO!!
I'M SO GLAD. YOU'RE POPULAR WITH WOMEN, MASTER HANZO!!
OKAY, LET'S GO TO THAT PLACE.
A LOT OF MY FAVORITE GIRLS ARE THERE. ♡
LONG TIME NO SEE, HANZOU! ♡
HANZOU...
...WE DIDN'T COME TO PLAY.
HA HA HA! ♡
TO TELL YOU THE TRUTH...
...WE CAME TO PLAY. ♡
YEAH! ♡
WHAT?!
YOU SHOULD LET OFF SOME STEAM AND GET RID OF THAT FROWN ON YOUR FACE. ♪
SO YOU TWO ARE IN THIS TOO?!
YOU'D NEVER COME TO A PLACE LIKE THIS UNLESS WE TRICKED YOU INTO IT, MASTER HANZO...
"A NINJA'S SECRET OUTING."
KRAK
KIDDING ...
UH?

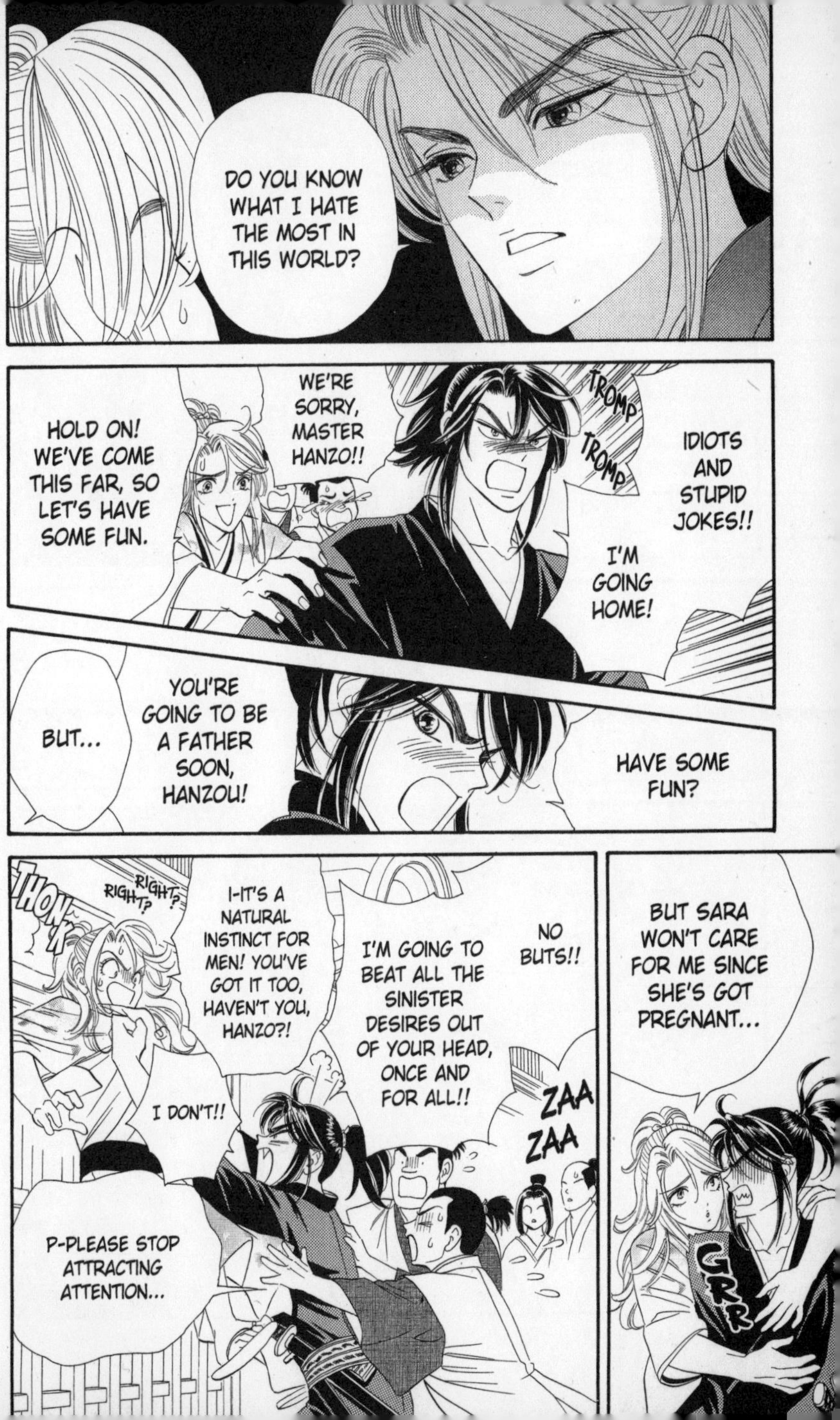
DO YOU KNOW WHAT I HATE THE MOST IN THIS WORLD?
IDIOTS AND STUPID JOKES!!
TROMP
TROMP
I'M GOING HOME!
WE'RE SORRY, MASTER HANZO!!
HOLD ON! WE'VE COME THIS FAR, SO LET'S HAVE SOME FUN.
HAVE SOME FUN?
YOU'RE GOING TO BE A FATHER SOON, HANZOU!
BUT...
BUT SARA WON'T CARE FOR ME SINCE SHE'S GOT PREGNANT...
GRR
NO BUTS!!
I'M GOING TO BEAT ALL THE SINISTER DESIRES OUT OF YOUR HEAD, ONCE AND FOR ALL!!
ZAA
ZAA
I-IT'S A NATURAL INSTINCT FOR MEN! YOU'VE GOT IT TOO, HAVEN'T YOU, HANZO?!
RIGHT? RIGHT?
THONK
I DON'T!!
P-PLEASE STOP ATTRACTING ATTENTION...

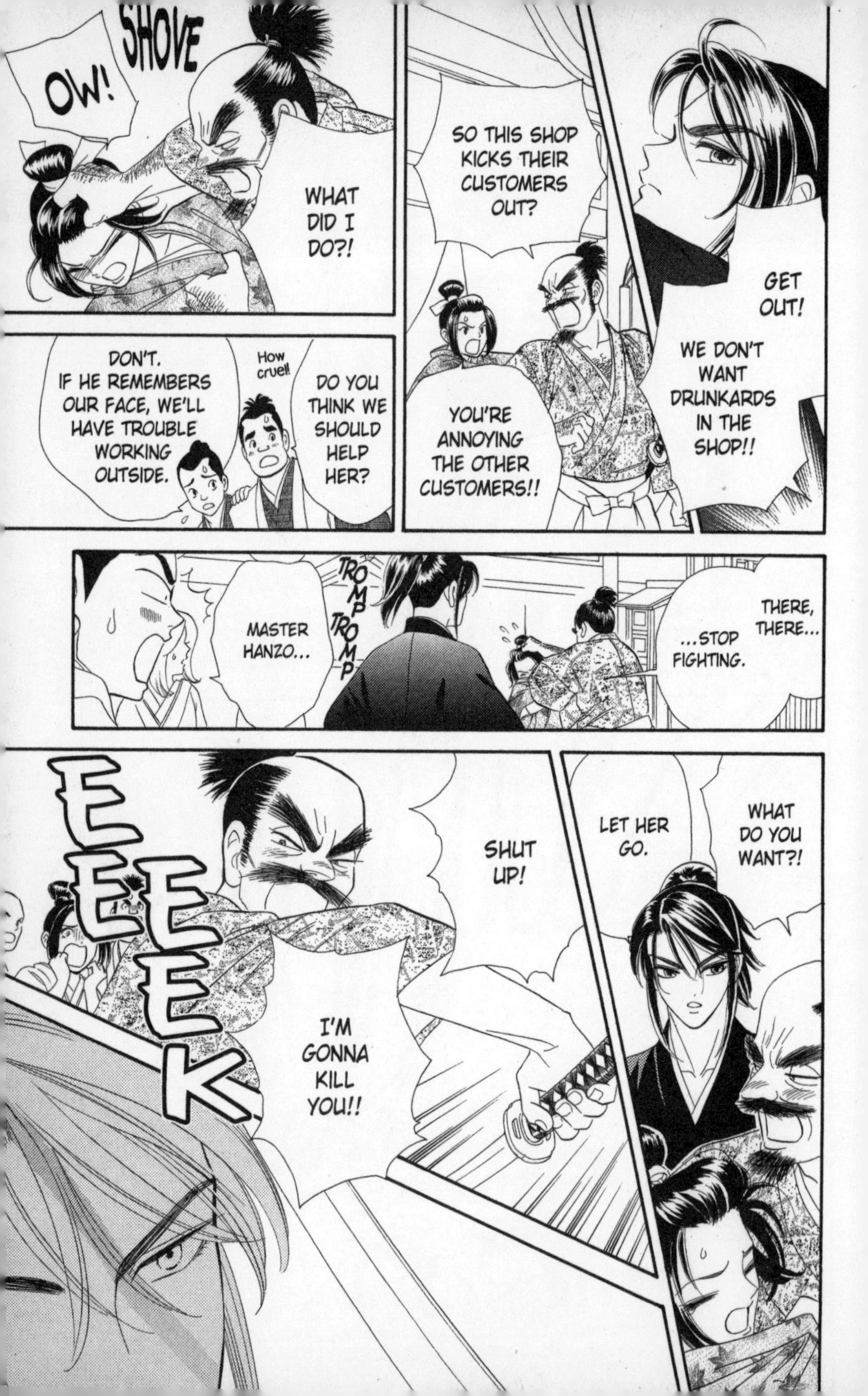
GET OUT!
WE DON'T WANT DRUNKARDS IN THE SHOP!!
SO THIS SHOP KICKS THEIR CUSTOMERS OUT?
YOU'RE ANNOYING THE OTHER CUSTOMERS!!
SHOVE
OW!
WHAT DID I DO?!
DO YOU THINK WE SHOULD HELP HER?
How cruel!
DON'T. IF HE REMEMBERS OUR FACE, WE'LL HAVE TROUBLE WORKING OUTSIDE.
THERE, THERE...
...STOP FIGHTING.
TROMP TROMP
MASTER HANZO...
WHAT DO YOU WANT?!
LET HER GO.
SHUT UP!
I'M GONNA KILL YOU!!
EEEEK

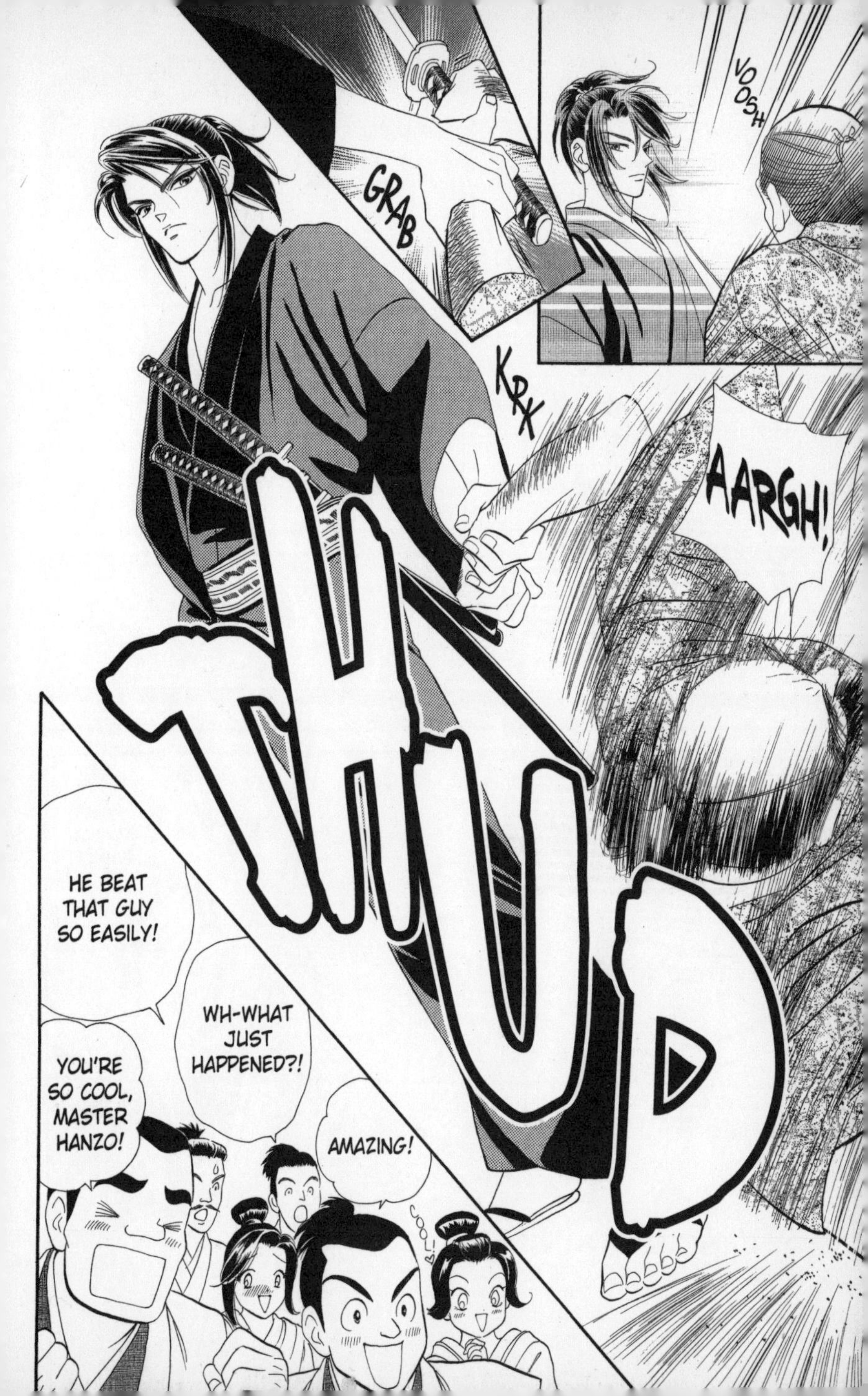
VOOSH
GRAB
KRK
AARGH!
THUD
HE BEAT THAT GUY SO EASILY!
WH-WHAT JUST HAPPENED?!
YOU'RE SO COOL, MASTER HANZO!
AMAZING!
COOL!

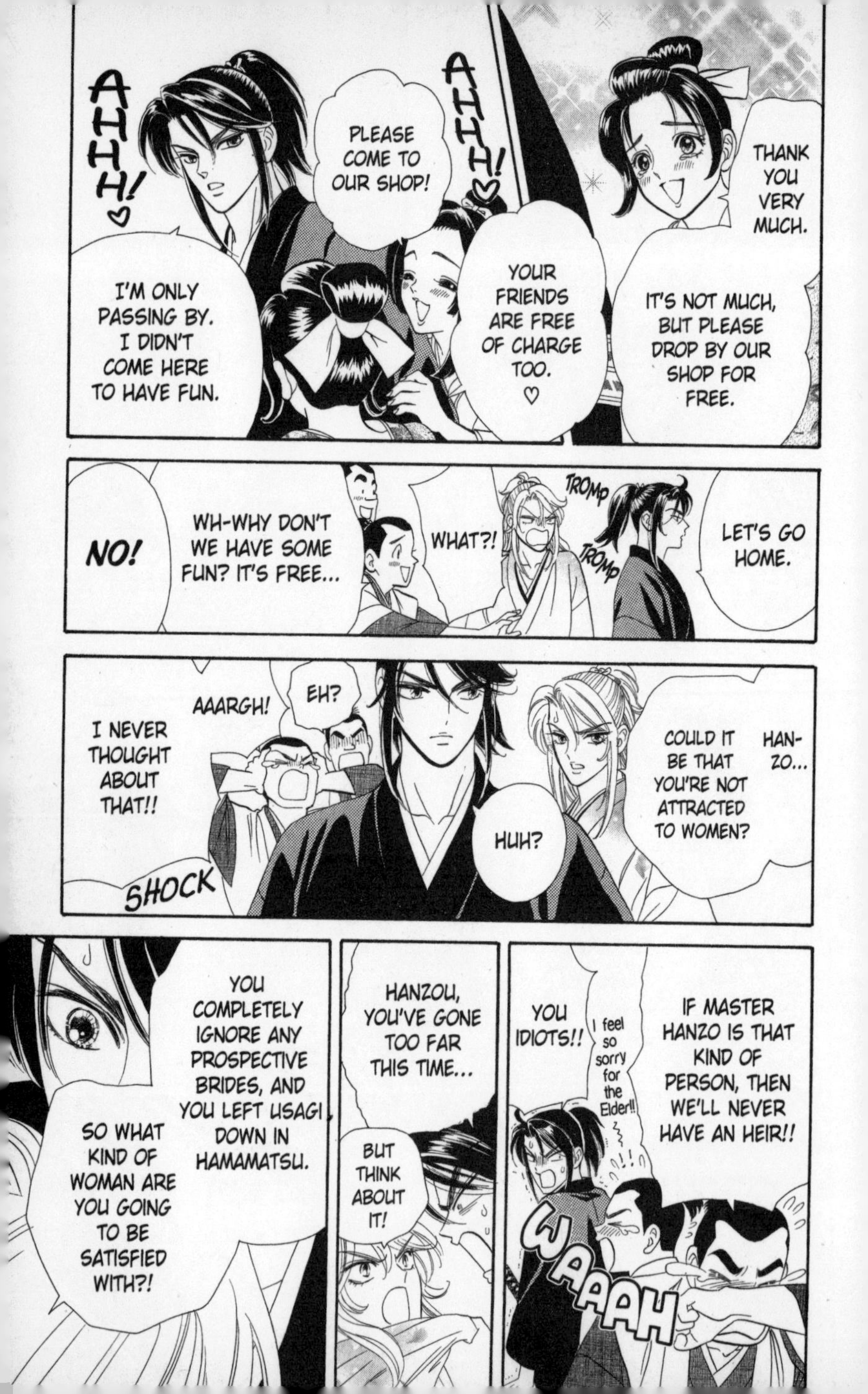
THANK YOU VERY MUCH.
IT'S NOT MUCH, BUT PLEASE DROP BY OUR SHOP FOR FREE.
AHHH! ♡
YOUR FRIENDS ARE FREE OF CHARGE TOO. ♡
PLEASE COME TO OUR SHOP!
AHHH! ♡
I'M ONLY PASSING BY. I DIDN'T COME HERE TO HAVE FUN.
LET'S GO HOME.
TROMP
TROMP
WHAT?!
WH-WHY DON'T WE HAVE SOME FUN? IT'S FREE...
NO!
HAN-ZO...
COULD IT BE THAT YOU'RE NOT ATTRACTED TO WOMEN?
HUH?
EH?
AAARGH!
I NEVER THOUGHT ABOUT THAT!!
SHOCK
IF MASTER HANZO IS THAT KIND OF PERSON, THEN WE'LL NEVER HAVE AN HEIR!!
I feel so sorry for the Elder!!
YOU IDIOTS!!
WAAAH
HANZOU, YOU'VE GONE TOO FAR THIS TIME...
BUT THINK ABOUT IT!
YOU COMPLETELY IGNORE ANY PROSPECTIVE BRIDES, AND YOU LEFT USAGI DOWN IN HAMAMATSU.
SO WHAT KIND OF WOMAN ARE YOU GOING TO BE SATISFIED WITH?!

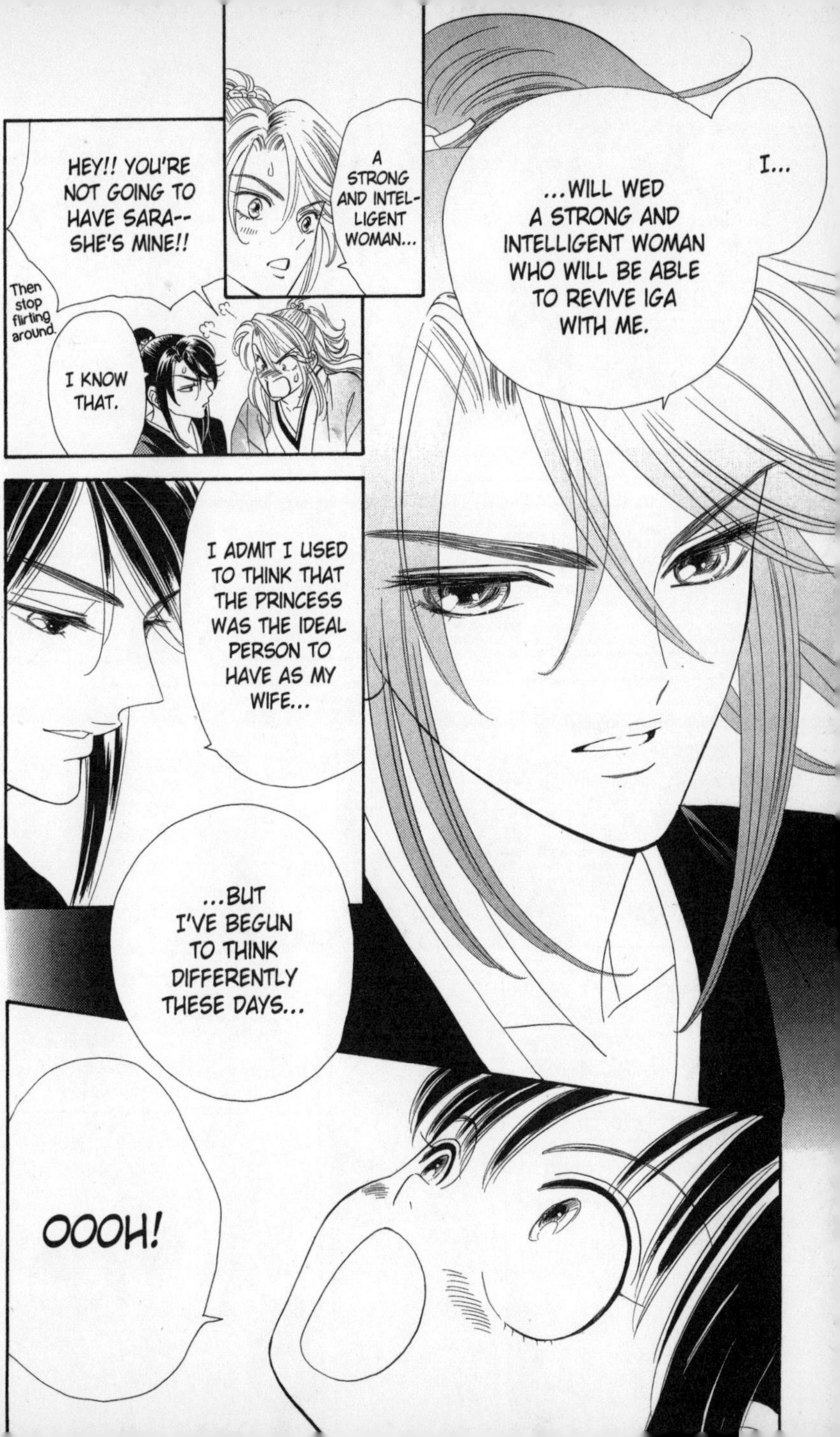
I...
...WILL WED A STRONG AND INTELLIGENT WOMAN WHO WILL BE ABLE TO REVIVE IGA WITH ME.
A STRONG AND INTELLIGENT WOMAN...
HEY!! YOU'RE NOT GOING TO HAVE SARA-- SHE'S MINE!!
I KNOW THAT.
Then stop flirting around.
I ADMIT I USED TO THINK THAT THE PRINCESS WAS THE IDEAL PERSON TO HAVE AS MY WIFE...
...BUT I'VE BEGUN TO THINK DIFFERENTLY THESE DAYS...
OOOH!

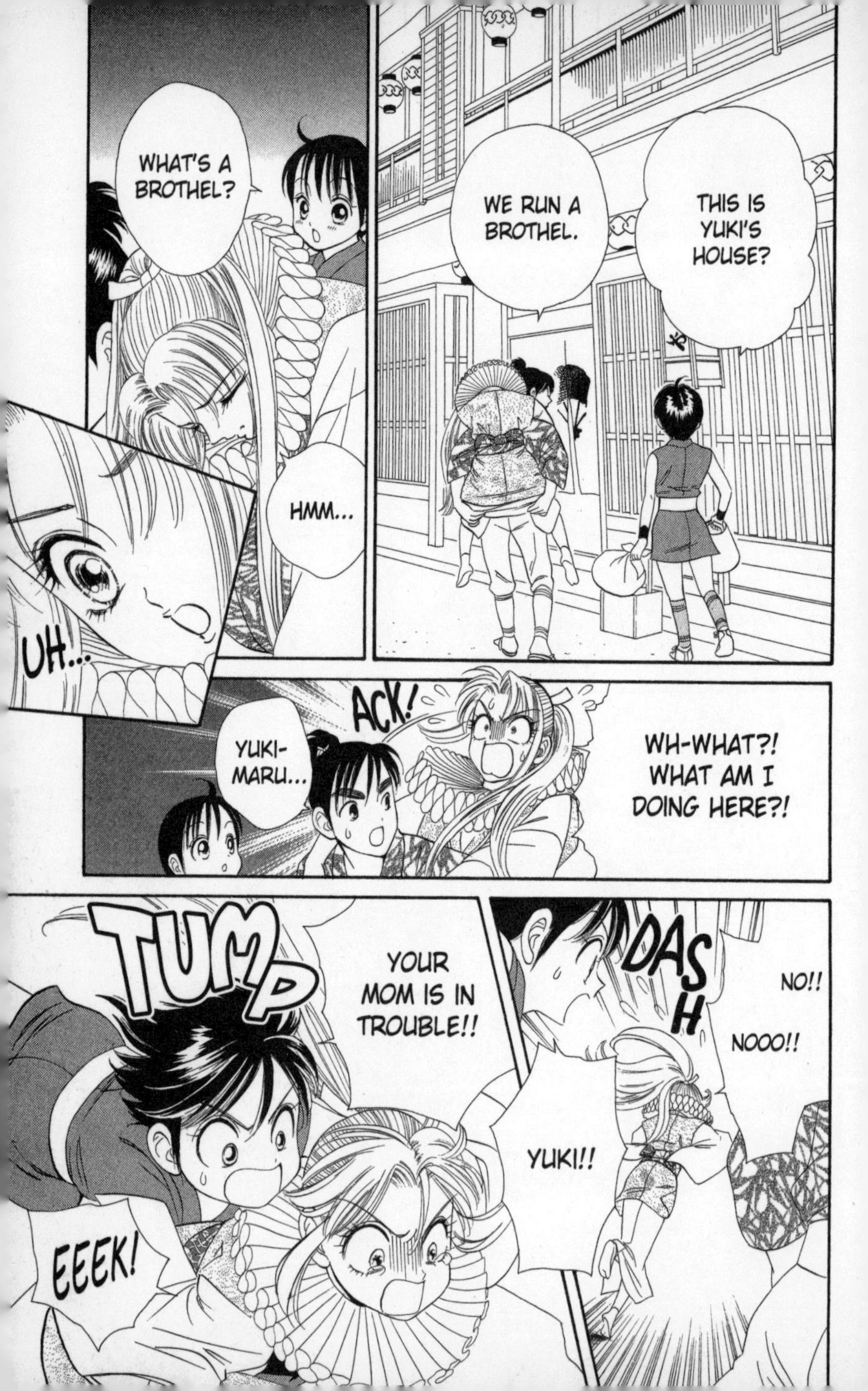
THIS IS YUKI'S HOUSE?
WE RUN A BROTHEL.
WHAT'S A BROTHEL?
HMM...
UH...
WH-WHAT?! WHAT AM I DOING HERE?!
ACK!
YUKI-MARU...
NO!!
NOOO!!
DASH
YUKI!!
YOUR MOM IS IN TROUBLE!!
TUMP
EEEK!

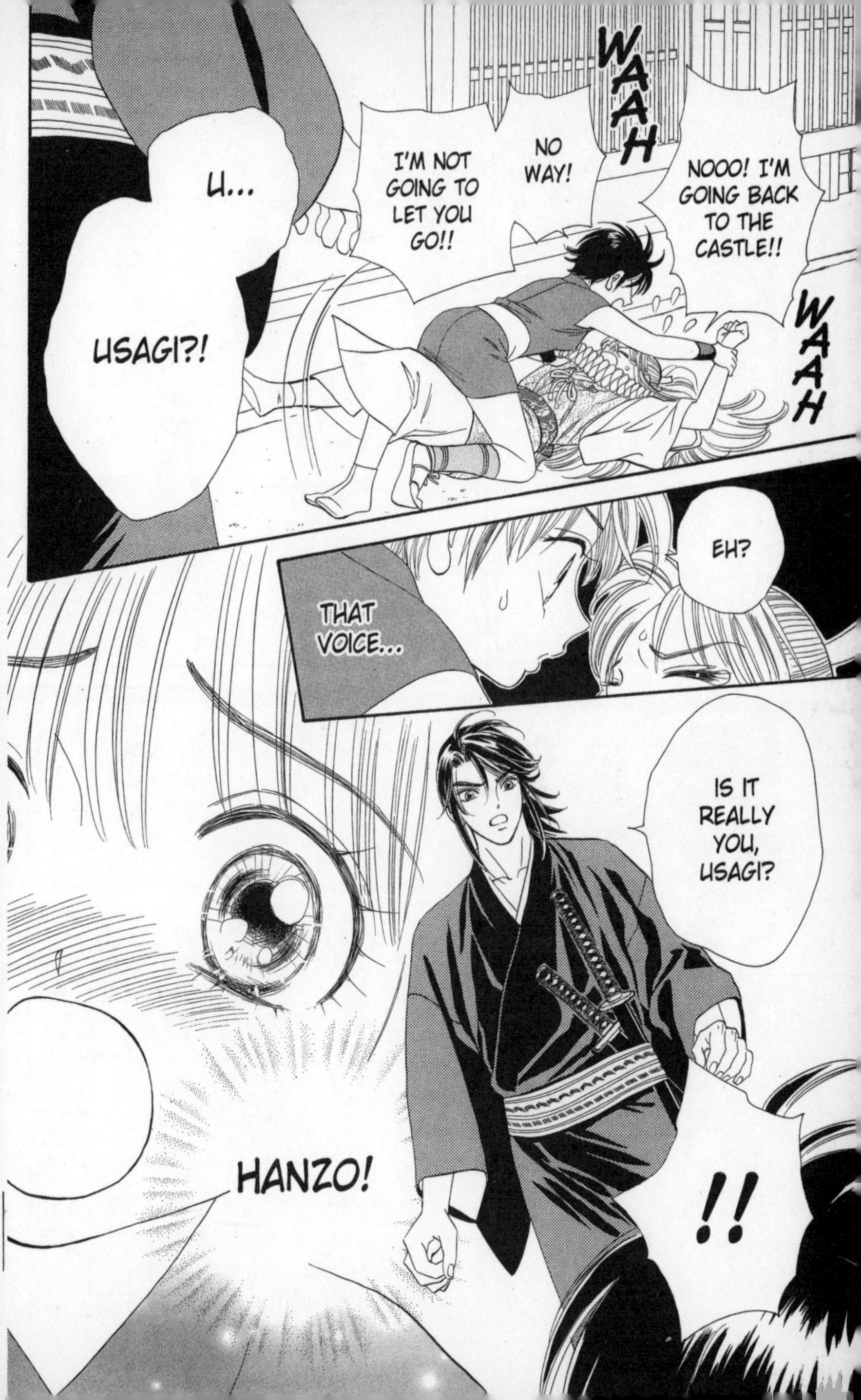
WAAH
NOOO! I'M GOING BACK TO THE CASTLE!!
WAAH
NO WAY!
I'M NOT GOING TO LET YOU GO!!
U...
USAGI?!
EH?
THAT VOICE...
IS IT REALLY YOU, USAGI?
!!
HANZO!

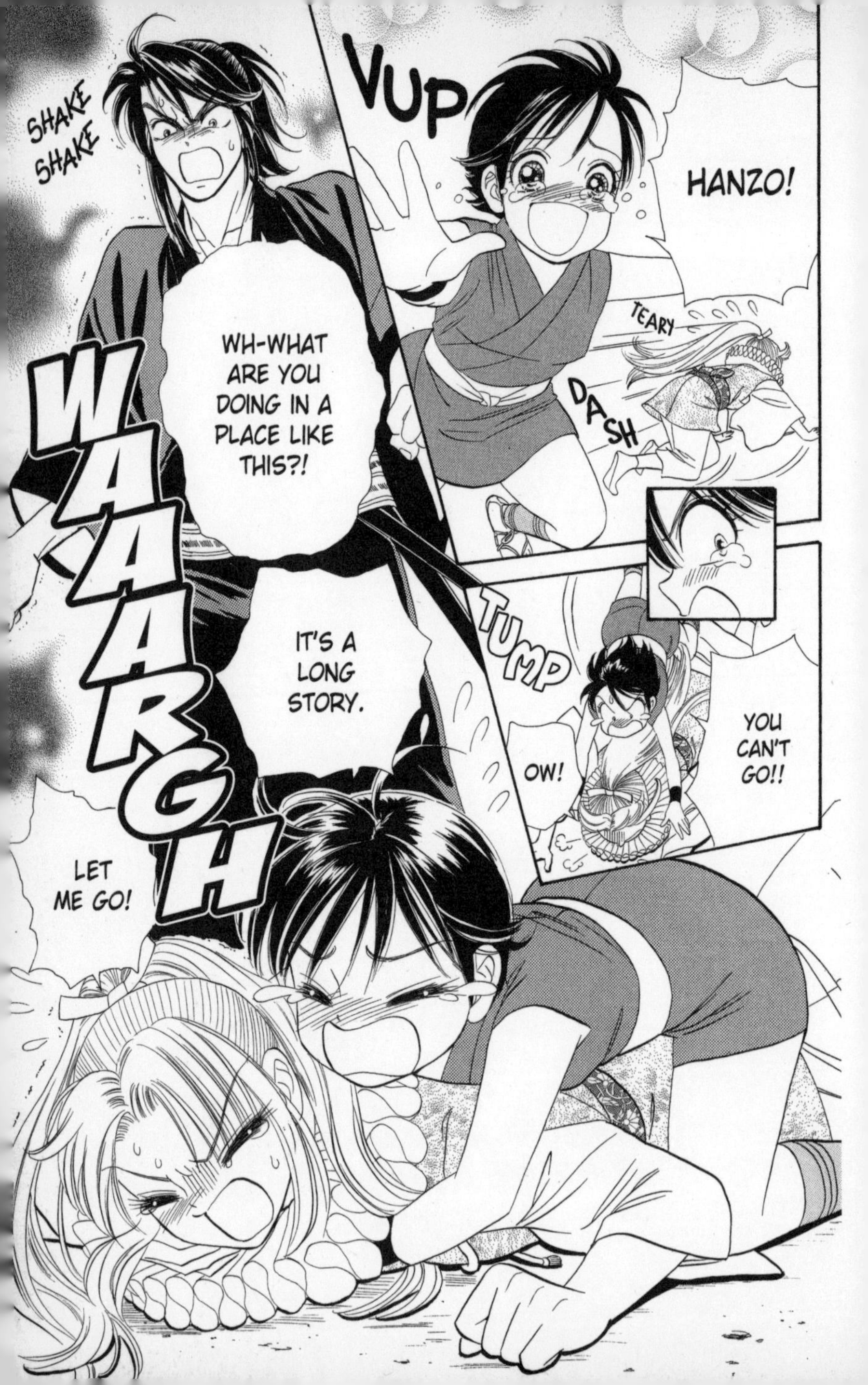
VUP
HANZO!
TEARY
DASH
TUMP
YOU CAN'T GO!!
OW!
SHAKE SHAKE
WH-WHAT ARE YOU DOING IN A PLACE LIKE THIS?!
IT'S A LONG STORY.
WAARGH
LET ME GO!

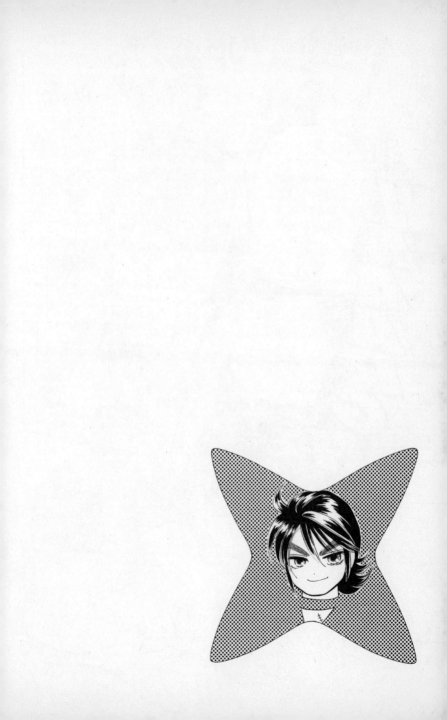

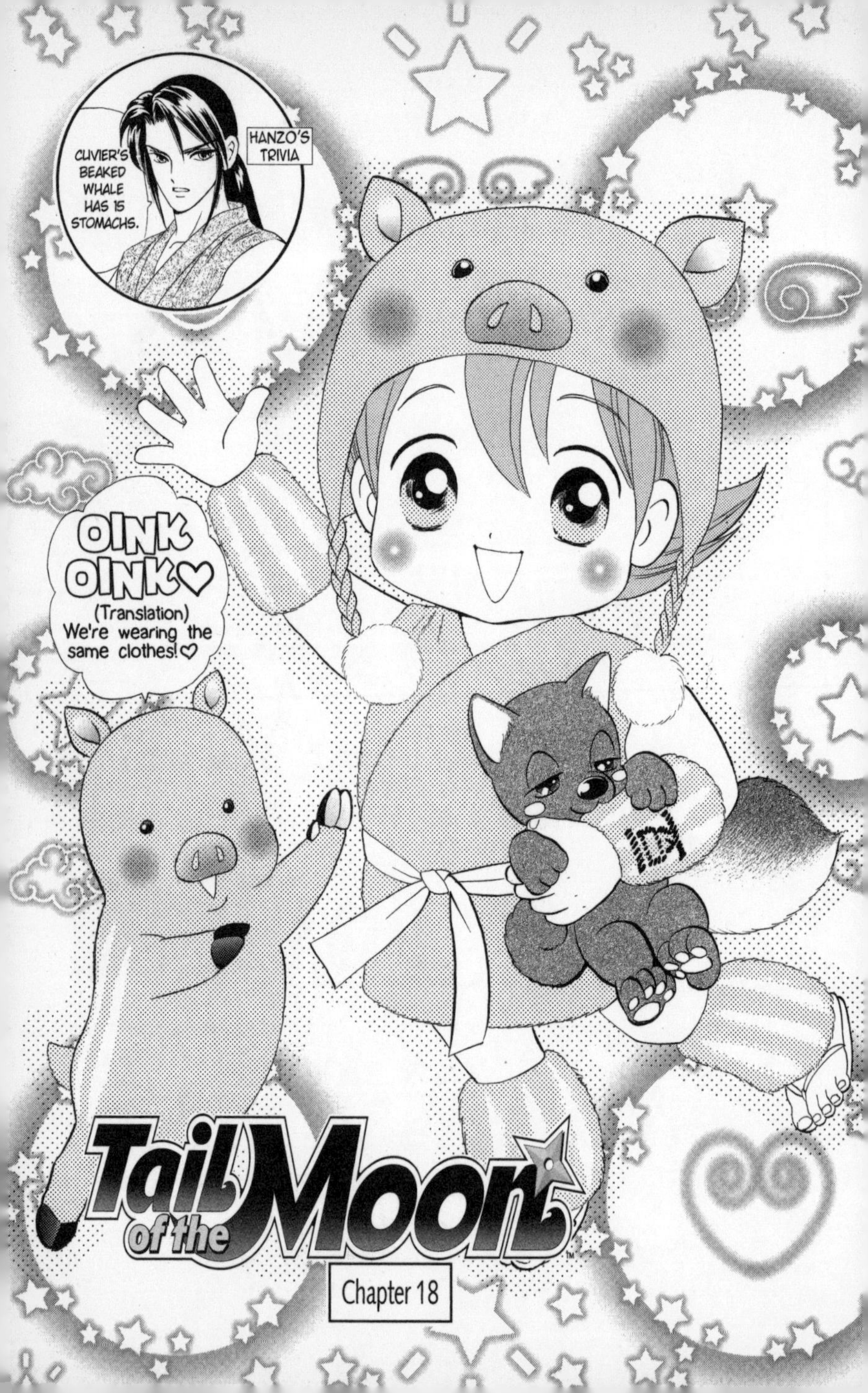
HANZO'S TRIVIA
CUVIER'S BEAKED WHALE HAS 15 STOMACHS.
OINK OINK♡ (Translation) We're wearing the same clothes!♡
Tail of the Moon™
Chapter 18

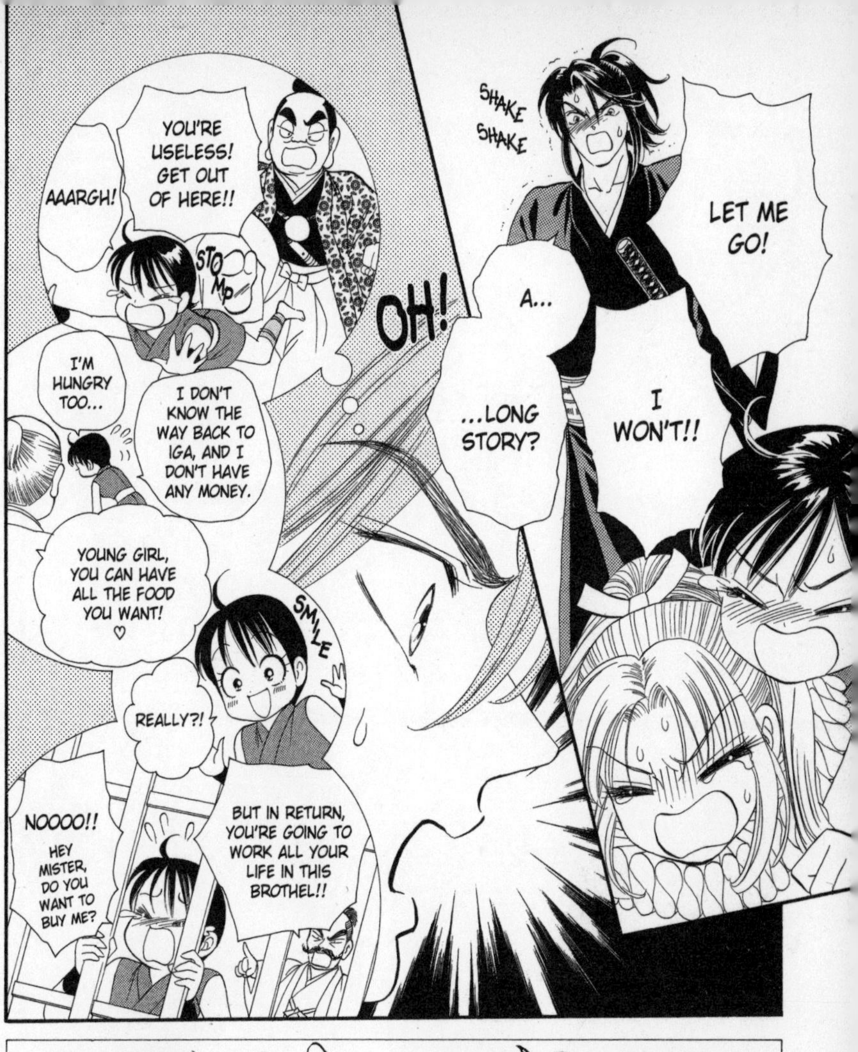
SHAKE SHAKE
LET ME GO!
I WON'T!!
A...
...LONG STORY?
OH!
YOU'RE USELESS! GET OUT OF HERE!!
AAARGH!
STOMP
I'M HUNGRY TOO...
I DON'T KNOW THE WAY BACK TO IGA, AND I DON'T HAVE ANY MONEY.
YOUNG GIRL, YOU CAN HAVE ALL THE FOOD YOU WANT! ♡
SMILE
REALLY?!
BUT IN RETURN, YOU'RE GOING TO WORK ALL YOUR LIFE IN THIS BROTHEL!!
NOOOO!!
HEY MISTER, DO YOU WANT TO BUY ME?

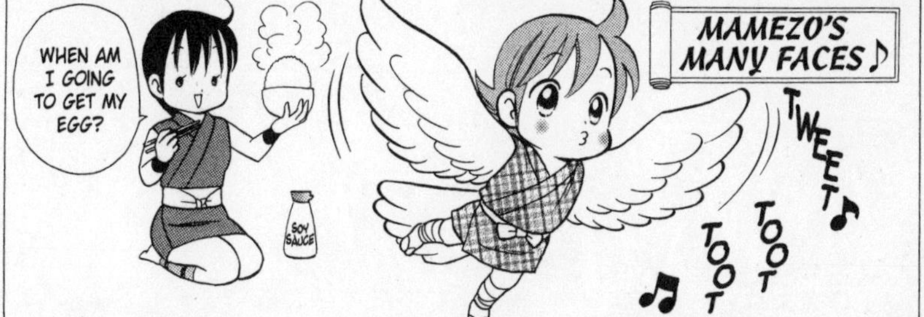
MAMEZO'S MANY FACES♪
TWEET♪
TOOT TOOT
WHEN AM I GOING TO GET MY EGG?
SOY SAUCE

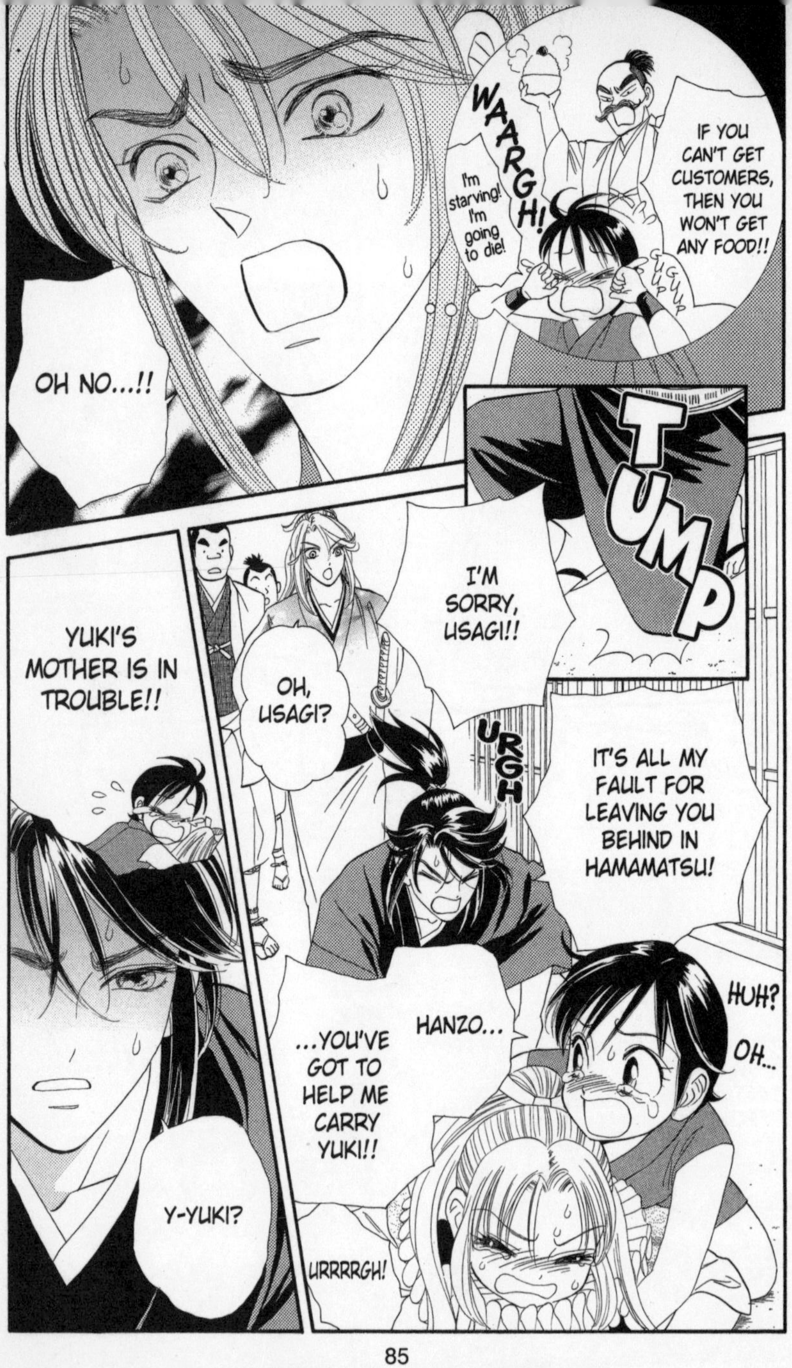
IF YOU CAN'T GET CUSTOMERS, THEN YOU WON'T GET ANY FOOD!!
WAARGH!
I'm starving! I'm going to die!
OH NO...!!
TUMP
I'M SORRY, USAGI!!
IT'S ALL MY FAULT FOR LEAVING YOU BEHIND IN HAMAMATSU!
URGH
OH, USAGI?
HUH?
OH...
HANZO...
...YOU'VE GOT TO HELP ME CARRY YUKI!!
URRRRGH!
YUKI'S MOTHER IS IN TROUBLE!!
Y-YUKI?

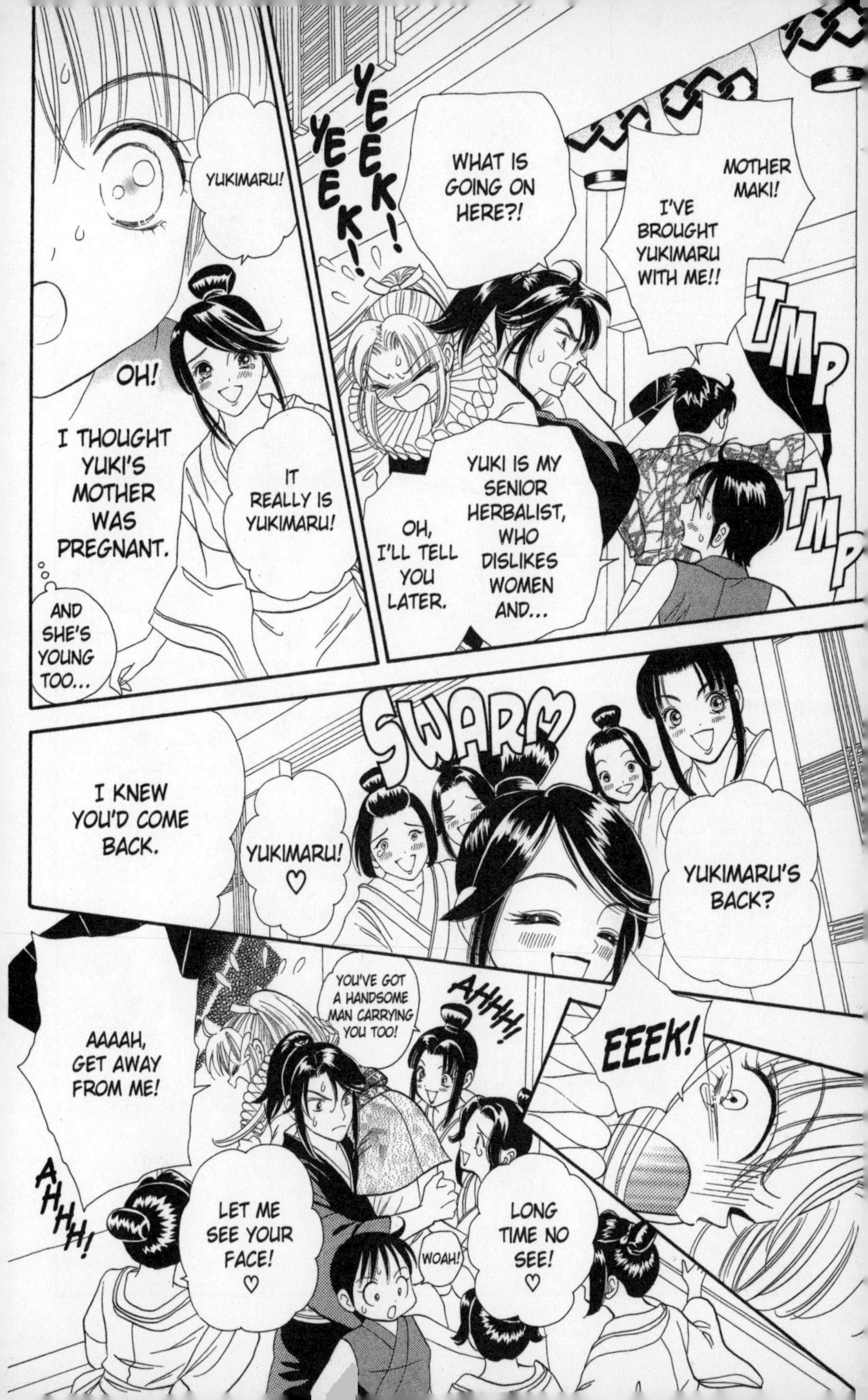
MOTHER MAKI!
I'VE BROUGHT YUKIMARU WITH ME!!
TMP
TMP
YEEK! YEEK!
WHAT IS GOING ON HERE?!
YUKI IS MY SENIOR HERBALIST, WHO DISLIKES WOMEN AND...
OH, I'LL TELL YOU LATER.
YUKIMARU!
IT REALLY IS YUKIMARU!
OH!
I THOUGHT YUKI'S MOTHER WAS PREGNANT.
AND SHE'S YOUNG TOO...
SWARM
YUKIMARU'S BACK?
YUKIMARU! ♡
I KNEW YOU'D COME BACK.
EEEK!
LONG TIME NO SEE! ♡
WOAH!
YOU'VE GOT A HANDSOME MAN CARRYING YOU TOO!
AHHH!
LET ME SEE YOUR FACE! ♡
AAAAH, GET AWAY FROM ME!
AHHH!

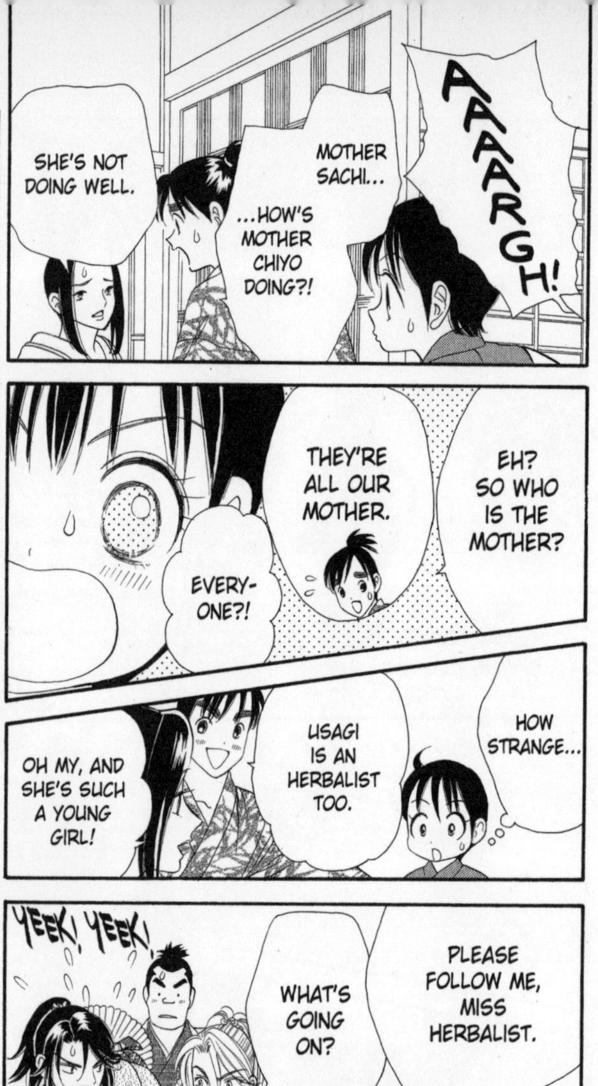
AAAARGH!
MOTHER SACHI...
...HOW'S MOTHER CHIYO DOING?!
SHE'S NOT DOING WELL.
EH? SO WHO IS THE MOTHER?
THEY'RE ALL OUR MOTHER.
EVERY-ONE?!
HOW STRANGE...
USAGI IS AN HERBALIST TOO.
OH MY, AND SHE'S SUCH A YOUNG GIRL!
PLEASE FOLLOW ME, MISS HERBALIST.
WHAT'S GOING ON?
YEEK! YEEK!
...
...OKAY.
YOU TELL ME!

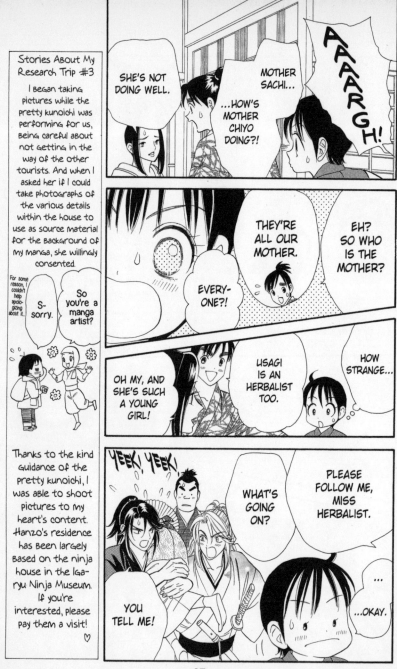

Stories About My Research Trip #3

I began taking pictures while the pretty kunoichi was performing for us, being careful about not getting in the way of the other tourists. And when I asked her if I could take photographs of the various details within the house to use as source material for the background of my manga, she willingly consented.

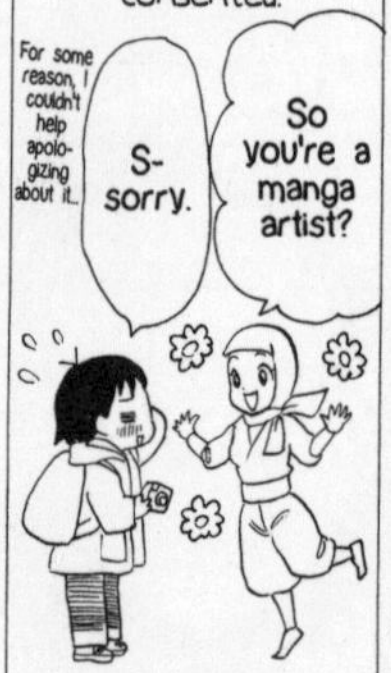
So you're a manga artist?
S-sorry.
For some reason, I couldn't help apologizing about it.

Thanks to the kind guidance of the pretty kunoichi, I was able to shoot pictures to my heart's content. Hanzo's residence has been largely based on the ninja house in the Iga-ryu Ninja Museum. If you're interested, please pay them a visit! ♡

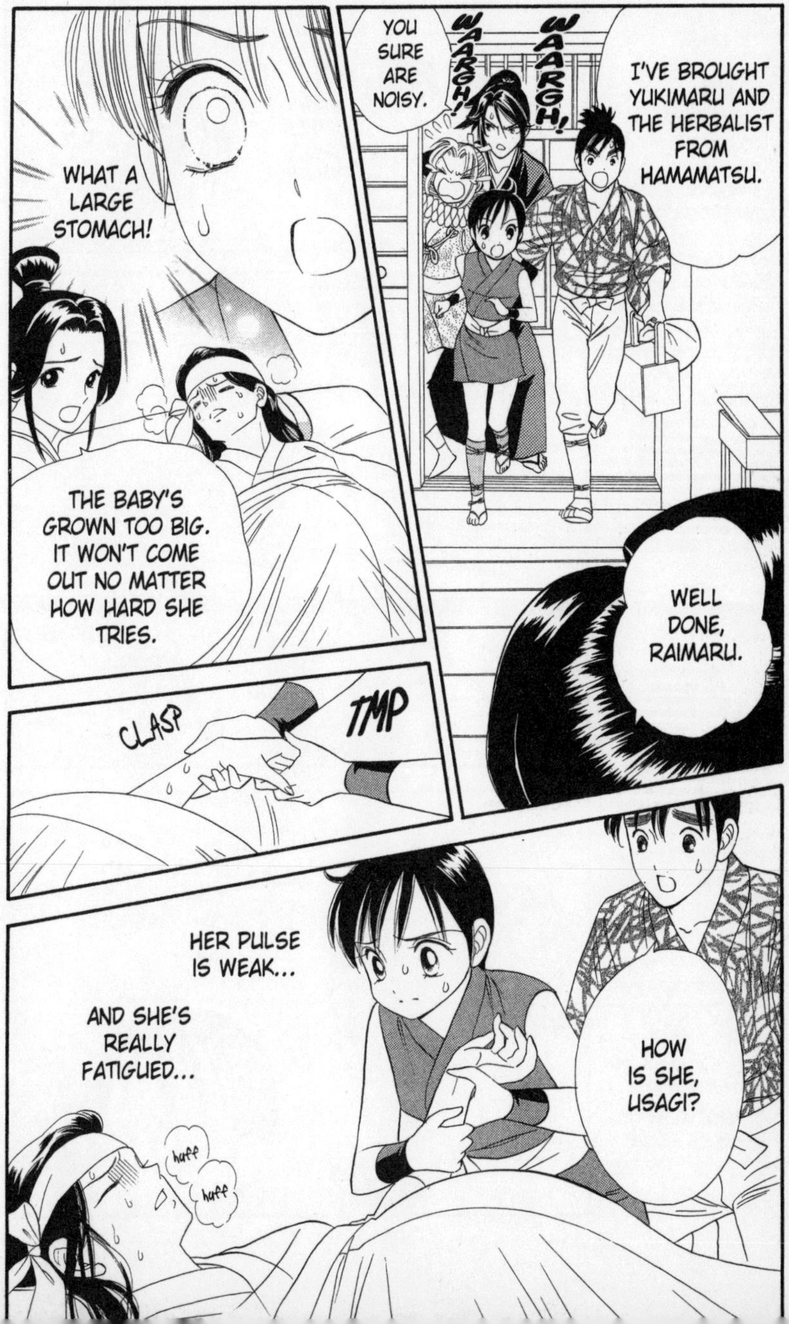

I'VE BROUGHT YUKIMARU AND THE HERBALIST FROM HAMAMATSU.
WAAARGH!
WAARGH!
YOU SURE ARE NOISY.
WELL DONE, RAIMARU.
WHAT A LARGE STOMACH!
THE BABY'S GROWN TOO BIG. IT WON'T COME OUT NO MATTER HOW HARD SHE TRIES.
TMP
CLASP
HOW IS SHE, USAGI?
HER PULSE IS WEAK...
AND SHE'S REALLY FATIGUED...
huff
huff

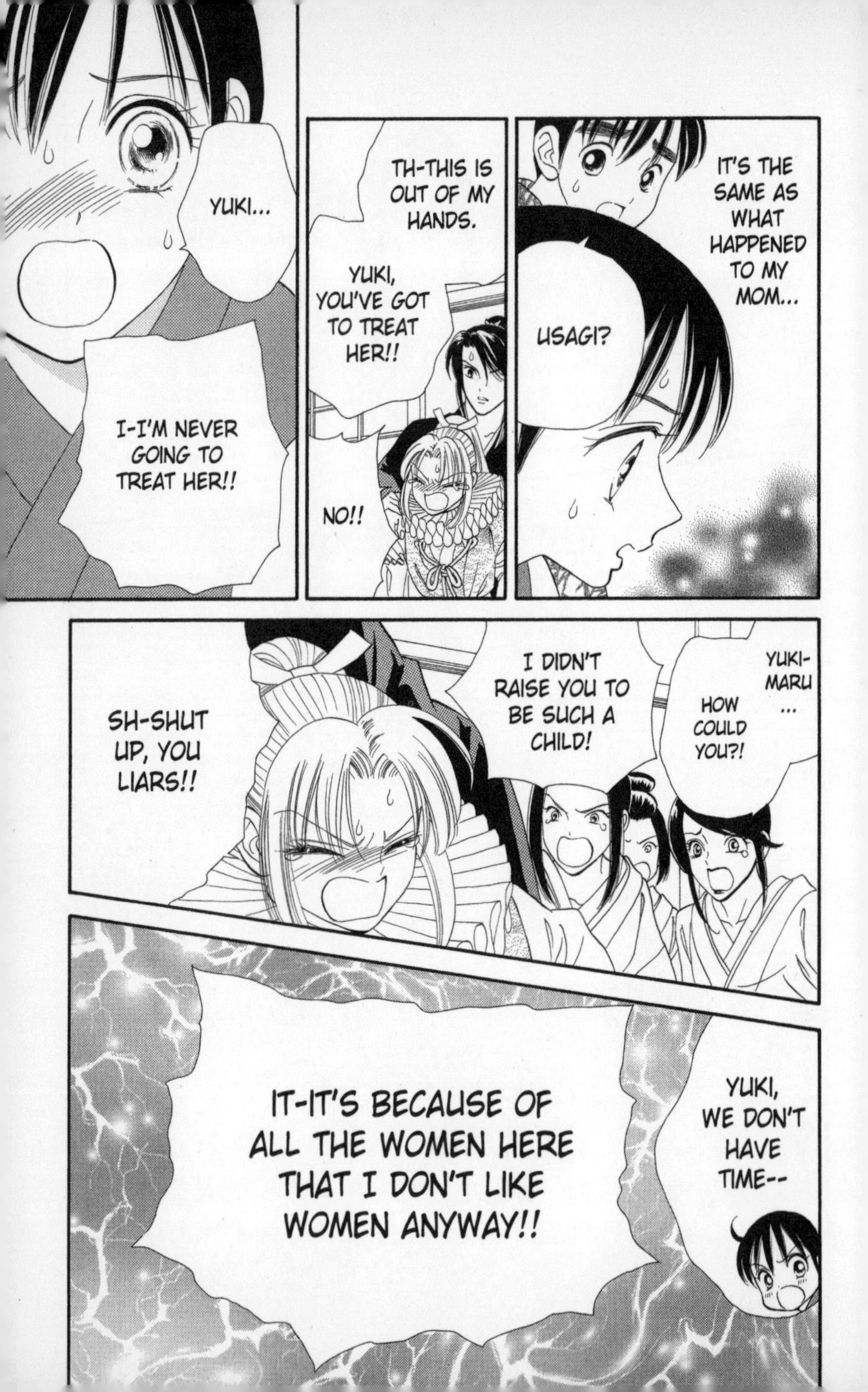
IT'S THE SAME AS WHAT HAPPENED TO MY MOM...
USAGI?
TH-THIS IS OUT OF MY HANDS.
YUKI, YOU'VE GOT TO TREAT HER!!
NO!!
YUKI...
I-I'M NEVER GOING TO TREAT HER!!
YUKI-MARU...
HOW COULD YOU?!
I DIDN'T RAISE YOU TO BE SUCH A CHILD!
SH-SHUT UP, YOU LIARS!!
YUKI, WE DON'T HAVE TIME--
IT-IT'S BECAUSE OF ALL THE WOMEN HERE THAT I DON'T LIKE WOMEN ANYWAY!!

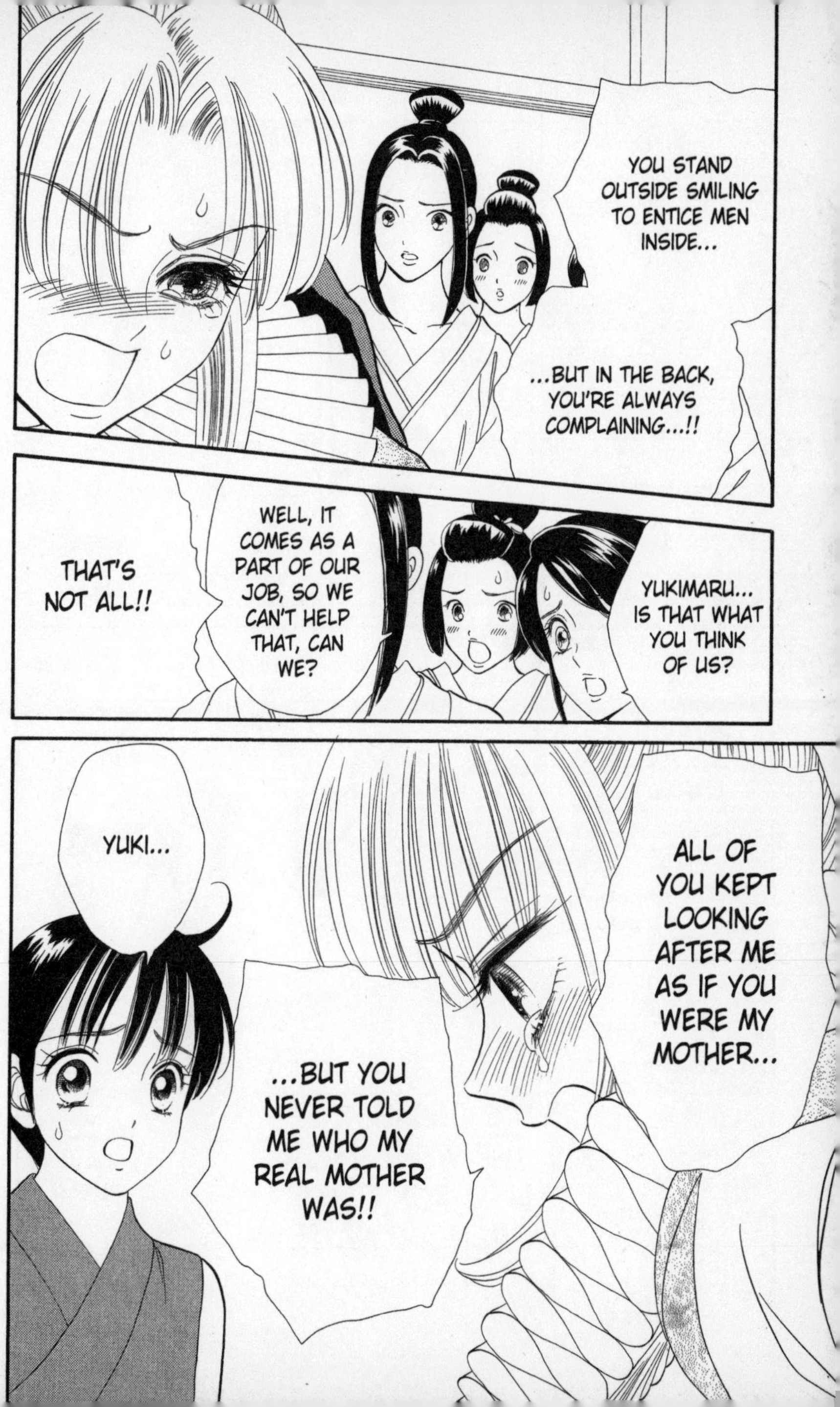
YOU STAND OUTSIDE SMILING TO ENTICE MEN INSIDE...
...BUT IN THE BACK, YOU'RE ALWAYS COMPLAINING...!!
YUKIMARU... IS THAT WHAT YOU THINK OF US?
WELL, IT COMES AS A PART OF OUR JOB, SO WE CAN'T HELP THAT, CAN WE?
THAT'S NOT ALL!!
ALL OF YOU KEPT LOOKING AFTER ME AS IF YOU WERE MY MOTHER...
...BUT YOU NEVER TOLD ME WHO MY REAL MOTHER WAS!!
YUKI...

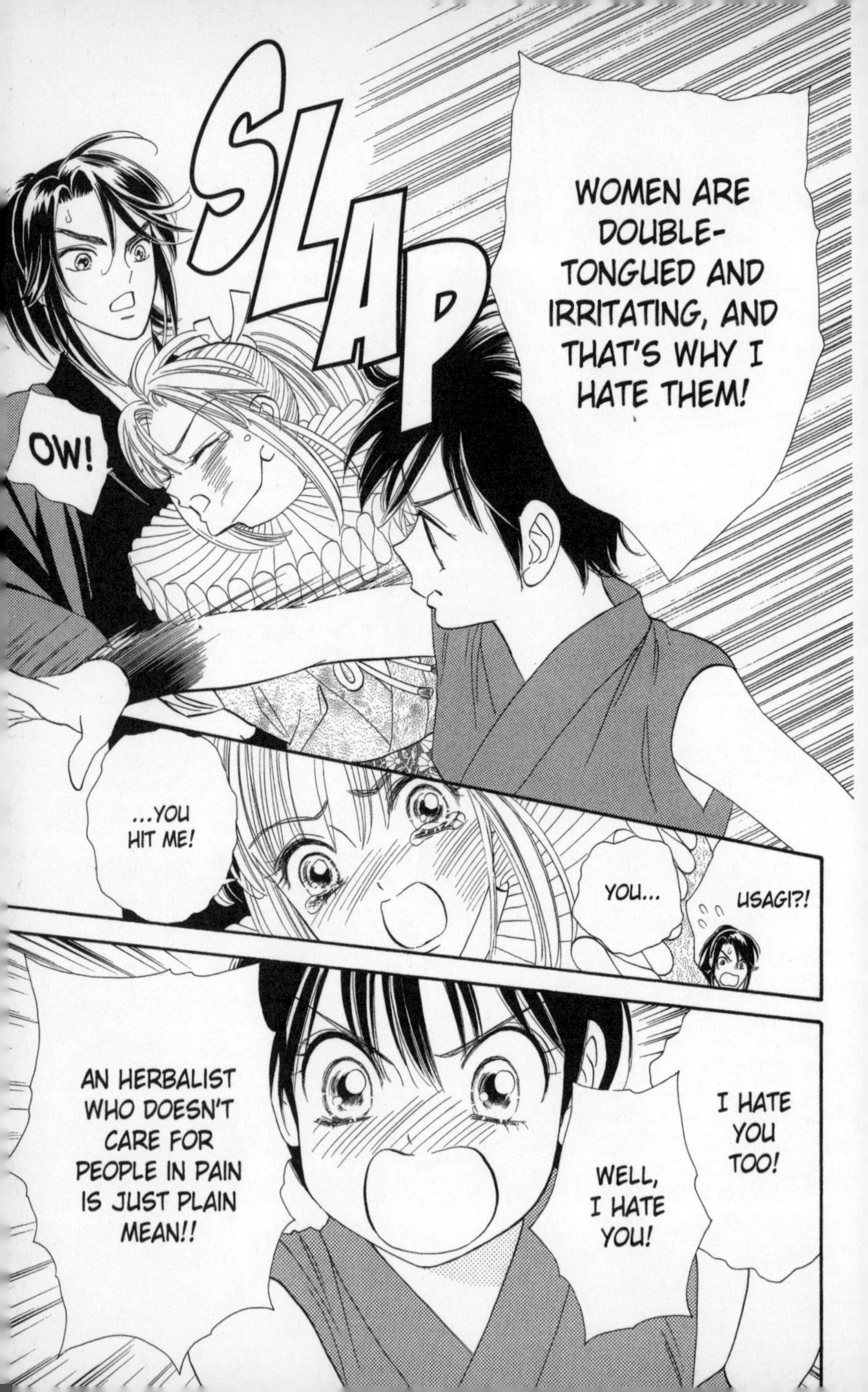
WOMEN ARE DOUBLE-TONGUED AND IRRITATING, AND THAT'S WHY I HATE THEM!
SLAP
OW!
USAGI?!
YOU...
...YOU HIT ME!
I HATE YOU TOO!
WELL, I HATE YOU!
AN HERBALIST WHO DOESN'T CARE FOR PEOPLE IN PAIN IS JUST PLAIN MEAN!!

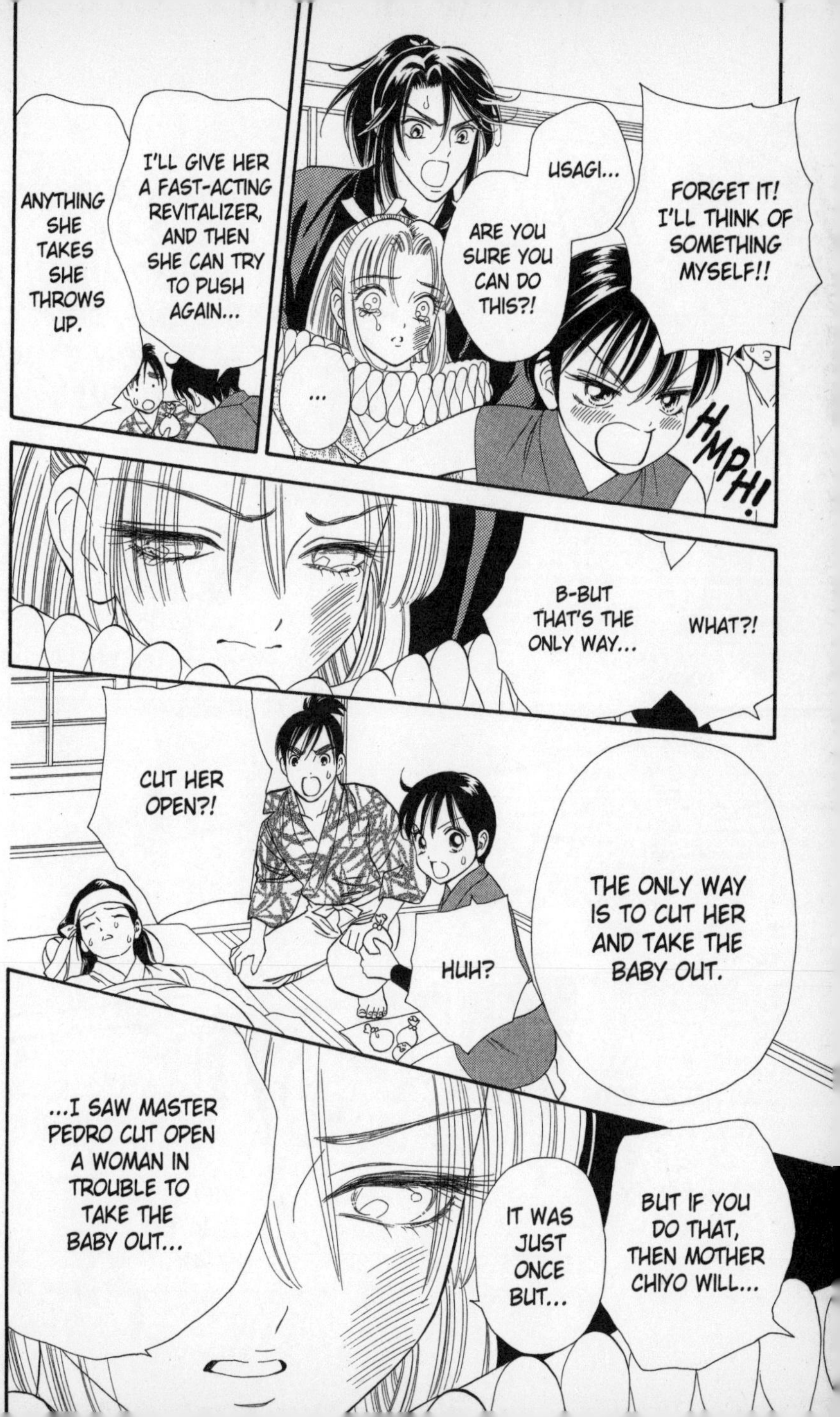
FORGET IT! I'LL THINK OF SOMETHING MYSELF!!
USAGI...
ARE YOU SURE YOU CAN DO THIS?!
HMPH!
...
I'LL GIVE HER A FAST-ACTING REVITALIZER, AND THEN SHE CAN TRY TO PUSH AGAIN...
ANYTHING SHE TAKES SHE THROWS UP.
WHAT?!
B-BUT THAT'S THE ONLY WAY...
THE ONLY WAY IS TO CUT HER AND TAKE THE BABY OUT.
HUH?
CUT HER OPEN?!
BUT IF YOU DO THAT, THEN MOTHER CHIYO WILL...
IT WAS JUST ONCE BUT...
...I SAW MASTER PEDRO CUT OPEN A WOMAN IN TROUBLE TO TAKE THE BABY OUT...

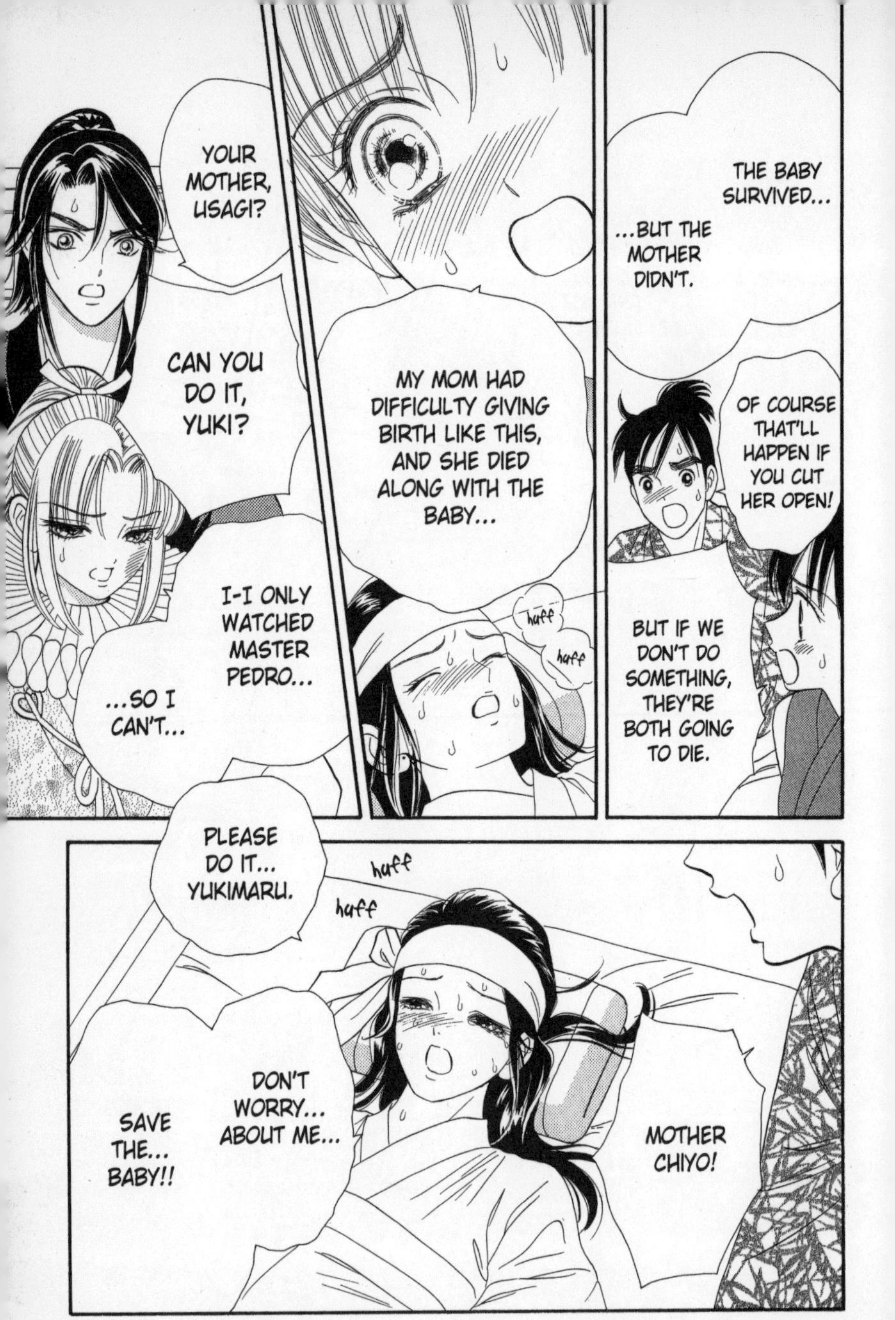
THE BABY SURVIVED...
...BUT THE MOTHER DIDN'T.
OF COURSE THAT'LL HAPPEN IF YOU CUT HER OPEN!
BUT IF WE DON'T DO SOMETHING, THEY'RE BOTH GOING TO DIE.
MY MOM HAD DIFFICULTY GIVING BIRTH LIKE THIS, AND SHE DIED ALONG WITH THE BABY...
huff
huff
YOUR MOTHER, USAGI?
CAN YOU DO IT, YUKI?
I-I ONLY WATCHED MASTER PEDRO...
...SO I CAN'T...
PLEASE DO IT... YUKIMARU.
huff
huff
MOTHER CHIYO!
DON'T WORRY... ABOUT ME...
SAVE THE... BABY!!

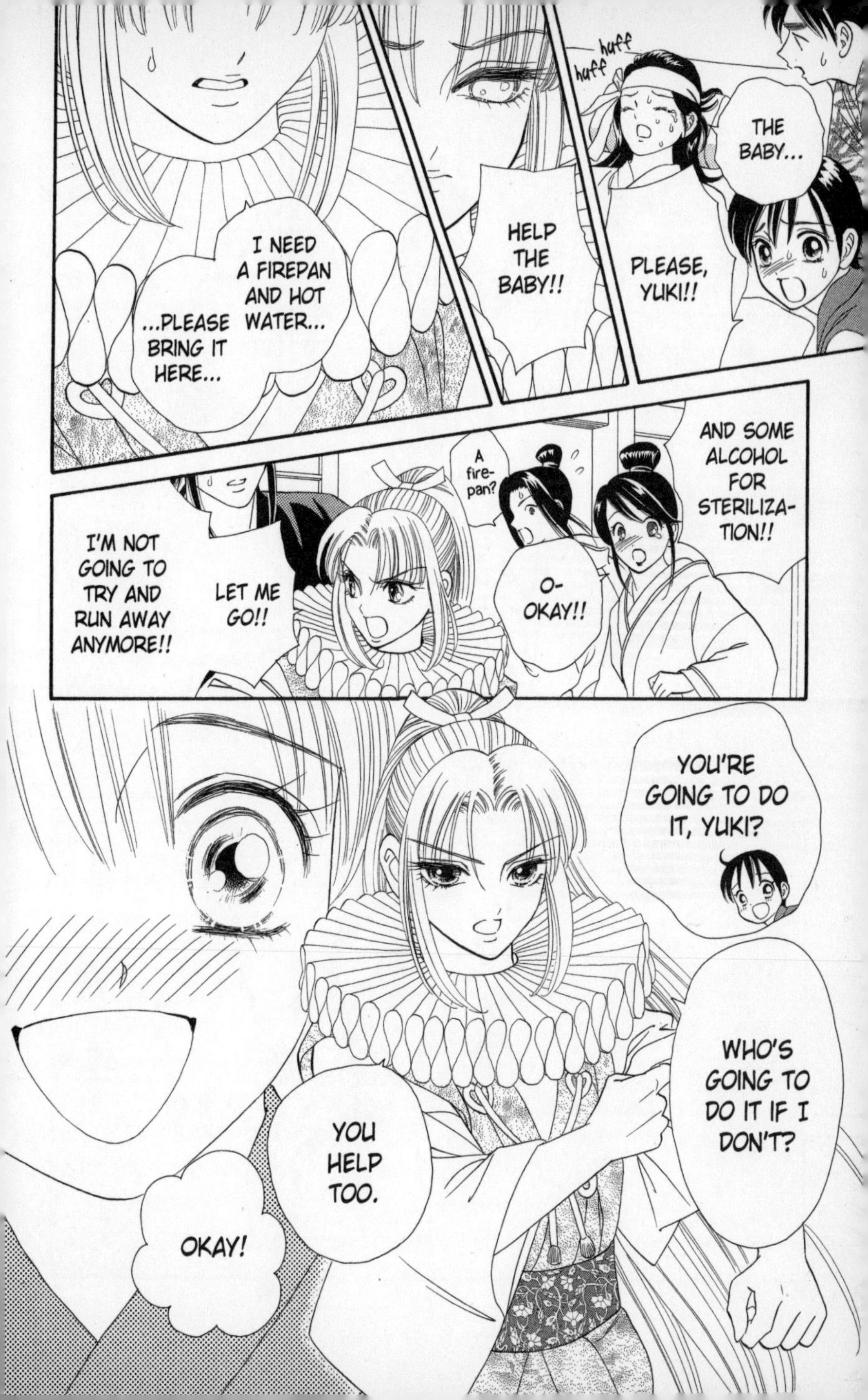
huff
huff
THE BABY...
PLEASE, YUKI!!
HELP THE BABY!!
I NEED A FIREPAN AND HOT WATER...
...PLEASE BRING IT HERE...
AND SOME ALCOHOL FOR STERILIZA-TION!!
A fire-pan?
O-OKAY!!
LET ME GO!!
I'M NOT GOING TO TRY AND RUN AWAY ANYMORE!!
YOU'RE GOING TO DO IT, YUKI?
WHO'S GOING TO DO IT IF I DON'T?
YOU HELP TOO.
OKAY!

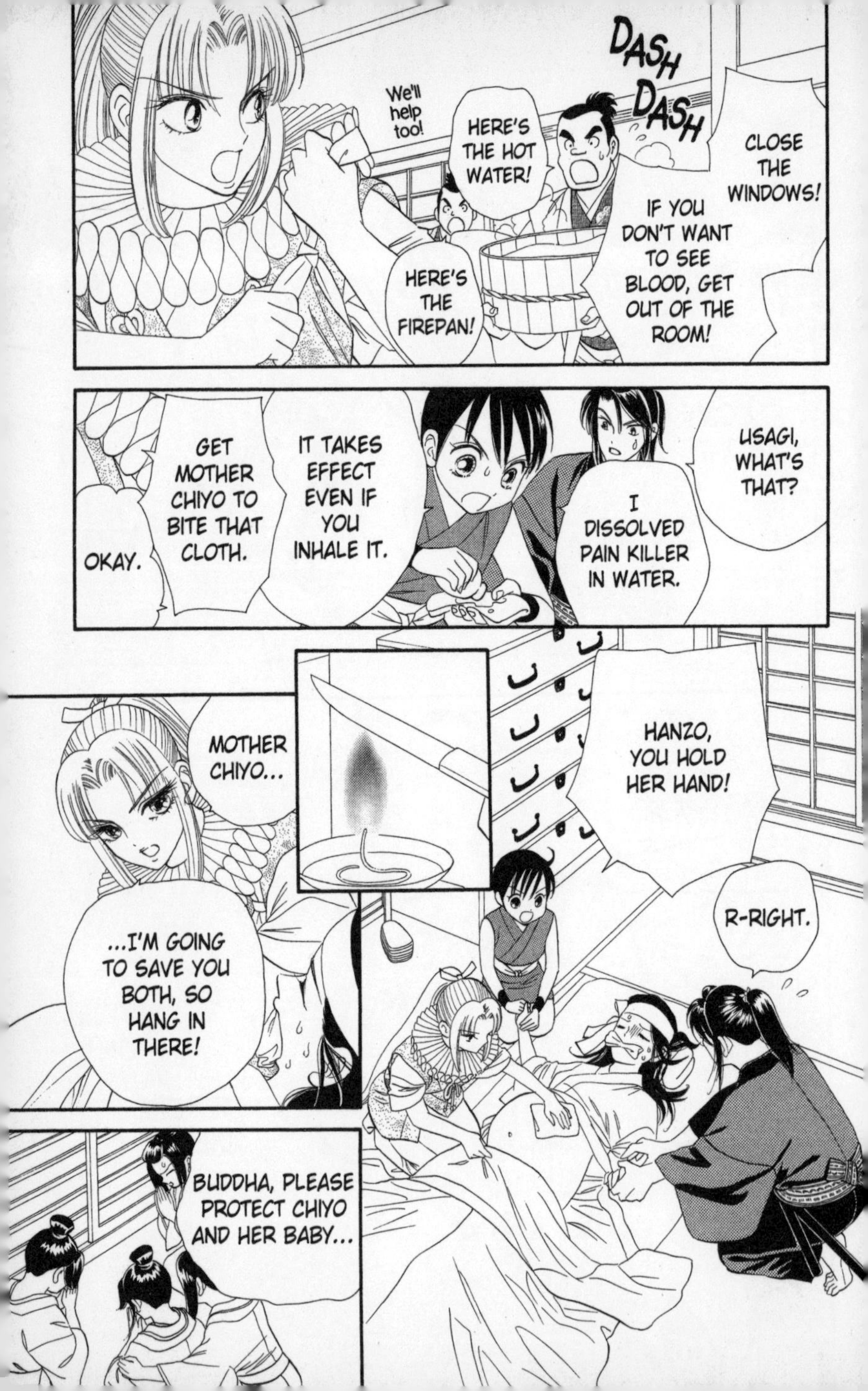
DASH DASH
CLOSE THE WINDOWS!
IF YOU DON'T WANT TO SEE BLOOD, GET OUT OF THE ROOM!
HERE'S THE HOT WATER!
We'll help too!
HERE'S THE FIREPAN!
USAGI, WHAT'S THAT?
I DISSOLVED PAIN KILLER IN WATER.
IT TAKES EFFECT EVEN IF YOU INHALE IT.
GET MOTHER CHIYO TO BITE THAT CLOTH.
OKAY.
HANZO, YOU HOLD HER HAND!
R-RIGHT.
MOTHER CHIYO...
...I'M GOING TO SAVE YOU BOTH, SO HANG IN THERE!
BUDDHA, PLEASE PROTECT CHIYO AND HER BABY...

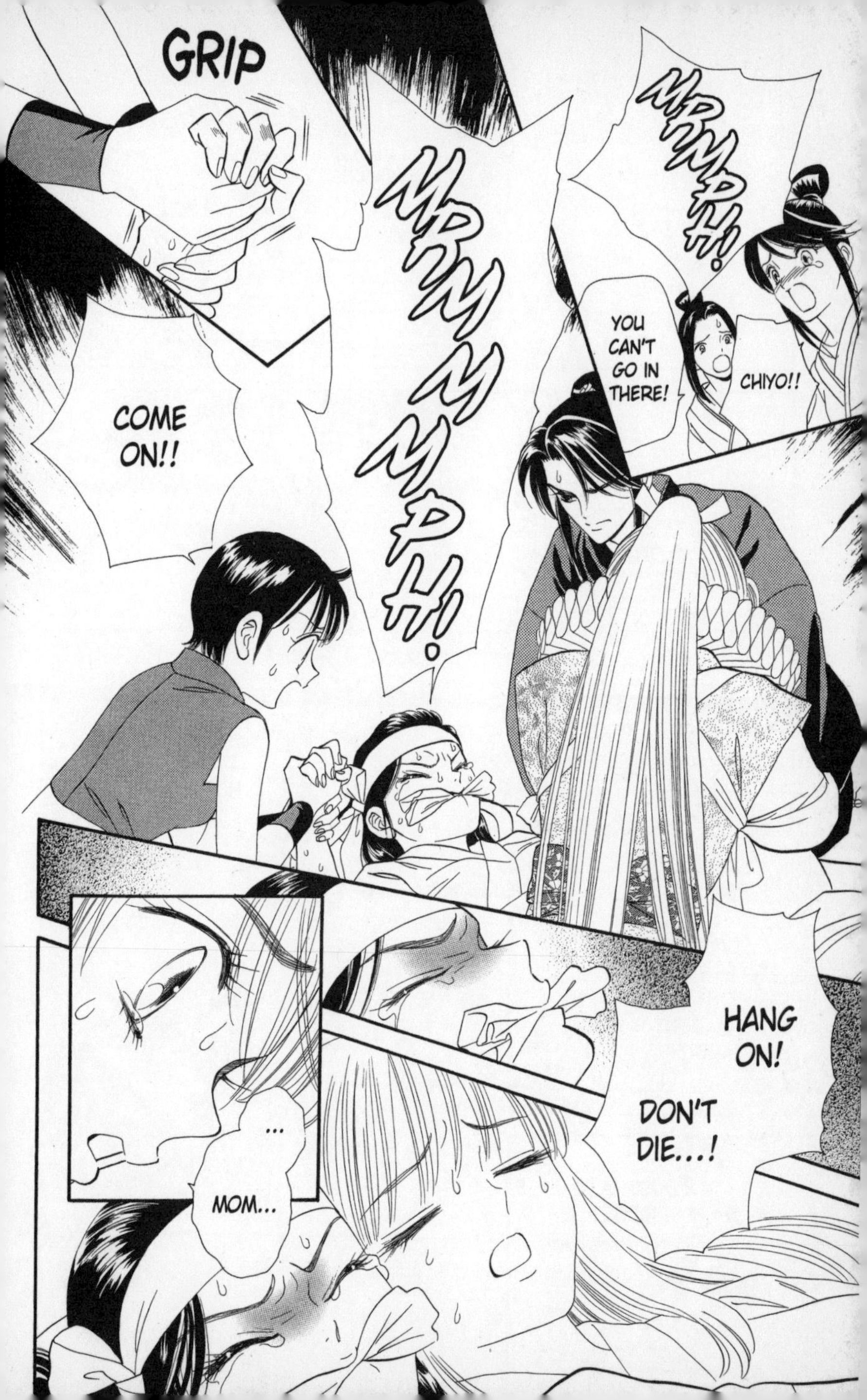

MRMPH!
CHIYO!!
YOU CAN'T GO IN THERE!
MRMMMMPH!
GRIP
COME ON!!
HANG ON!
DON'T DIE...!
...
MOM...

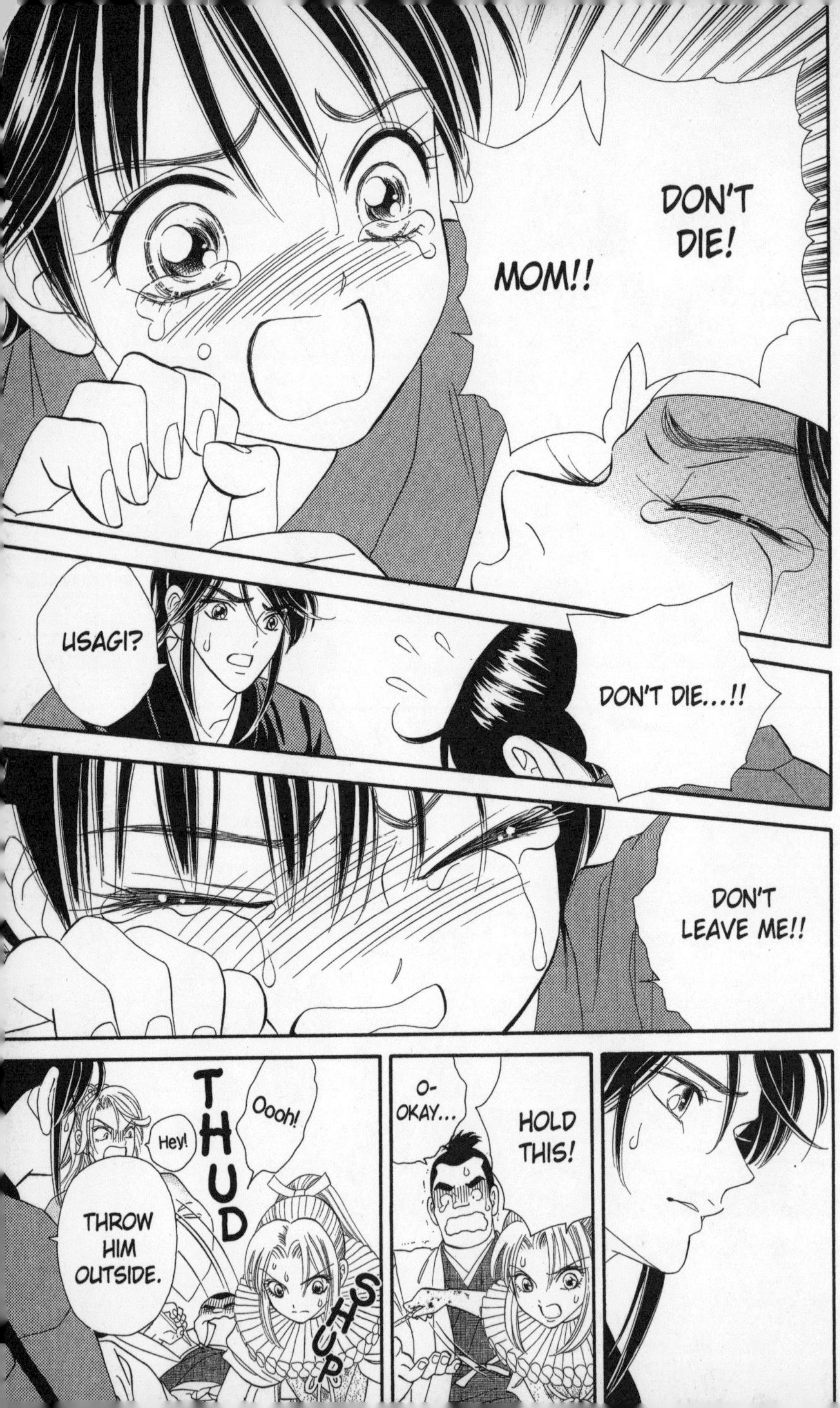
DON'T DIE!
MOM!!
DON'T DIE...!!
USAGI?
DON'T LEAVE ME!!
HOLD THIS!
O- OKAY...
Oooh!
THUD
Hey!
THROW HIM OUTSIDE.
SHUP

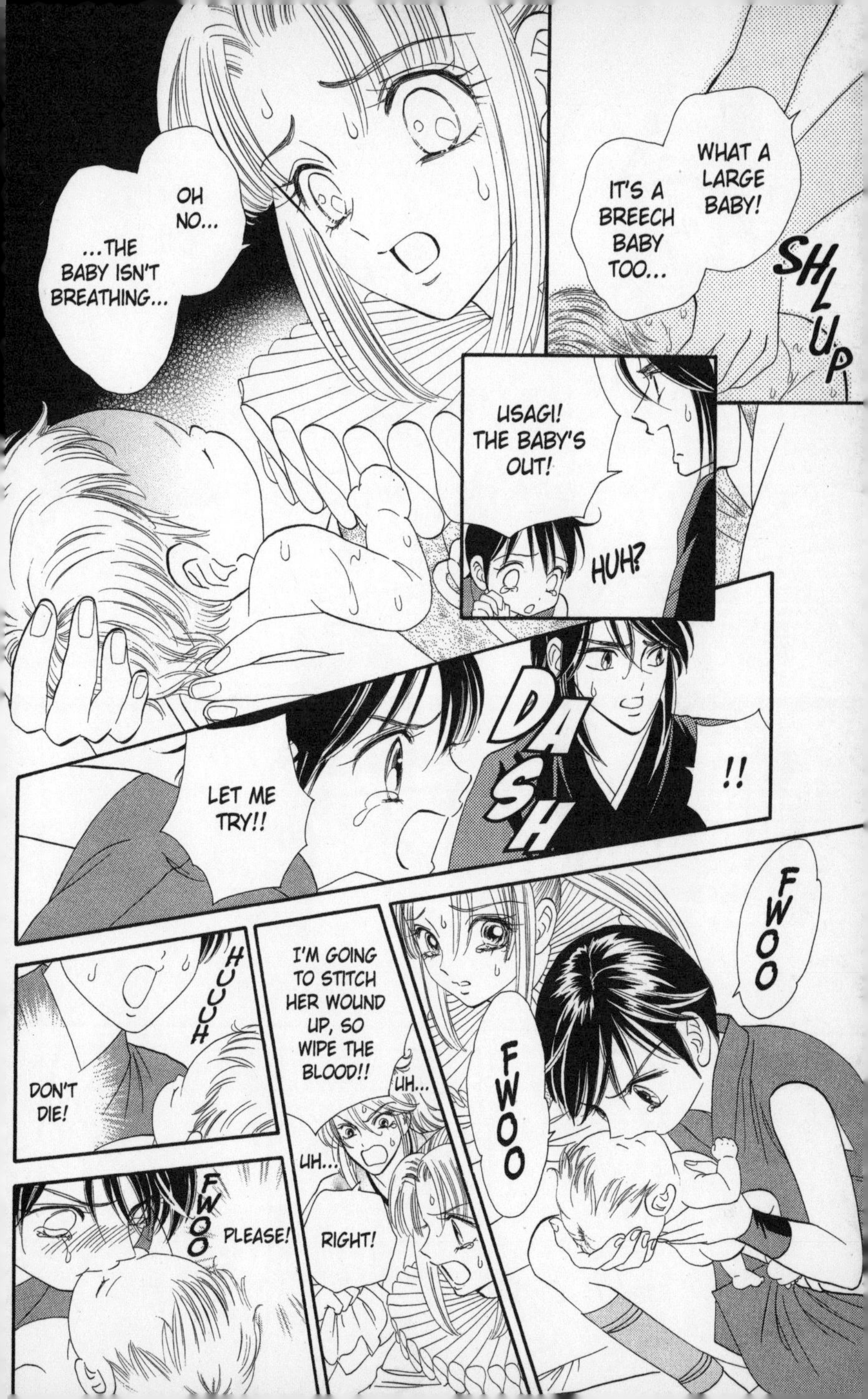
WHAT A LARGE BABY!
IT'S A BREECH BABY TOO...
SHLUP
USAGI! THE BABY'S OUT!
HUH?
OH NO...
...THE BABY ISN'T BREATHING...
!!
DASH
LET ME TRY!!
FWOO
FWOO
I'M GOING TO STITCH HER WOUND UP, SO WIPE THE BLOOD!!
UH...
UH...
RIGHT!
HUUUUH
DON'T DIE!
FWOO
PLEASE!

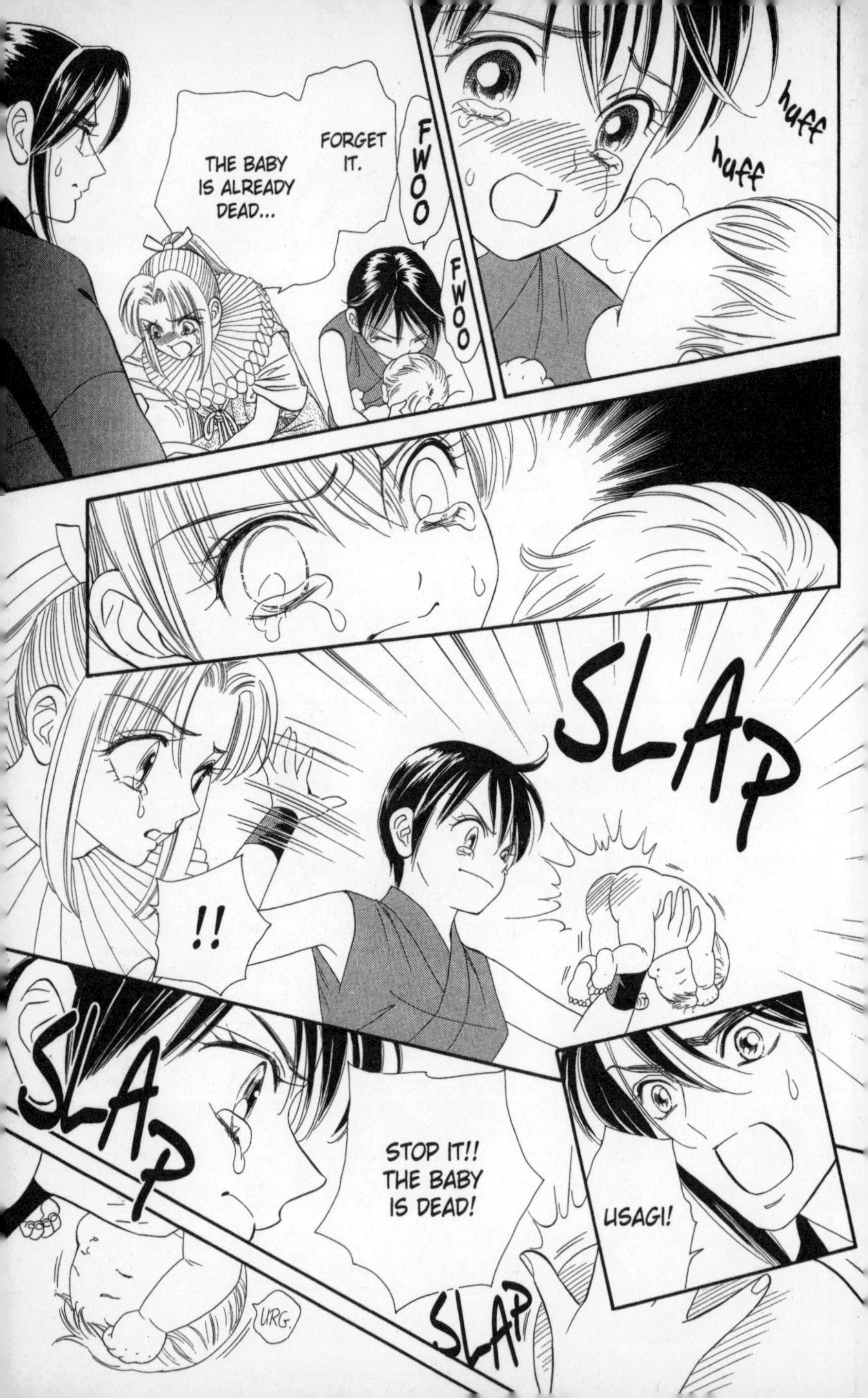
huff
huff
FWOO
FWOO
FORGET IT.
THE BABY IS ALREADY DEAD...
SLAP
!!
USAGI!
STOP IT!! THE BABY IS DEAD!
SLAP
SLAP
URG.

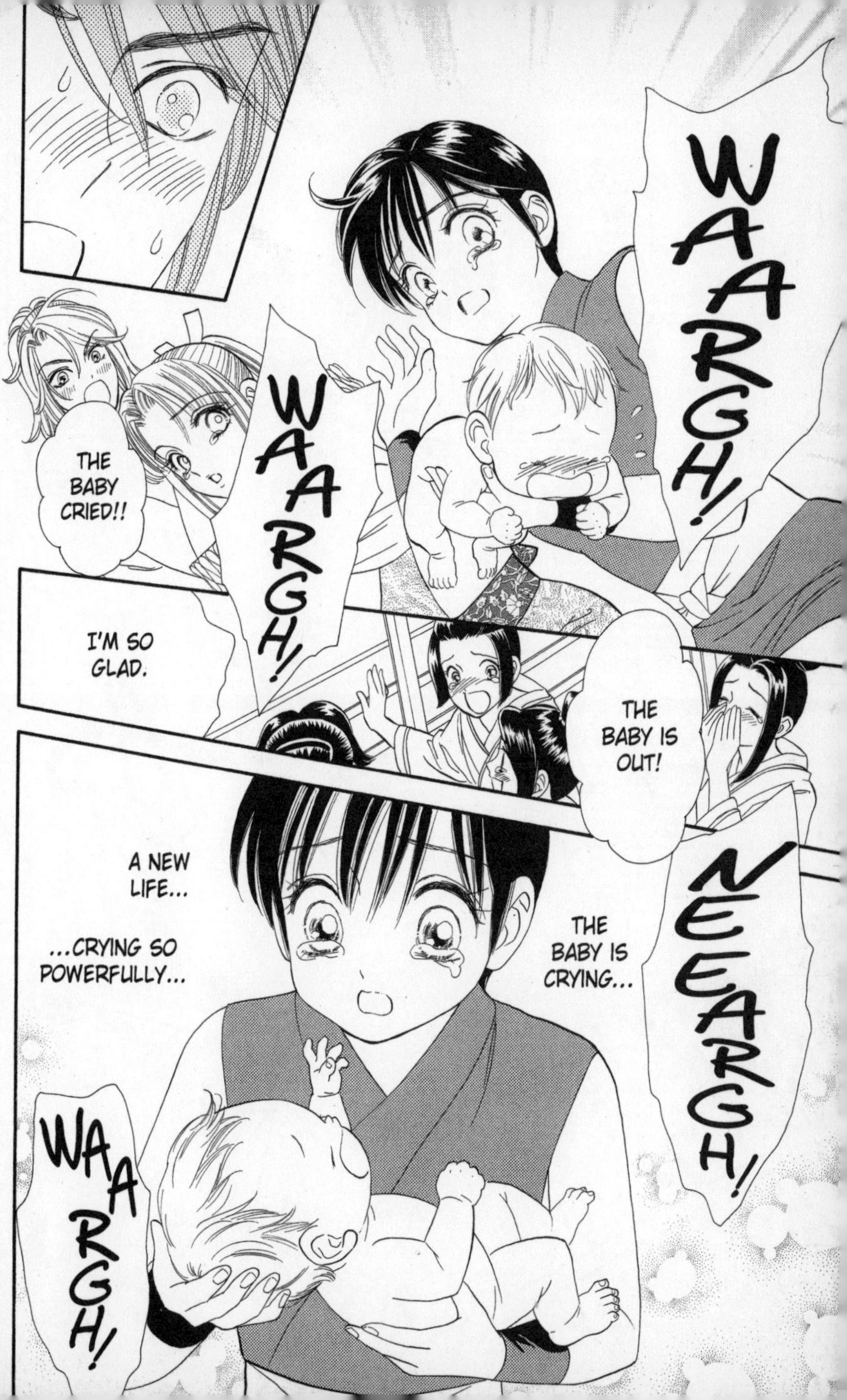
WAARGH!
WAARGH!
THE BABY CRIED!!
THE BABY IS OUT!
I'M SO GLAD.
NEEARGH!
THE BABY IS CRYING...
A NEW LIFE...
...CRYING SO POWERFULLY...
WAARGH!

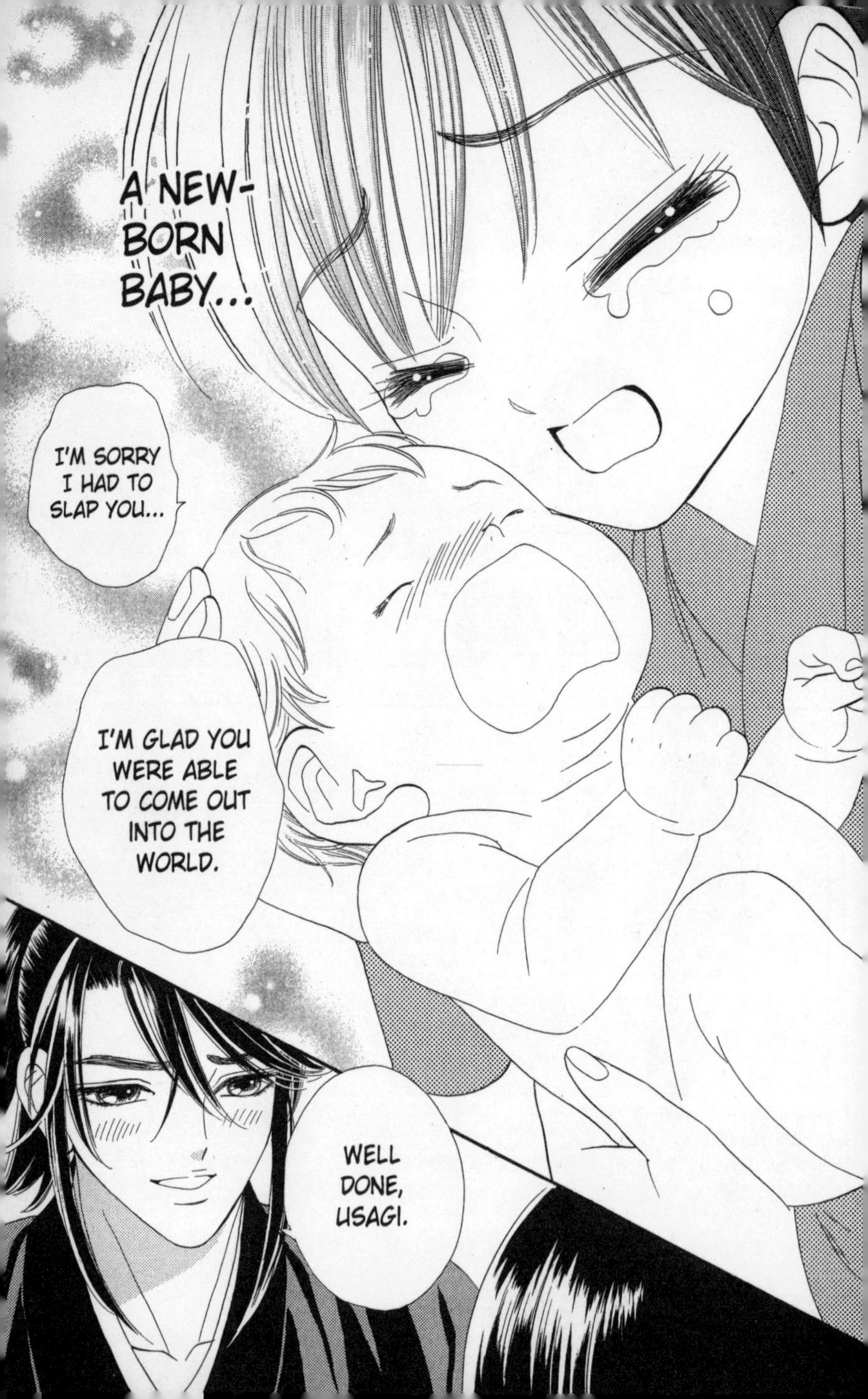
A NEW-BORN BABY...
I'M SORRY I HAD TO SLAP YOU...
I'M GLAD YOU WERE ABLE TO COME OUT INTO THE WORLD.
WELL DONE, USAGI.

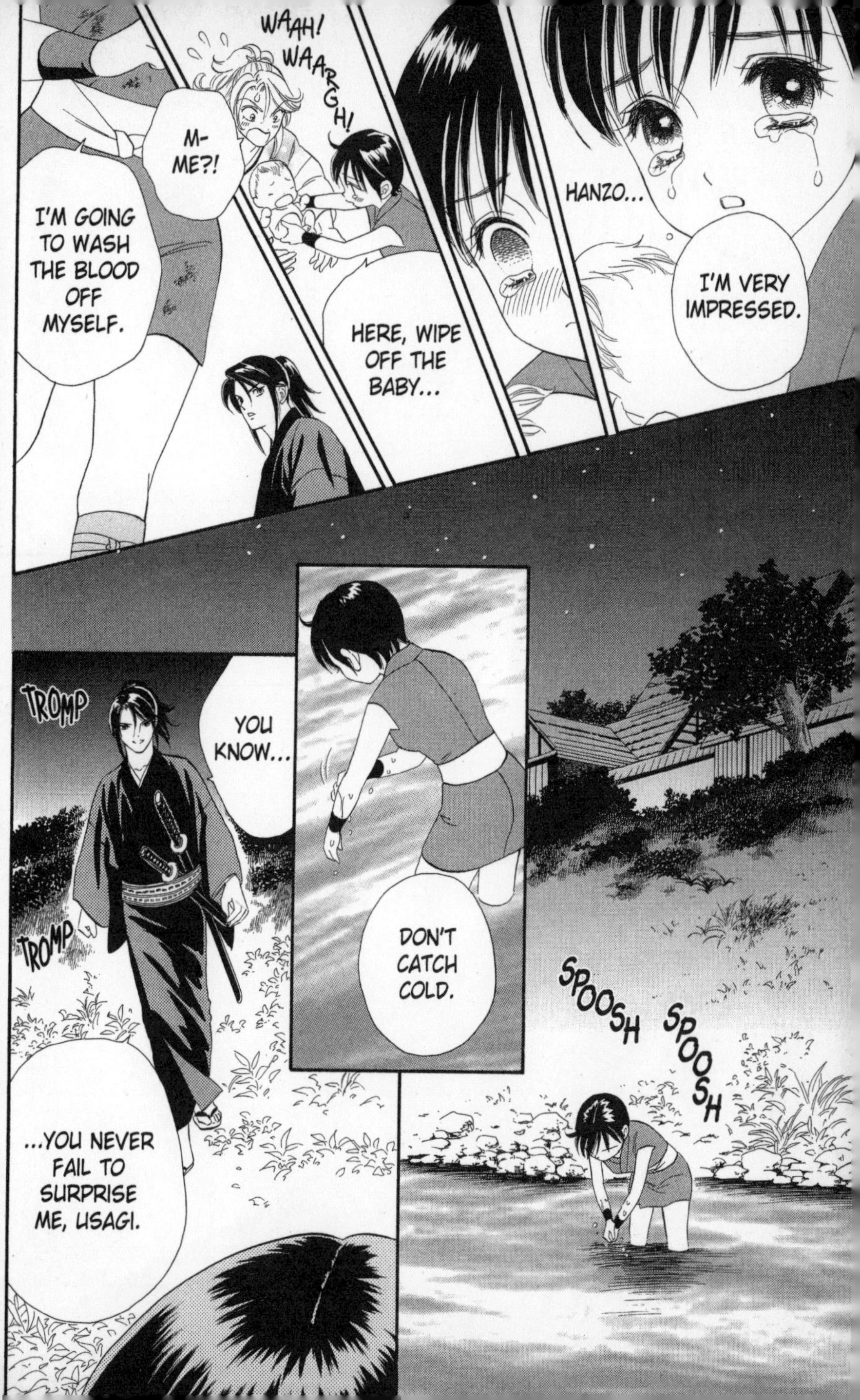
HANZO...
I'M VERY IMPRESSED.
HERE, WIPE OFF THE BABY...
WAAH! WAARGH!
M-ME?!
I'M GOING TO WASH THE BLOOD OFF MYSELF.
SPOOSH SPOOSH
DON'T CATCH COLD.
TROMP
YOU KNOW...
TROMP
...YOU NEVER FAIL TO SURPRISE ME, USAGI.

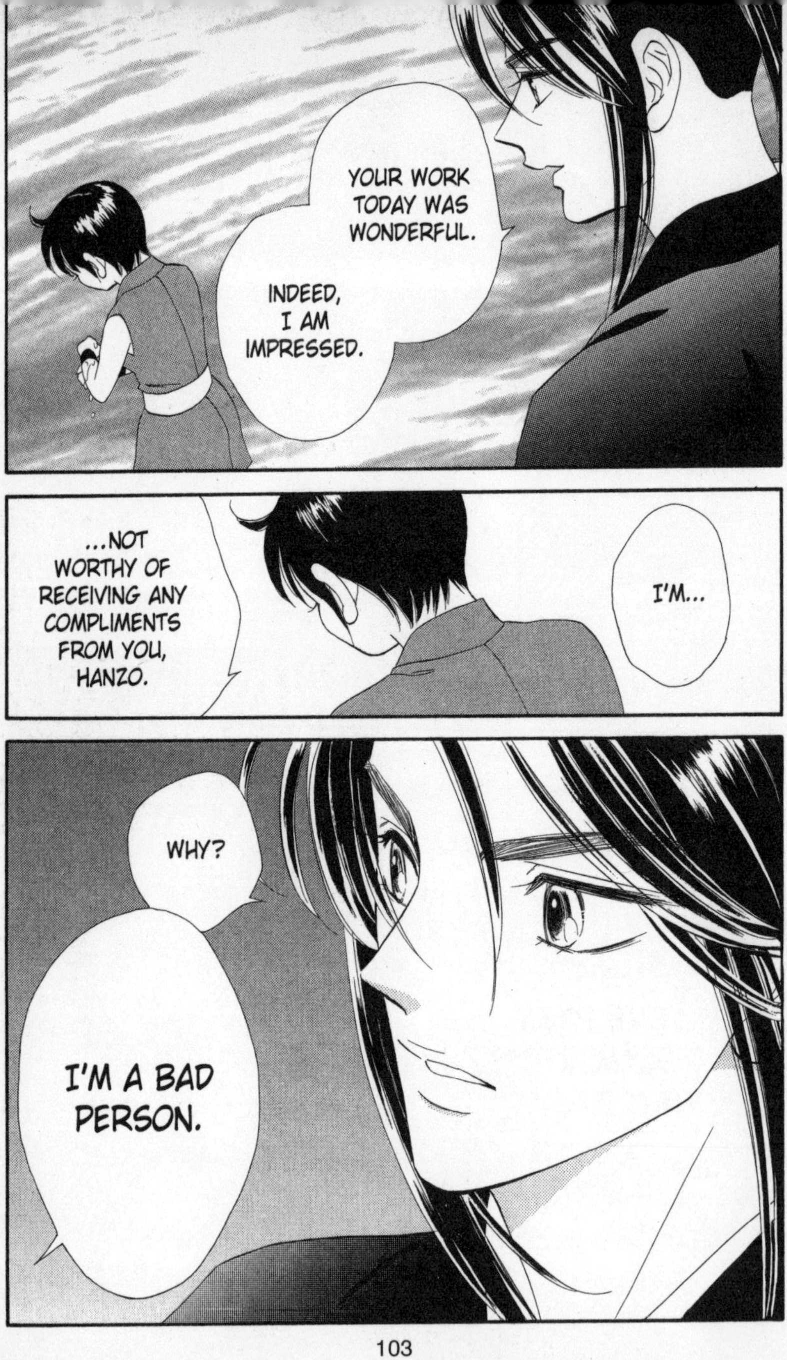
YOUR WORK TODAY WAS WONDERFUL.
INDEED, I AM IMPRESSED.
I'M...
...NOT WORTHY OF RECEIVING ANY COMPLIMENTS FROM YOU, HANZO.
WHY?
I'M A BAD PERSON.

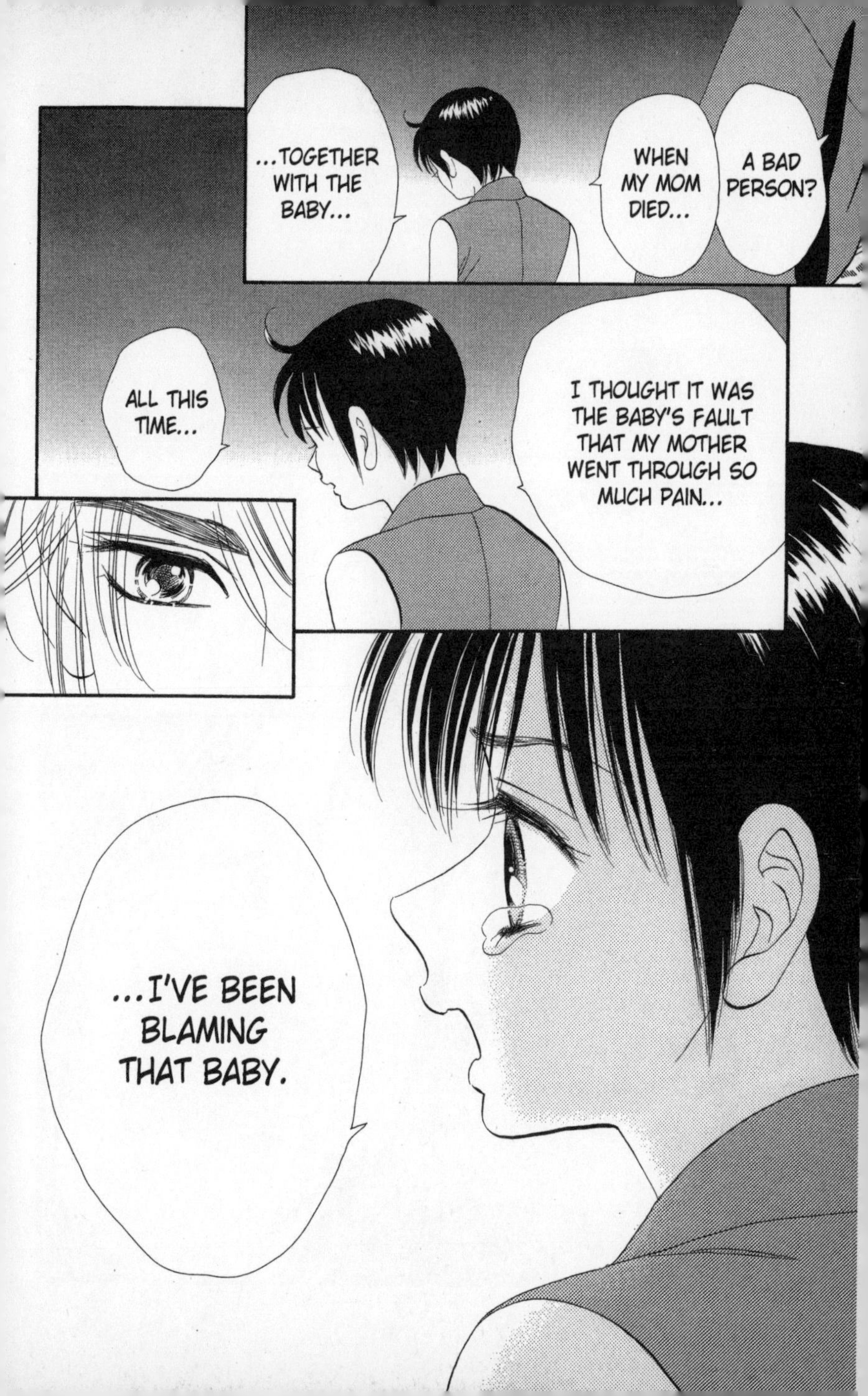
A BAD PERSON?
WHEN MY MOM DIED...
...TOGETHER WITH THE BABY...
I THOUGHT IT WAS THE BABY'S FAULT THAT MY MOTHER WENT THROUGH SO MUCH PAIN...
ALL THIS TIME...
...I'VE BEEN BLAMING THAT BABY.

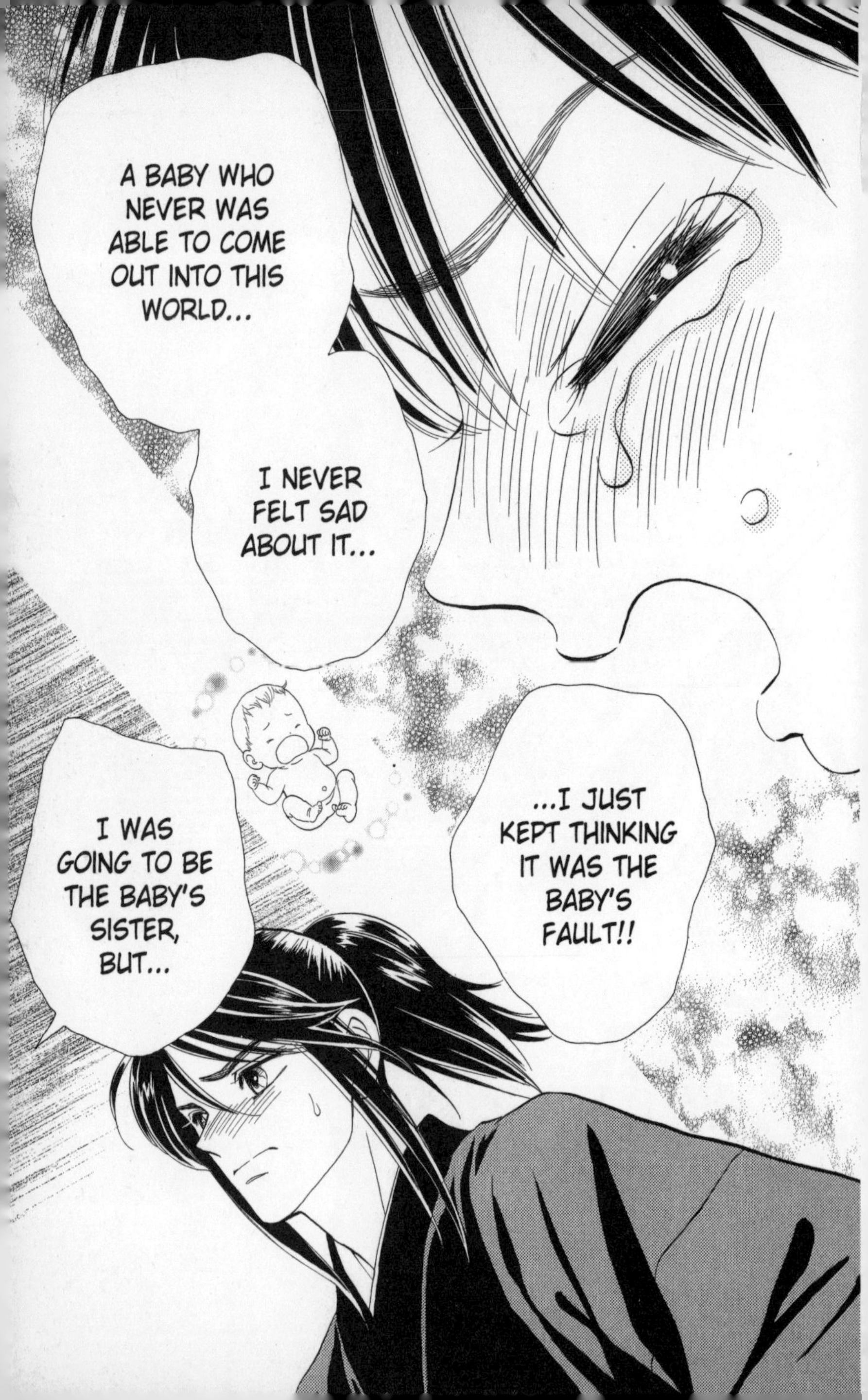
A BABY WHO NEVER WAS ABLE TO COME OUT INTO THIS WORLD...
I NEVER FELT SAD ABOUT IT...
...I JUST KEPT THINKING IT WAS THE BABY'S FAULT!!
I WAS GOING TO BE THE BABY'S SISTER, BUT...

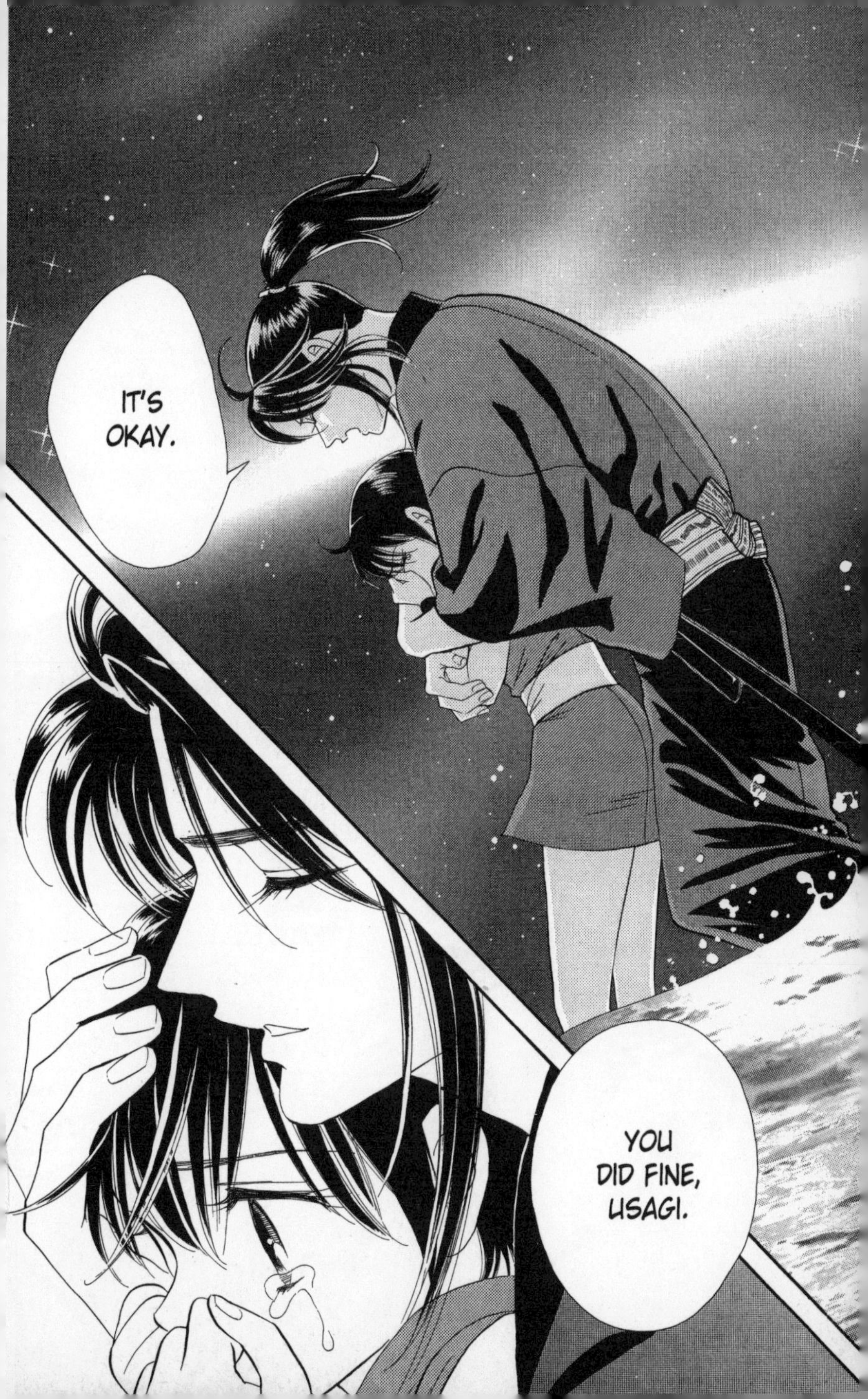
IT'S OKAY.
YOU DID FINE, USAGI.

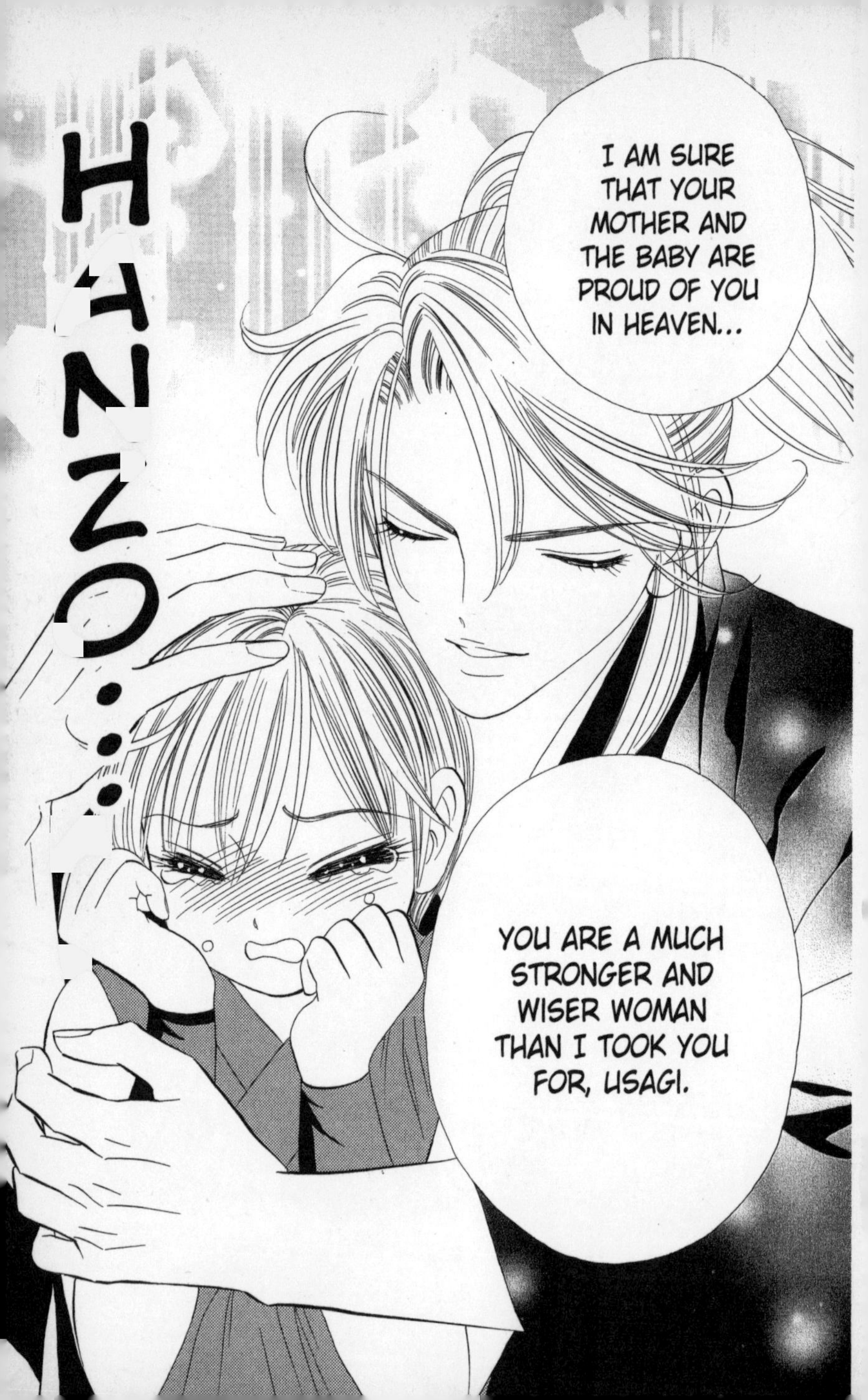
I AM SURE THAT YOUR MOTHER AND THE BABY ARE PROUD OF YOU IN HEAVEN...
YOU ARE A MUCH STRONGER AND WISER WOMAN THAN I TOOK YOU FOR, USAGI.
HANZO...

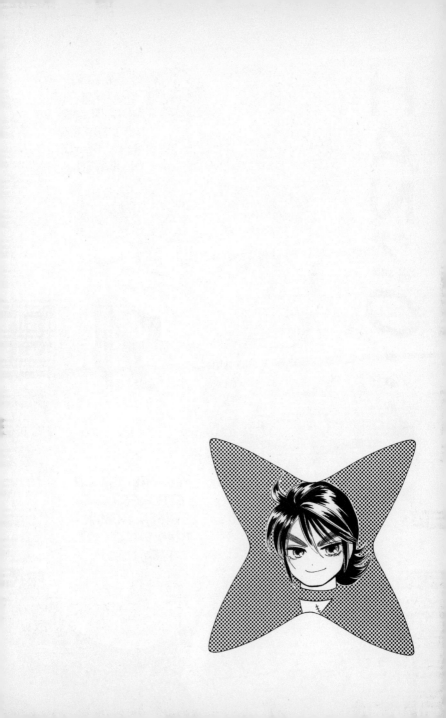

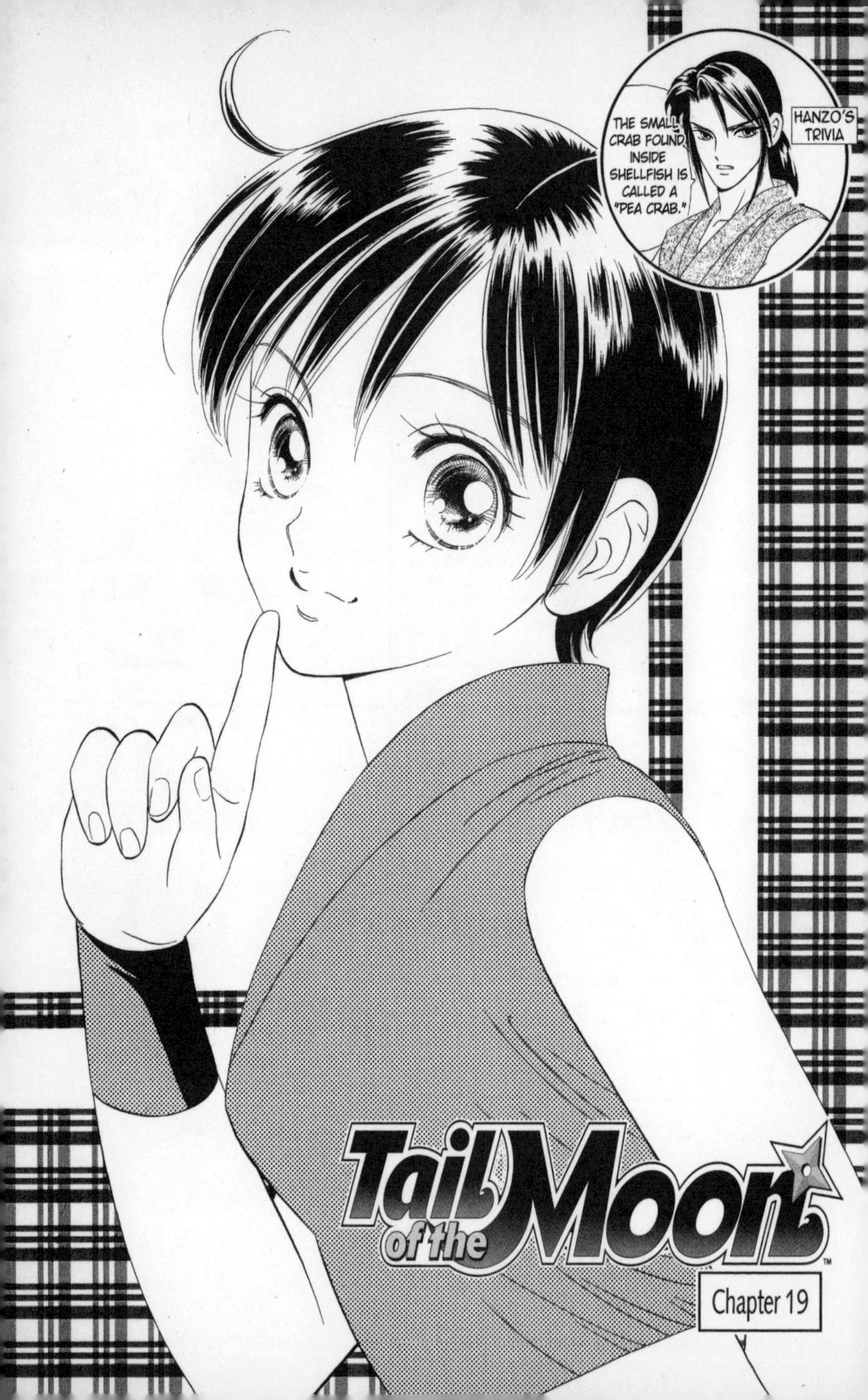
HANZO'S TRIVIA
THE SMALL CRAB FOUND INSIDE SHELLFISH IS CALLED A "PEA CRAB."
Tail of the Moon™
Chapter 19

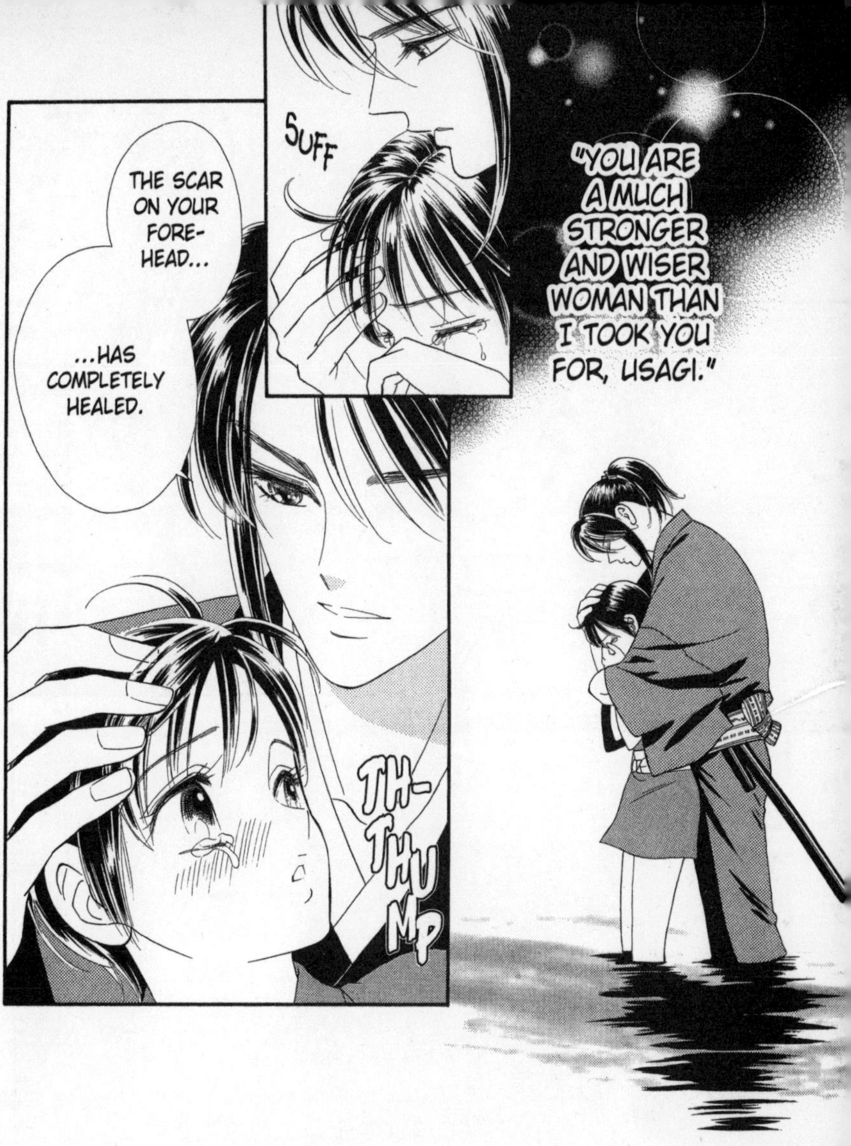
"YOU ARE A MUCH STRONGER AND WISER WOMAN THAN I TOOK YOU FOR, USAGI."
SUFF
THE SCAR ON YOUR FORE-HEAD...
...HAS COMPLETELY HEALED.
TH-THUMP

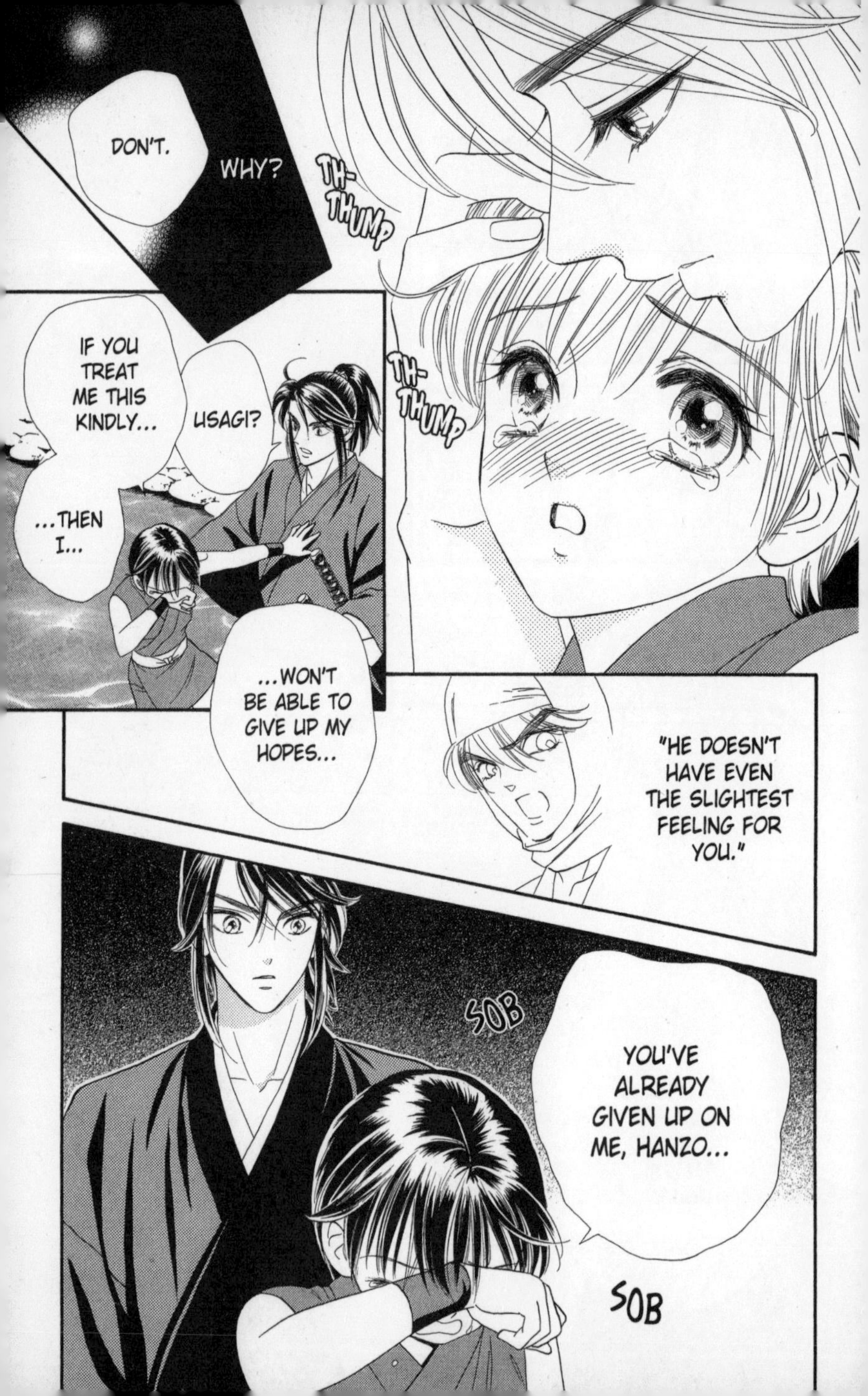
TH-THUMP
TH-THUMP
DON'T.
WHY?
USAGI?
IF YOU TREAT ME THIS KINDLY...
...THEN I...
...WON'T BE ABLE TO GIVE UP MY HOPES...
"HE DOESN'T HAVE EVEN THE SLIGHTEST FEELING FOR YOU."
SOB
YOU'VE ALREADY GIVEN UP ON ME, HANZO...
SOB

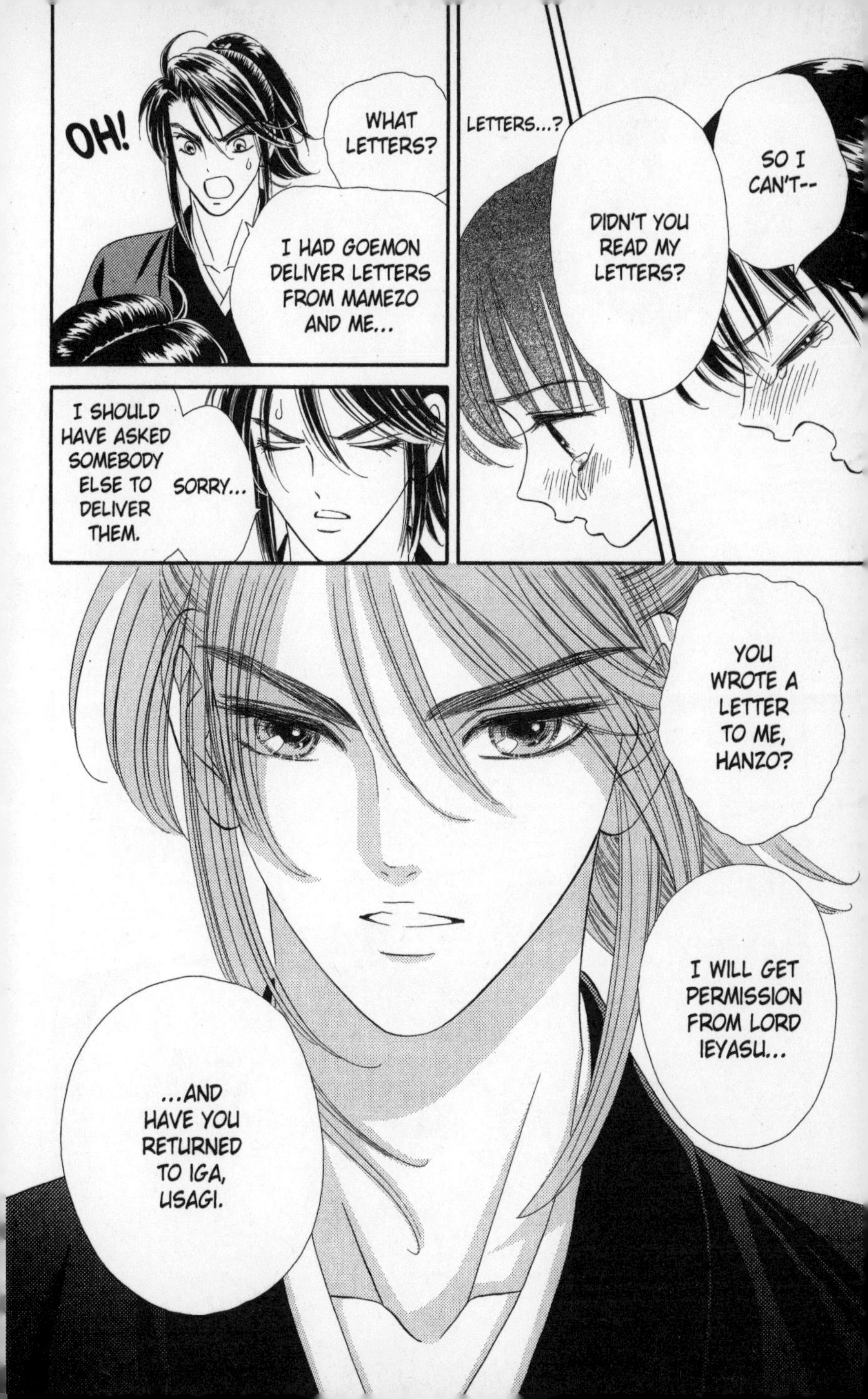
SO I CAN'T--
DIDN'T YOU READ MY LETTERS?
LETTERS...?
WHAT LETTERS?
OH!
I HAD GOEMON DELIVER LETTERS FROM MAMEZO AND ME...
SORRY...
I SHOULD HAVE ASKED SOMEBODY ELSE TO DELIVER THEM.
YOU WROTE A LETTER TO ME, HANZO?
I WILL GET PERMISSION FROM LORD IEYASU...
...AND HAVE YOU RETURNED TO IGA, USAGI.

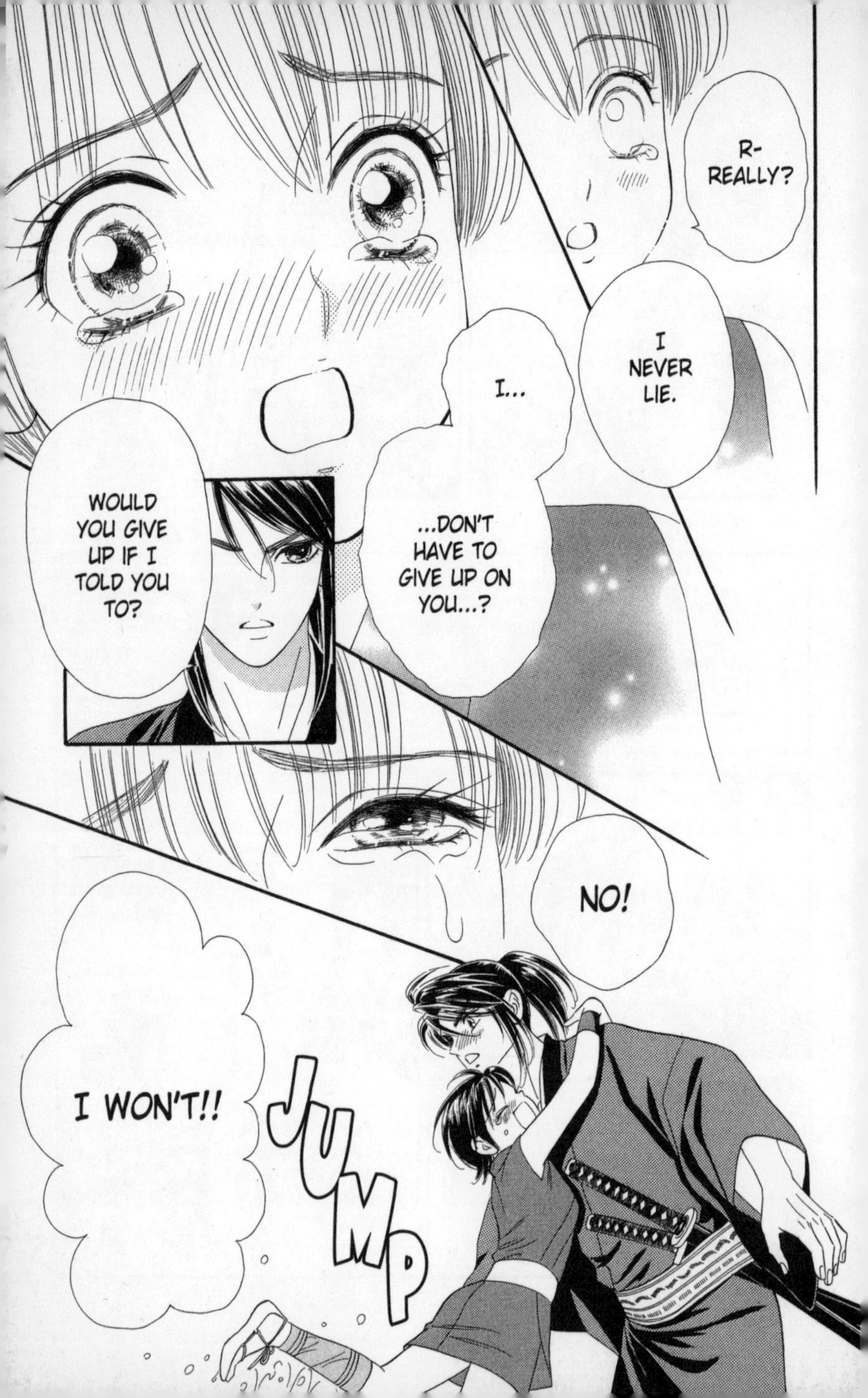
R- REALLY?
I NEVER LIE.
I...
...DON'T HAVE TO GIVE UP ON YOU...?
WOULD YOU GIVE UP IF I TOLD YOU TO?
NO!
I WON'T!!
JUMP

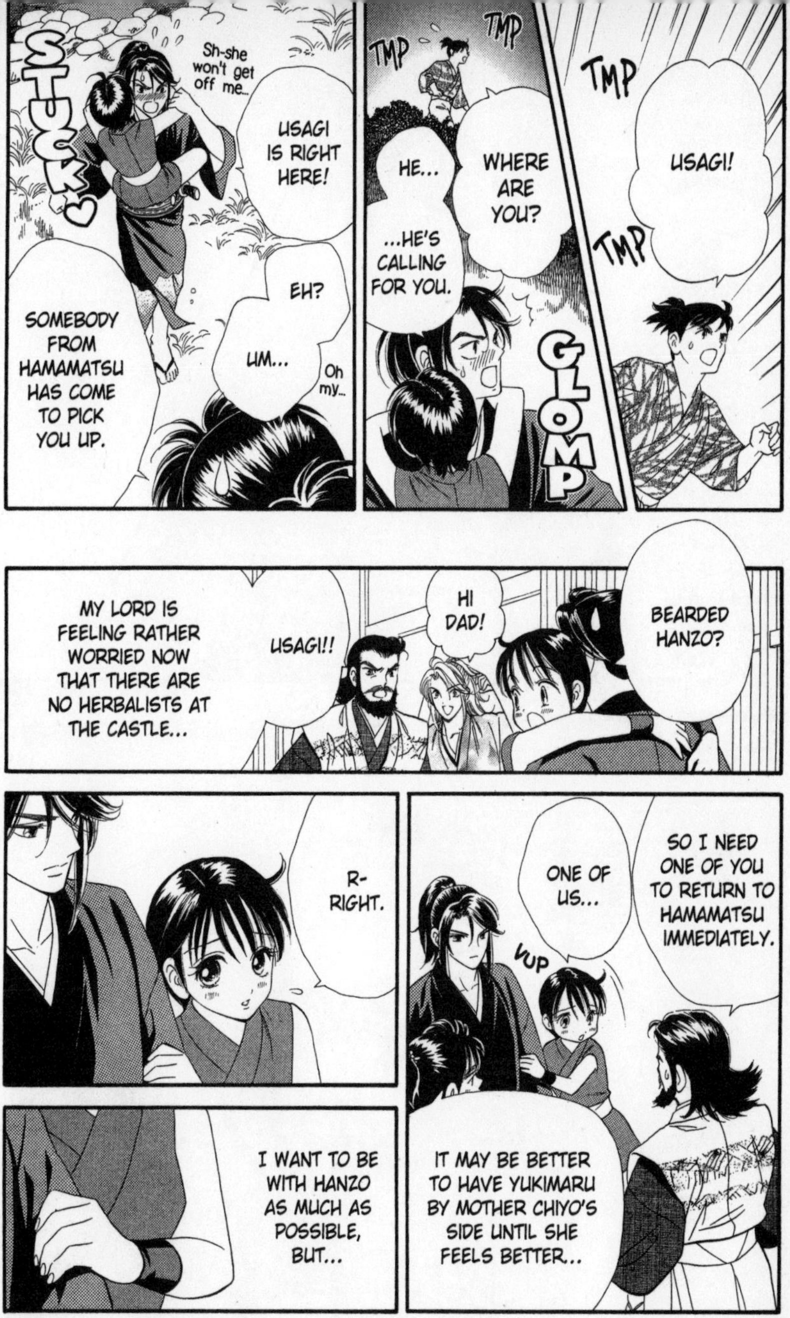
TMP
USAGI!
TMP
TMP
TMP
TMP
WHERE ARE YOU?
HE...
...HE'S CALLING FOR YOU.
GLOMP
Sh-she won't get off me...
STUCK
USAGI IS RIGHT HERE!
EH?
UM...
Oh my...
SOMEBODY FROM HAMAMATSU HAS COME TO PICK YOU UP.
BEARDED HANZO?
HI DAD!
USAGI!!
MY LORD IS FEELING RATHER WORRIED NOW THAT THERE ARE NO HERBALISTS AT THE CASTLE...
SO I NEED ONE OF YOU TO RETURN TO HAMAMATSU IMMEDIATELY.
ONE OF US...
VUP
IT MAY BE BETTER TO HAVE YUKIMARU BY MOTHER CHIYO'S SIDE UNTIL SHE FEELS BETTER...
R-RIGHT.
I WANT TO BE WITH HANZO AS MUCH AS POSSIBLE, BUT...

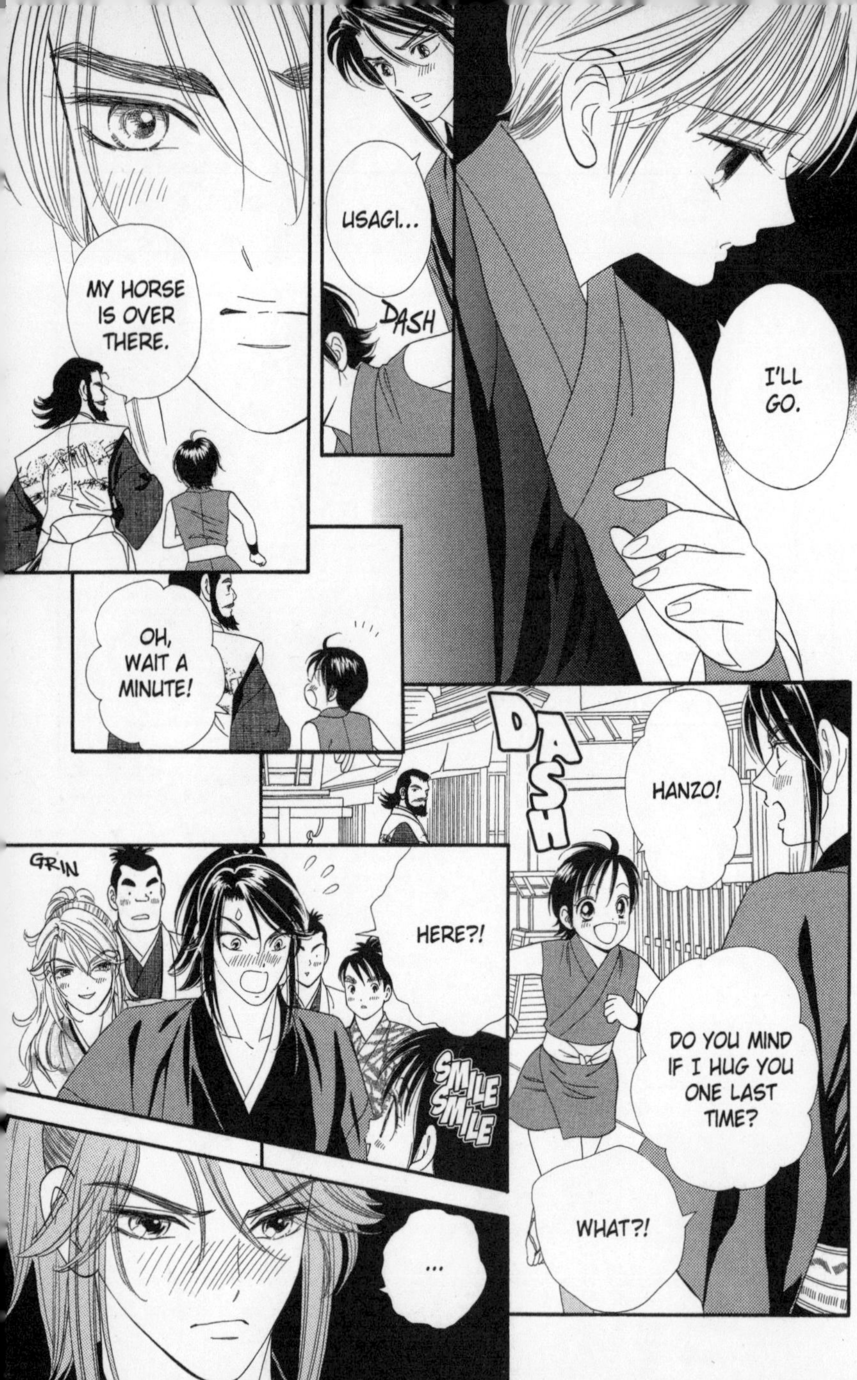
I'LL GO.
USAGI...
DASH
MY HORSE IS OVER THERE.
OH, WAIT A MINUTE!
DASH
HANZO!
DO YOU MIND IF I HUG YOU ONE LAST TIME?
WHAT?!
HERE?!
GRIN
SMILE SMILE
...

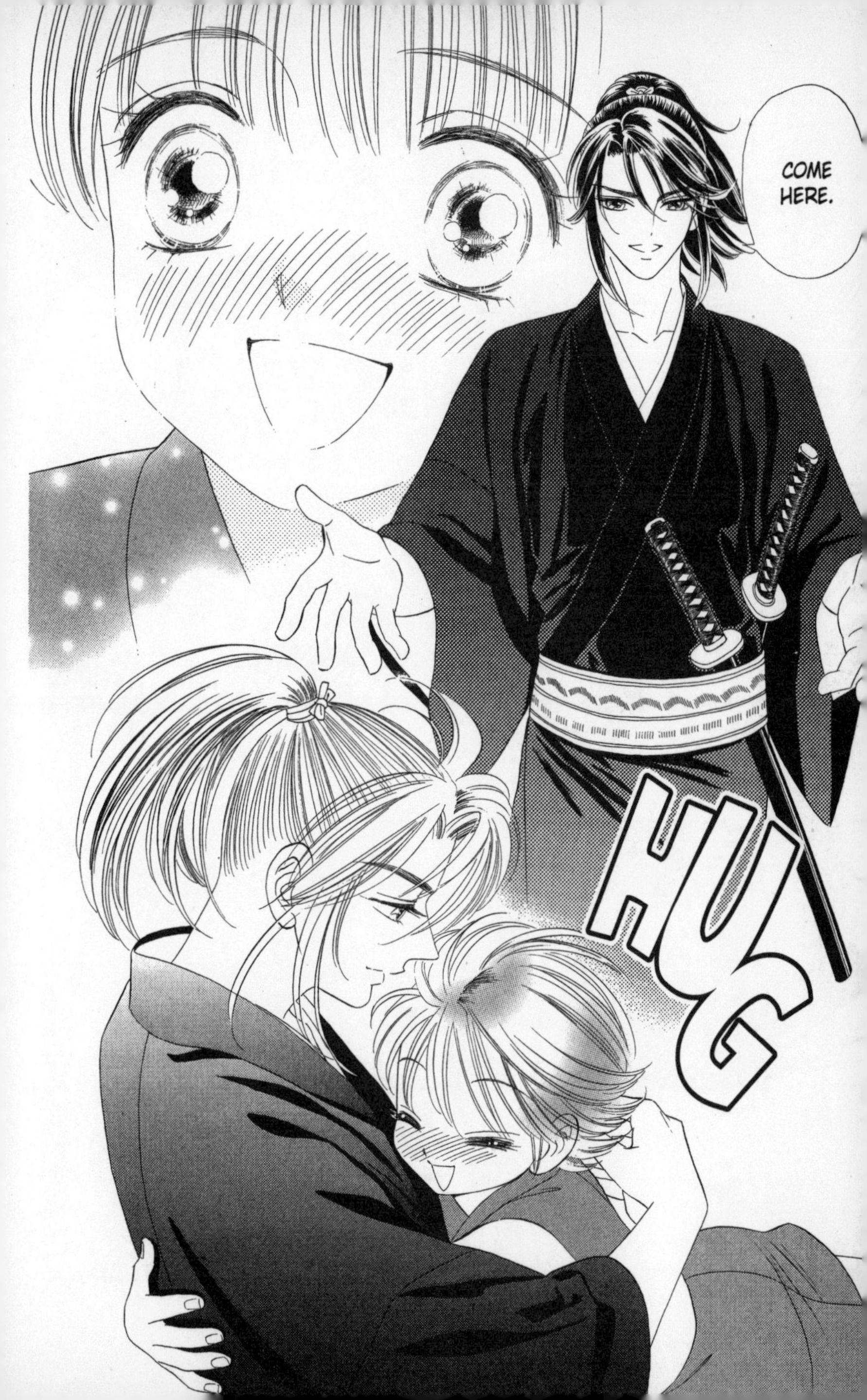
COME HERE.
HUG

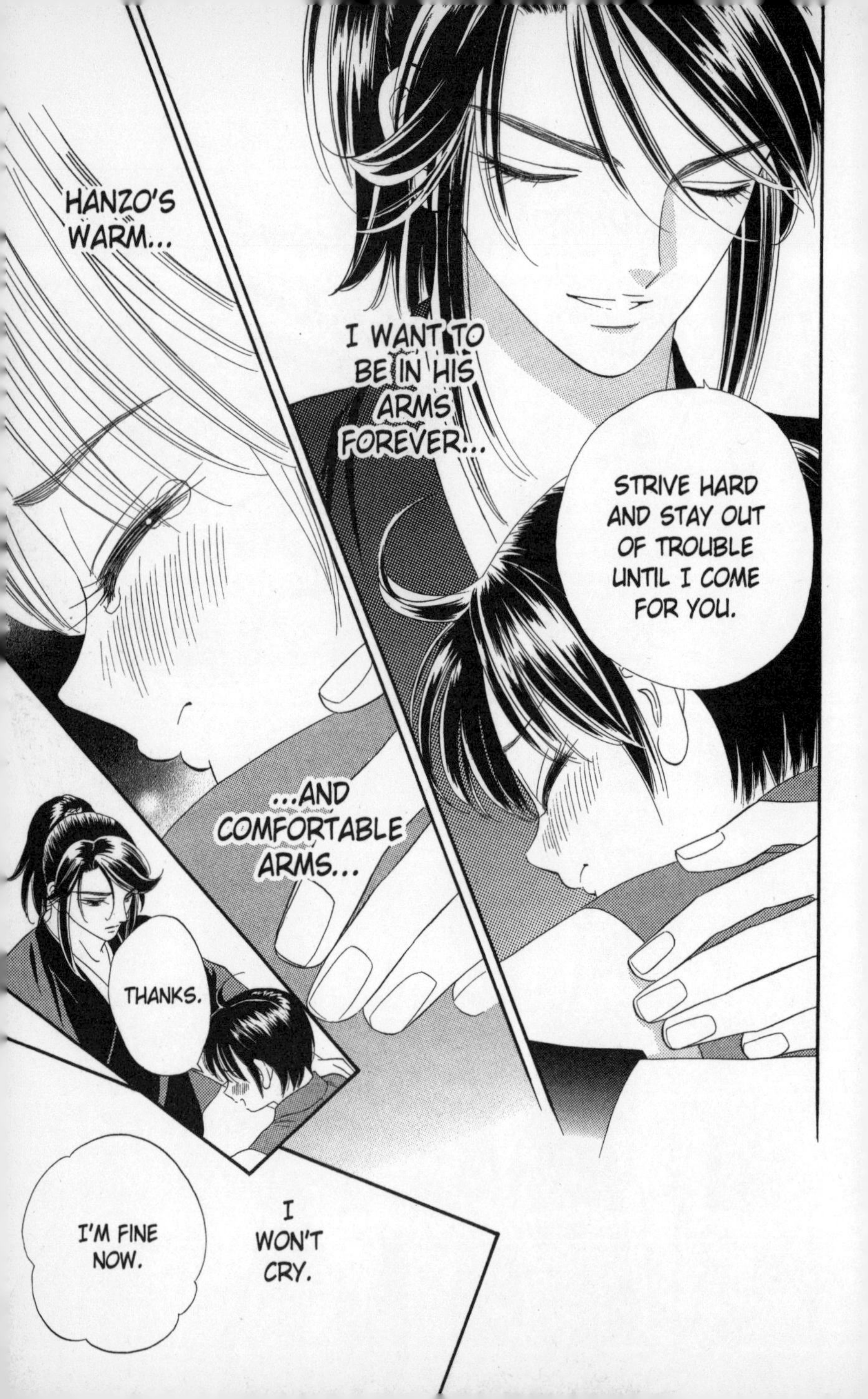
STRIVE HARD AND STAY OUT OF TROUBLE UNTIL I COME FOR YOU.
I WANT TO BE IN HIS ARMS FOREVER...
HANZO'S WARM...
...AND COMFORTABLE ARMS...
THANKS.
I WON'T CRY.
I'M FINE NOW.

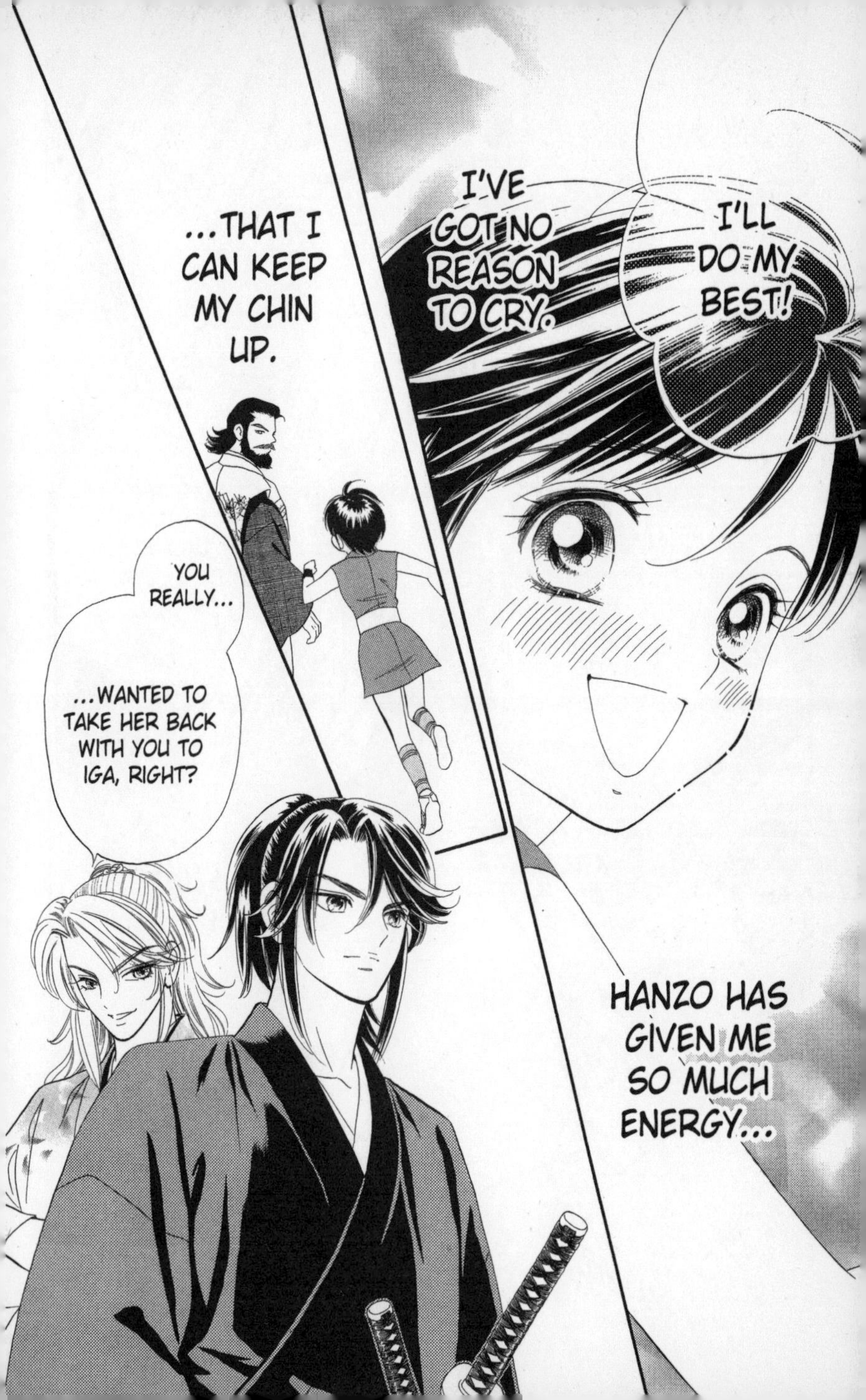
I'LL DO MY BEST!
I'VE GOT NO REASON TO CRY.
HANZO HAS GIVEN ME SO MUCH ENERGY...
...THAT I CAN KEEP MY CHIN UP.
YOU REALLY...
...WANTED TO TAKE HER BACK WITH YOU TO IGA, RIGHT?

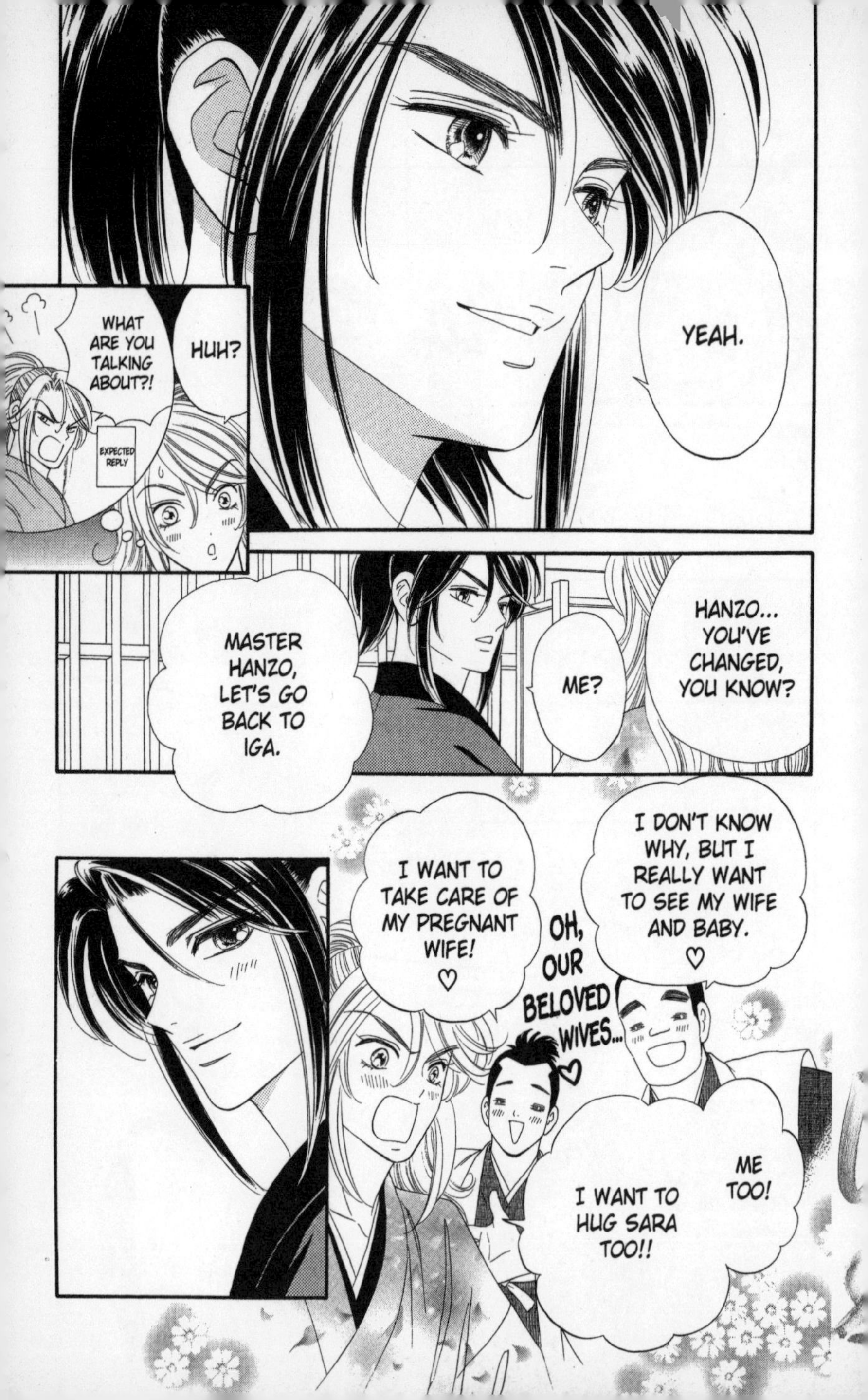
YEAH.
HUH?
WHAT ARE YOU TALKING ABOUT?!
EXPECTED REPLY
HANZO... YOU'VE CHANGED, YOU KNOW?
ME?
MASTER HANZO, LET'S GO BACK TO IGA.
I DON'T KNOW WHY, BUT I REALLY WANT TO SEE MY WIFE AND BABY. ♡
I WANT TO TAKE CARE OF MY PREGNANT WIFE! ♡
OH, OUR BELOVED WIVES... ♡
ME TOO!
I WANT TO HUG SARA TOO!!

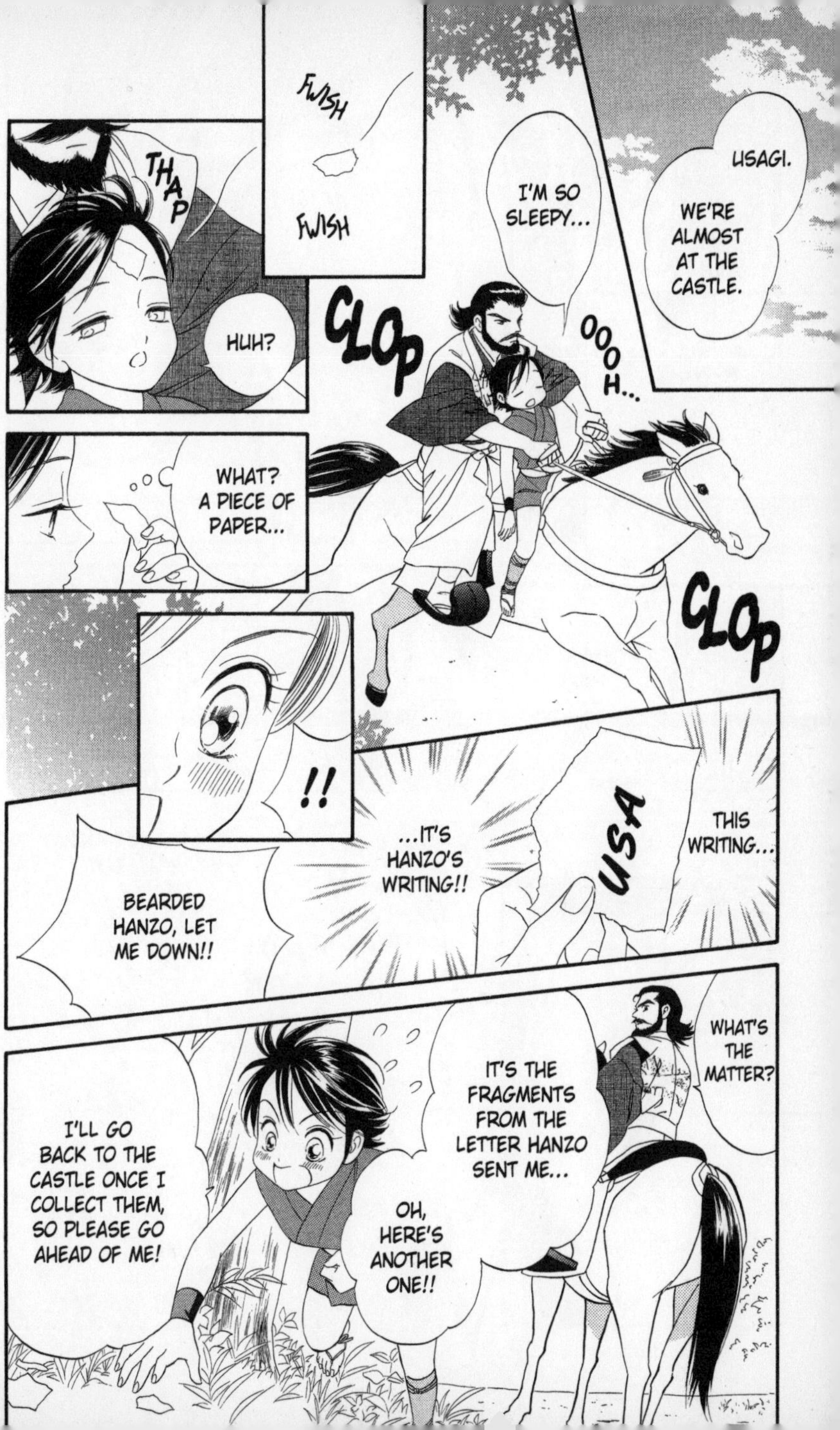
USAGI.
WE'RE ALMOST AT THE CASTLE.
I'M SO SLEEPY...
OOOH...
CLOP
CLOP
FWISH
FWISH
THAP
HUH?
WHAT? A PIECE OF PAPER...
!!
THIS WRITING...
USA
...IT'S HANZO'S WRITING!!
BEARDED HANZO, LET ME DOWN!!
WHAT'S THE MATTER?
IT'S THE FRAGMENTS FROM THE LETTER HANZO SENT ME...
OH, HERE'S ANOTHER ONE!!
I'LL GO BACK TO THE CASTLE ONCE I COLLECT THEM, SO PLEASE GO AHEAD OF ME!

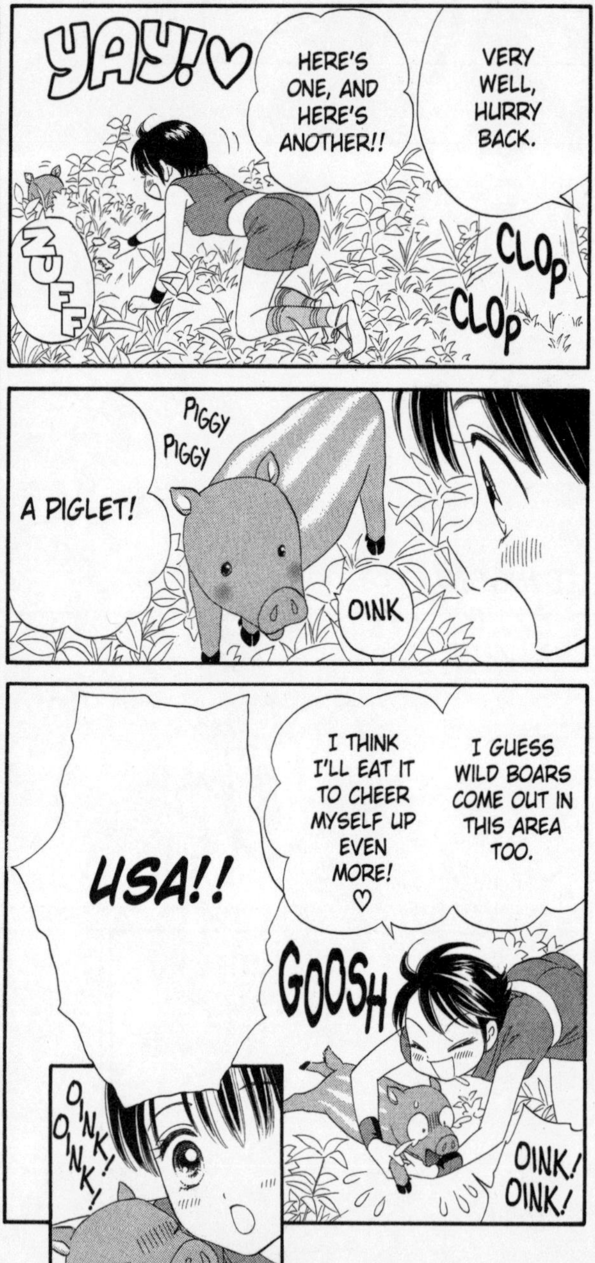
VERY WELL, HURRY BACK.
CLOP CLOP
HERE'S ONE, AND HERE'S ANOTHER!!
YAY!♡
ZUFF
OINK
A PIGLET!
PIGGY PIGGY
I GUESS WILD BOARS COME OUT IN THIS AREA TOO.
I THINK I'LL EAT IT TO CHEER MYSELF UP EVEN MORE! ♡
GOOSH
OINK! OINK!
USA!!
OINK! OINK!

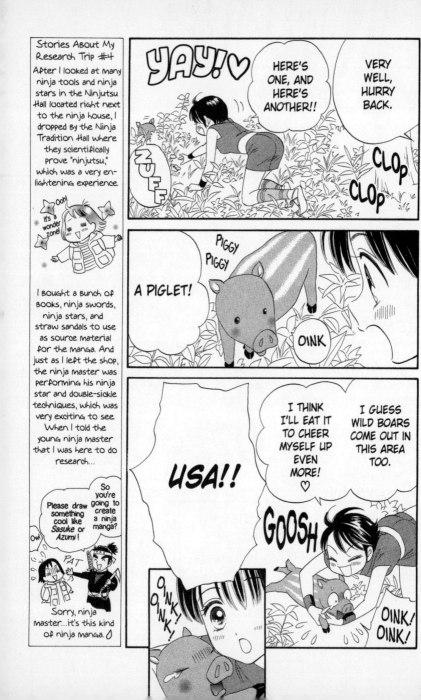

Stories About My Research Trip #4

After I looked at many ninja tools and ninja stars in the Ninjutsu Hall located right next to the ninja house, I dropped by the Ninja Tradition Hall where they scientifically prove "ninjutsu," which was a very enlightening experience.

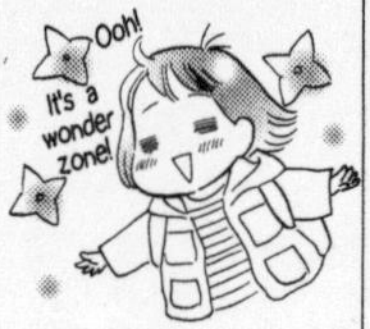
Ooh!
It's a wonder zone!

I bought a bunch of books, ninja swords, ninja stars, and straw sandals to use as source material for the manga. And just as I left the shop, the ninja master was performing his ninja star and double-sickle techniques, which was very exciting to see. When I told the young ninja master that I was here to do research...

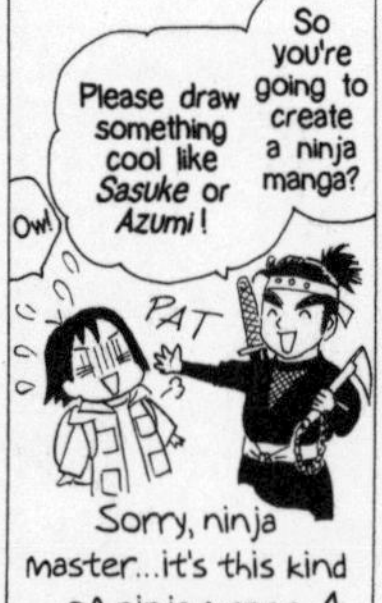
So you're going to create a ninja manga?
Please draw something cool like *Sasuke* or *Azumi*!
Ow!
PAT

Sorry, ninja master...it's this kind of ninja manga.

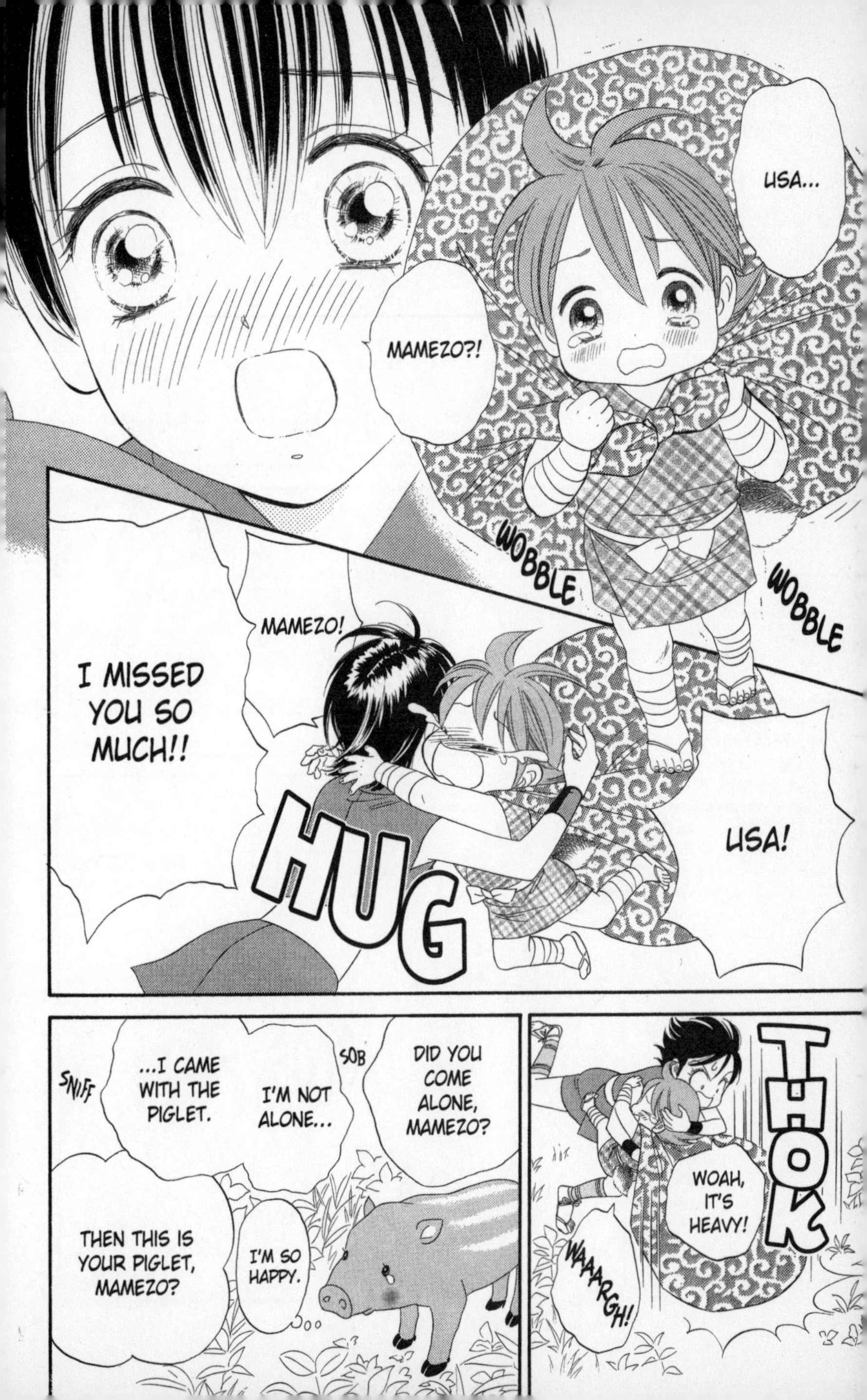
USA...
MAMEZO?!
WOBBLE
WOBBLE
USA!
HUG
MAMEZO!
I MISSED YOU SO MUCH!!
THOK
WOAH, IT'S HEAVY!
WAAARGH!
DID YOU COME ALONE, MAMEZO?
SOB
I'M NOT ALONE...
...I CAME WITH THE PIGLET.
SNIFF
I'M SO HAPPY.
THEN THIS IS YOUR PIGLET, MAMEZO?

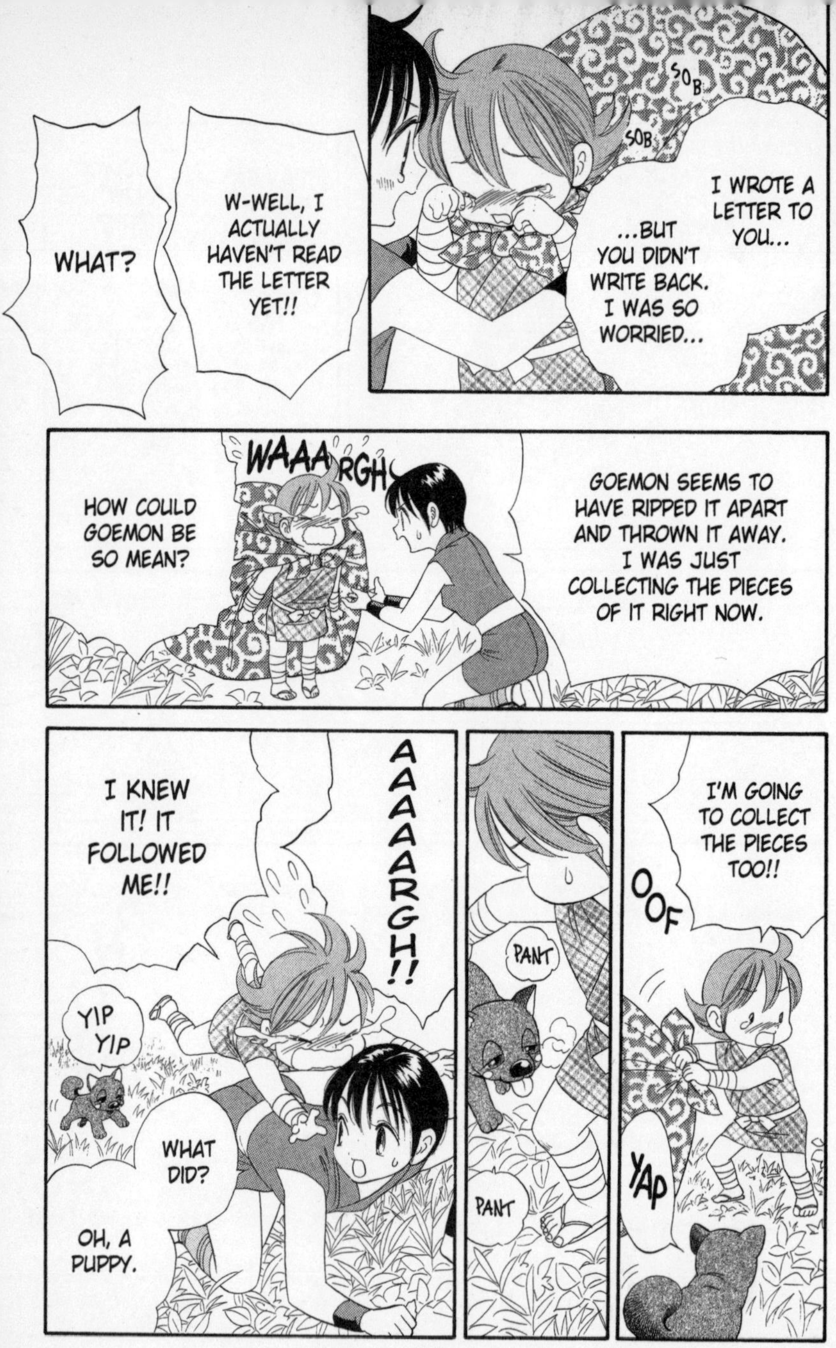
SOB
SOB
I WROTE A LETTER TO YOU...
...BUT YOU DIDN'T WRITE BACK. I WAS SO WORRIED...
W-WELL, I ACTUALLY HAVEN'T READ THE LETTER YET!!
WHAT?
GOEMON SEEMS TO HAVE RIPPED IT APART AND THROWN IT AWAY. I WAS JUST COLLECTING THE PIECES OF IT RIGHT NOW.
WAAARGH
HOW COULD GOEMON BE SO MEAN?
I'M GOING TO COLLECT THE PIECES TOO!!
OOF
YAP
PANT
PANT
AAAAAARGH!!
I KNEW IT! IT FOLLOWED ME!!
YIP YIP
WHAT DID?
OH, A PUPPY.

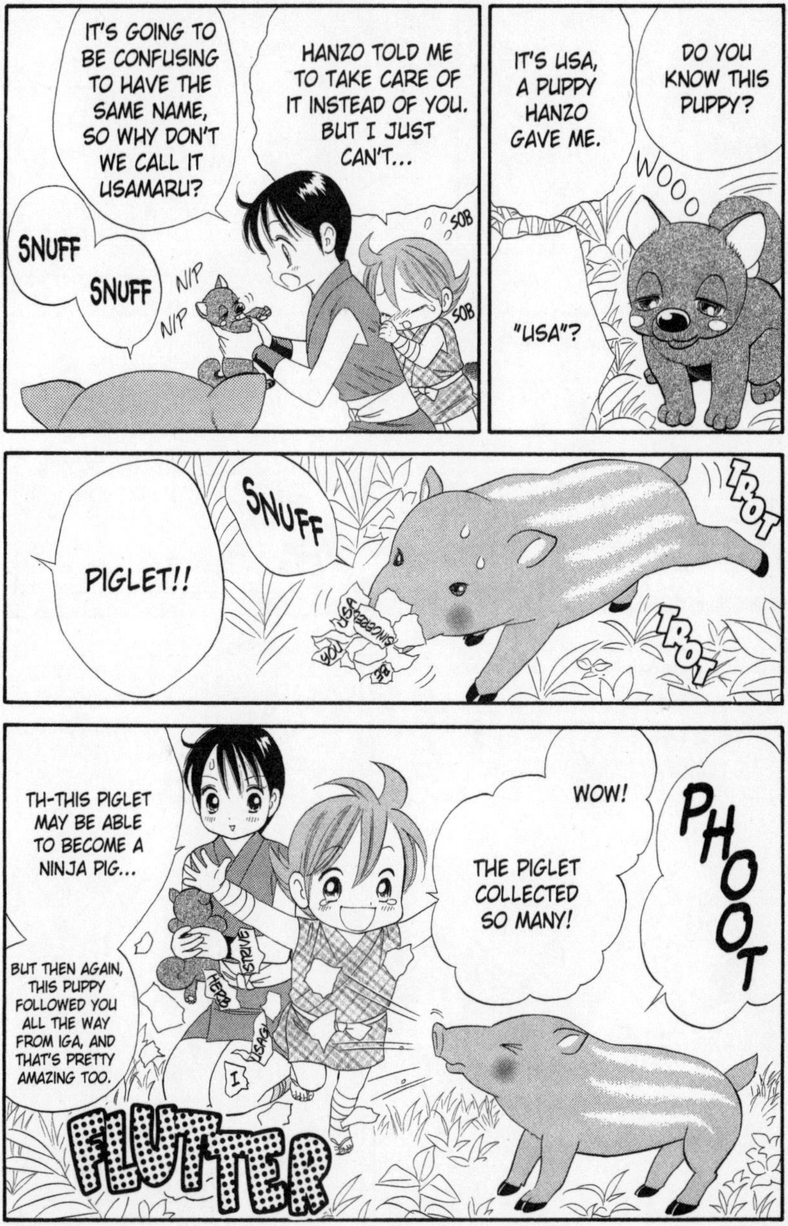
DO YOU KNOW THIS PUPPY?
IT'S USA, A PUPPY HANZO GAVE ME.
WOOO
"USA"?
HANZO TOLD ME TO TAKE CARE OF IT INSTEAD OF YOU. BUT I JUST CAN'T...
SOB
SOB
IT'S GOING TO BE CONFUSING TO HAVE THE SAME NAME, SO WHY DON'T WE CALL IT USAMARU?
NIP
NIP
SNUFF
SNUFF
TROT
TROT
SNUFF
USA
SINCERELY
YOU
BE
PIGLET!!
PHOOT
WOW!
THE PIGLET COLLECTED SO MANY!
TH-THIS PIGLET MAY BE ABLE TO BECOME A NINJA PIG...
STRIVE
HERB
USAGI
I
BUT THEN AGAIN, THIS PUPPY FOLLOWED YOU ALL THE WAY FROM IGA, AND THAT'S PRETTY AMAZING TOO.
FLUTTER

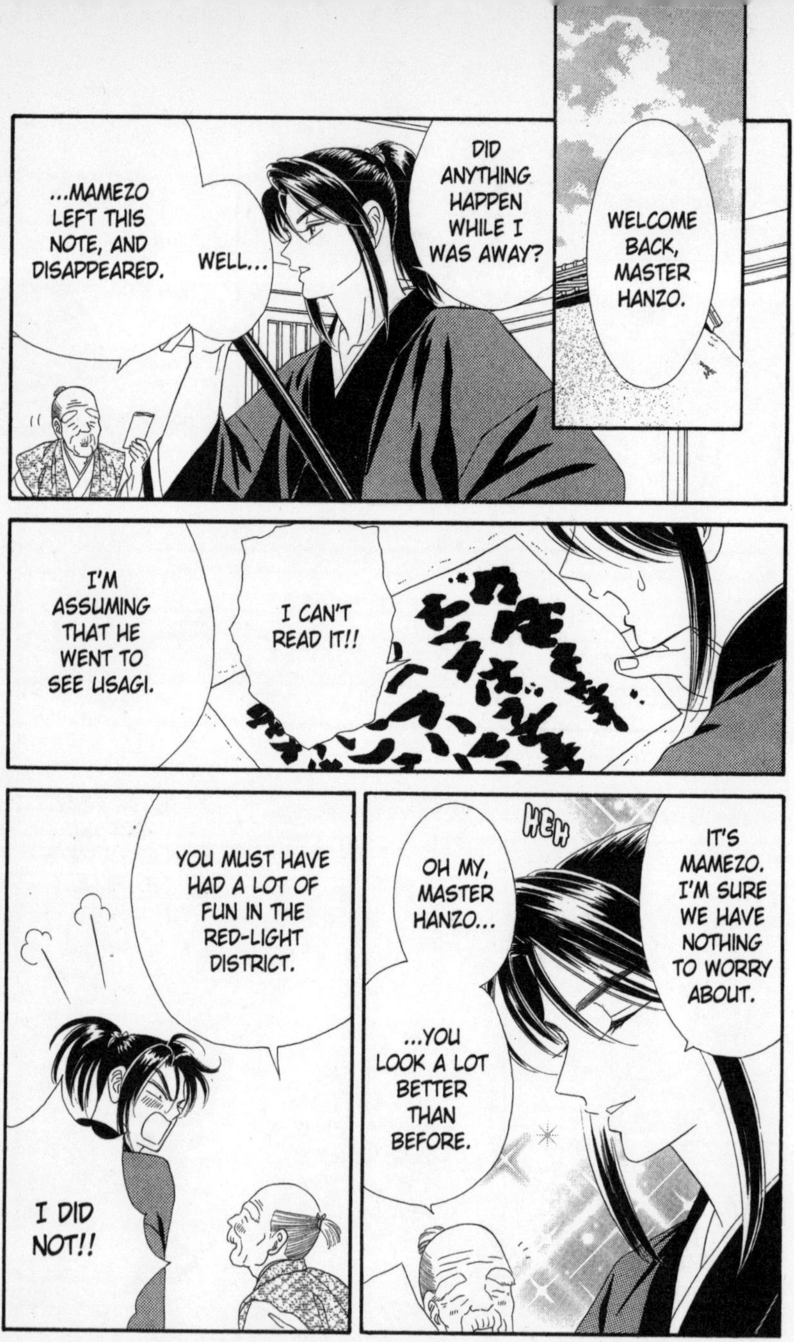
WELCOME BACK, MASTER HANZO.
DID ANYTHING HAPPEN WHILE I WAS AWAY?
WELL...
...MAMEZO LEFT THIS NOTE, AND DISAPPEARED.
I CAN'T READ IT!!
I'M ASSUMING THAT HE WENT TO SEE USAGI.
IT'S MAMEZO. I'M SURE WE HAVE NOTHING TO WORRY ABOUT.
HEH
OH MY, MASTER HANZO...
...YOU LOOK A LOT BETTER THAN BEFORE.
YOU MUST HAVE HAD A LOT OF FUN IN THE RED-LIGHT DISTRICT.
I DID NOT!!

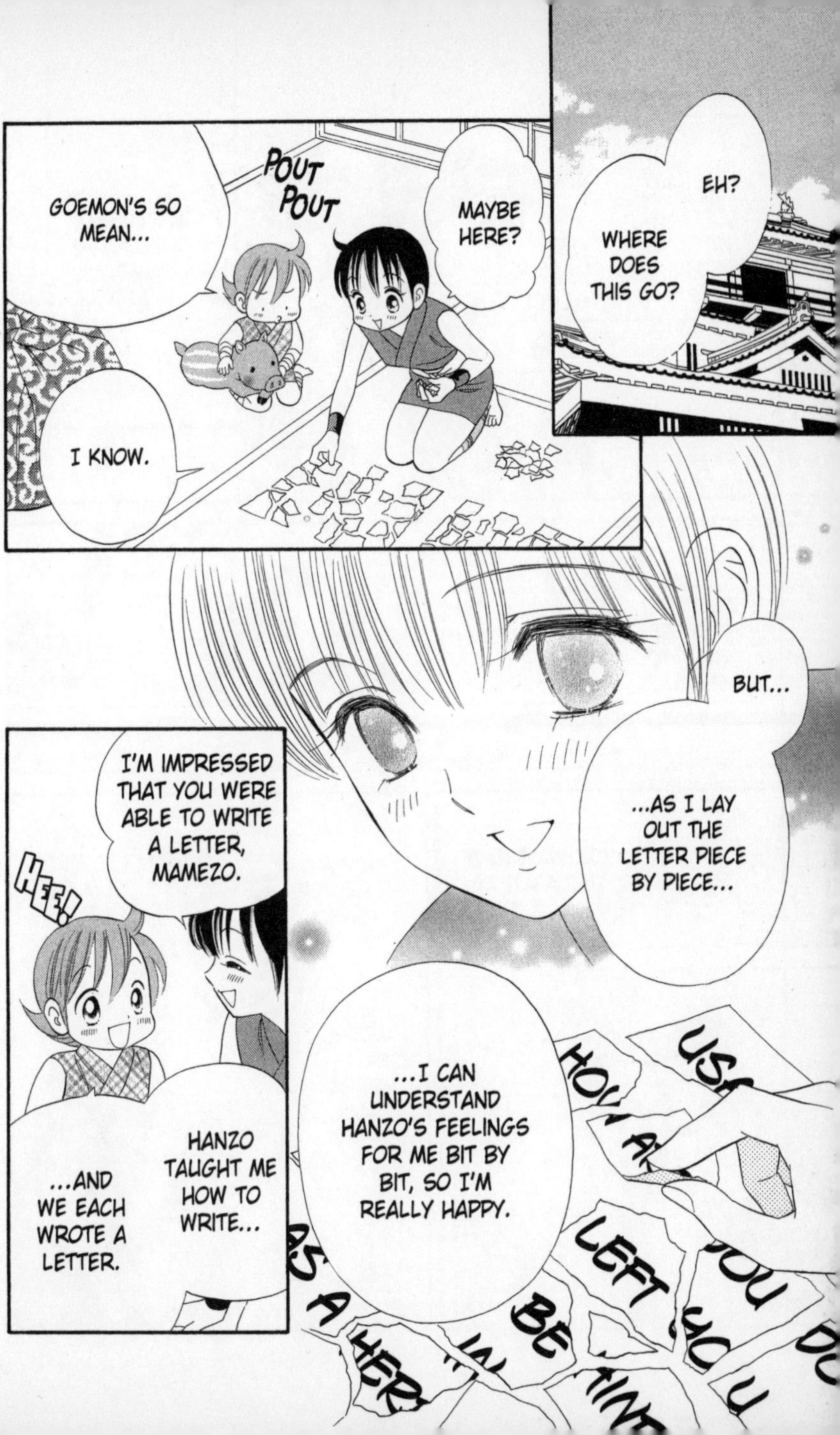
EH?
WHERE DOES THIS GO?
MAYBE HERE?
POUT POUT
GOEMON'S SO MEAN...
I KNOW.
BUT...
...AS I LAY OUT THE LETTER PIECE BY PIECE...
...I CAN UNDERSTAND HANZO'S FEELINGS FOR ME BIT BY BIT, SO I'M REALLY HAPPY.
YOU
LEFT
BE
AS A
I'M IMPRESSED THAT YOU WERE ABLE TO WRITE A LETTER, MAMEZO.
HEE!
HANZO TAUGHT ME HOW TO WRITE...
...AND WE EACH WROTE A LETTER.

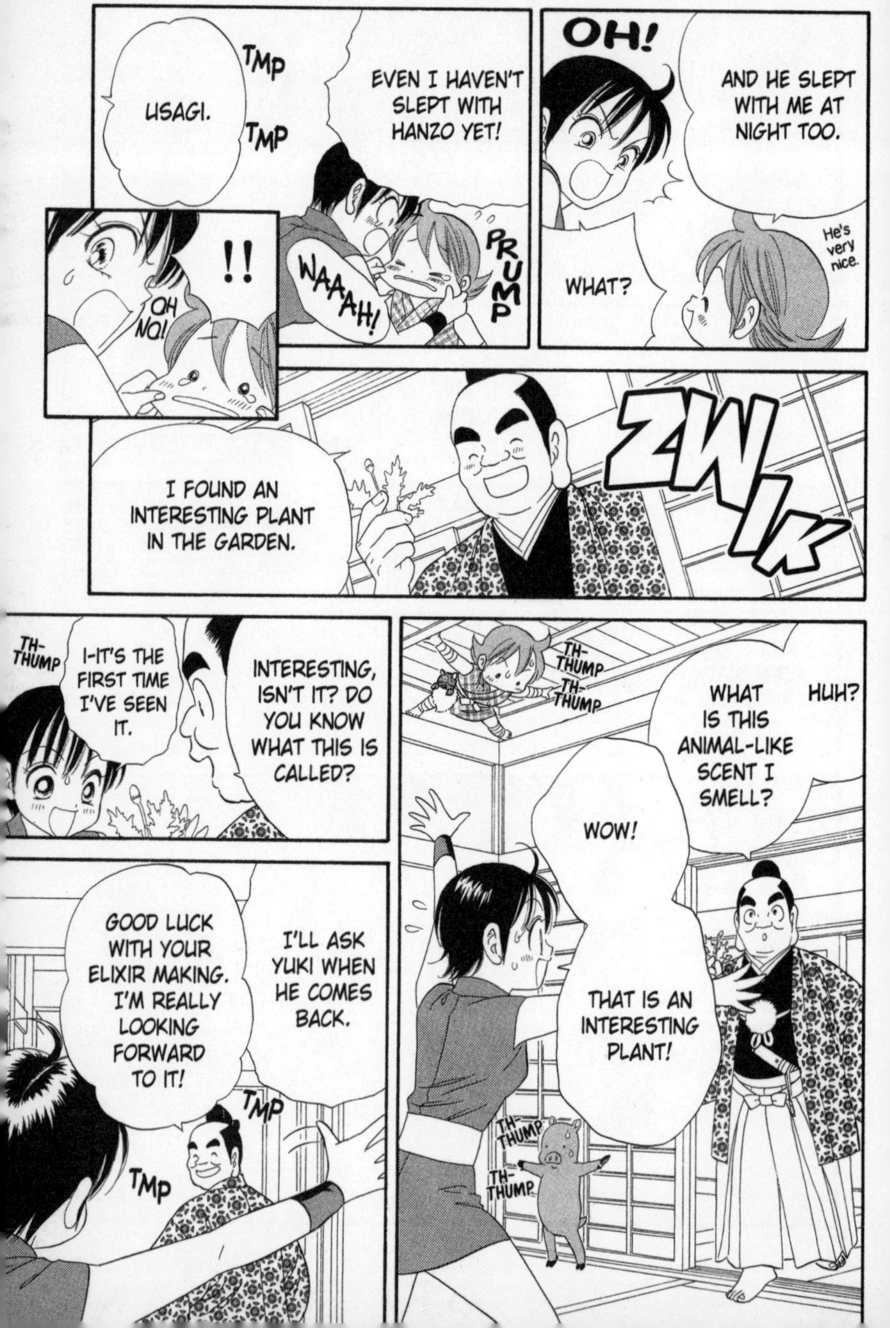
OH!
AND HE SLEPT WITH ME AT NIGHT TOO.
He's very nice.
WHAT?
EVEN I HAVEN'T SLEPT WITH HANZO YET!
TMP
TMP
USAGI.
PRUMP
WAAAAH!
!!
OH NO!
ZWIK
I FOUND AN INTERESTING PLANT IN THE GARDEN.
HUH?
WHAT IS THIS ANIMAL-LIKE SCENT I SMELL?
TH-THUMP
TH-THUMP
WOW!
THAT IS AN INTERESTING PLANT!
TH-THUMP
TH-THUMP
INTERESTING, ISN'T IT? DO YOU KNOW WHAT THIS IS CALLED?
I-IT'S THE FIRST TIME I'VE SEEN IT.
TH-THUMP
I'LL ASK YUKI WHEN HE COMES BACK.
GOOD LUCK WITH YOUR ELIXIR MAKING. I'M REALLY LOOKING FORWARD TO IT!
TMP
TMP

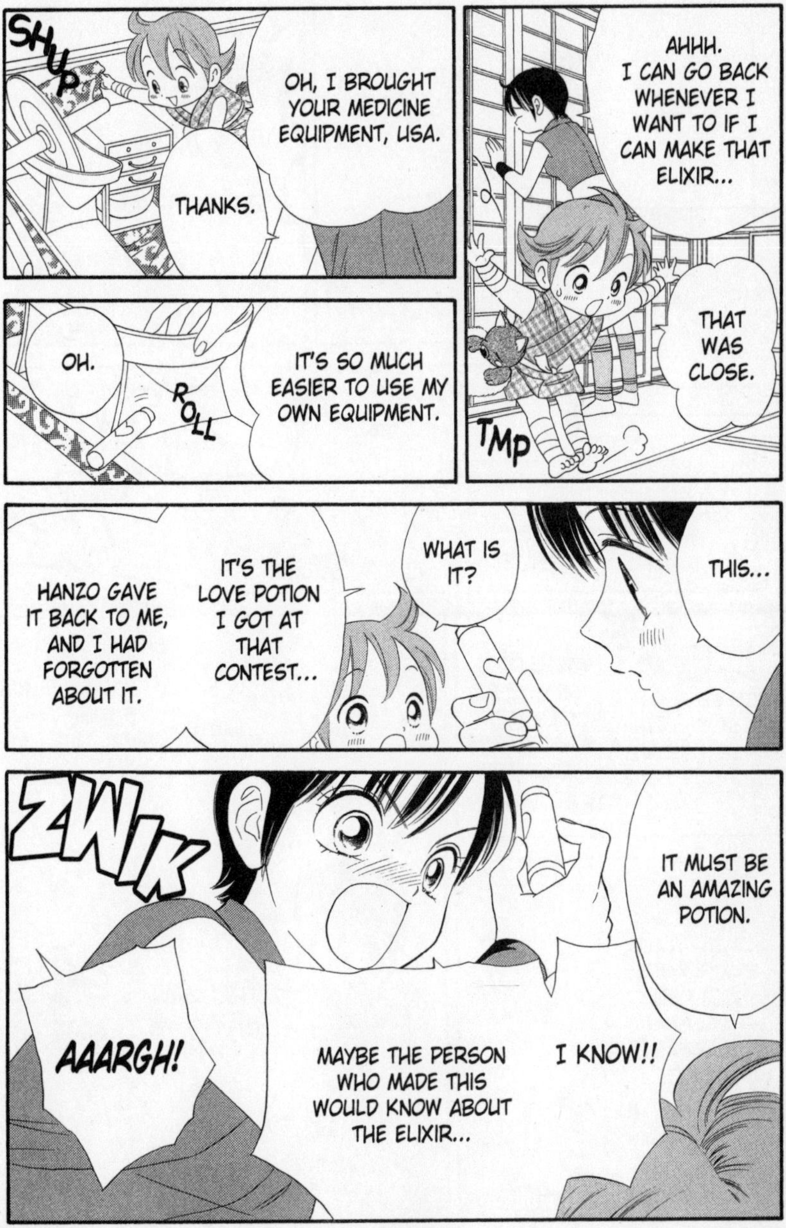
AHHH.
I CAN GO BACK WHENEVER I WANT TO IF I CAN MAKE THAT ELIXIR...
THAT WAS CLOSE.
TMP
OH, I BROUGHT YOUR MEDICINE EQUIPMENT, USA.
THANKS.
SHUP
IT'S SO MUCH EASIER TO USE MY OWN EQUIPMENT.
OH.
ROLL
THIS...
WHAT IS IT?
IT'S THE LOVE POTION I GOT AT THAT CONTEST...
HANZO GAVE IT BACK TO ME, AND I HAD FORGOTTEN ABOUT IT.
IT MUST BE AN AMAZING POTION.
ZWIK
I KNOW!!
MAYBE THE PERSON WHO MADE THIS WOULD KNOW ABOUT THE ELIXIR...
AAARGH!

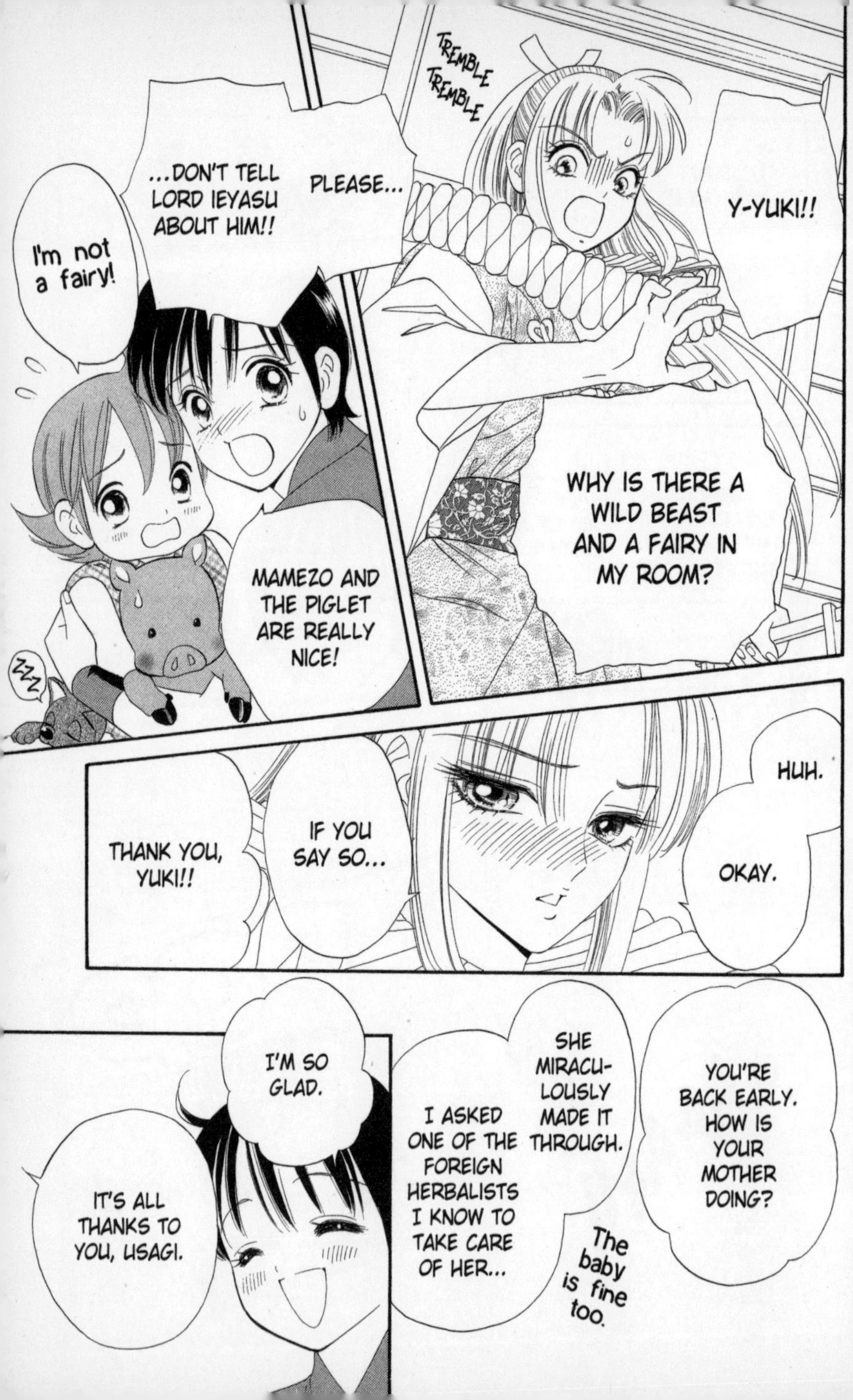
TREMBLE TREMBLE
Y-YUKI!!
WHY IS THERE A WILD BEAST AND A FAIRY IN MY ROOM?
PLEASE...
...DON'T TELL LORD IEYASU ABOUT HIM!!
I'm not a fairy!
MAMEZO AND THE PIGLET ARE REALLY NICE!
ZZZ
HUH.
OKAY.
IF YOU SAY SO...
THANK YOU, YUKI!!
YOU'RE BACK EARLY. HOW IS YOUR MOTHER DOING?
SHE MIRACULOUSLY MADE IT THROUGH.
I ASKED ONE OF THE FOREIGN HERBALISTS I KNOW TO TAKE CARE OF HER...
The baby is fine too.
I'M SO GLAD.
IT'S ALL THANKS TO YOU, USAGI.

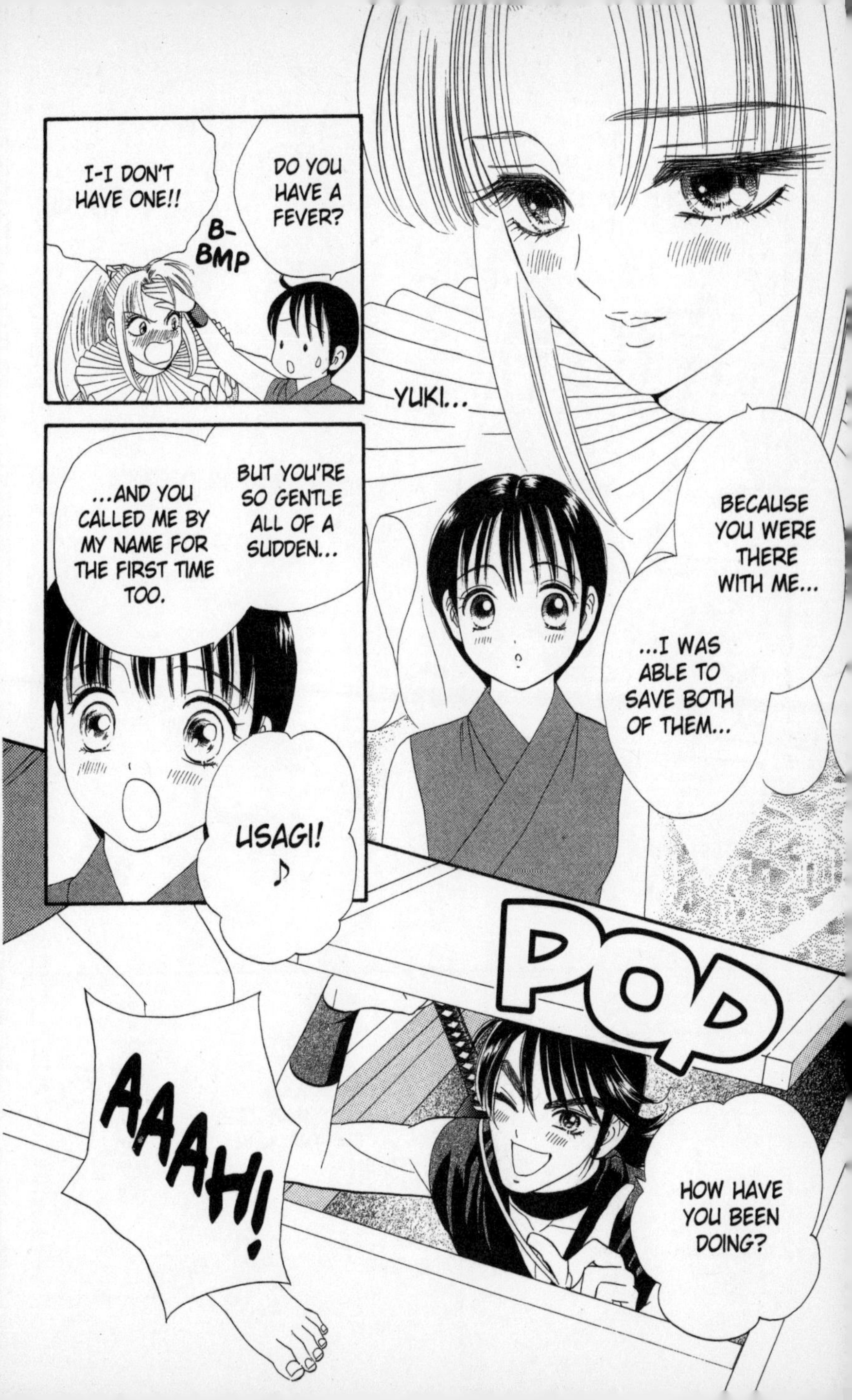
YUKI...
BECAUSE YOU WERE THERE WITH ME...
...I WAS ABLE TO SAVE BOTH OF THEM...
DO YOU HAVE A FEVER?
B-BMP
I-I DON'T HAVE ONE!!
BUT YOU'RE SO GENTLE ALL OF A SUDDEN...
...AND YOU CALLED ME BY MY NAME FOR THE FIRST TIME TOO.
USAGI! ♪
POP
HOW HAVE YOU BEEN DOING?
AAAH!

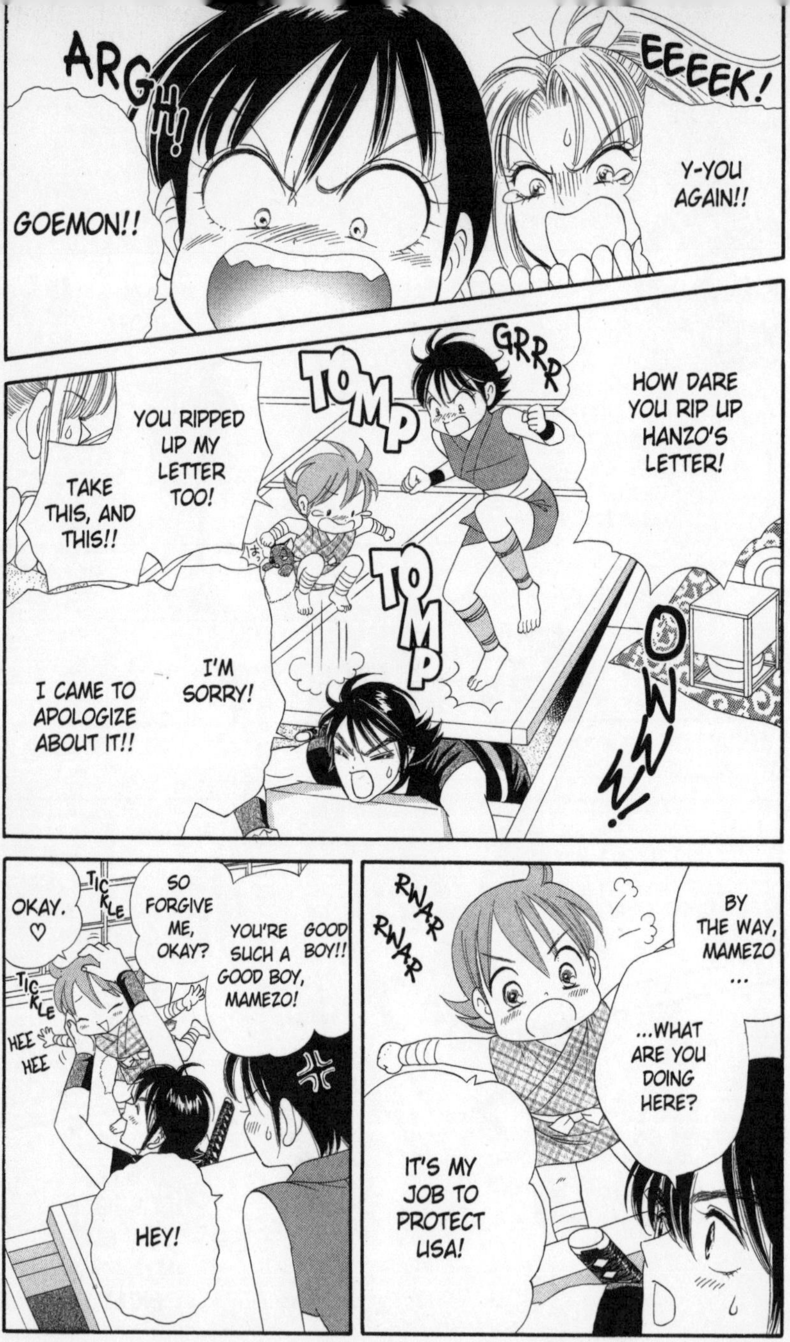
EEEEEK!
Y-YOU AGAIN!!
ARGH!
GOEMON!!
HOW DARE YOU RIP UP HANZO'S LETTER!
GRRR
TOMP
YOU RIPPED UP MY LETTER TOO!
TAKE THIS, AND THIS!!
DOWWW!!
TOMP
I'M SORRY!
I CAME TO APOLOGIZE ABOUT IT!!
BY THE WAY, MAMEZO ...
RWAR RWAR
...WHAT ARE YOU DOING HERE?
IT'S MY JOB TO PROTECT USA!
GOOD BOY!!
YOU'RE SUCH A GOOD BOY, MAMEZO!
SO FORGIVE ME, OKAY?
TICKLE
OKAY. ♡
TICKLE
HEE HEE
HEY!

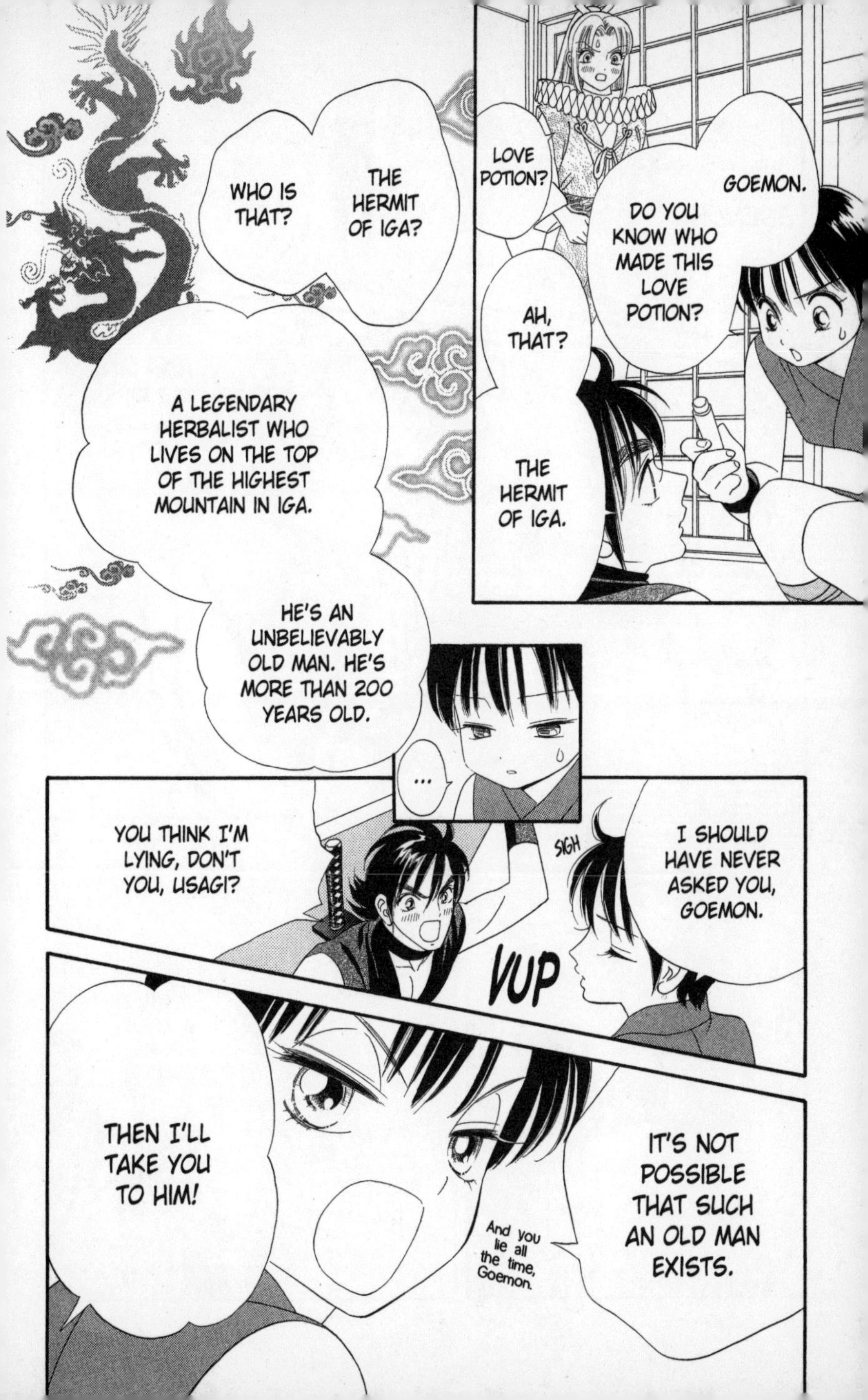
GOEMON.
DO YOU KNOW WHO MADE THIS LOVE POTION?
LOVE POTION?
AH, THAT?
THE HERMIT OF IGA.
THE HERMIT OF IGA?
WHO IS THAT?
A LEGENDARY HERBALIST WHO LIVES ON THE TOP OF THE HIGHEST MOUNTAIN IN IGA.
HE'S AN UNBELIEVABLY OLD MAN. HE'S MORE THAN 200 YEARS OLD.
...
I SHOULD HAVE NEVER ASKED YOU, GOEMON.
SIGH
YOU THINK I'M LYING, DON'T YOU, USAGI?
VUP
IT'S NOT POSSIBLE THAT SUCH AN OLD MAN EXISTS.
And you lie all the time, Goemon.
THEN I'LL TAKE YOU TO HIM!

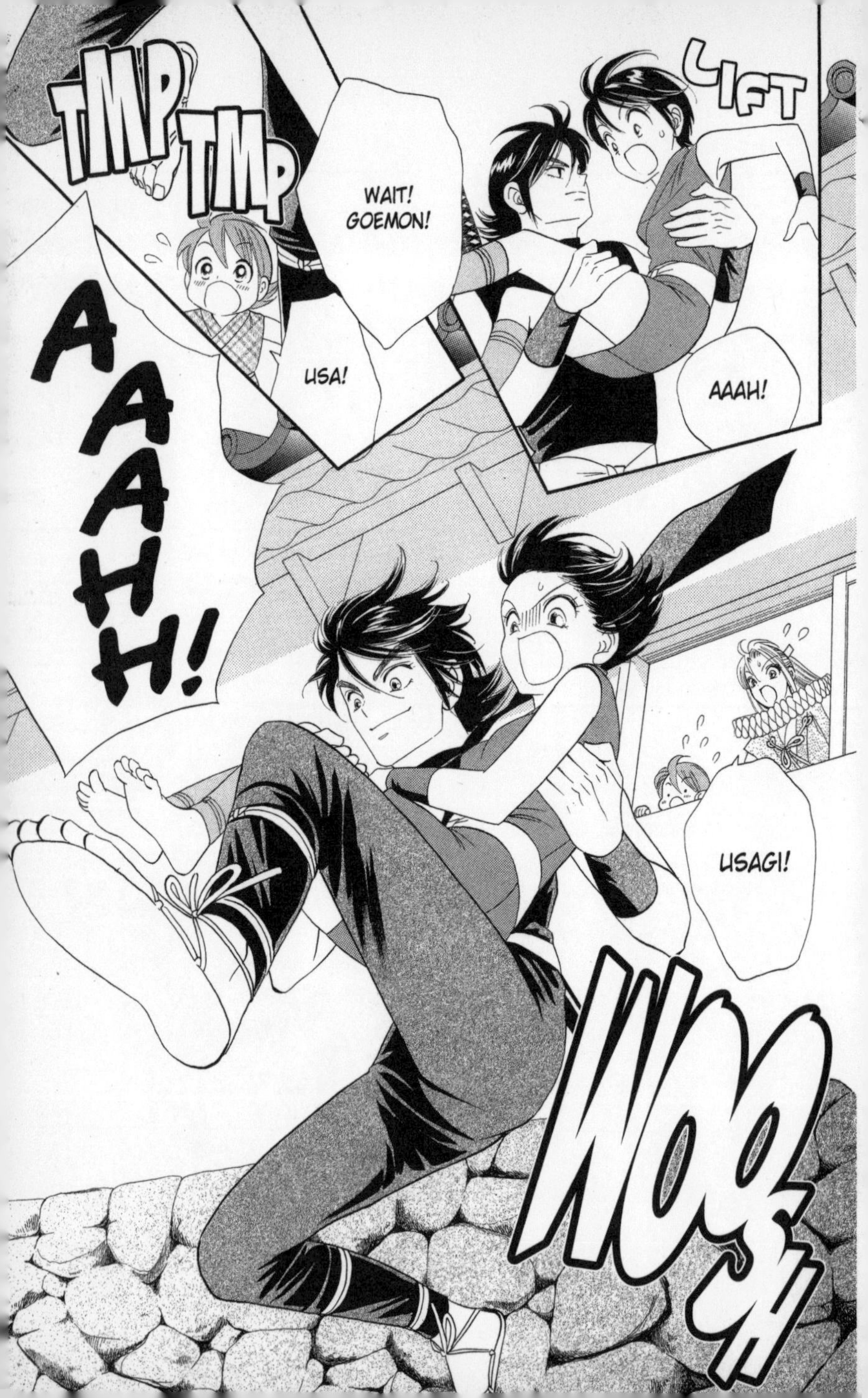
LIFT
AAAH!
WAIT! GOEMON!
TMP TMP
USA!
AAAAH!
USAGI!
WHOOSH

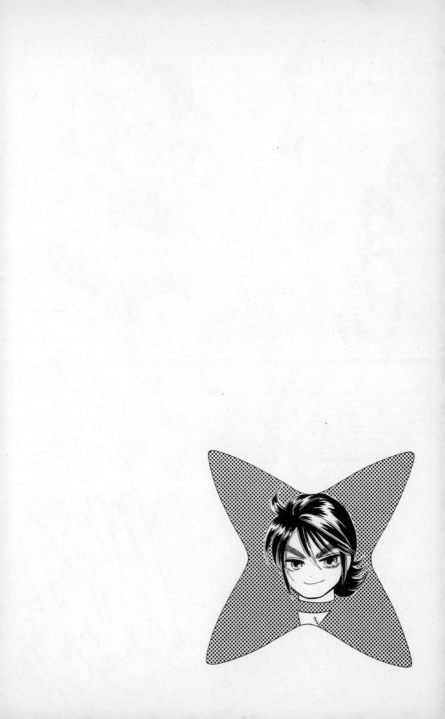

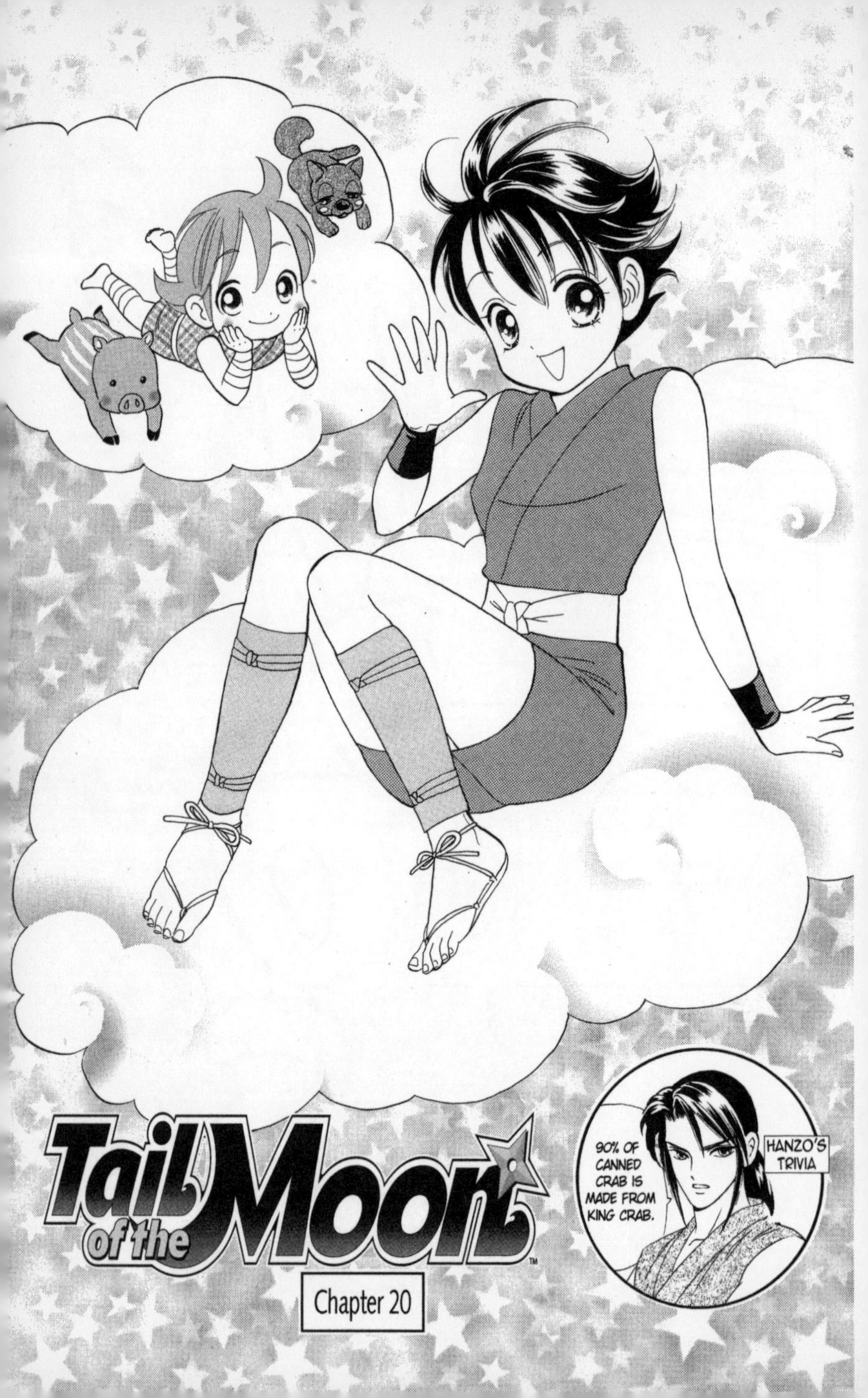
Tail of the Moon™
Chapter 20
HANZO'S TRIVIA
90% OF CANNED CRAB IS MADE FROM KING CRAB.

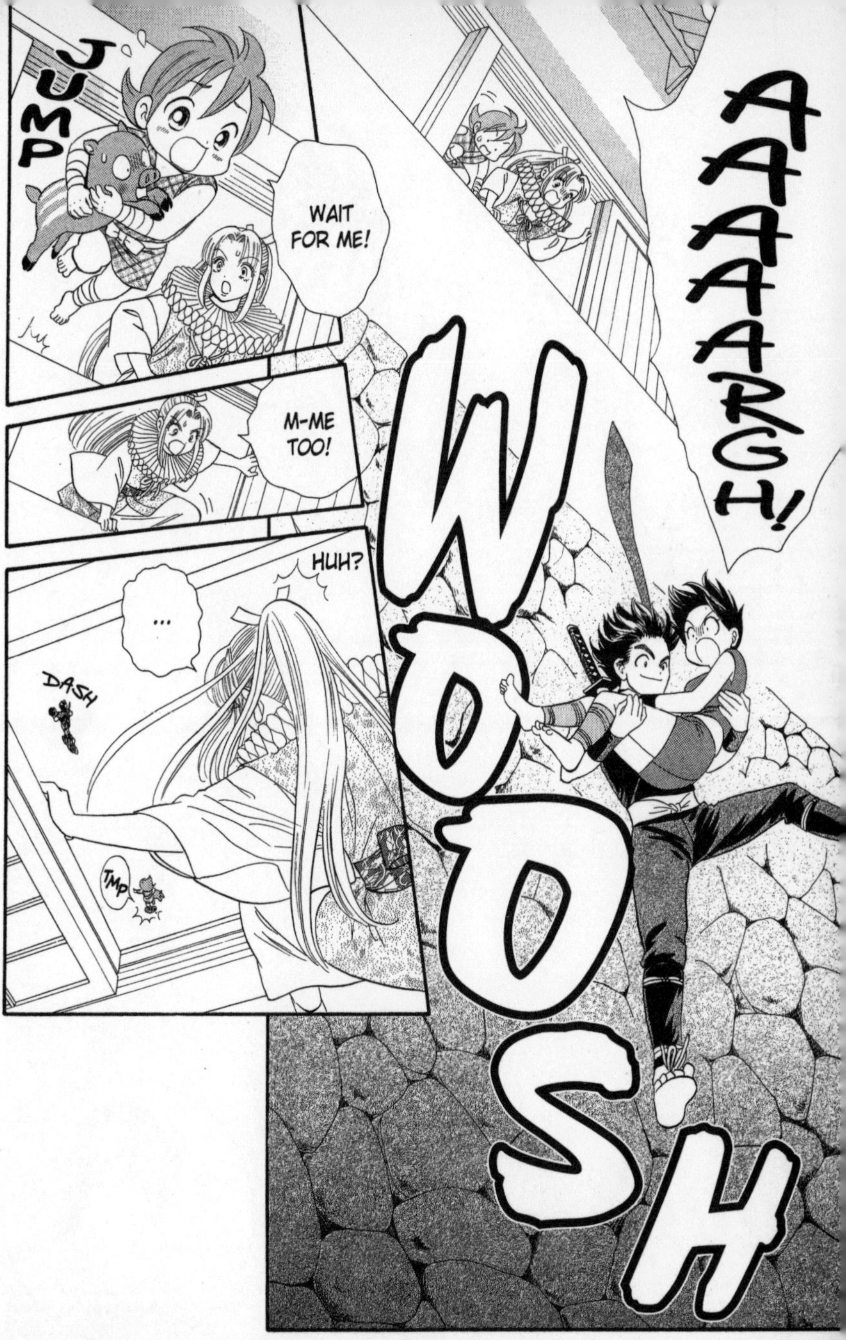
AAAAAARGH!
WOOSH
WAIT FOR ME!
JUMP
M-ME TOO!
HUH?
...
DASH
TMP

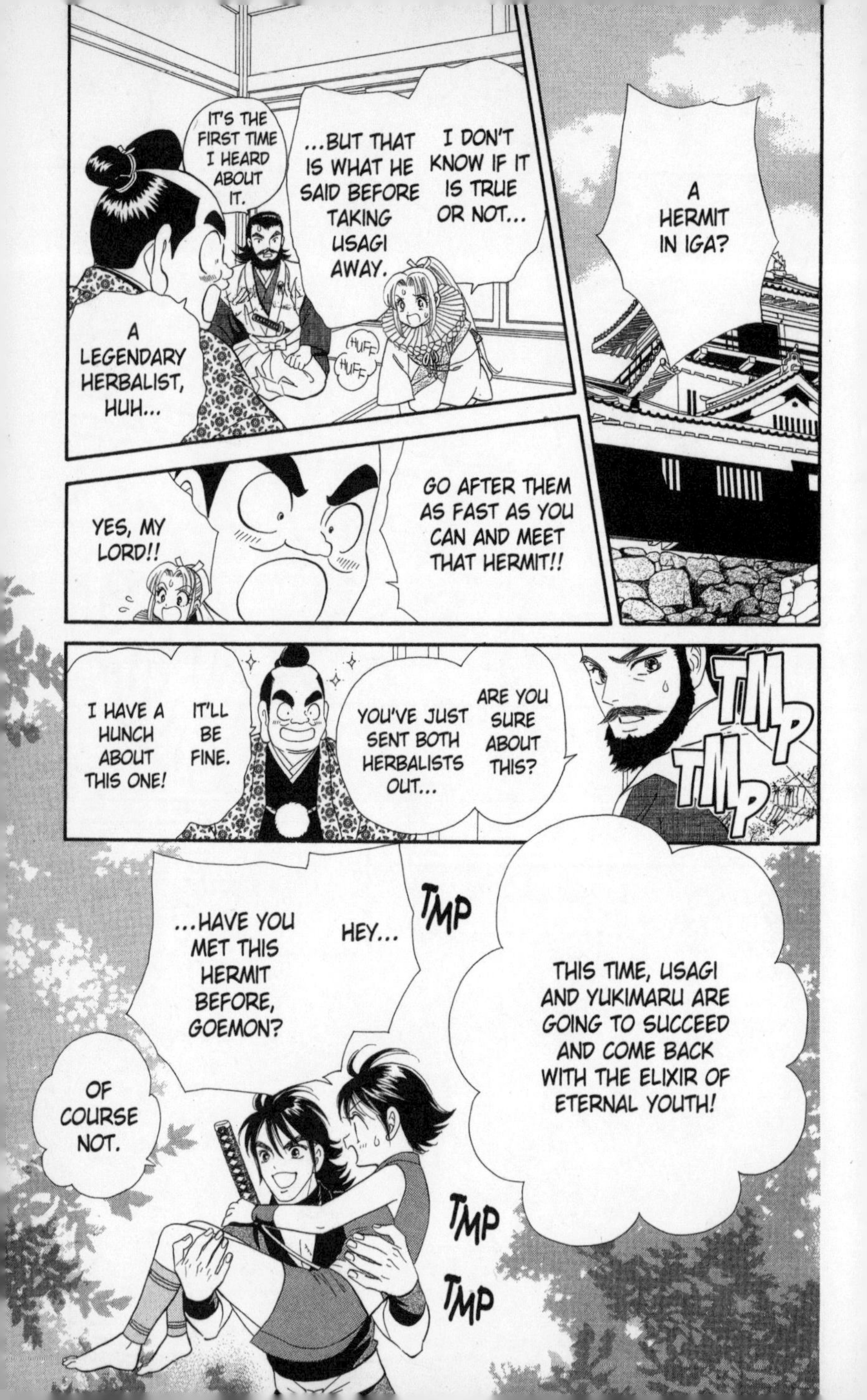
A HERMIT IN IGA?
I DON'T KNOW IF IT IS TRUE OR NOT...
...BUT THAT IS WHAT HE SAID BEFORE TAKING USAGI AWAY.
IT'S THE FIRST TIME I HEARD ABOUT IT.
HUFF
HUFF
A LEGENDARY HERBALIST, HUH...
GO AFTER THEM AS FAST AS YOU CAN AND MEET THAT HERMIT!!
YES, MY LORD!!
TMP
TMP
ARE YOU SURE ABOUT THIS?
YOU'VE JUST SENT BOTH HERBALISTS OUT...
IT'LL BE FINE.
I HAVE A HUNCH ABOUT THIS ONE!
THIS TIME, USAGI AND YUKIMARU ARE GOING TO SUCCEED AND COME BACK WITH THE ELIXIR OF ETERNAL YOUTH!
TMP
HEY...
...HAVE YOU MET THIS HERMIT BEFORE, GOEMON?
TMP
TMP
OF COURSE NOT.

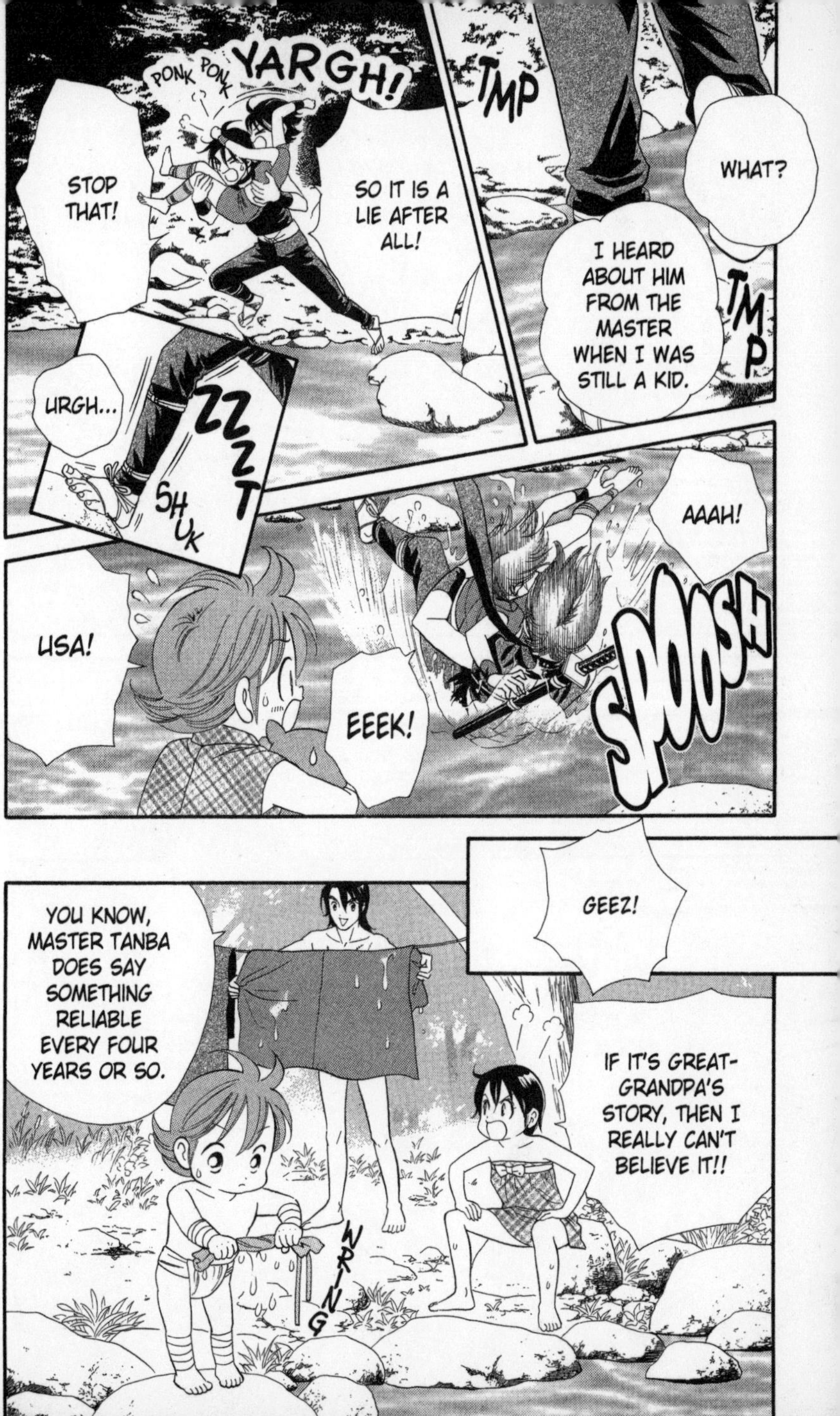
TMP
WHAT?
I HEARD ABOUT HIM FROM THE MASTER WHEN I WAS STILL A KID.
TMP
YARGH!
PONK PONK
SO IT IS A LIE AFTER ALL!
STOP THAT!
URGH...
ZZZT
SHUK
AAAH!
SPOOSH
EEEK!
USA!
GEEZ!
IF IT'S GREAT-GRANDPA'S STORY, THEN I REALLY CAN'T BELIEVE IT!!
WRING
YOU KNOW, MASTER TANBA DOES SAY SOMETHING RELIABLE EVERY FOUR YEARS OR SO.

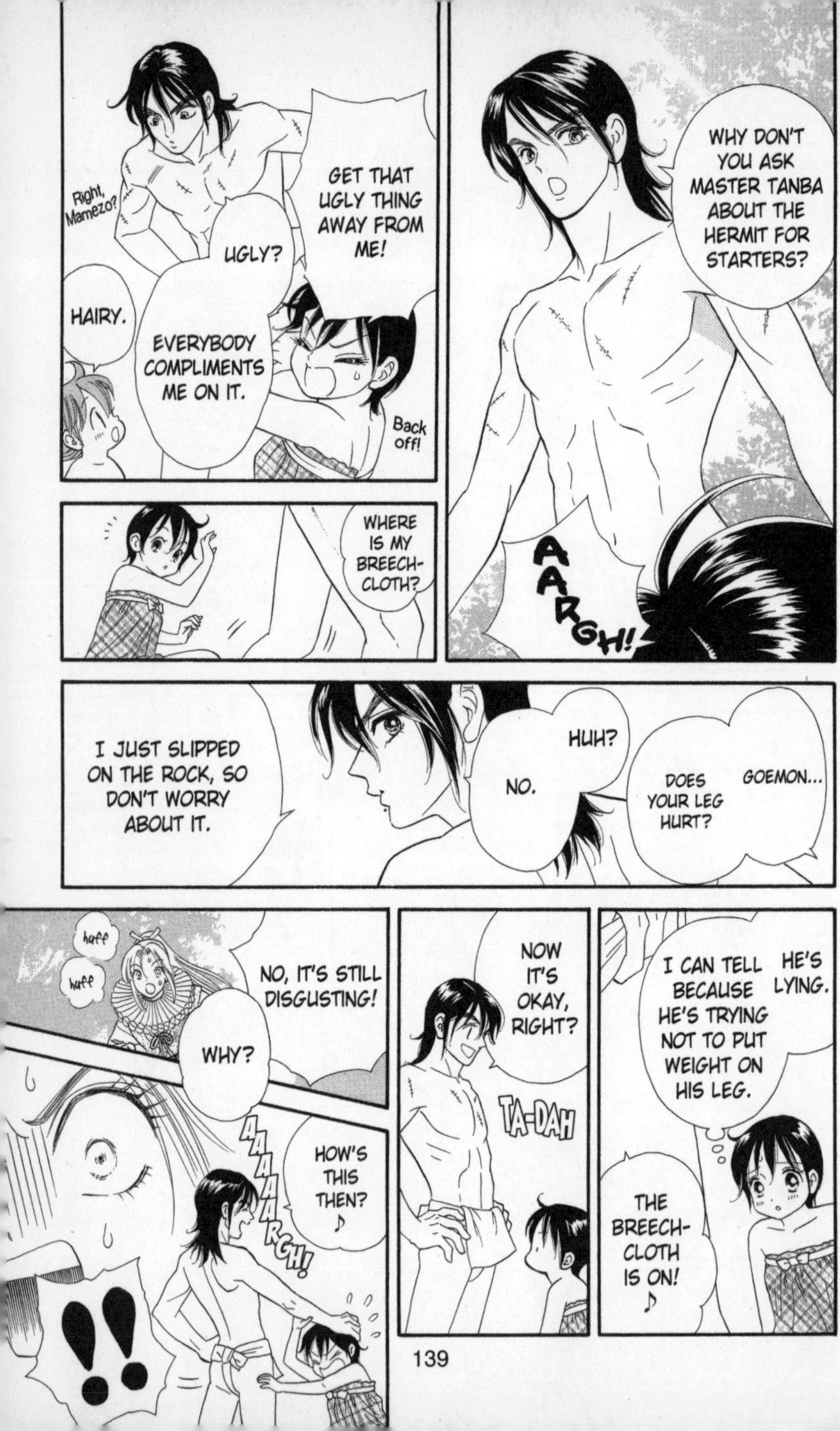
WHY DON'T YOU ASK MASTER TANBA ABOUT THE HERMIT FOR STARTERS?
AARGH!
GET THAT UGLY THING AWAY FROM ME!
UGLY?
EVERYBODY COMPLIMENTS ME ON IT.
Right, Mamezo?
HAIRY.
Back off!
WHERE IS MY BREECH-CLOTH?
GOEMON...
DOES YOUR LEG HURT?
HUH?
NO.
I JUST SLIPPED ON THE ROCK, SO DON'T WORRY ABOUT IT.
HE'S LYING.
I CAN TELL BECAUSE HE'S TRYING NOT TO PUT WEIGHT ON HIS LEG.
THE BREECH-CLOTH IS ON! ♪
NOW IT'S OKAY, RIGHT?
TA-DAH
NO, IT'S STILL DISGUSTING!
huff
huff
WHY?
HOW'S THIS THEN? ♪
AAAAAARGH!

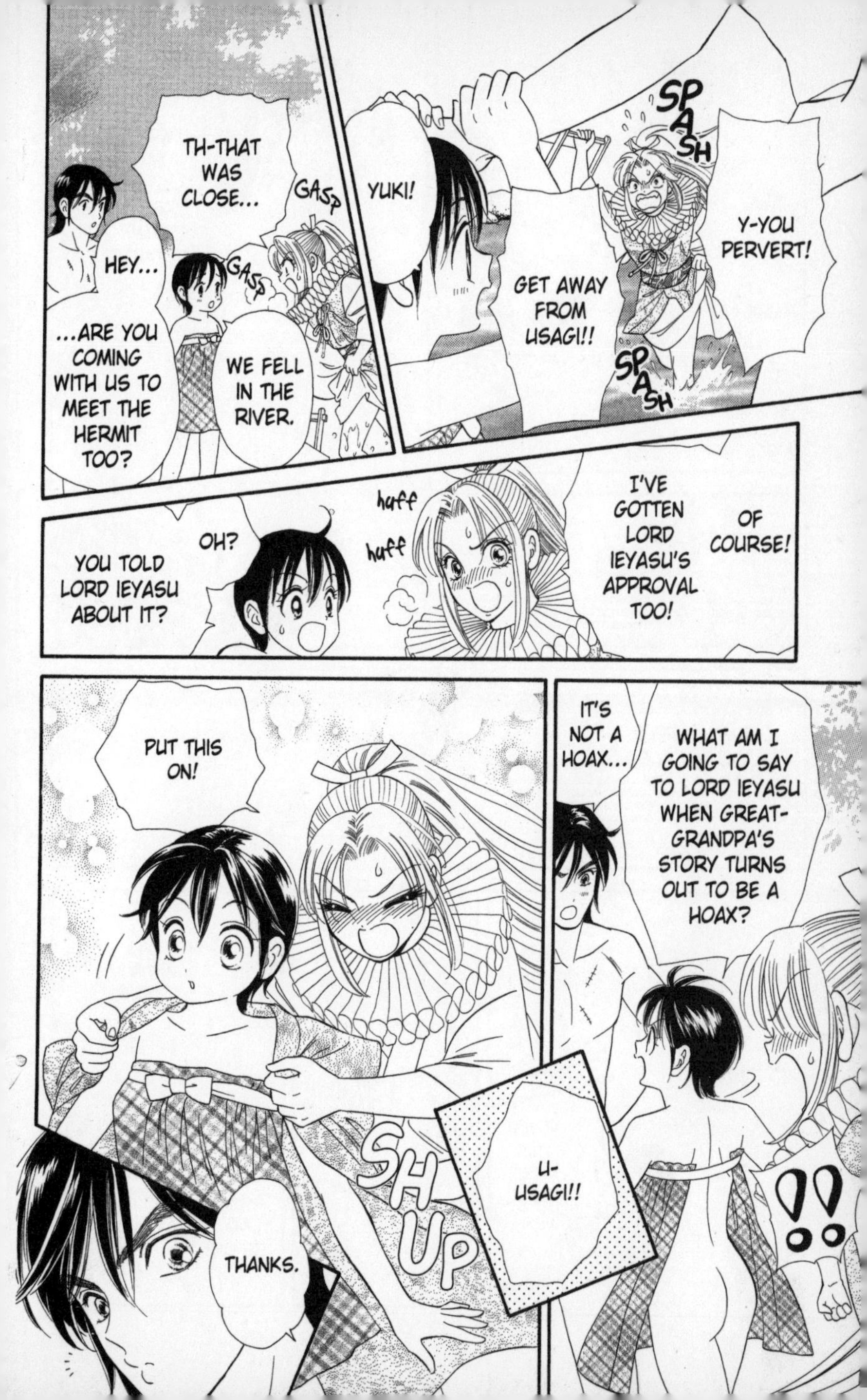
SPASH
Y-YOU PERVERT!
GET AWAY FROM USAGI!!
SPASH
YUKI!
GASP
TH-THAT WAS CLOSE...
GASP
WE FELL IN THE RIVER.
HEY...
...ARE YOU COMING WITH US TO MEET THE HERMIT TOO?
OF COURSE!
I'VE GOTTEN LORD IEYASU'S APPROVAL TOO!
huff
huff
OH?
YOU TOLD LORD IEYASU ABOUT IT?
WHAT AM I GOING TO SAY TO LORD IEYASU WHEN GREAT-GRANDPA'S STORY TURNS OUT TO BE A HOAX?
IT'S NOT A HOAX...
!!
PUT THIS ON!
SHUP
U-USAGI!!
THANKS.

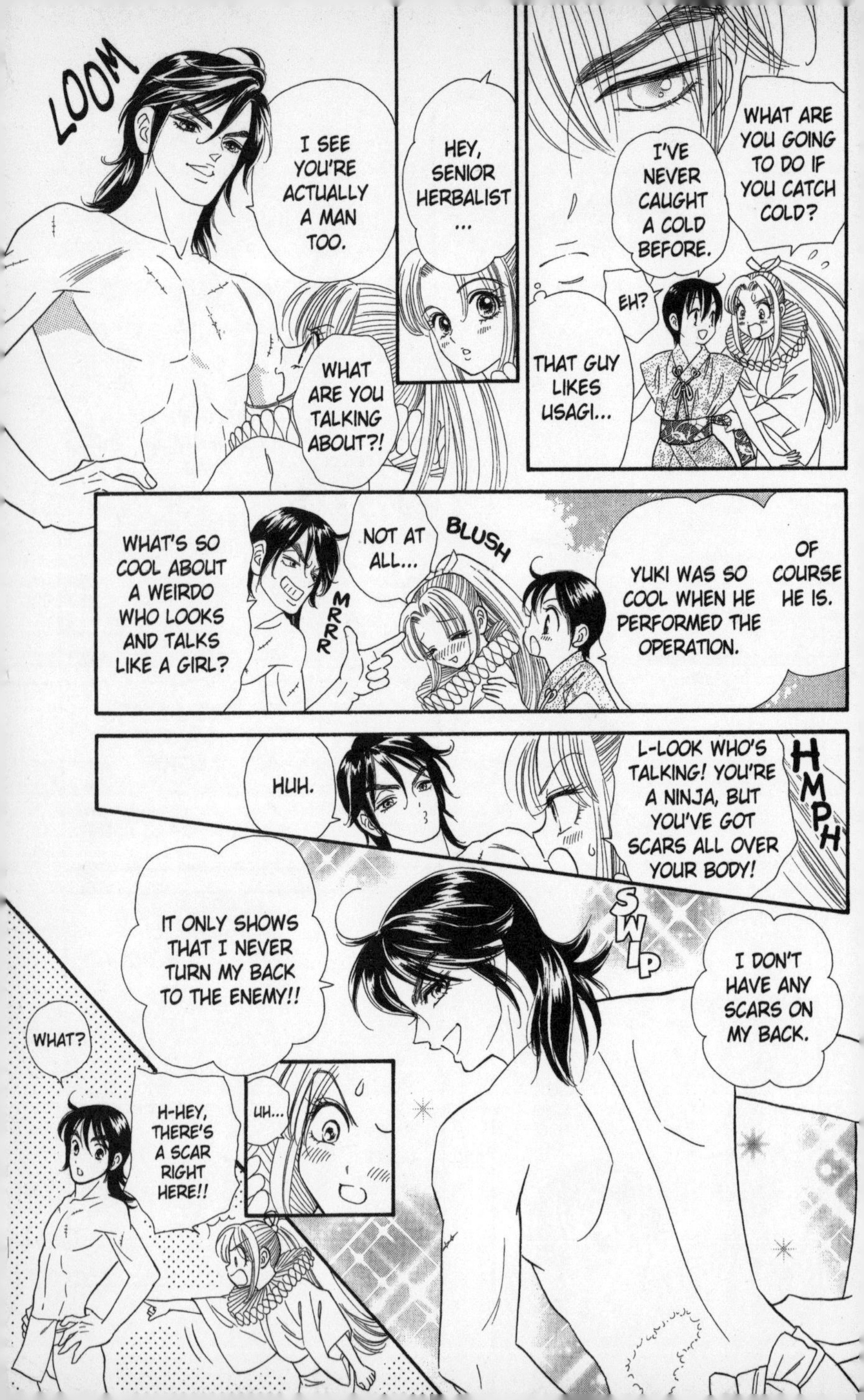
WHAT ARE YOU GOING TO DO IF YOU CATCH COLD?
I'VE NEVER CAUGHT A COLD BEFORE.
EH?
THAT GUY LIKES USAGI...
HEY, SENIOR HERBALIST...
LOOM
I SEE YOU'RE ACTUALLY A MAN TOO.
WHAT ARE YOU TALKING ABOUT?!
OF COURSE HE IS.
YUKI WAS SO COOL WHEN HE PERFORMED THE OPERATION.
BLUSH
NOT AT ALL...
MRRR
WHAT'S SO COOL ABOUT A WEIRDO WHO LOOKS AND TALKS LIKE A GIRL?
HMPH
L-LOOK WHO'S TALKING! YOU'RE A NINJA, BUT YOU'VE GOT SCARS ALL OVER YOUR BODY!
HUH.
SWIP
I DON'T HAVE ANY SCARS ON MY BACK.
IT ONLY SHOWS THAT I NEVER TURN MY BACK TO THE ENEMY!!
UH...
H-HEY, THERE'S A SCAR RIGHT HERE!!
WHAT?

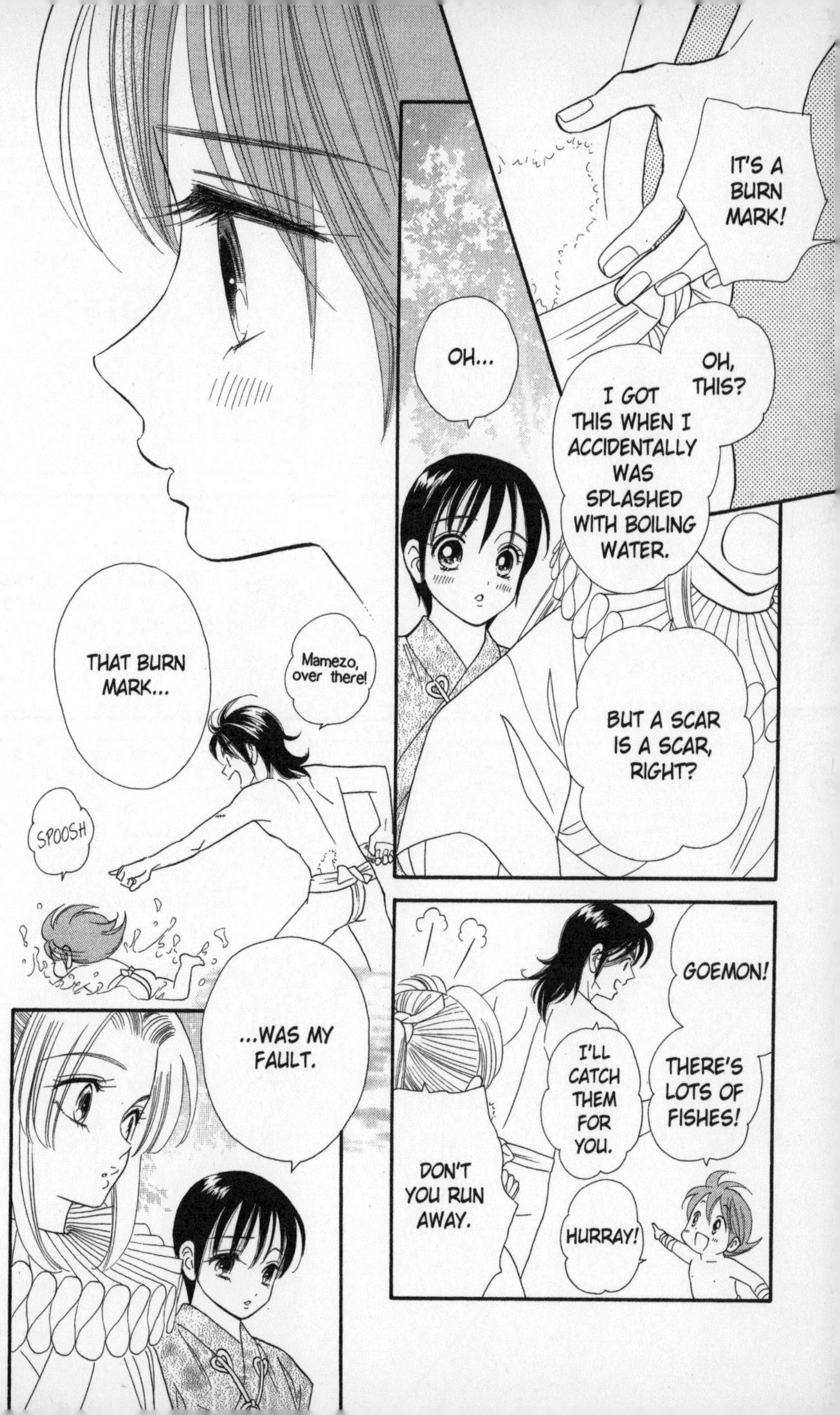
IT'S A BURN MARK!
OH, THIS?
I GOT THIS WHEN I ACCIDENTALLY WAS SPLASHED WITH BOILING WATER.
OH...
BUT A SCAR IS A SCAR, RIGHT?
THAT BURN MARK...
Mamezo, over there!
SPOOSH
GOEMON!
THERE'S LOTS OF FISHES!
I'LL CATCH THEM FOR YOU.
HURRAY!
DON'T YOU RUN AWAY.
...WAS MY FAULT.

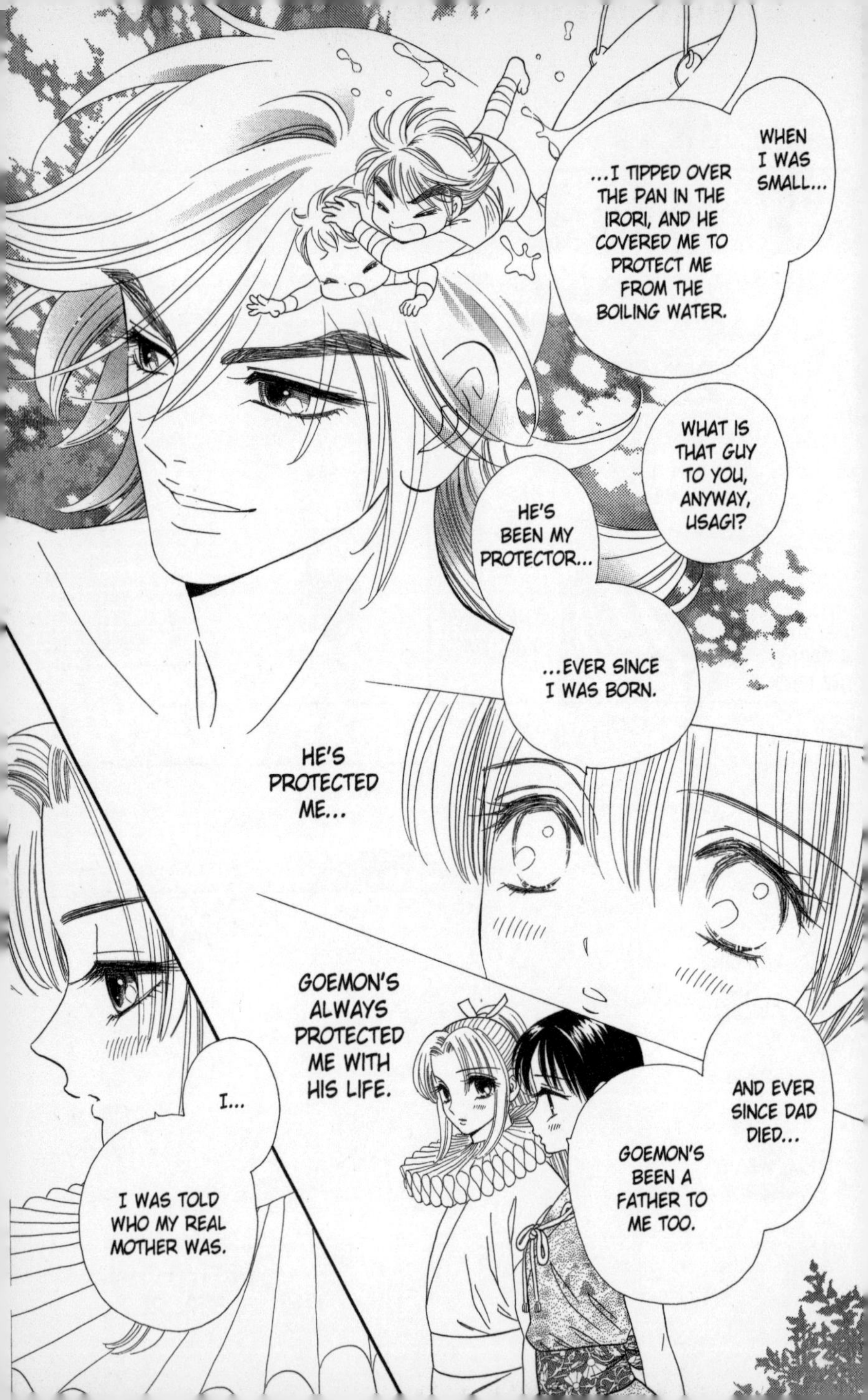
WHEN I WAS SMALL...
...I TIPPED OVER THE PAN IN THE IRORI, AND HE COVERED ME TO PROTECT ME FROM THE BOILING WATER.
WHAT IS THAT GUY TO YOU, ANYWAY, USAGI?
HE'S BEEN MY PROTECTOR...
...EVER SINCE I WAS BORN.
HE'S PROTECTED ME...
AND EVER SINCE DAD DIED...
GOEMON'S BEEN A FATHER TO ME TOO.
GOEMON'S ALWAYS PROTECTED ME WITH HIS LIFE.
I...
I WAS TOLD WHO MY REAL MOTHER WAS.

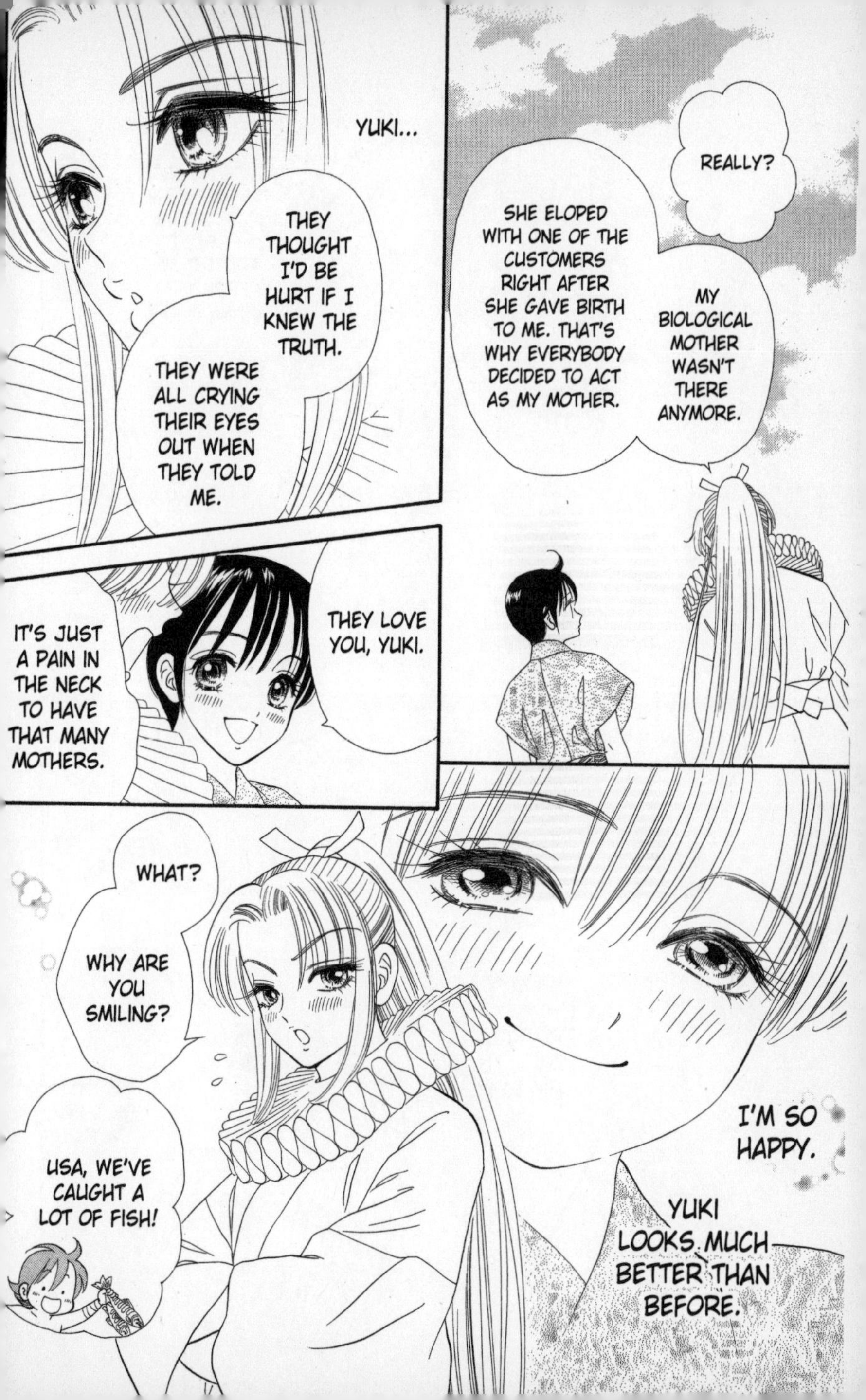
REALLY?
MY BIOLOGICAL MOTHER WASN'T THERE ANYMORE.
SHE ELOPED WITH ONE OF THE CUSTOMERS RIGHT AFTER SHE GAVE BIRTH TO ME. THAT'S WHY EVERYBODY DECIDED TO ACT AS MY MOTHER.
YUKI...
THEY THOUGHT I'D BE HURT IF I KNEW THE TRUTH.
THEY WERE ALL CRYING THEIR EYES OUT WHEN THEY TOLD ME.
THEY LOVE YOU, YUKI.
IT'S JUST A PAIN IN THE NECK TO HAVE THAT MANY MOTHERS.
I'M SO HAPPY.
YUKI LOOKS MUCH BETTER THAN BEFORE.
WHAT?
WHY ARE YOU SMILING?
USA, WE'VE CAUGHT A LOT OF FISH!

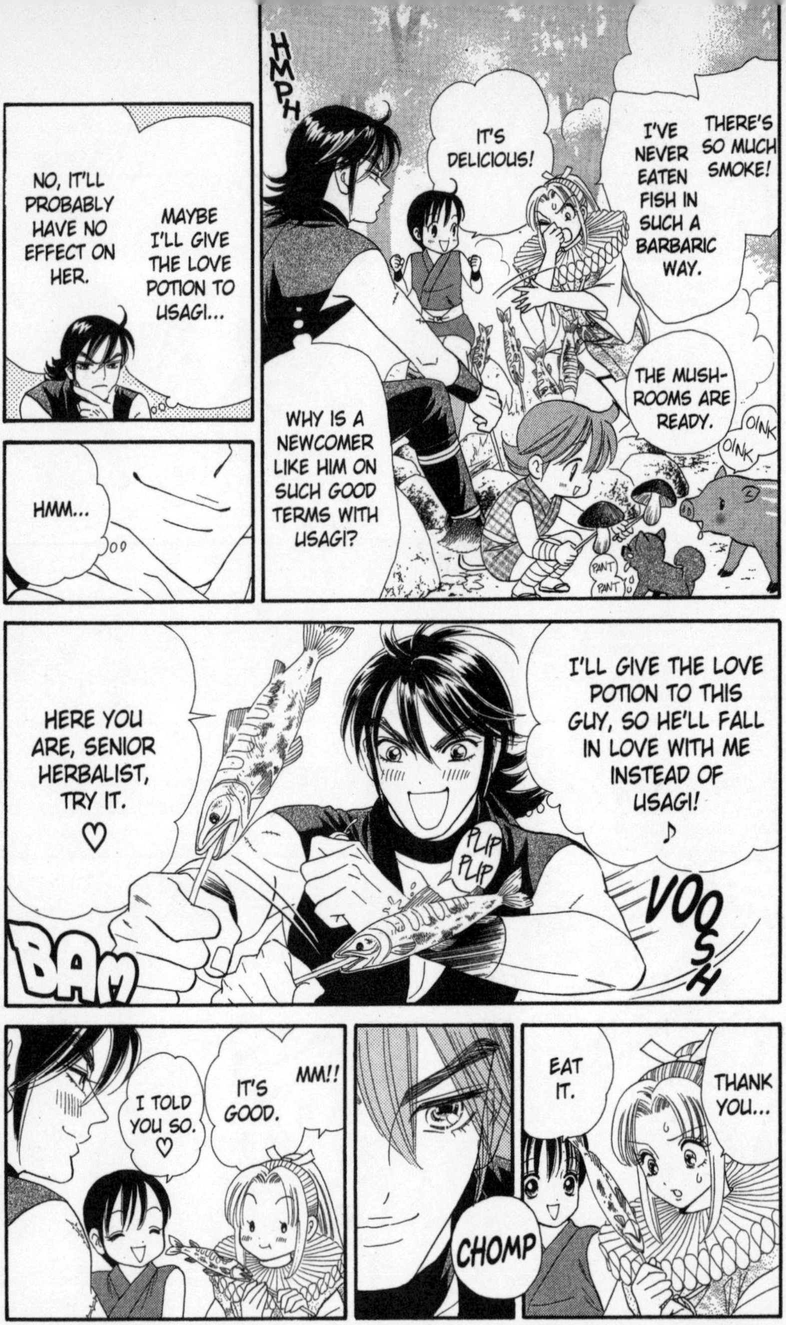
THERE'S SO MUCH SMOKE!
I'VE NEVER EATEN FISH IN SUCH A BARBARIC WAY.
IT'S DELICIOUS!
HMPH
THE MUSH-ROOMS ARE READY.
OINK OINK
WHY IS A NEWCOMER LIKE HIM ON SUCH GOOD TERMS WITH USAGI?
PANT PANT
MAYBE I'LL GIVE THE LOVE POTION TO USAGI...
NO, IT'LL PROBABLY HAVE NO EFFECT ON HER.
HMM...
I'LL GIVE THE LOVE POTION TO THIS GUY, SO HE'LL FALL IN LOVE WITH ME INSTEAD OF USAGI! ♪
VOOSH
PLIP PLIP
HERE YOU ARE, SENIOR HERBALIST, TRY IT. ♡
BAM
THANK YOU...
EAT IT.
CHOMP
MM!!
IT'S GOOD.
I TOLD YOU SO. ♡

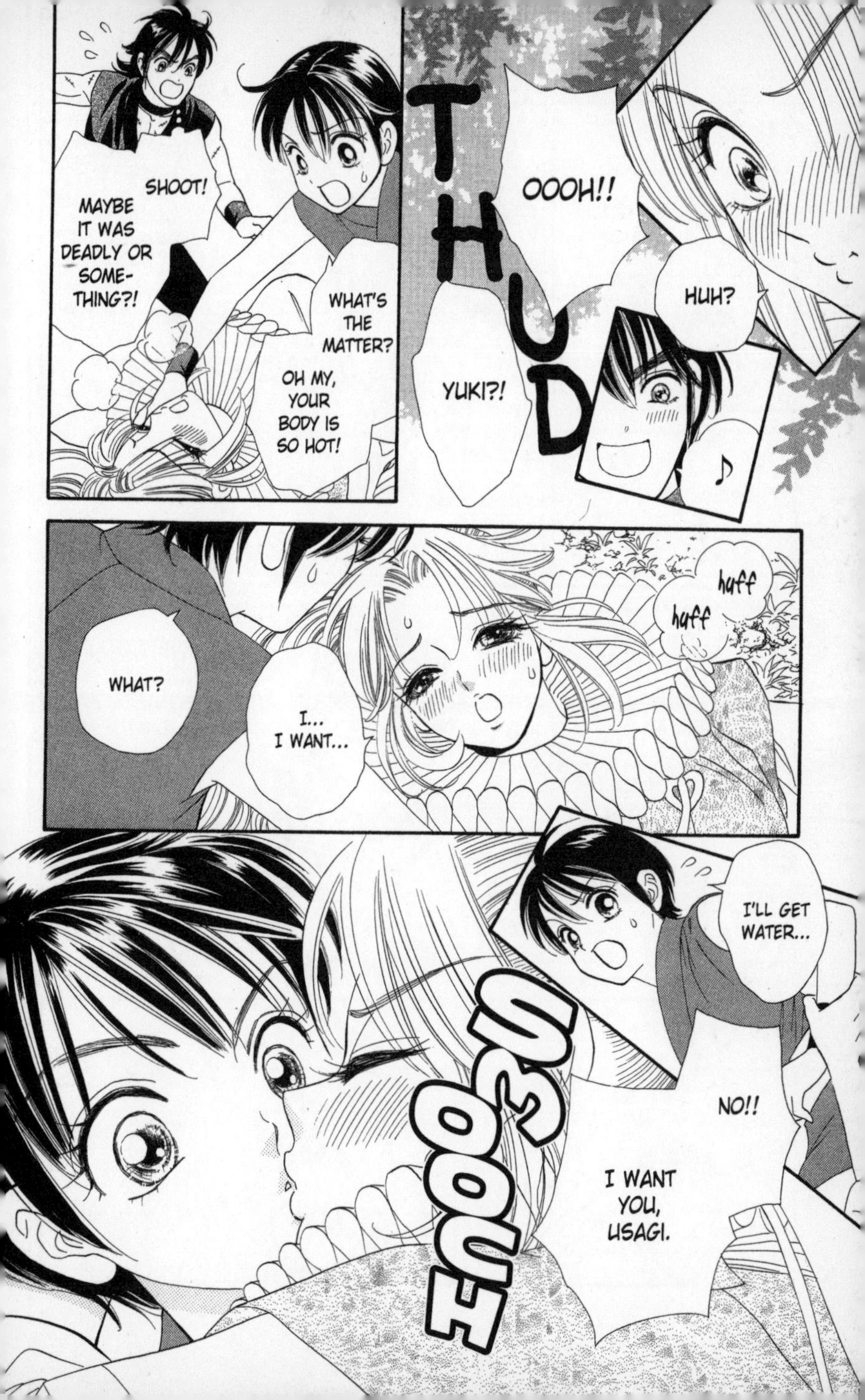
HUH?
♪
OOOH!!
THUD
YUKI?!
WHAT'S THE MATTER?
OH MY, YOUR BODY IS SO HOT!
SHOOT!
MAYBE IT WAS DEADLY OR SOME-THING?!
huff huff
I... I WANT...
WHAT?
I'LL GET WATER...
NO!!
I WANT YOU, USAGI.
SMOOCH

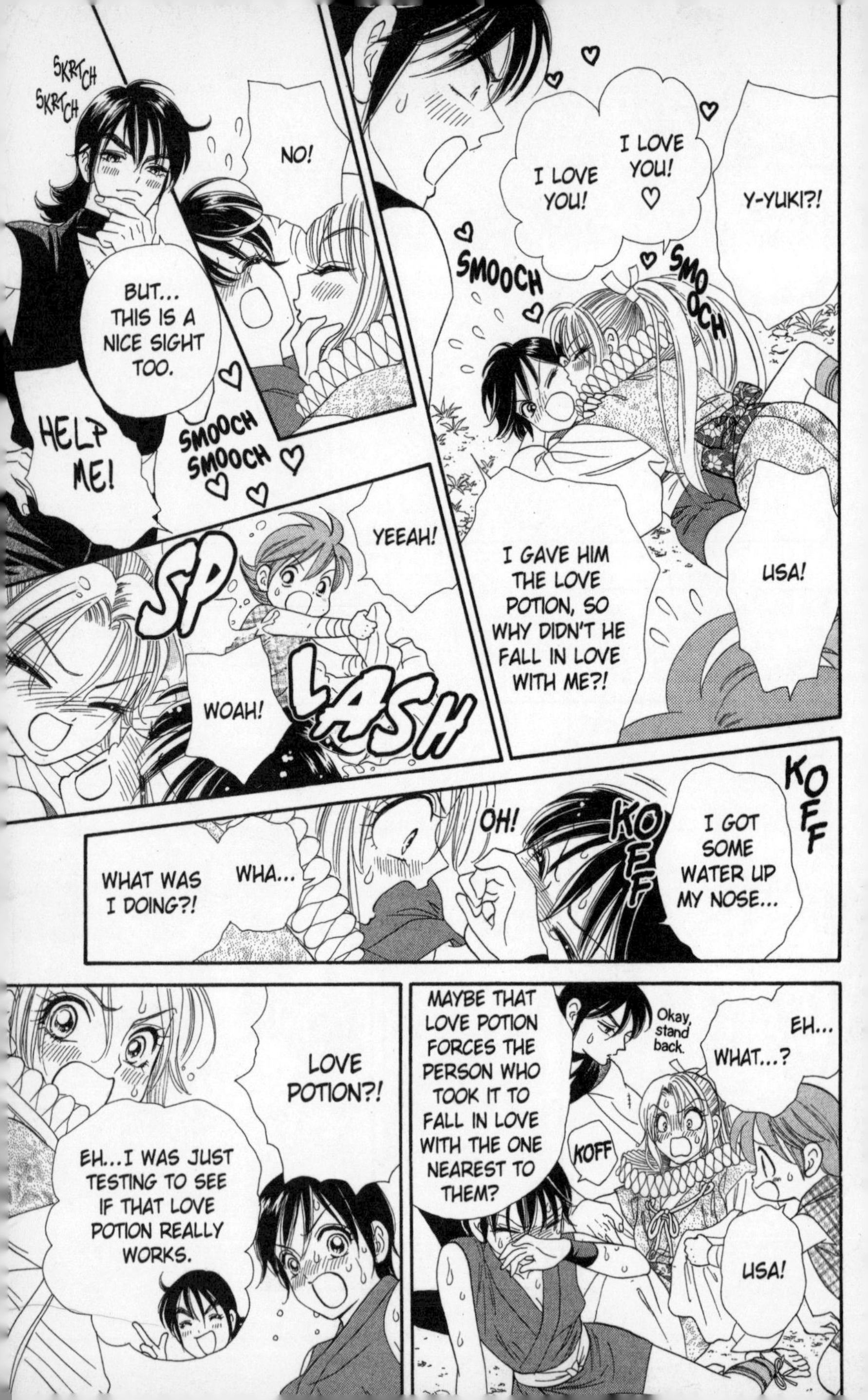
Y-YUKI?!
I LOVE YOU!
I LOVE YOU!
SMOOCH
SMOOCH
USA!
I GAVE HIM THE LOVE POTION, SO WHY DIDN'T HE FALL IN LOVE WITH ME?!
NO!
SKRTCH SKRTCH
BUT... THIS IS A NICE SIGHT TOO.
SMOOCH SMOOCH
HELP ME!
YEEAH!
SPLASH
WOAH!
KOFF KOFF
I GOT SOME WATER UP MY NOSE...
OH!
WHA...
WHAT WAS I DOING?!
EH... WHAT...?
Okay, stand back.
MAYBE THAT LOVE POTION FORCES THE PERSON WHO TOOK IT TO FALL IN LOVE WITH THE ONE NEAREST TO THEM?
USA!
KOFF
LOVE POTION?!
EH...I WAS JUST TESTING TO SEE IF THAT LOVE POTION REALLY WORKS.

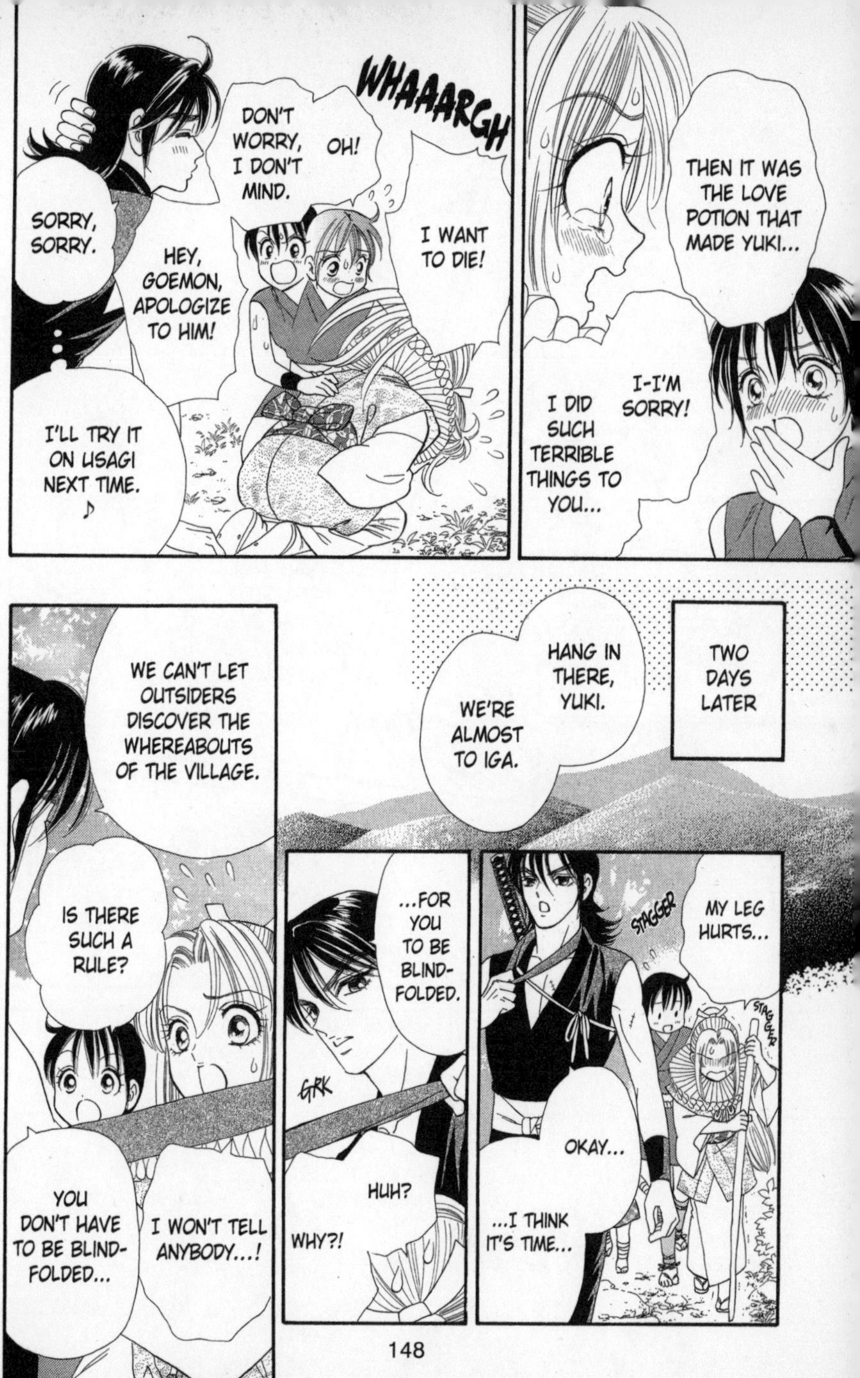
THEN IT WAS THE LOVE POTION THAT MADE YUKI...
I-I'M SORRY!
I DID SUCH TERRIBLE THINGS TO YOU...
WHAAARGH
I WANT TO DIE!
OH!
DON'T WORRY, I DON'T MIND.
HEY, GOEMON, APOLOGIZE TO HIM!
SORRY, SORRY.
I'LL TRY IT ON USAGI NEXT TIME. ♪
TWO DAYS LATER
HANG IN THERE, YUKI.
WE'RE ALMOST TO IGA.
MY LEG HURTS...
STAGGER
STAGGER
OKAY...
...I THINK IT'S TIME...
...FOR YOU TO BE BLIND-FOLDED.
GRK
HUH?
WHY?!
WE CAN'T LET OUTSIDERS DISCOVER THE WHEREABOUTS OF THE VILLAGE.
IS THERE SUCH A RULE?
I WON'T TELL ANYBODY...!
YOU DON'T HAVE TO BE BLIND-FOLDED...

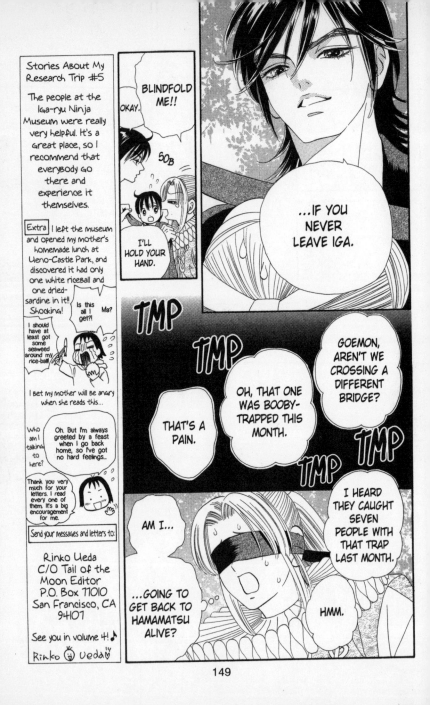

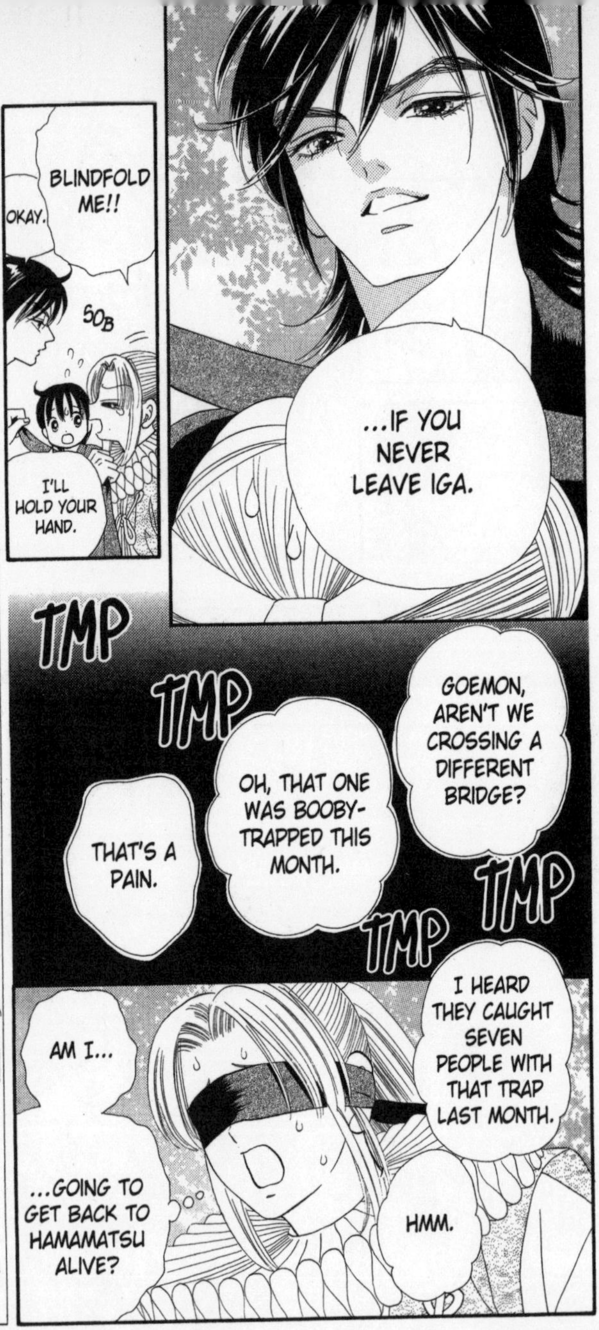
...IF YOU NEVER LEAVE IGA.
BLINDFOLD ME!!
OKAY.
SOB
I'LL HOLD YOUR HAND.
TMP
TMP
GOEMON, AREN'T WE CROSSING A DIFFERENT BRIDGE?
OH, THAT ONE WAS BOOBY-TRAPPED THIS MONTH.
THAT'S A PAIN.
TMP
TMP
I HEARD THEY CAUGHT SEVEN PEOPLE WITH THAT TRAP LAST MONTH.
HMM.
AM I...
...GOING TO GET BACK TO HAMAMATSU ALIVE?

Stories About My Research Trip #5

The people at the Iga-ryu Ninja Museum were really very helpful. It's a great place, so I recommend that everybody go there and experience it themselves.

Extra I left the museum and opened my mother's homemade lunch at Ueno-Castle Park, and discovered it had only one white riceball and one dried-sardine in it!! Shocking!

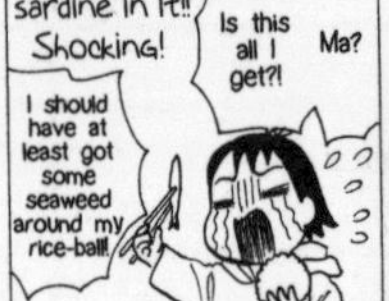
Is this all I get?!
Ma?
I should have at least got some seaweed around my rice-ball!

I bet my mother will be angry when she reads this...

Who am I talking to here?

Oh. But I'm always greeted by a feast when I go back home, so I've got no hard feelings...

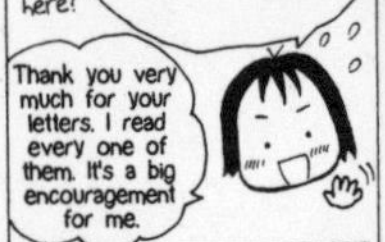
Thank you very much for your letters. I read every one of them. It's a big encouragement for me.

Send your messages and letters to:

Rinko Ueda
C/O Tail of the Moon Editor
P.O. Box 77010
San Francisco, CA 94107

See you in volume 4! ♪

Rinko Ueda

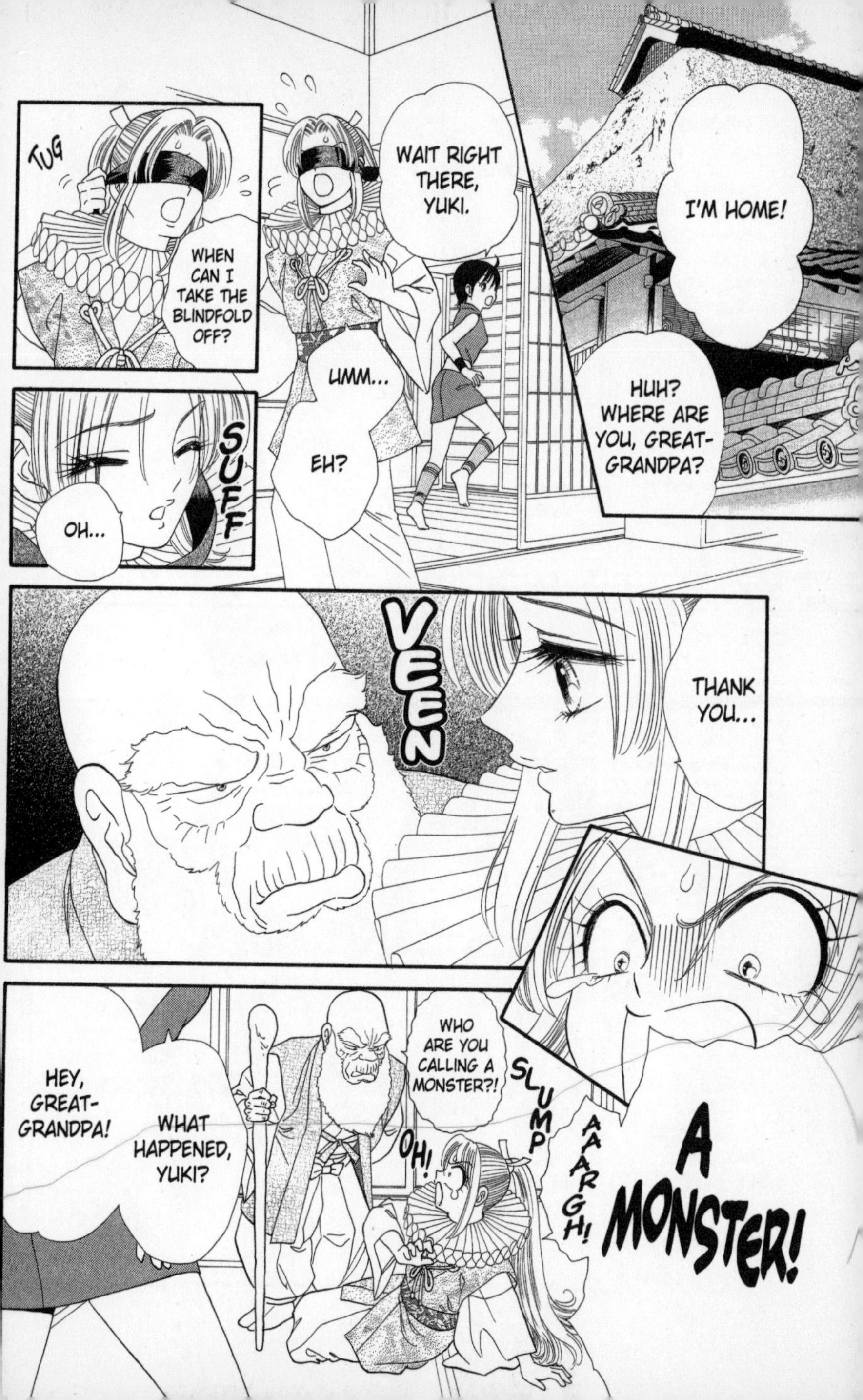
I'M HOME!
HUH? WHERE ARE YOU, GREAT-GRANDPA?
WAIT RIGHT THERE, YUKI.
TUG
WHEN CAN I TAKE THE BLINDFOLD OFF?
UMM...
EH?
SUFF
OH...
VEEN
THANK YOU...
A MONSTER!
AAARGH!
SLUMP
WHO ARE YOU CALLING A MONSTER?!
OH!
WHAT HAPPENED, YUKI?
HEY, GREAT-GRANDPA!

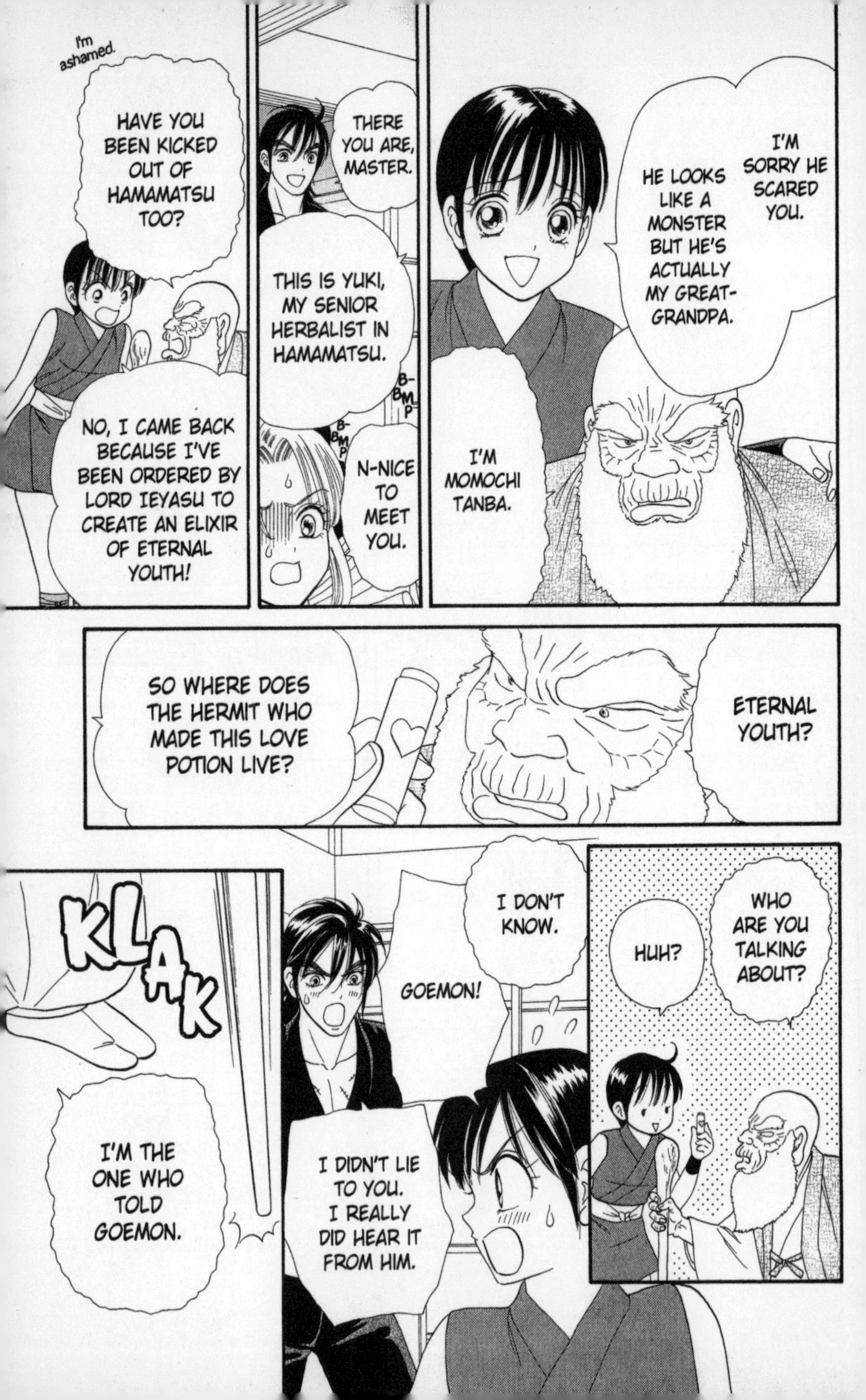

I'M SORRY HE SCARED YOU.
HE LOOKS LIKE A MONSTER BUT HE'S ACTUALLY MY GREAT-GRANDPA.
I'M MOMOCHI TANBA.
THERE YOU ARE, MASTER.
THIS IS YUKI, MY SENIOR HERBALIST IN HAMAMATSU.
B-BMP
B-BMP
N-NICE TO MEET YOU.
I'm ashamed.
HAVE YOU BEEN KICKED OUT OF HAMAMATSU TOO?
NO, I CAME BACK BECAUSE I'VE BEEN ORDERED BY LORD IEYASU TO CREATE AN ELIXIR OF ETERNAL YOUTH!
ETERNAL YOUTH?
SO WHERE DOES THE HERMIT WHO MADE THIS LOVE POTION LIVE?
WHO ARE YOU TALKING ABOUT?
HUH?
I DON'T KNOW.
GOEMON!
I DIDN'T LIE TO YOU. I REALLY DID HEAR IT FROM HIM.
KLAK
I'M THE ONE WHO TOLD GOEMON.

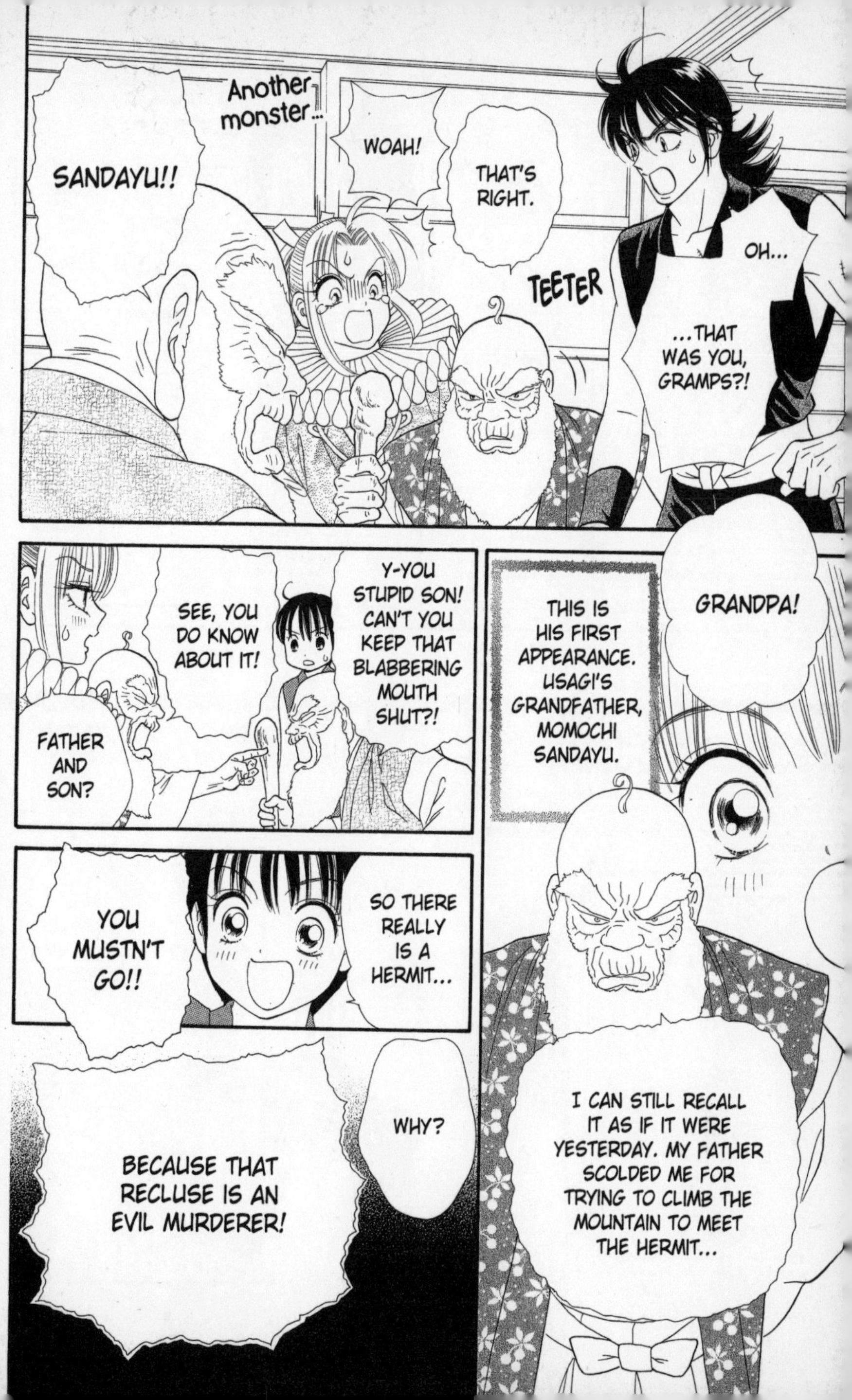
OH...
...THAT WAS YOU, GRAMPS?!
THAT'S RIGHT.
TEETER
WOAH!
Another monster...
SANDAYU!!
GRANDPA!
THIS IS HIS FIRST APPEARANCE. USAGI'S GRANDFATHER, MOMOCHI SANDAYU.
I CAN STILL RECALL IT AS IF IT WERE YESTERDAY. MY FATHER SCOLDED ME FOR TRYING TO CLIMB THE MOUNTAIN TO MEET THE HERMIT...
Y-YOU STUPID SON! CAN'T YOU KEEP THAT BLABBERING MOUTH SHUT?!
SEE, YOU DO KNOW ABOUT IT!
FATHER AND SON?
SO THERE REALLY IS A HERMIT...
YOU MUSTN'T GO!!
WHY?
BECAUSE THAT RECLUSE IS AN EVIL MURDERER!

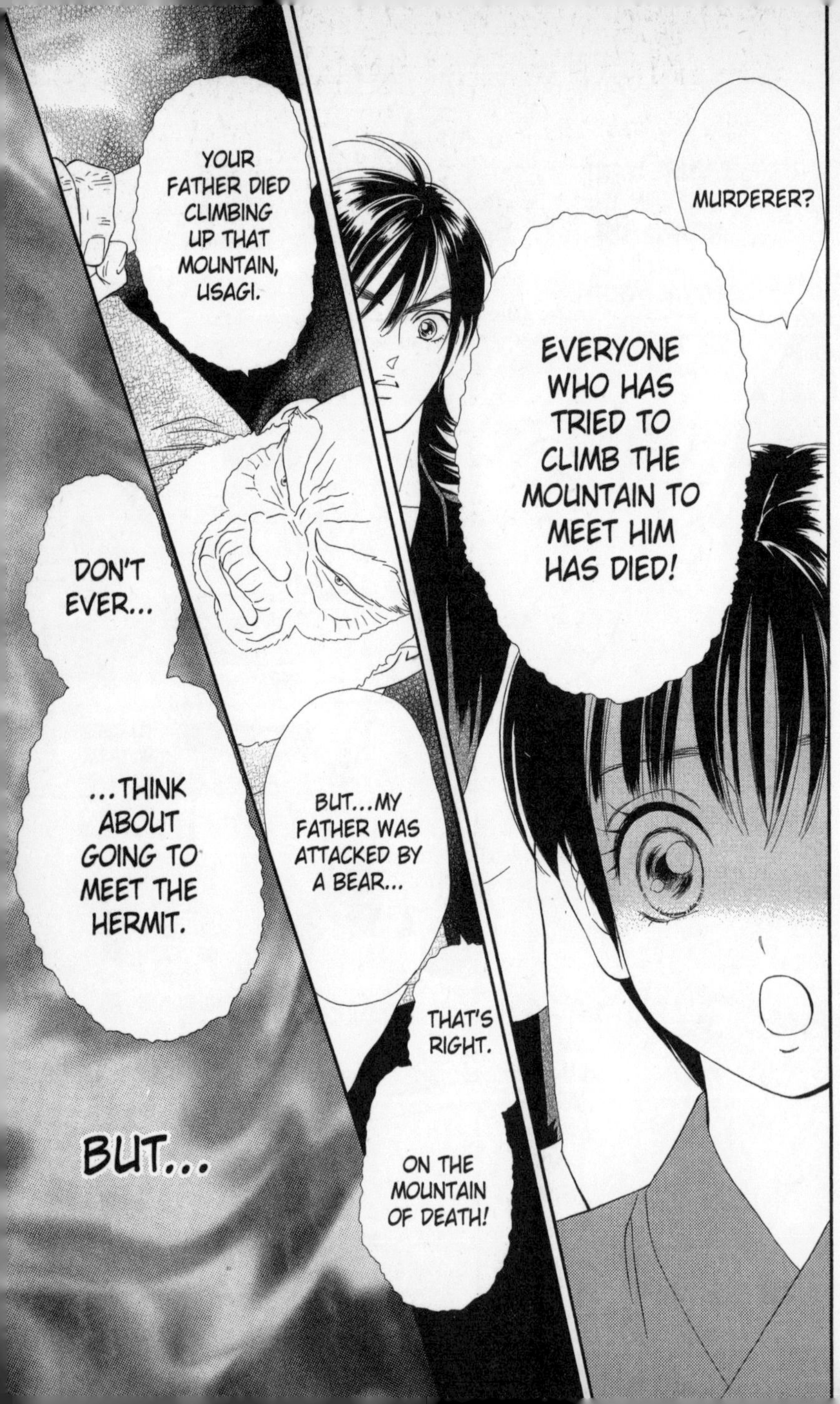
MURDERER?
EVERYONE WHO HAS TRIED TO CLIMB THE MOUNTAIN TO MEET HIM HAS DIED!
YOUR FATHER DIED CLIMBING UP THAT MOUNTAIN, USAGI.
BUT...MY FATHER WAS ATTACKED BY A BEAR...
THAT'S RIGHT.
ON THE MOUNTAIN OF DEATH!
DON'T EVER...
...THINK ABOUT GOING TO MEET THE HERMIT.
BUT...

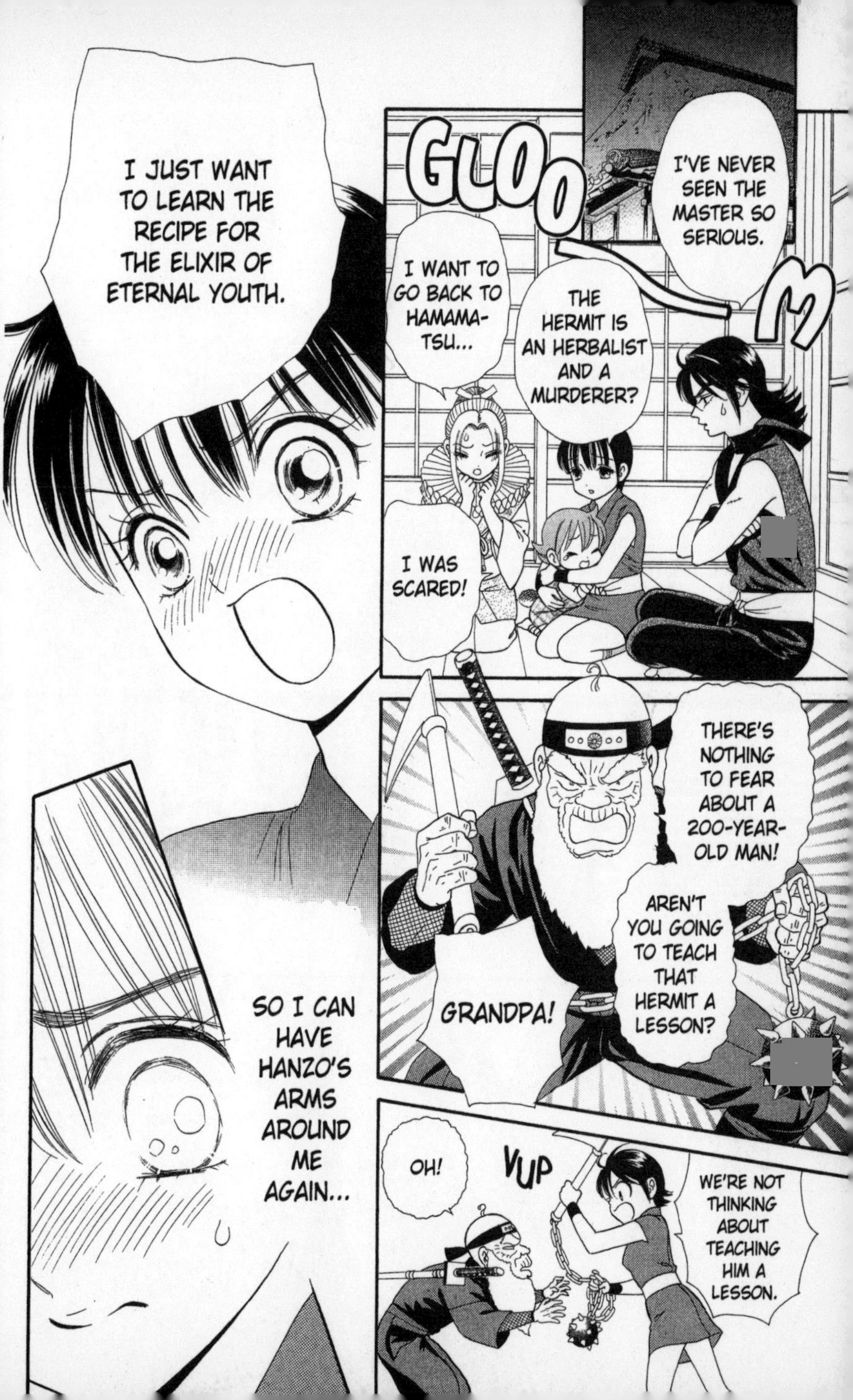
I'VE NEVER SEEN THE MASTER SO SERIOUS.
GLOO~M
THE HERMIT IS AN HERBALIST AND A MURDERER?
I WANT TO GO BACK TO HAMAMA-TSU...
I WAS SCARED!
I JUST WANT TO LEARN THE RECIPE FOR THE ELIXIR OF ETERNAL YOUTH.
THERE'S NOTHING TO FEAR ABOUT A 200-YEAR-OLD MAN!
AREN'T YOU GOING TO TEACH THAT HERMIT A LESSON?
GRANDPA!
WE'RE NOT THINKING ABOUT TEACHING HIM A LESSON.
VUP
OH!
SO I CAN HAVE HANZO'S ARMS AROUND ME AGAIN...

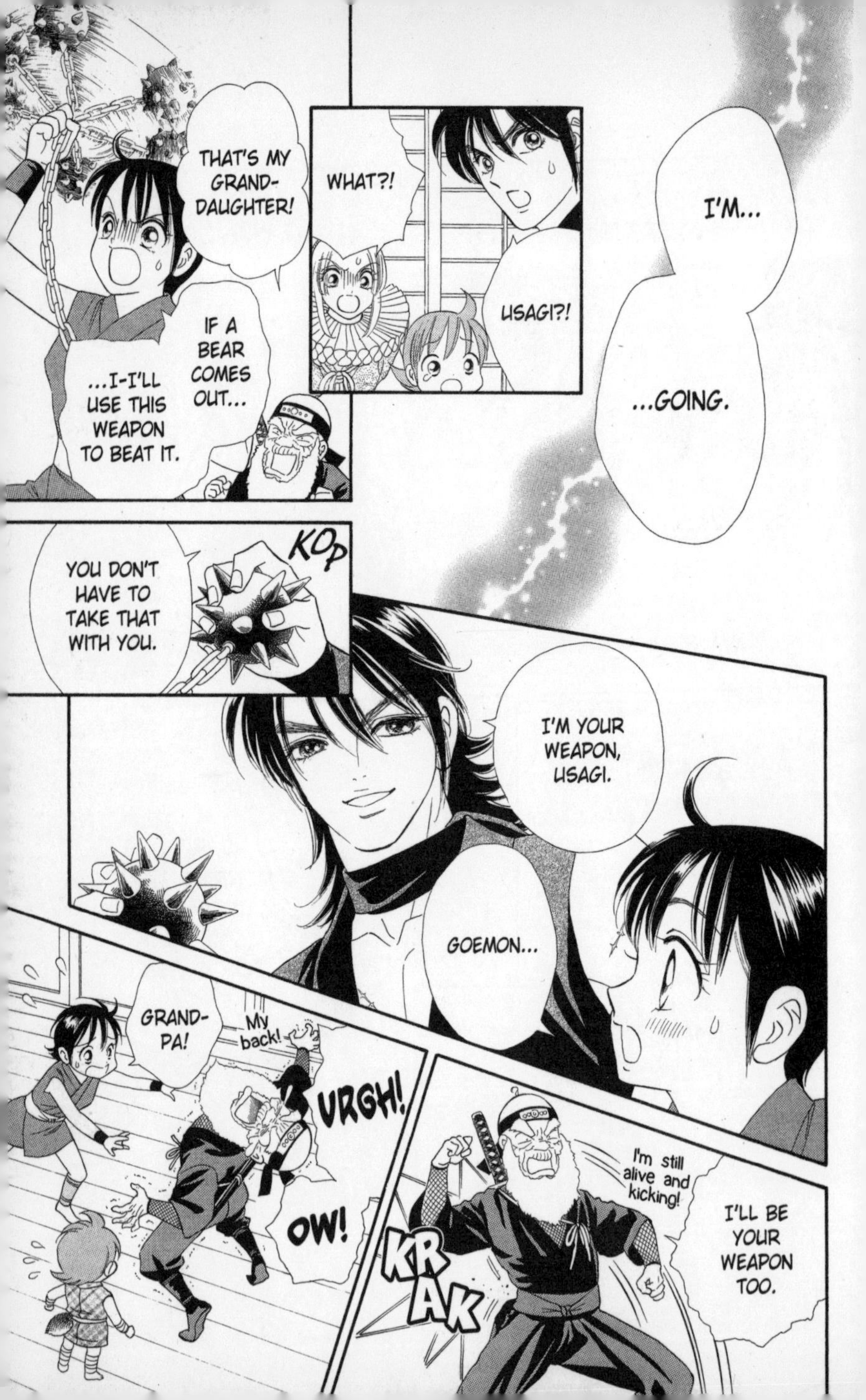
I'M...
...GOING.
WHAT?!
USAGI?!
THAT'S MY GRAND-DAUGHTER!
IF A BEAR COMES OUT...
...I-I'LL USE THIS WEAPON TO BEAT IT.
KOP
YOU DON'T HAVE TO TAKE THAT WITH YOU.
I'M YOUR WEAPON, USAGI.
GOEMON...
I'LL BE YOUR WEAPON TOO.
I'm still alive and kicking!
KRAK
URGH!
My back!
GRAND-PA!
OW!

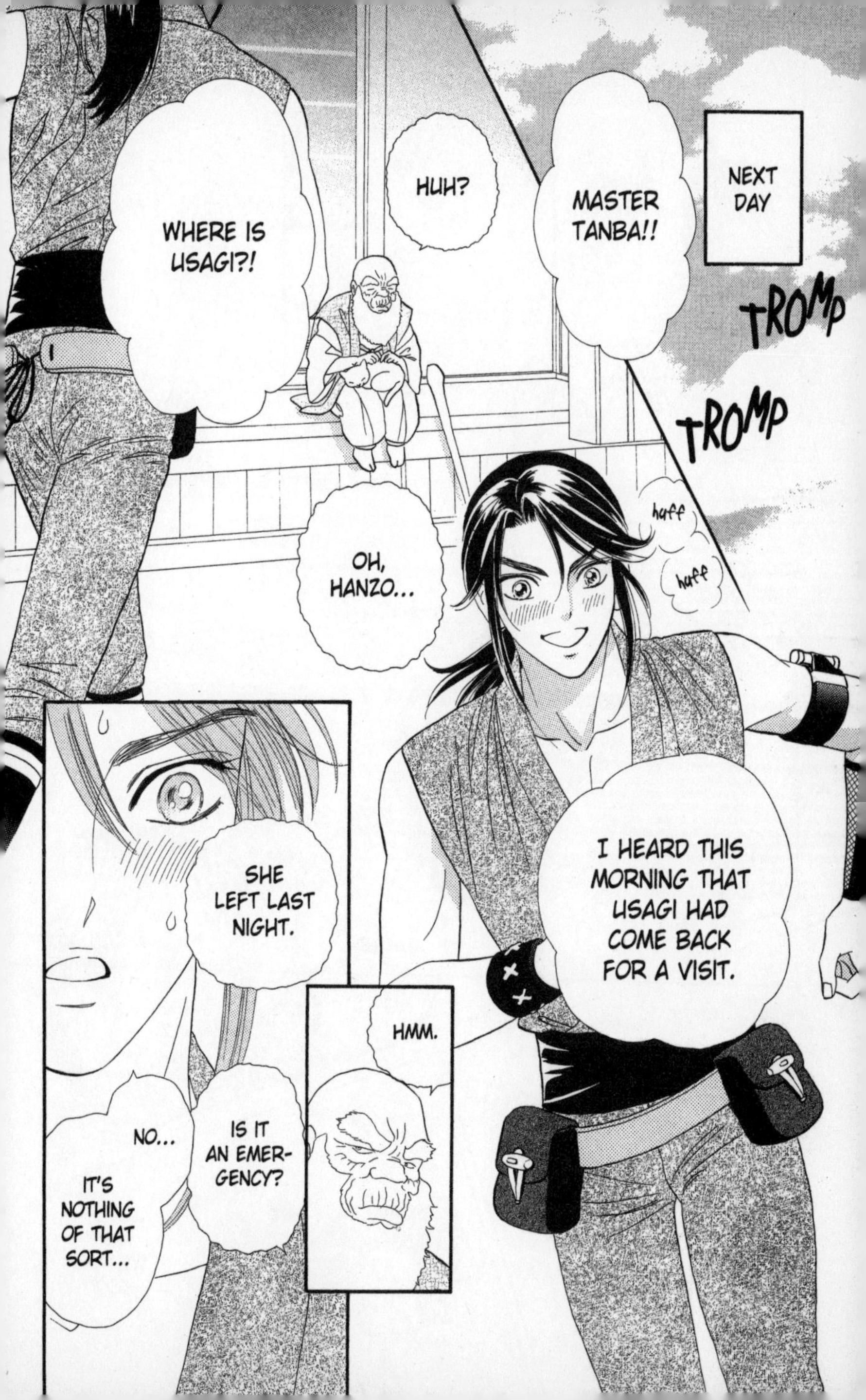
NEXT DAY
TROMP
TROMP
MASTER TANBA!!
huff
huff
HUH?
OH, HANZO...
I HEARD THIS MORNING THAT USAGI HAD COME BACK FOR A VISIT.
WHERE IS USAGI?!
HMM.
SHE LEFT LAST NIGHT.
IS IT AN EMERGENCY?
NO...
IT'S NOTHING OF THAT SORT...

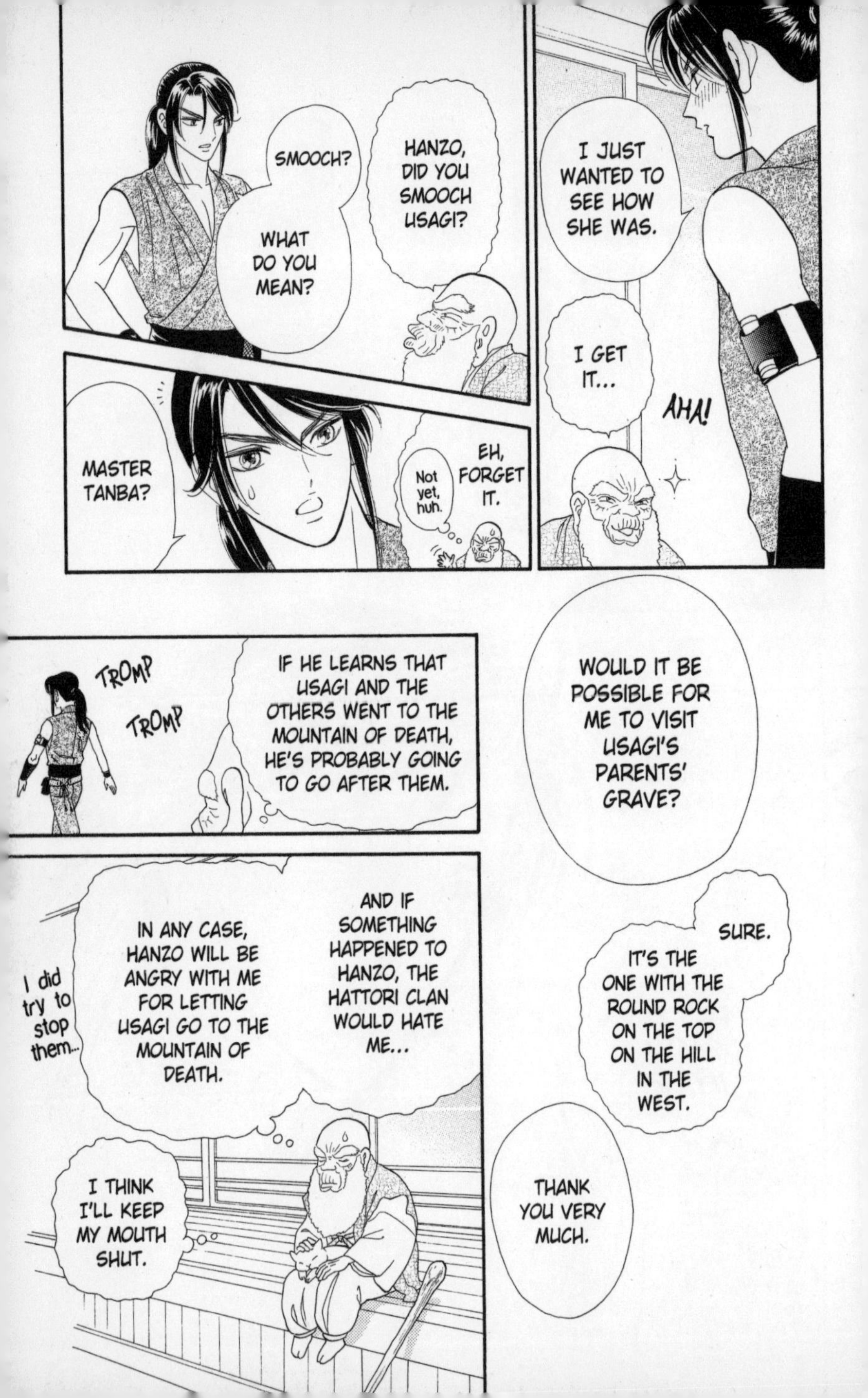
I JUST WANTED TO SEE HOW SHE WAS.
I GET IT...
AHA!
HANZO, DID YOU SMOOCH USAGI?
SMOOCH?
WHAT DO YOU MEAN?
EH, FORGET IT.
Not yet, huh.
MASTER TANBA?
WOULD IT BE POSSIBLE FOR ME TO VISIT USAGI'S PARENTS' GRAVE?
SURE.
IT'S THE ONE WITH THE ROUND ROCK ON THE TOP ON THE HILL IN THE WEST.
THANK YOU VERY MUCH.
IF HE LEARNS THAT USAGI AND THE OTHERS WENT TO THE MOUNTAIN OF DEATH, HE'S PROBABLY GOING TO GO AFTER THEM.
TROMP
TROMP
AND IF SOMETHING HAPPENED TO HANZO, THE HATTORI CLAN WOULD HATE ME...
IN ANY CASE, HANZO WILL BE ANGRY WITH ME FOR LETTING USAGI GO TO THE MOUNTAIN OF DEATH.
I did try to stop them...
I THINK I'LL KEEP MY MOUTH SHUT.

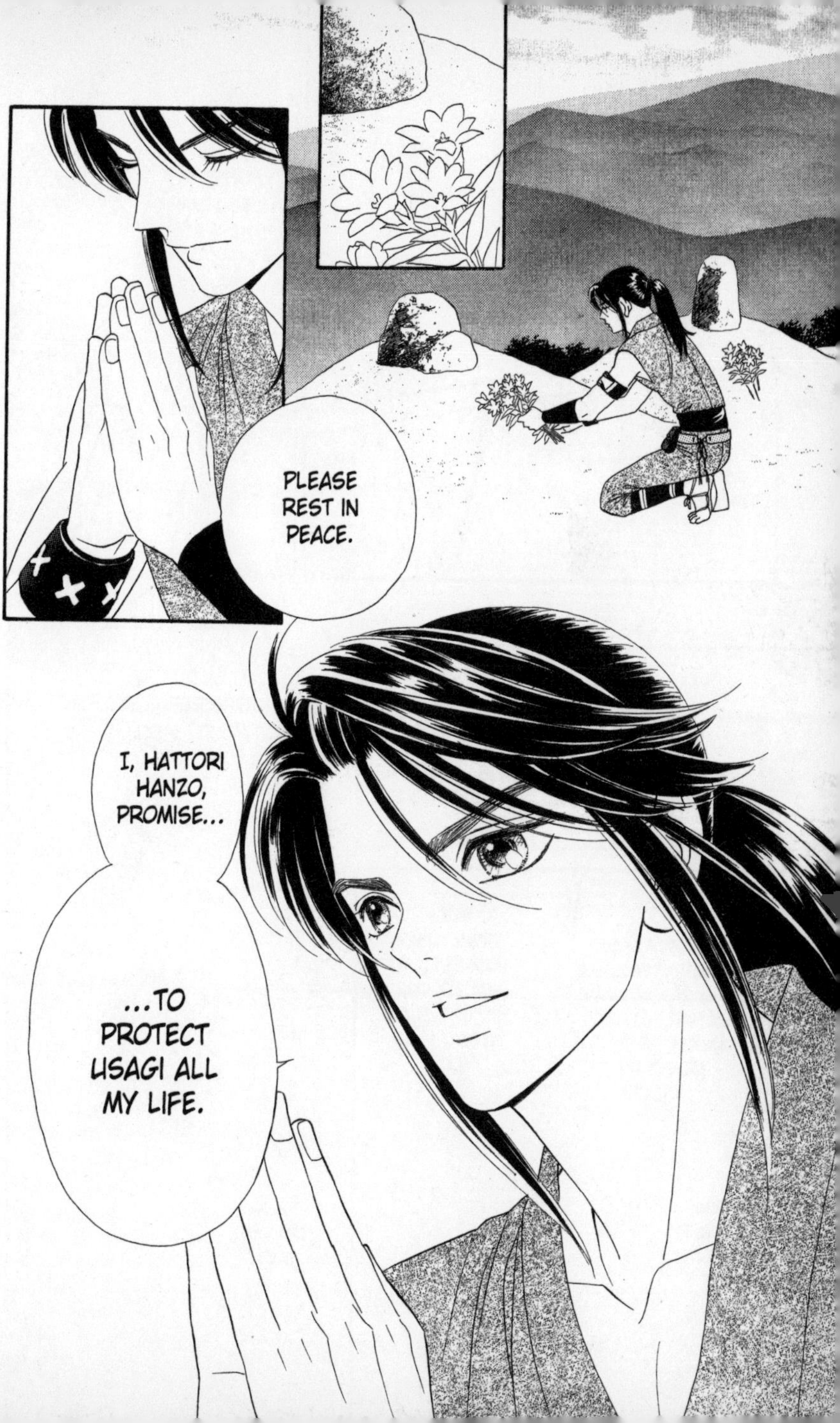
PLEASE REST IN PEACE.
I, HATTORI HANZO, PROMISE...
...TO PROTECT USAGI ALL MY LIFE.

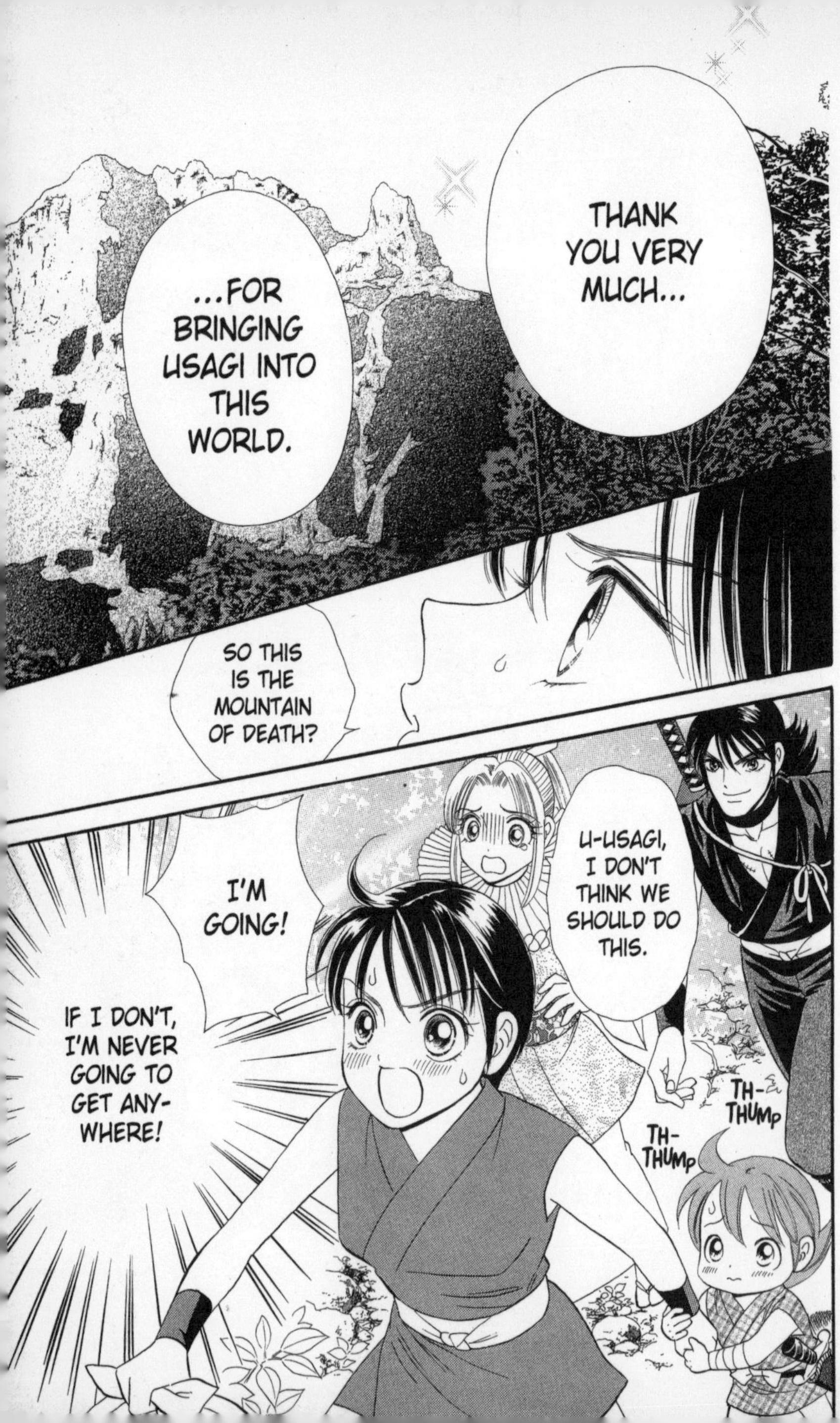
THANK YOU VERY MUCH...
...FOR BRINGING USAGI INTO THIS WORLD.
SO THIS IS THE MOUNTAIN OF DEATH?
U-USAGI, I DON'T THINK WE SHOULD DO THIS.
I'M GOING!
IF I DON'T, I'M NEVER GOING TO GET ANY-WHERE!
TH-THUMP
TH-THUMP

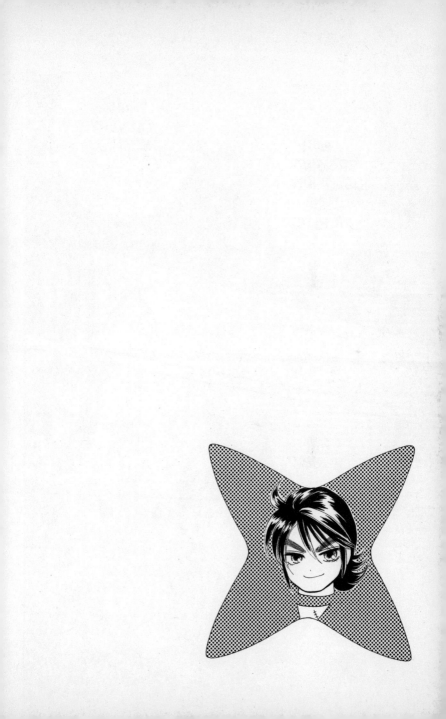

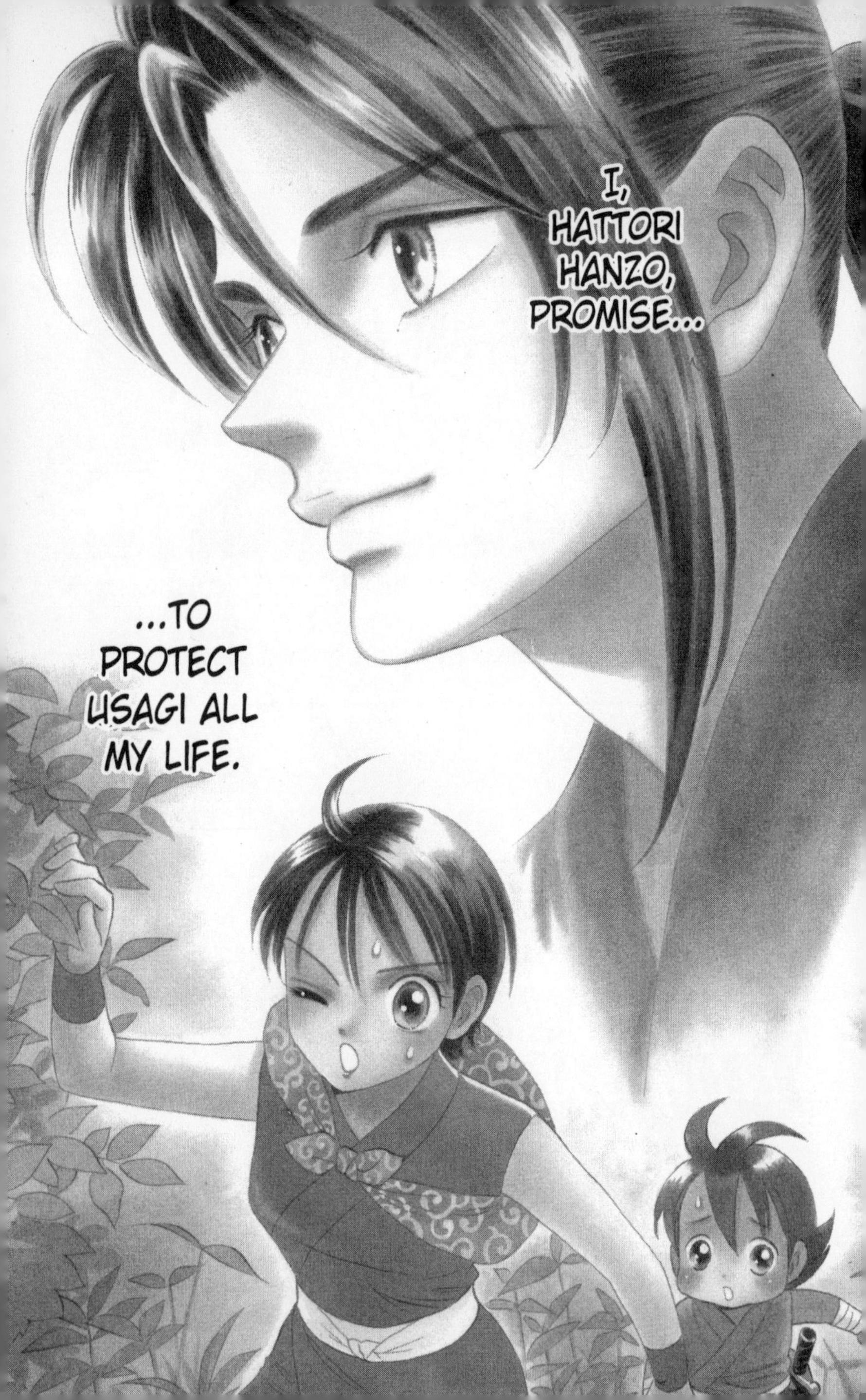
I, HATTORI HANZO, PROMISE...
...TO PROTECT USAGI ALL MY LIFE.

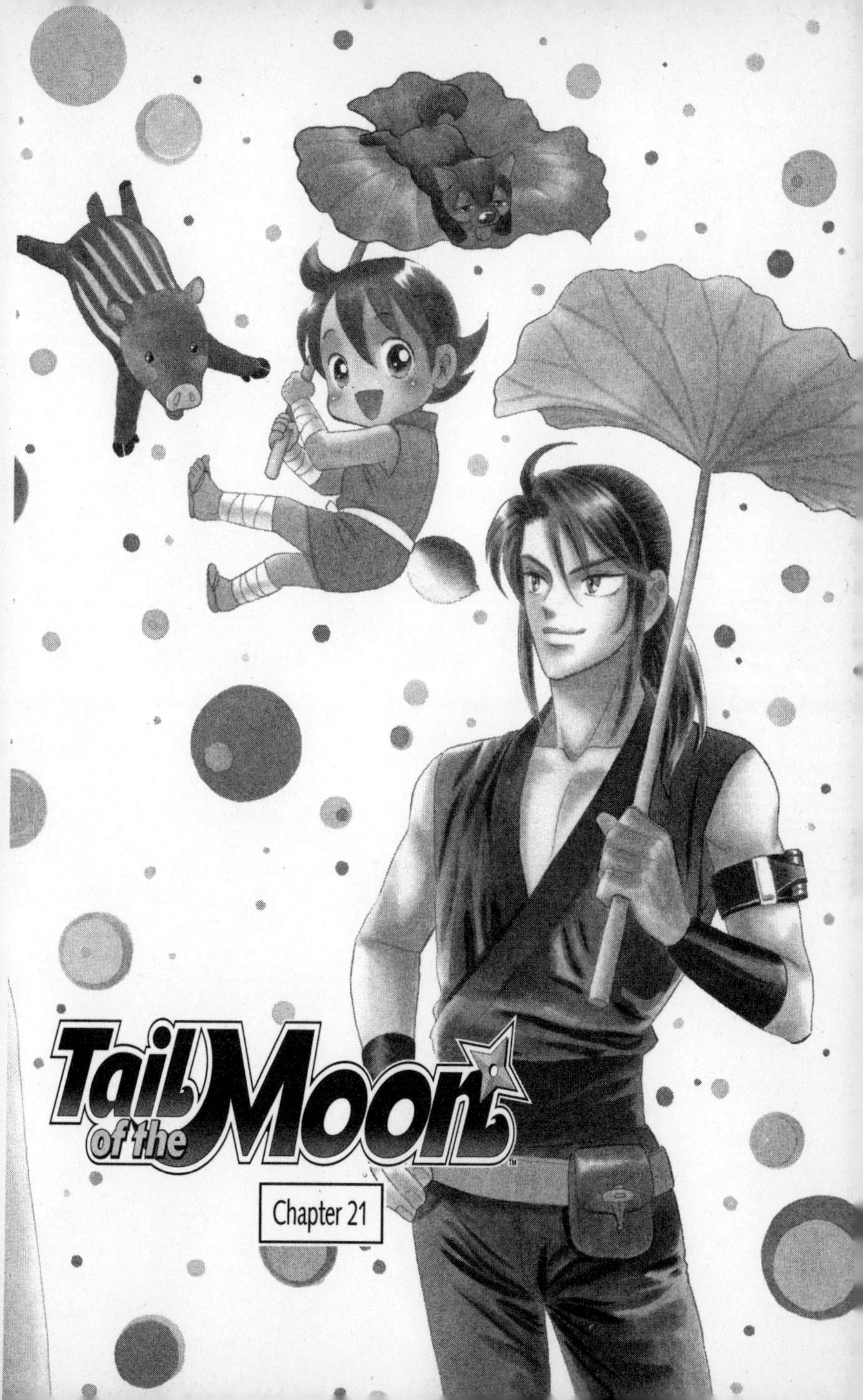
Tail of the Moon™
Chapter 21

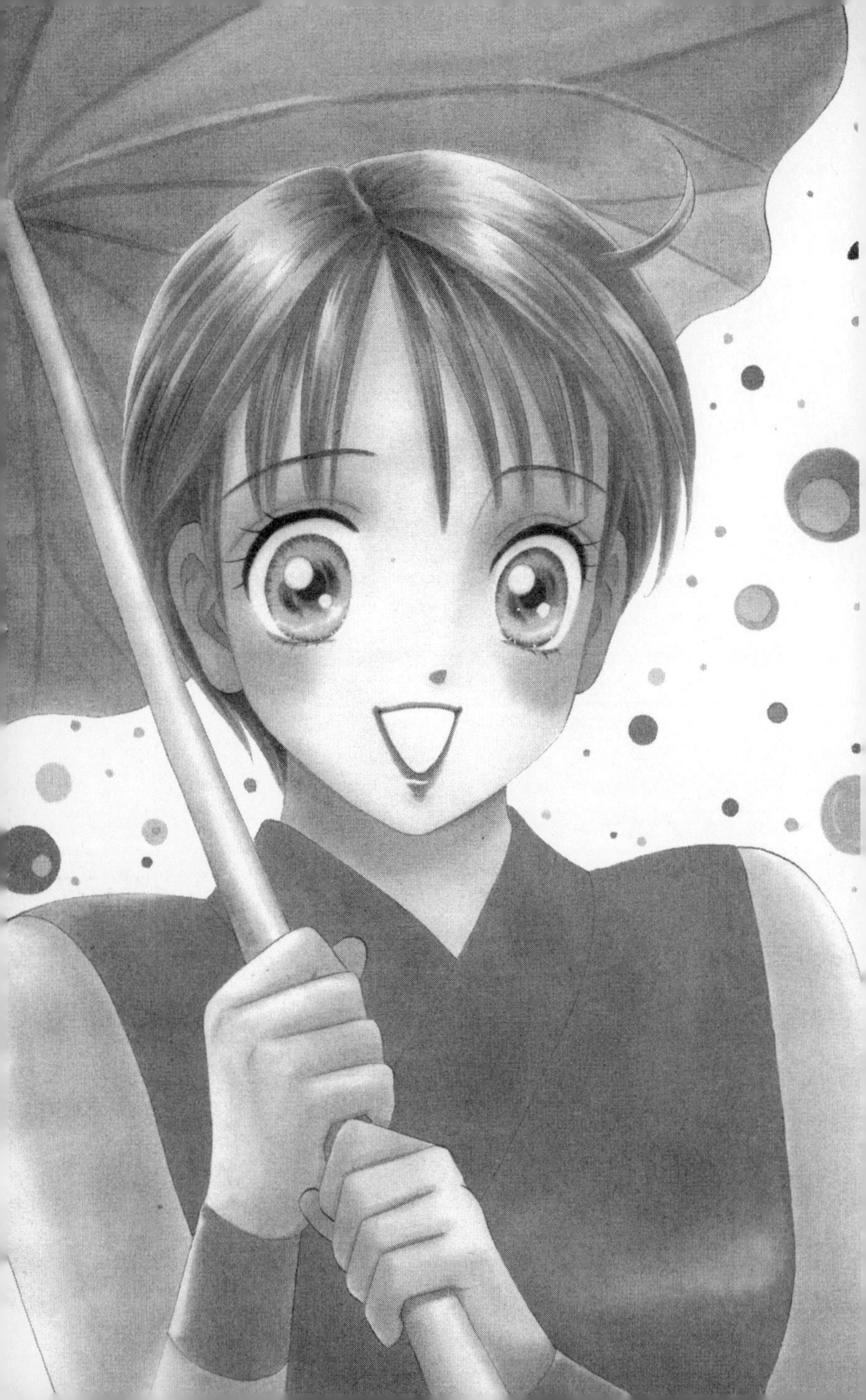

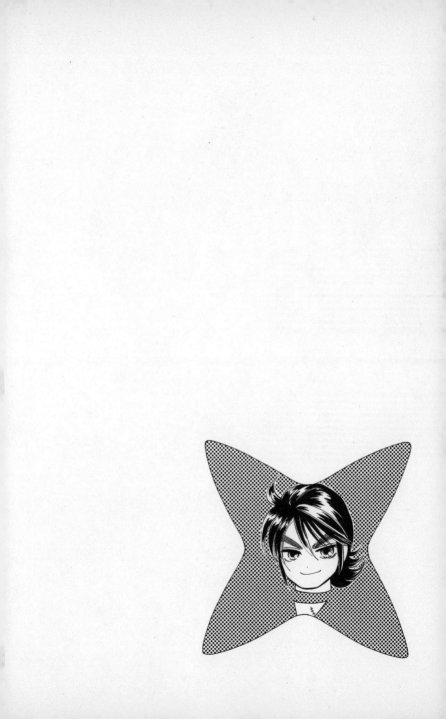

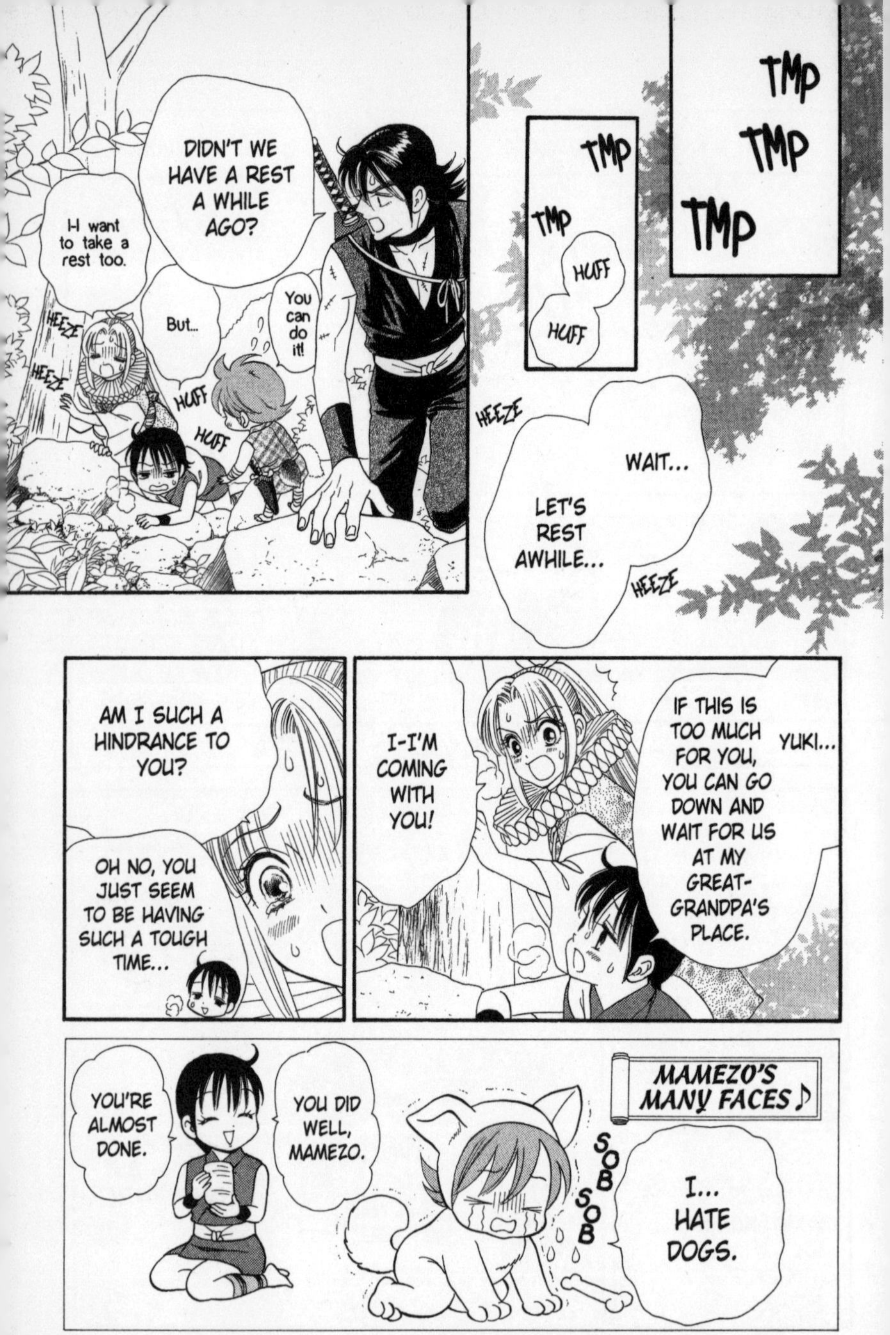
TMP
TMP
TMP
TMP
TMP
HUFF
HUFF
HEEZE
WAIT...
LET'S REST AWHILE...
HEEZE
DIDN'T WE HAVE A REST A WHILE AGO?
I-I want to take a rest too.
You can do it!
But...
HEEZE
HEEZE
HUFF
HUFF
YUKI...
IF THIS IS TOO MUCH FOR YOU, YOU CAN GO DOWN AND WAIT FOR US AT MY GREAT-GRANDPA'S PLACE.
I-I'M COMING WITH YOU!
AM I SUCH A HINDRANCE TO YOU?
OH NO, YOU JUST SEEM TO BE HAVING SUCH A TOUGH TIME...
MAMEZO'S MANY FACES♪
I... HATE DOGS.
SOB
SOB
YOU DID WELL, MAMEZO.
YOU'RE ALMOST DONE.

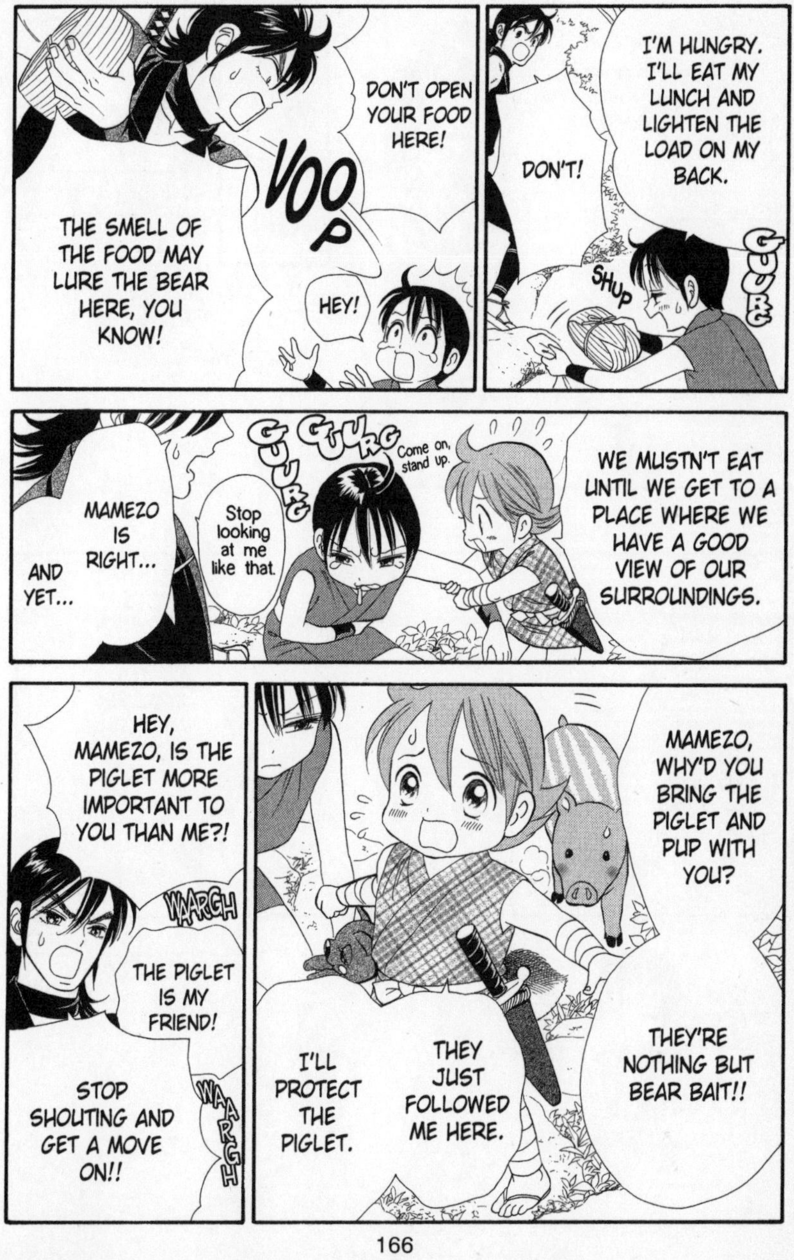
I'M HUNGRY. I'LL EAT MY LUNCH AND LIGHTEN THE LOAD ON MY BACK.
DON'T!
GUURG
SHUP
DON'T OPEN YOUR FOOD HERE!
VOOP
HEY!
THE SMELL OF THE FOOD MAY LURE THE BEAR HERE, YOU KNOW!
WE MUSTN'T EAT UNTIL WE GET TO A PLACE WHERE WE HAVE A GOOD VIEW OF OUR SURROUNDINGS.
Come on, stand up.
GUURG
GUURG
Stop looking at me like that.
MAMEZO IS RIGHT...
AND YET...
MAMEZO, WHY'D YOU BRING THE PIGLET AND PUP WITH YOU?
THEY'RE NOTHING BUT BEAR BAIT!!
THEY JUST FOLLOWED ME HERE.
I'LL PROTECT THE PIGLET.
HEY, MAMEZO, IS THE PIGLET MORE IMPORTANT TO YOU THAN ME?!
WAARGH
THE PIGLET IS MY FRIEND!
WAARGH
STOP SHOUTING AND GET A MOVE ON!!

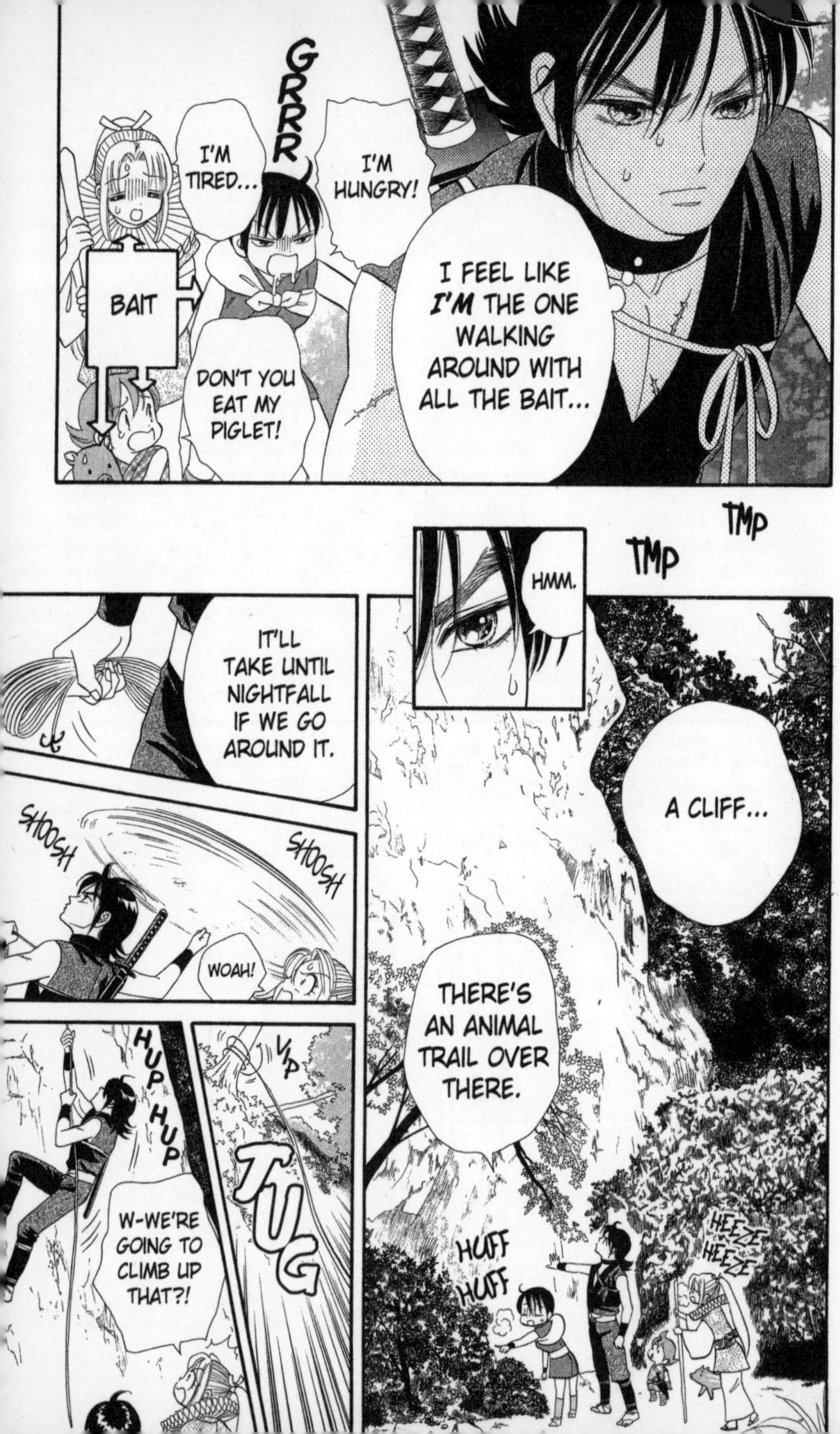
GRRR
I'M HUNGRY!
I'M TIRED...
BAIT
DON'T YOU EAT MY PIGLET!
I FEEL LIKE *I'M* THE ONE WALKING AROUND WITH ALL THE BAIT...
TMP
TMP
HMM.
A CLIFF...
THERE'S AN ANIMAL TRAIL OVER THERE.
HUFF HUFF
HEEZE HEEZE
IT'LL TAKE UNTIL NIGHTFALL IF WE GO AROUND IT.
SHOOSH
SHOOSH
WOAH!
VIP
TUG
HUP HUP
W-WE'RE GOING TO CLIMB UP THAT?!

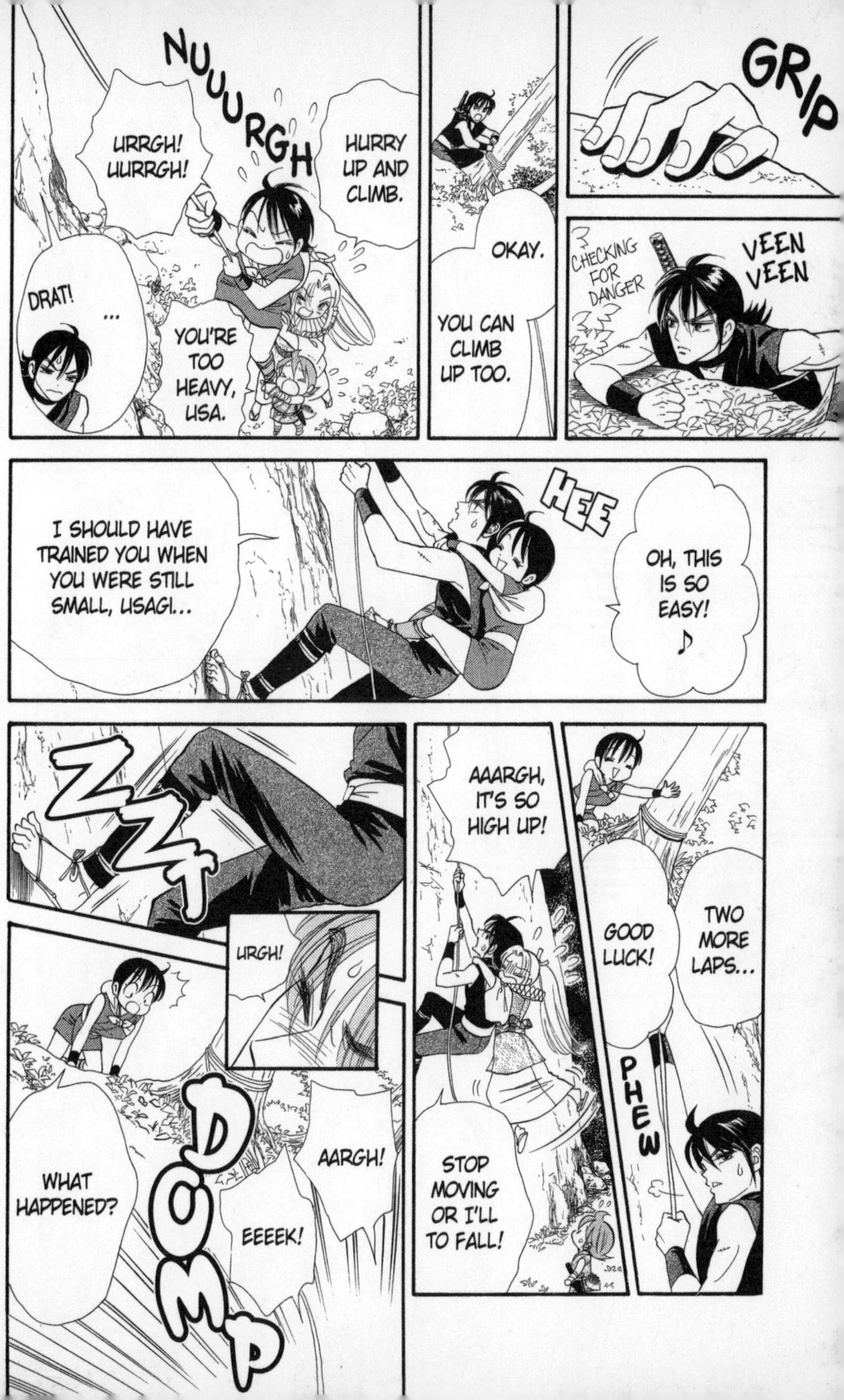
GRIP
CHECKING FOR DANGER
VEEN VEEN
OKAY.
YOU CAN CLIMB UP TOO.
HURRY UP AND CLIMB.
NUUURGH
URRGH! UURRGH!
YOU'RE TOO HEAVY, USA.
DRAT!
...
OH, THIS IS SO EASY! ♪
HEE
I SHOULD HAVE TRAINED YOU WHEN YOU WERE STILL SMALL, USAGI...
TWO MORE LAPS...
GOOD LUCK!
PHEW
AAARGH, IT'S SO HIGH UP!
STOP MOVING OR I'LL TO FALL!
ZZNT
URGH!
AARGH!
EEEEK!
DOMP
WHAT HAPPENED?

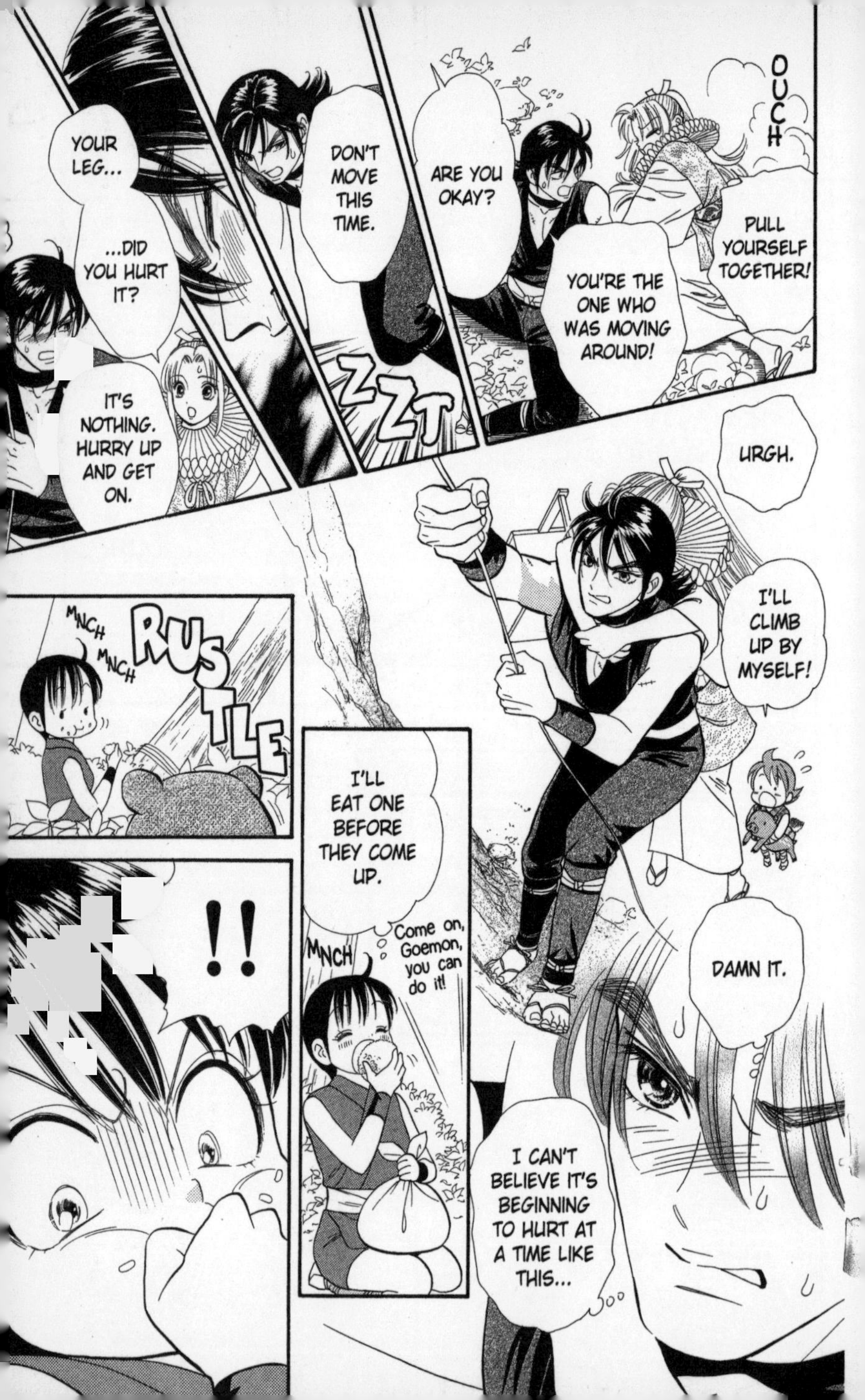
OUCH
ARE YOU OKAY?
PULL YOURSELF TOGETHER!
YOU'RE THE ONE WHO WAS MOVING AROUND!
DON'T MOVE THIS TIME.
ZZZT
YOUR LEG...
...DID YOU HURT IT?
IT'S NOTHING. HURRY UP AND GET ON.
URGH.
I'LL CLIMB UP BY MYSELF!
DAMN IT.
I CAN'T BELIEVE IT'S BEGINNING TO HURT AT A TIME LIKE THIS...
I'LL EAT ONE BEFORE THEY COME UP.
MNCH
Come on, Goemon, you can do it!
MNCH MNCH
RUSTLE
!!

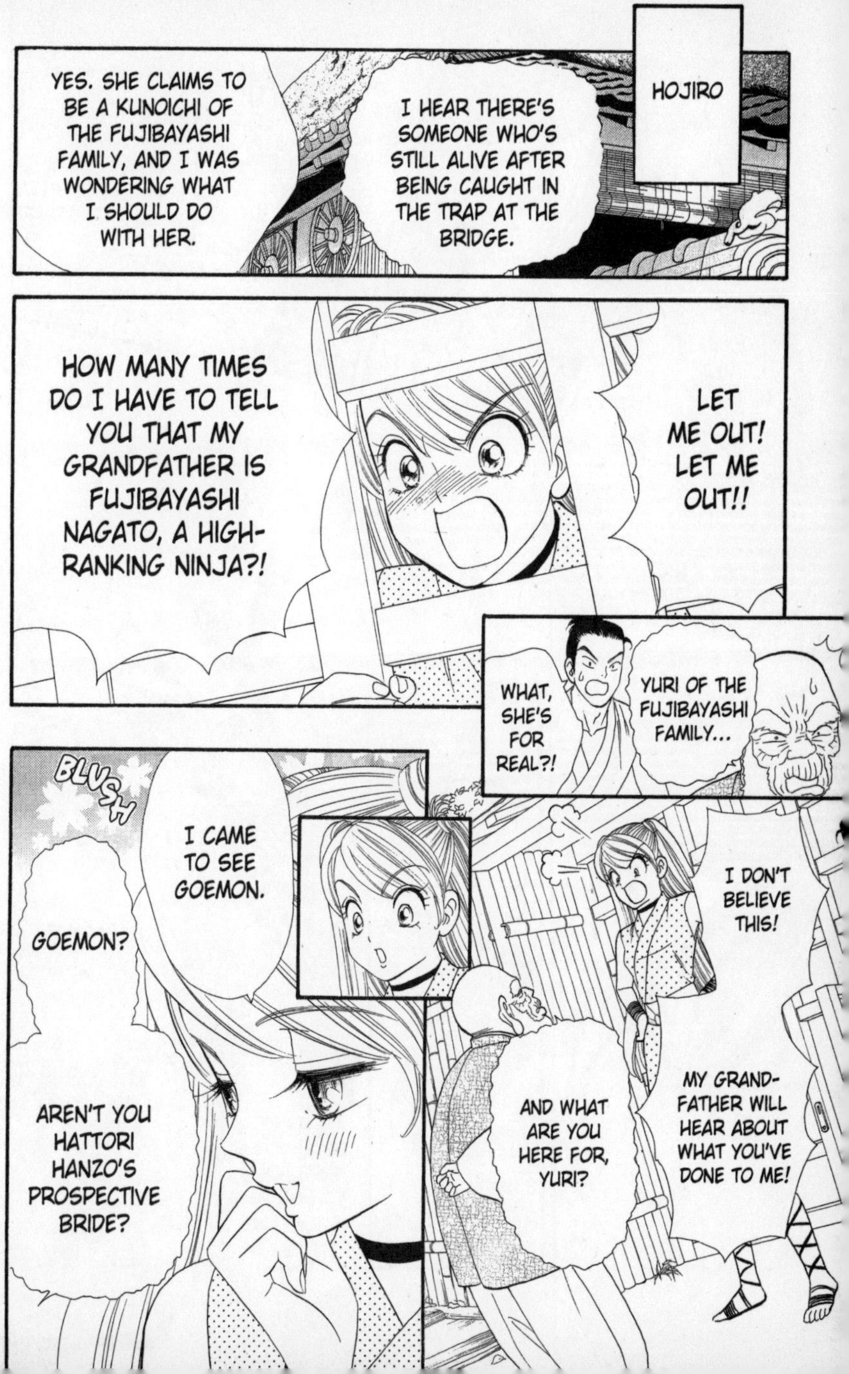
HOJIRO
I HEAR THERE'S SOMEONE WHO'S STILL ALIVE AFTER BEING CAUGHT IN THE TRAP AT THE BRIDGE.
YES. SHE CLAIMS TO BE A KUNOICHI OF THE FUJIBAYASHI FAMILY, AND I WAS WONDERING WHAT I SHOULD DO WITH HER.
LET ME OUT! LET ME OUT!!
HOW MANY TIMES DO I HAVE TO TELL YOU THAT MY GRANDFATHER IS FUJIBAYASHI NAGATO, A HIGH-RANKING NINJA?!
YURI OF THE FUJIBAYASHI FAMILY...
WHAT, SHE'S FOR REAL?!
I DON'T BELIEVE THIS!
MY GRAND-FATHER WILL HEAR ABOUT WHAT YOU'VE DONE TO ME!
AND WHAT ARE YOU HERE FOR, YURI?
BLUSH
I CAME TO SEE GOEMON.
GOEMON?
AREN'T YOU HATTORI HANZO'S PROSPECTIVE BRIDE?

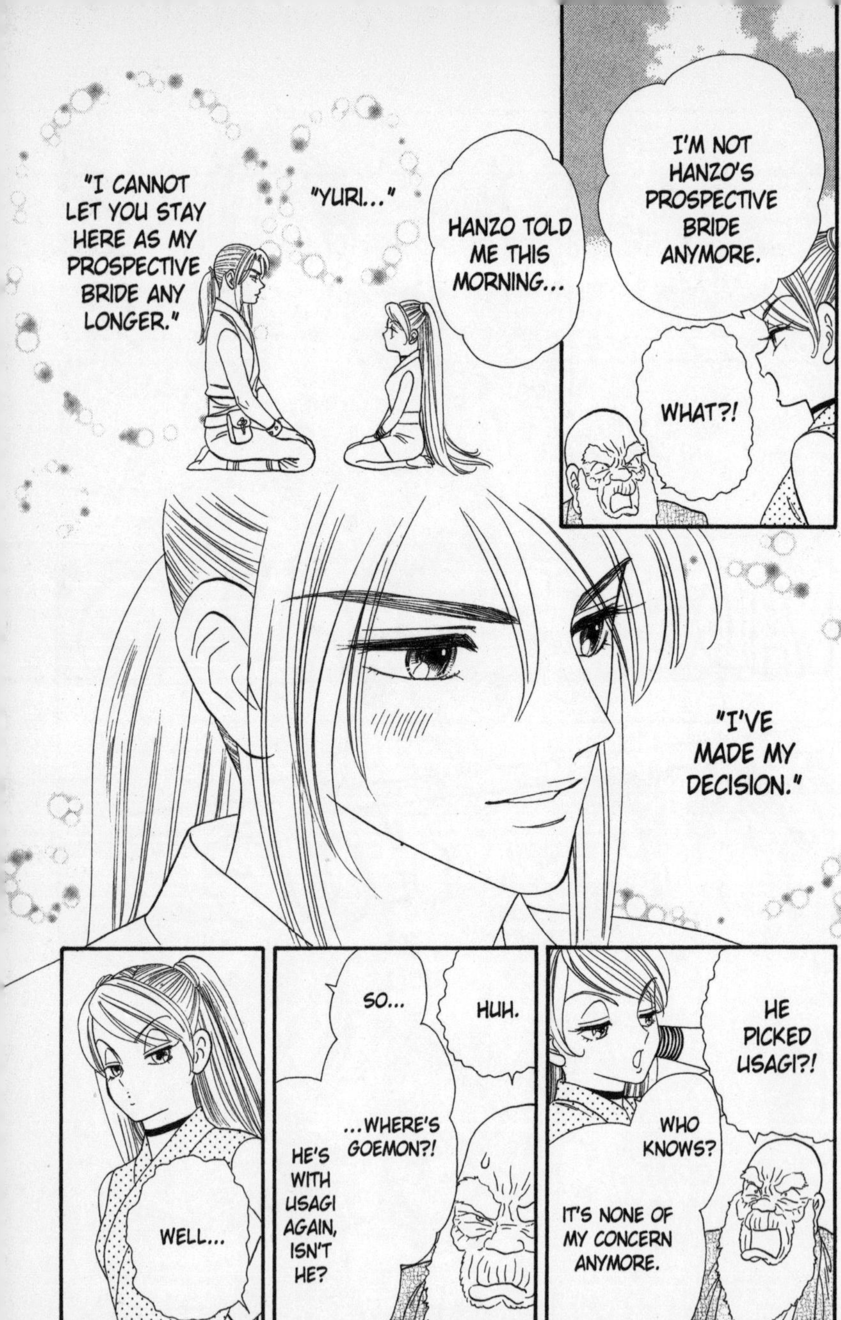
I'M NOT HANZO'S PROSPECTIVE BRIDE ANYMORE.
WHAT?!
HANZO TOLD ME THIS MORNING...
"YURI..."
"I CANNOT LET YOU STAY HERE AS MY PROSPECTIVE BRIDE ANY LONGER."
"I'VE MADE MY DECISION."
HE PICKED USAGI?!
WHO KNOWS?
IT'S NONE OF MY CONCERN ANYMORE.
HUH.
SO...
...WHERE'S GOEMON?!
HE'S WITH USAGI AGAIN, ISN'T HE?
WELL...

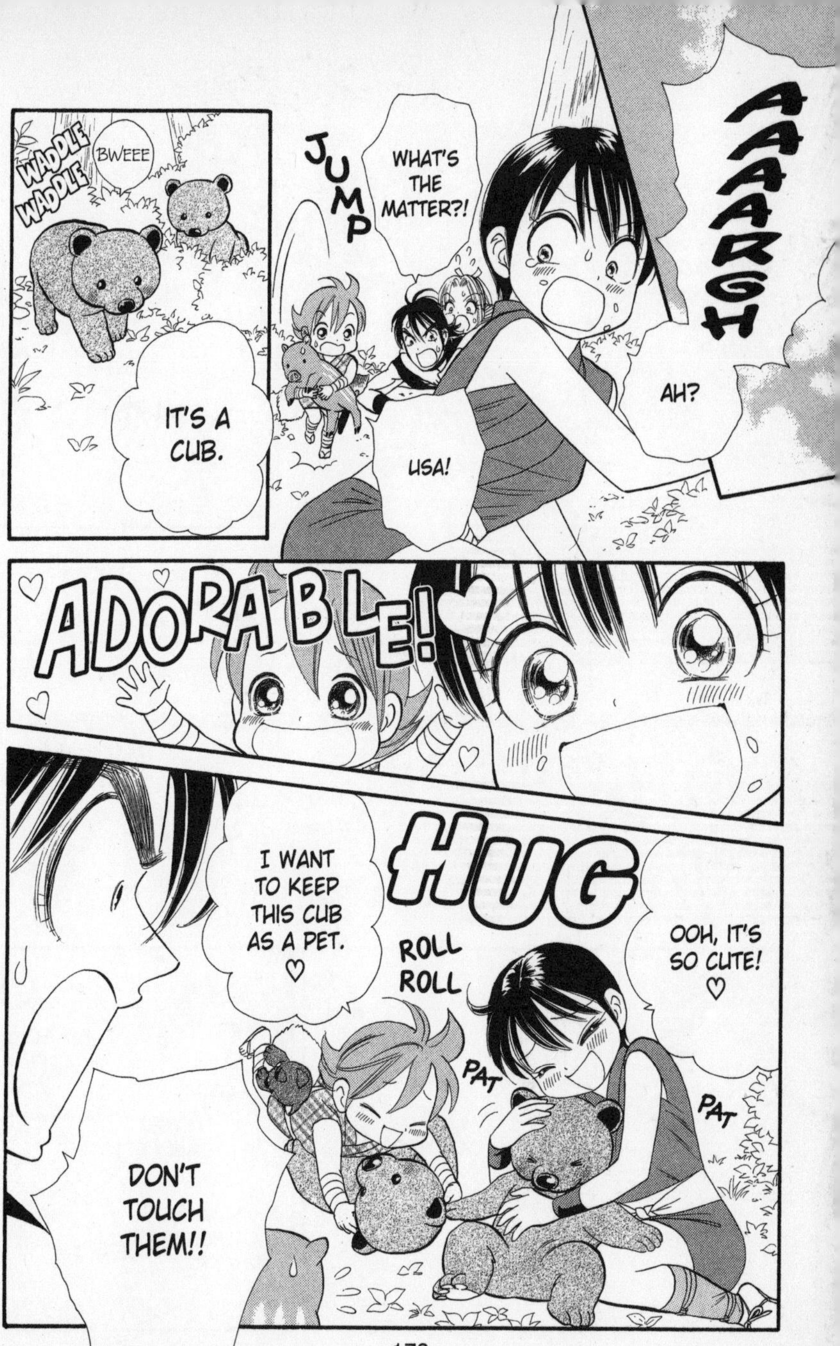
AAAARGH
AH?
WHAT'S THE MATTER?!
JUMP
USA!
WADDLE WADDLE
BWEEE
IT'S A CUB.
ADORABLE!
HUG
OOH, IT'S SO CUTE! ♡
I WANT TO KEEP THIS CUB AS A PET. ♡
ROLL ROLL
PAT PAT
DON'T TOUCH THEM!!

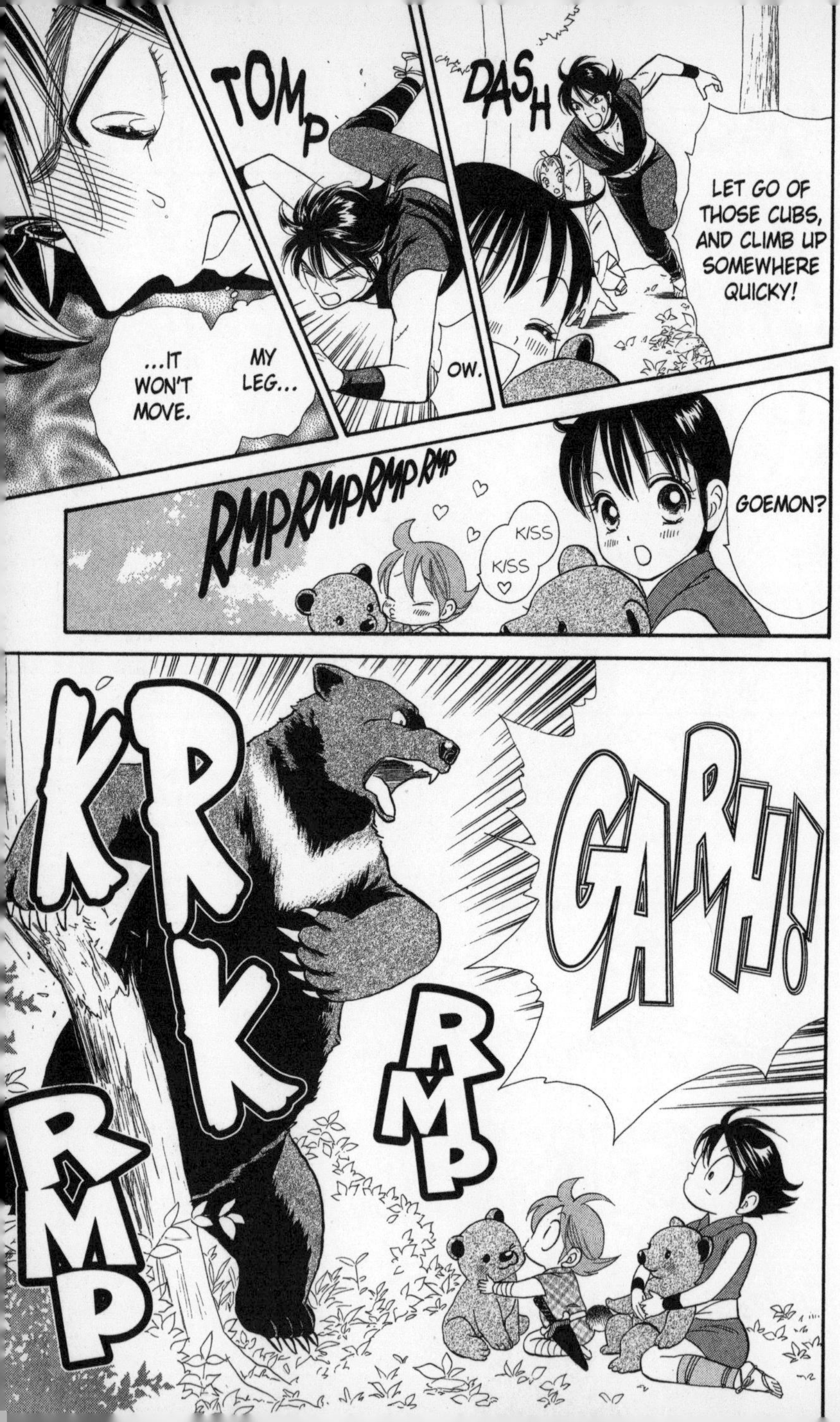
DASH
LET GO OF THOSE CUBS, AND CLIMB UP SOMEWHERE QUICKY!
OW.
TOMP
MY LEG...
...IT WON'T MOVE.
GOEMON?
KISS KISS
RMPRMPRMPRMP
GARH!
KRK
RMP
RMP

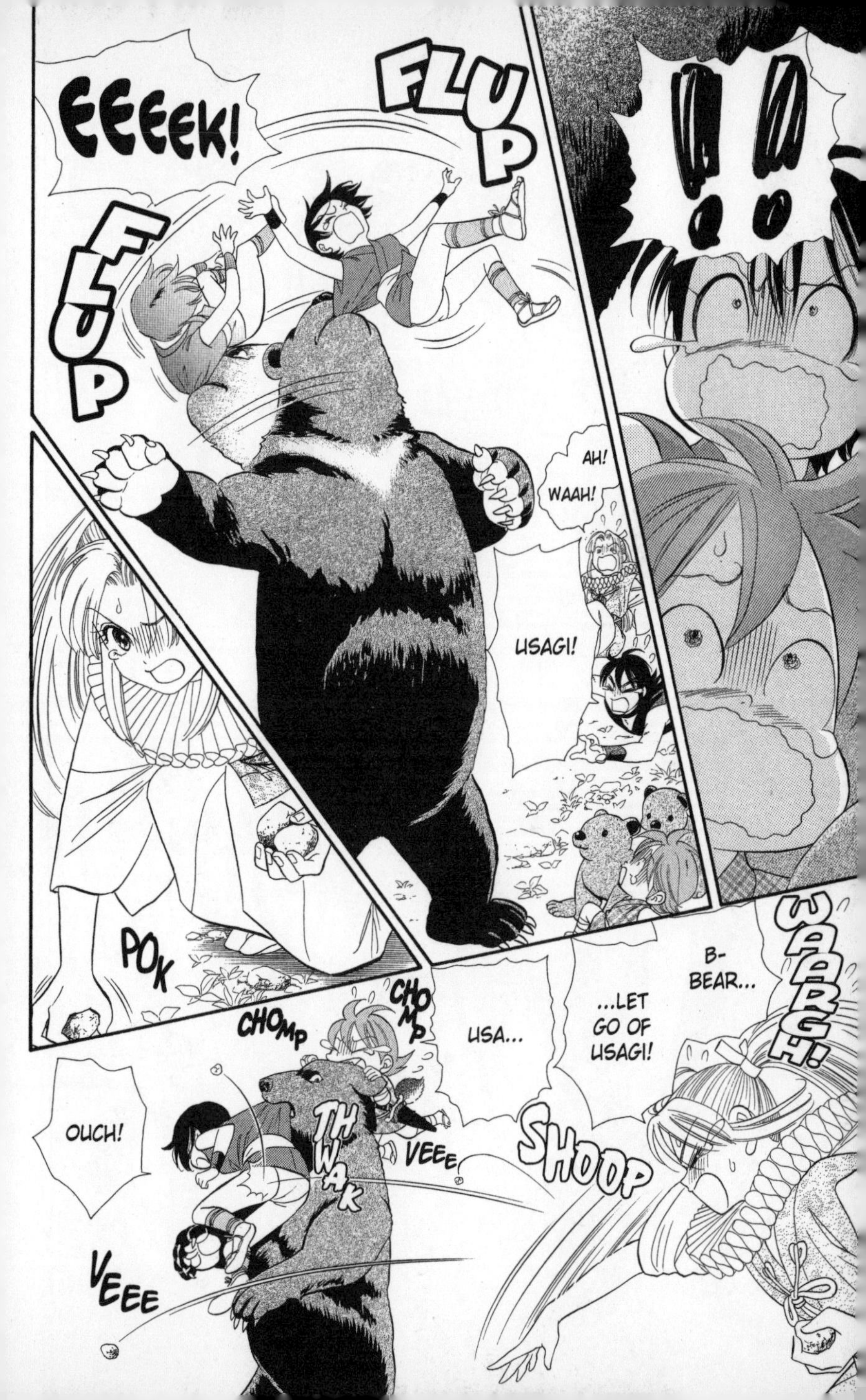
!!
EEEEK!
FLUP
FLUP
AH!
WAAH!
USAGI!
POK
WAARGH!
B-BEAR...
...LET GO OF USAGI!
USA...
SHOOP
CHOMP
CHOMP
THWAK
VEEE
OUCH!
VEEE

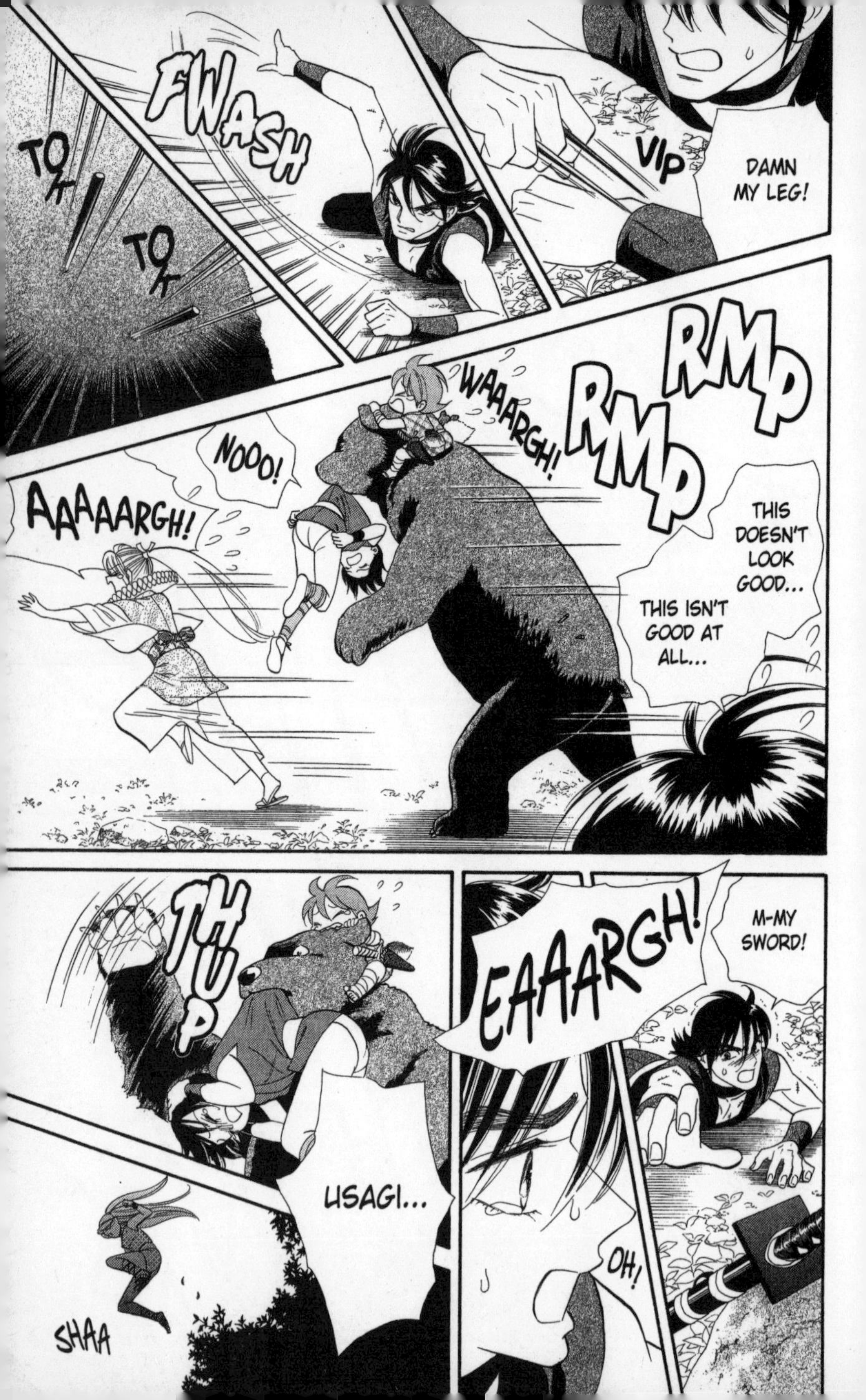
VIP
DAMN MY LEG!
FWASH
TOK
TOK
RMP
RMP
WAAARGH!
THIS DOESN'T LOOK GOOD...
THIS ISN'T GOOD AT ALL...
NOOO!
AAAAARGH!
M-MY SWORD!
EAAARGH!
OH!
THUP
USAGI...
SHAA

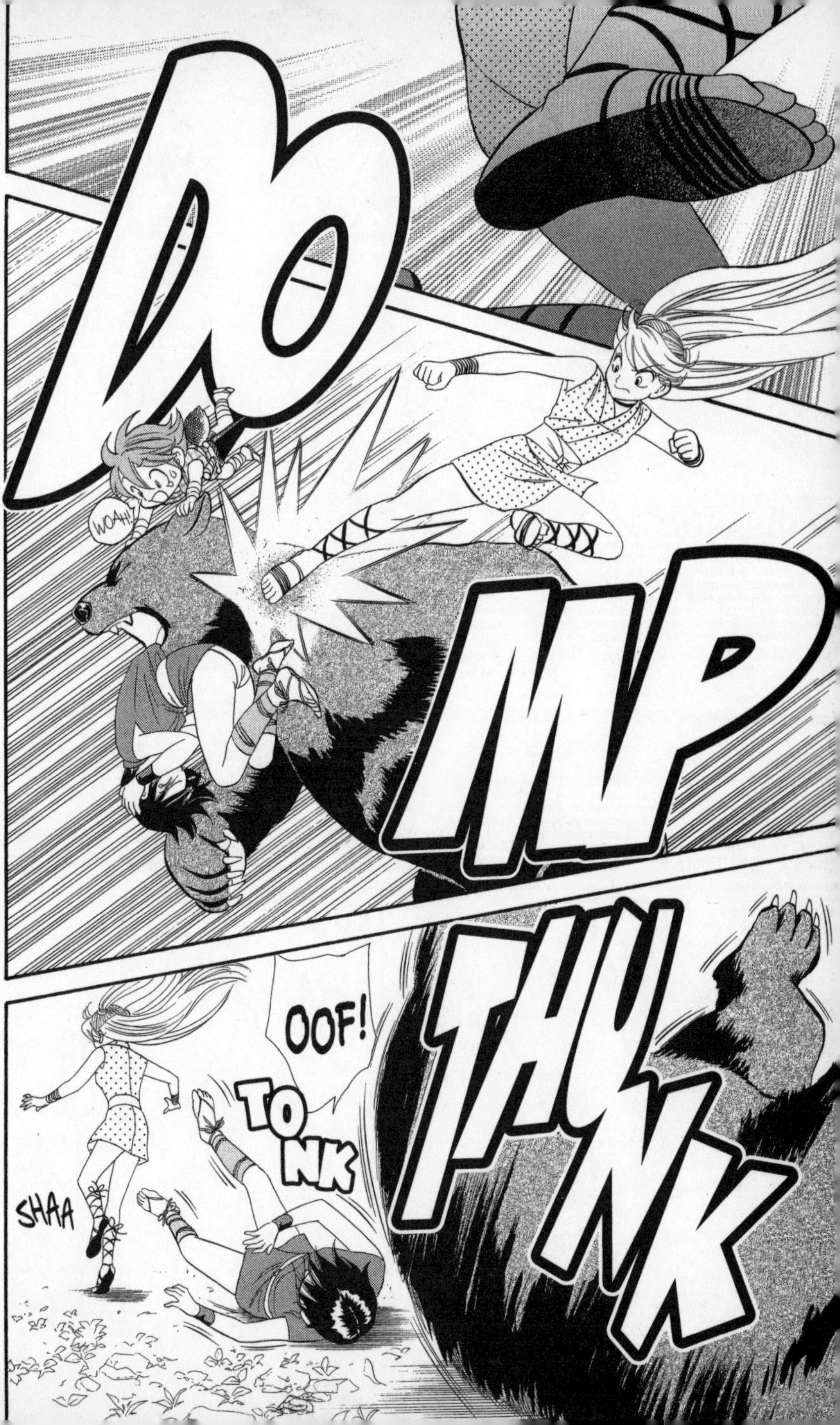
DO
MP
WOAH!!
THUNK
OOF!
TONK
SHAA

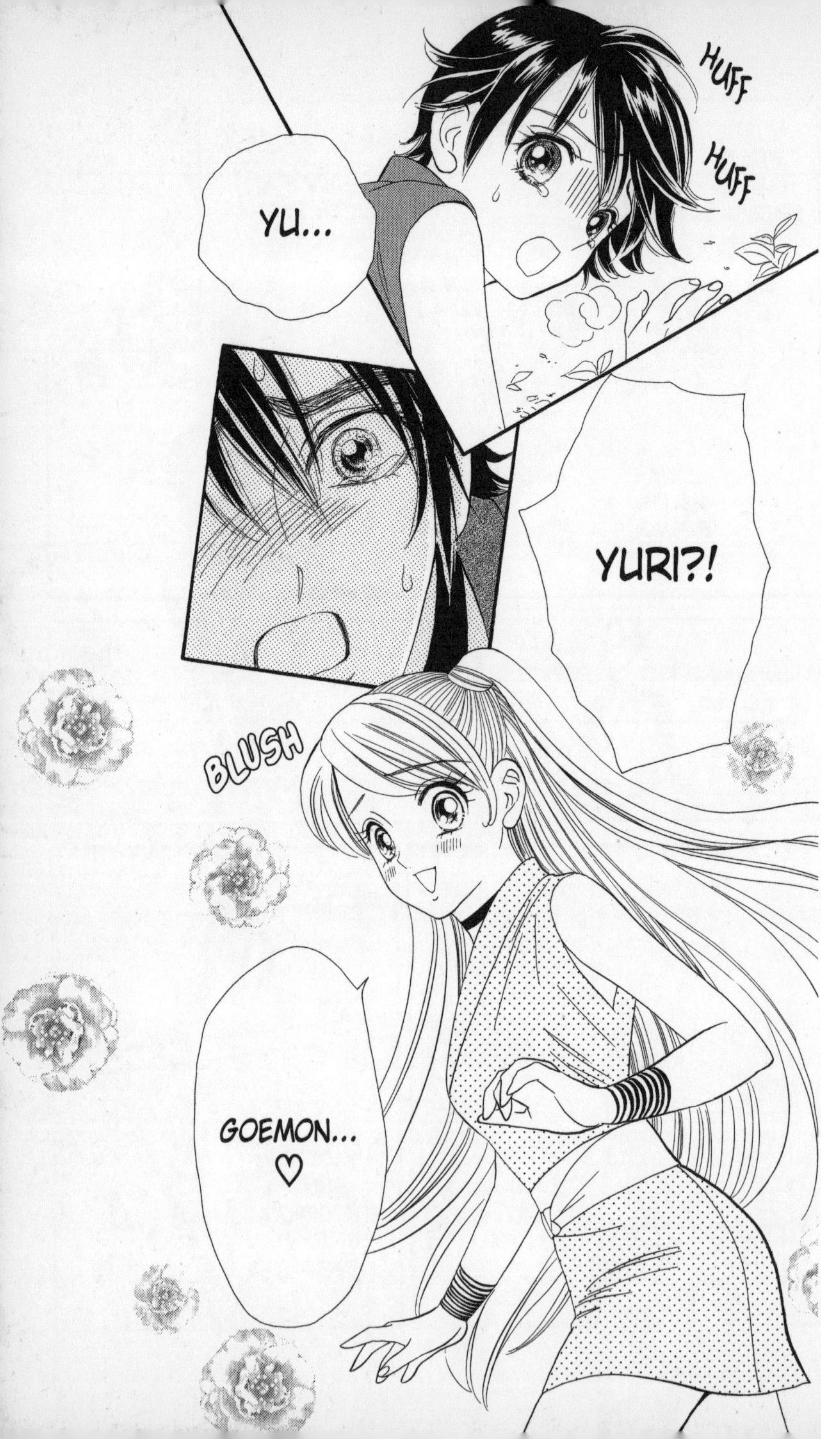
HUFF
HUFF
YU...
YURI?!
BLUSH
GOEMON... ♥

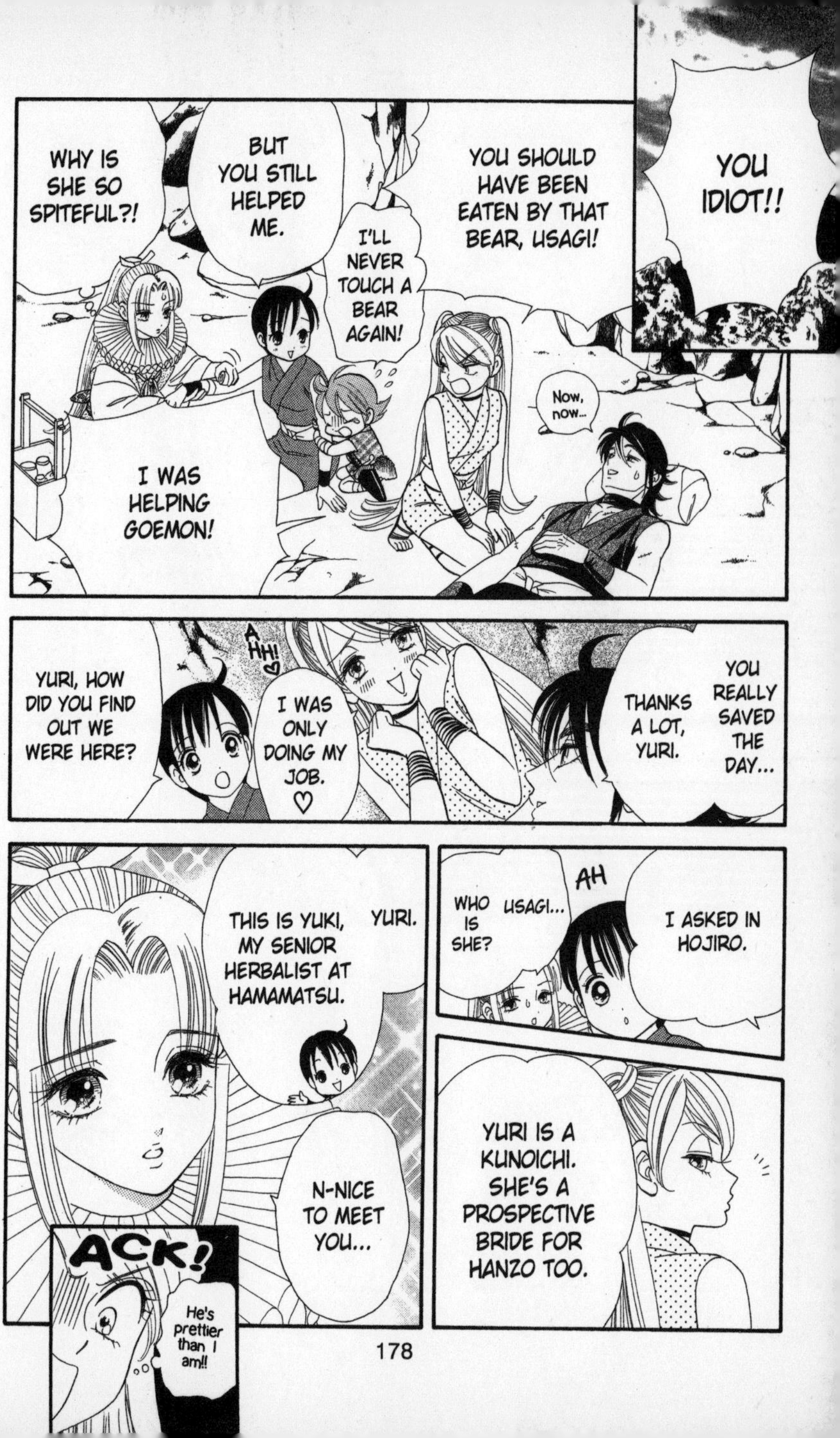
YOU IDIOT!!
YOU SHOULD HAVE BEEN EATEN BY THAT BEAR, USAGI!
Now, now...
I'LL NEVER TOUCH A BEAR AGAIN!
BUT YOU STILL HELPED ME.
WHY IS SHE SO SPITEFUL?!
I WAS HELPING GOEMON!
YOU REALLY SAVED THE DAY...
THANKS A LOT, YURI.
AHH! ♥
I WAS ONLY DOING MY JOB. ♡
YURI, HOW DID YOU FIND OUT WE WERE HERE?
I ASKED IN HOJIRO.
AH
USAGI...
WHO IS SHE?
YURI IS A KUNOICHI. SHE'S A PROSPECTIVE BRIDE FOR HANZO TOO.
YURI.
THIS IS YUKI, MY SENIOR HERBALIST AT HAMAMATSU.
N-NICE TO MEET YOU...
ACK!
He's prettier than I am!!

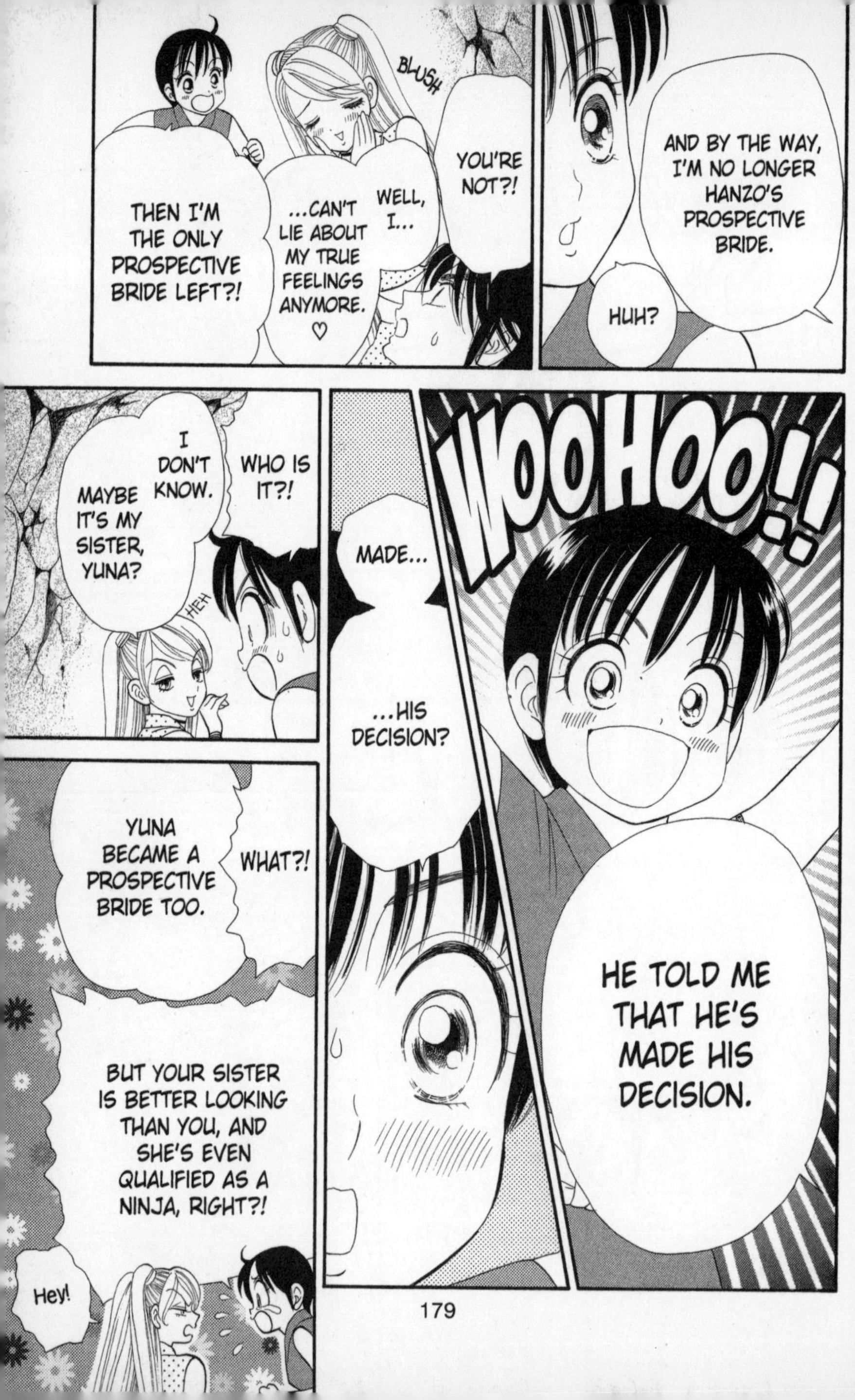
AND BY THE WAY, I'M NO LONGER HANZO'S PROSPECTIVE BRIDE.
HUH?
BLUSH
YOU'RE NOT?!
WELL, I...
...CAN'T LIE ABOUT MY TRUE FEELINGS ANYMORE. ♡
THEN I'M THE ONLY PROSPECTIVE BRIDE LEFT?!
WOOHOO!!
HE TOLD ME THAT HE'S MADE HIS DECISION.
MADE...
...HIS DECISION?
WHO IS IT?!
I DON'T KNOW.
MAYBE IT'S MY SISTER, YUNA?
HEH
WHAT?!
YUNA BECAME A PROSPECTIVE BRIDE TOO.
BUT YOUR SISTER IS BETTER LOOKING THAN YOU, AND SHE'S EVEN QUALIFIED AS A NINJA, RIGHT?!
Hey!

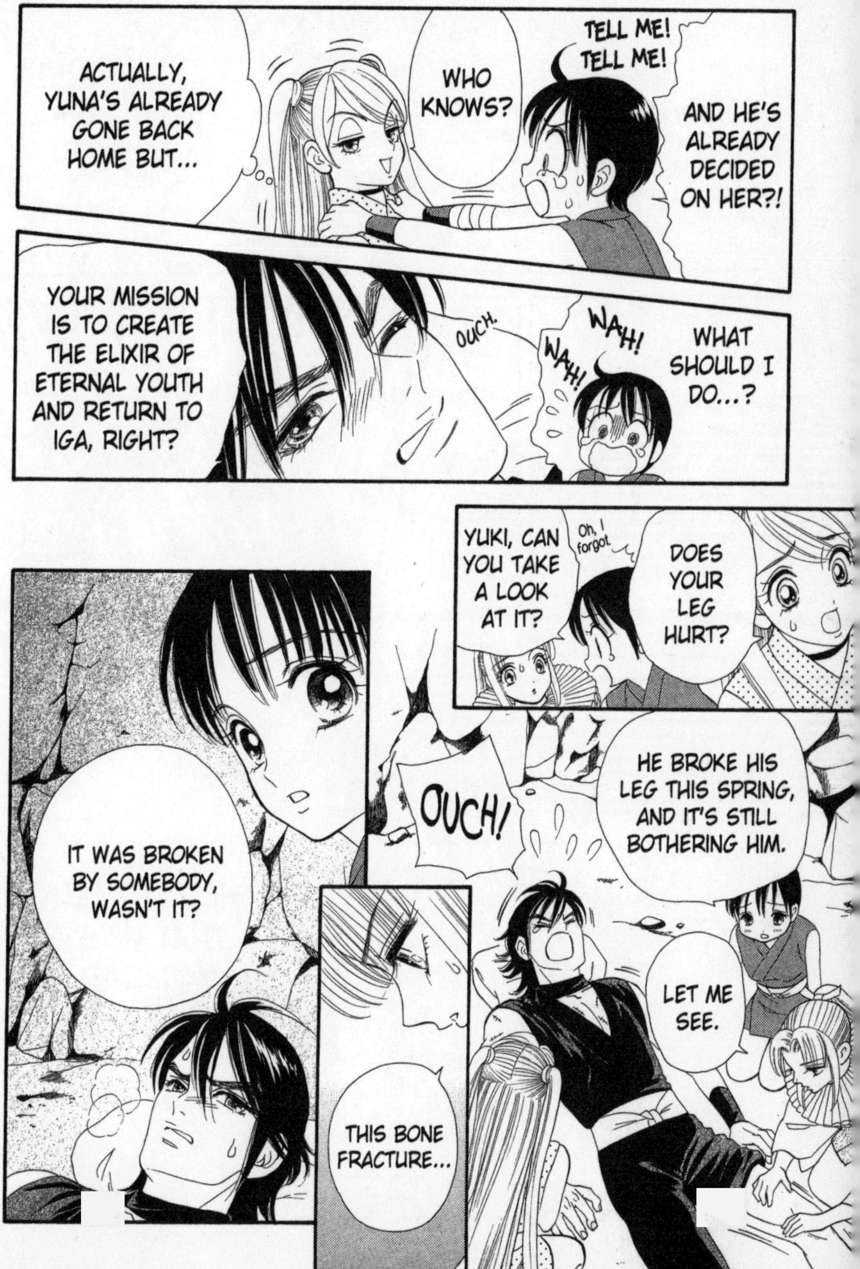
AND HE'S ALREADY DECIDED ON HER?!
TELL ME! TELL ME!
WHO KNOWS?
ACTUALLY, YUNA'S ALREADY GONE BACK HOME BUT...
WHAT SHOULD I DO...?
WAH! WAH!
OUCH.
YOUR MISSION IS TO CREATE THE ELIXIR OF ETERNAL YOUTH AND RETURN TO IGA, RIGHT?
DOES YOUR LEG HURT?
Oh, I forgot.
YUKI, CAN YOU TAKE A LOOK AT IT?
HE BROKE HIS LEG THIS SPRING, AND IT'S STILL BOTHERING HIM.
OUCH!
LET ME SEE.
THIS BONE FRACTURE...
IT WAS BROKEN BY SOMEBODY, WASN'T IT?

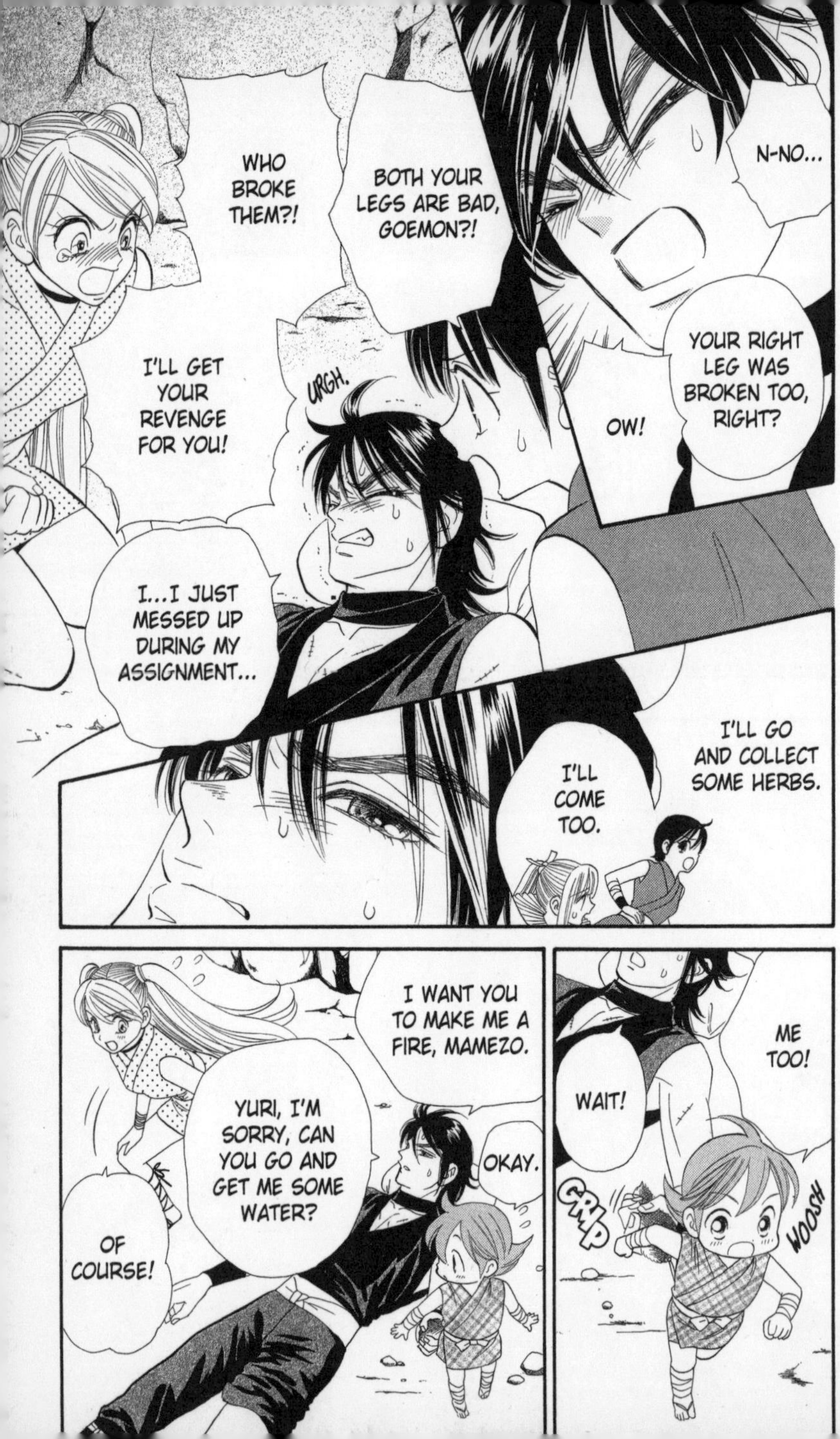
N-NO...
YOUR RIGHT LEG WAS BROKEN TOO, RIGHT?
OW!
BOTH YOUR LEGS ARE BAD, GOEMON?!
WHO BROKE THEM?!
URGH.
I'LL GET YOUR REVENGE FOR YOU!
I...I JUST MESSED UP DURING MY ASSIGNMENT...
I'LL GO AND COLLECT SOME HERBS.
I'LL COME TOO.
ME TOO!
WAIT!
WOOSH
GRAP
I WANT YOU TO MAKE ME A FIRE, MAMEZO.
OKAY.
YURI, I'M SORRY, CAN YOU GO AND GET ME SOME WATER?
OF COURSE!

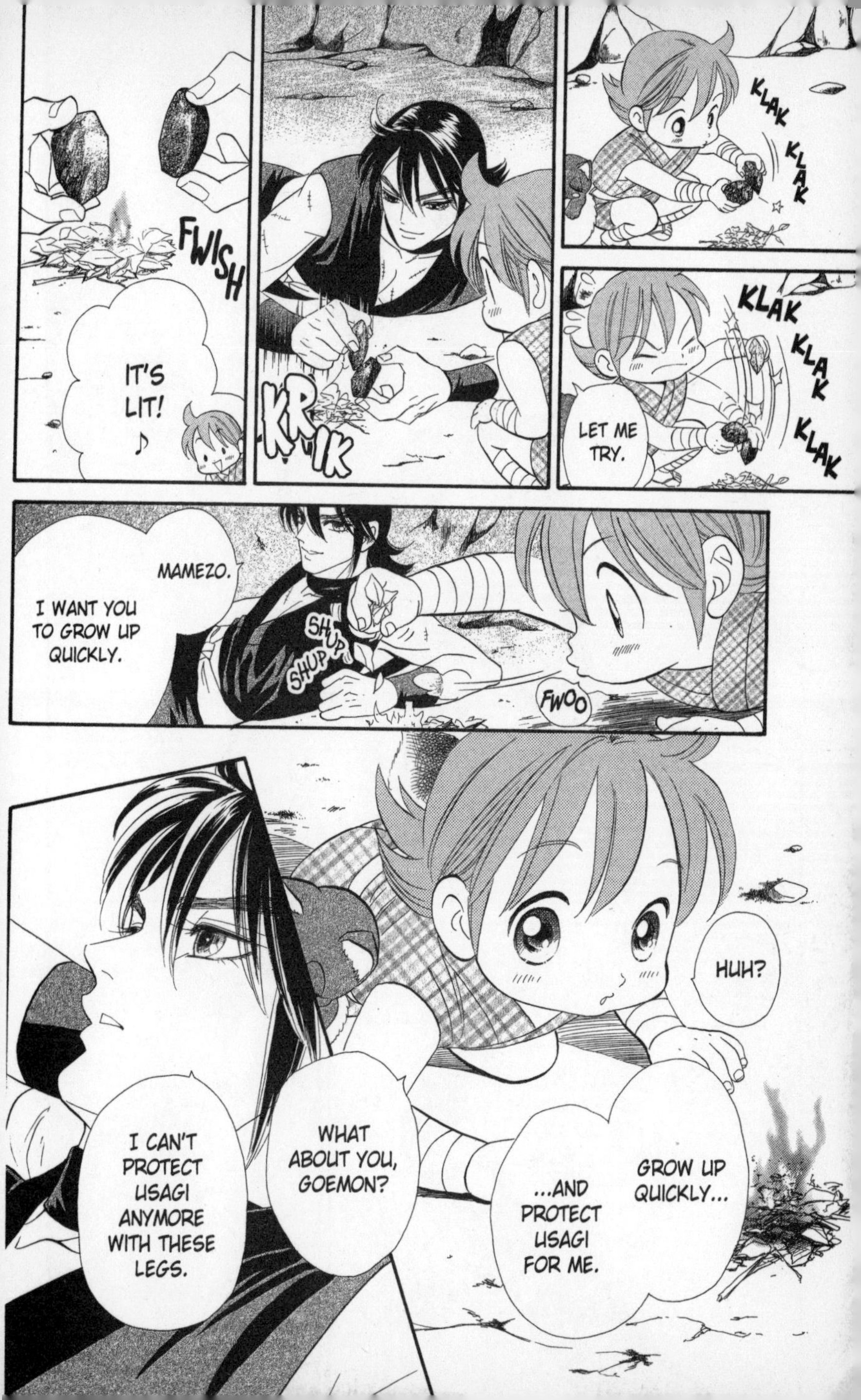
KLAK KLAK KLAK
KLAK KLAK KLAK
LET ME TRY.
KRIK
FWISH
IT'S LIT! ♪
FWOO
MAMEZO.
I WANT YOU TO GROW UP QUICKLY.
SHUP SHUP
HUH?
GROW UP QUICKLY...
...AND PROTECT USAGI FOR ME.
WHAT ABOUT YOU, GOEMON?
I CAN'T PROTECT USAGI ANYMORE WITH THESE LEGS.

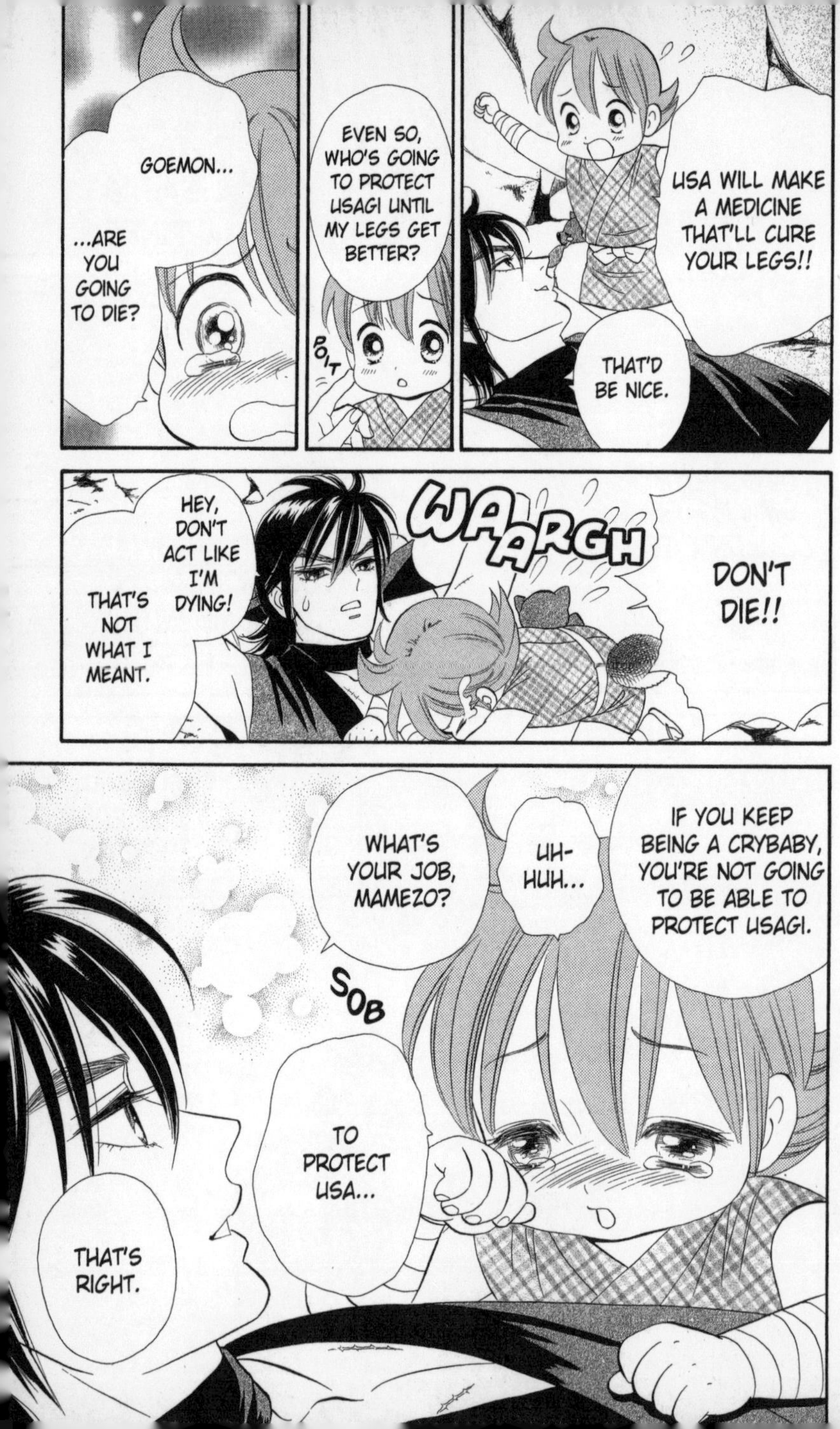
USA WILL MAKE A MEDICINE THAT'LL CURE YOUR LEGS!!
THAT'D BE NICE.
EVEN SO, WHO'S GOING TO PROTECT USAGI UNTIL MY LEGS GET BETTER?
POIT
GOEMON...
...ARE YOU GOING TO DIE?
DON'T DIE!!
WAARGH
HEY, DON'T ACT LIKE I'M DYING!
THAT'S NOT WHAT I MEANT.
IF YOU KEEP BEING A CRYBABY, YOU'RE NOT GOING TO BE ABLE TO PROTECT USAGI.
UH-HUH...
WHAT'S YOUR JOB, MAMEZO?
SOB
TO PROTECT USA...
THAT'S RIGHT.

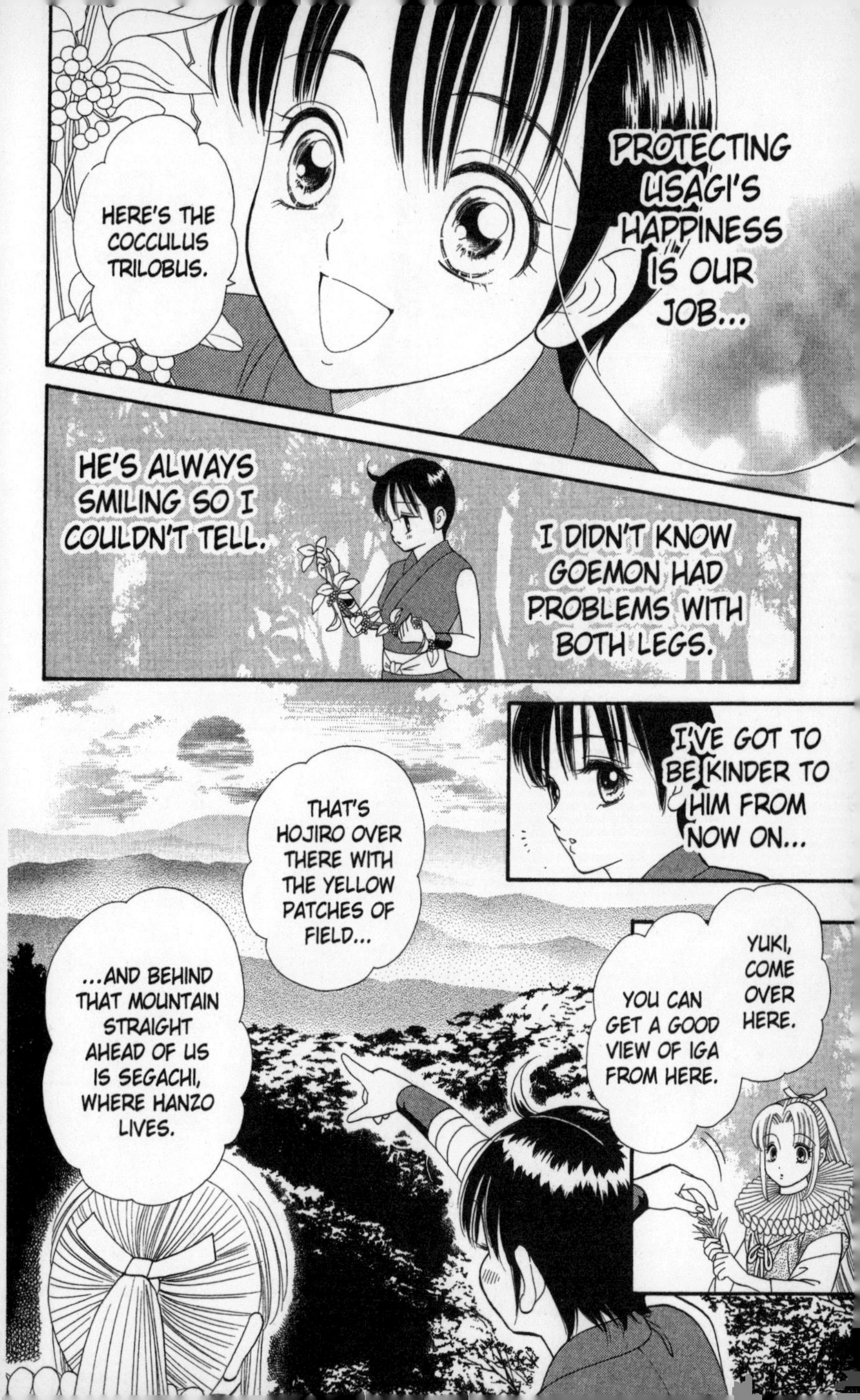
PROTECTING USAGI'S HAPPINESS IS OUR JOB...
HERE'S THE COCCULUS TRILOBUS.
I DIDN'T KNOW GOEMON HAD PROBLEMS WITH BOTH LEGS.
HE'S ALWAYS SMILING SO I COULDN'T TELL.
I'VE GOT TO BE KINDER TO HIM FROM NOW ON...
YUKI, COME OVER HERE.
YOU CAN GET A GOOD VIEW OF IGA FROM HERE.
THAT'S HOJIRO OVER THERE WITH THE YELLOW PATCHES OF FIELD...
...AND BEHIND THAT MOUNTAIN STRAIGHT AHEAD OF US IS SEGACHI, WHERE HANZO LIVES.

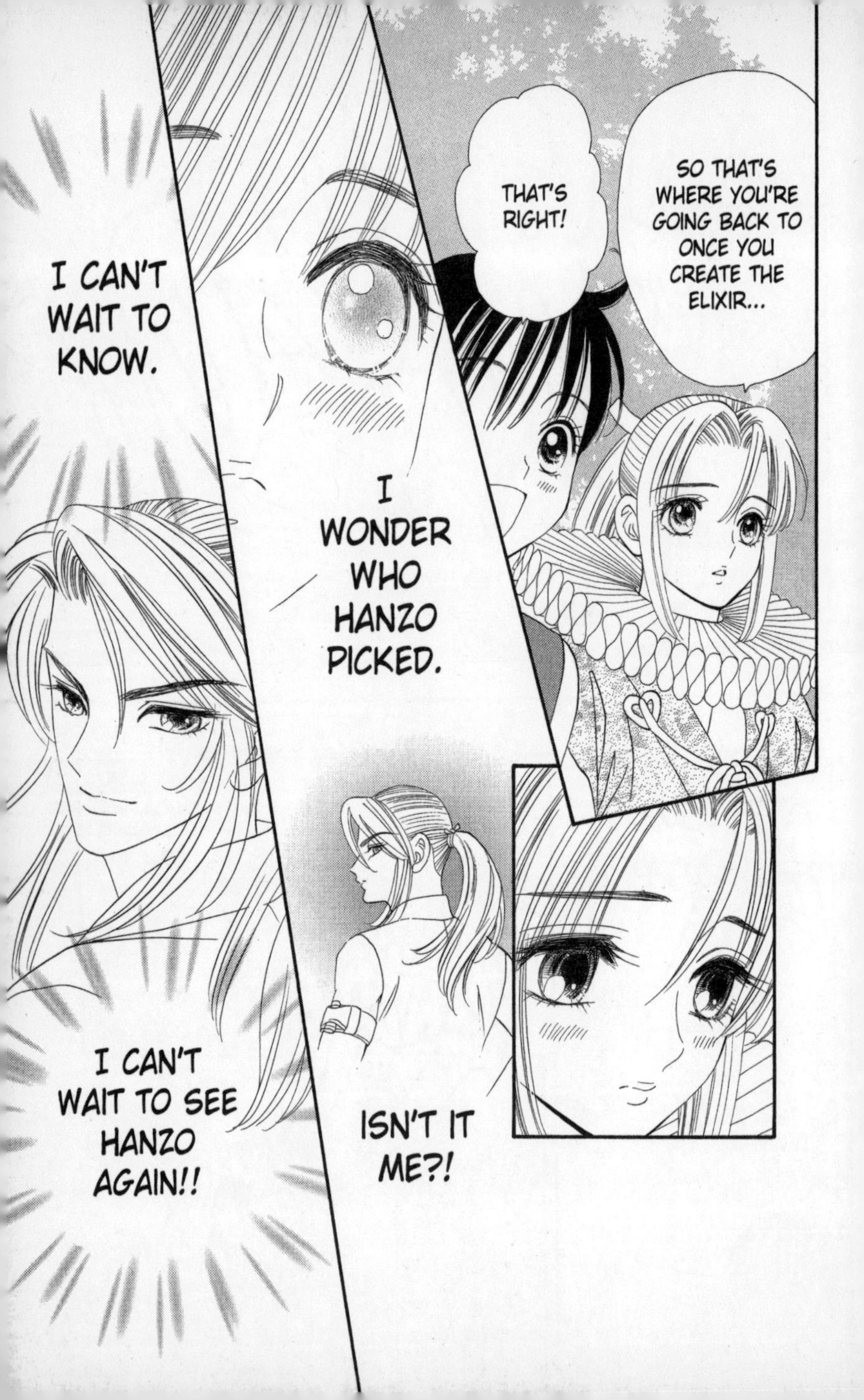
SO THAT'S WHERE YOU'RE GOING BACK TO ONCE YOU CREATE THE ELIXIR...
THAT'S RIGHT!
I WONDER WHO HANZO PICKED.
ISN'T IT ME?!
I CAN'T WAIT TO KNOW.
I CAN'T WAIT TO SEE HANZO AGAIN!!

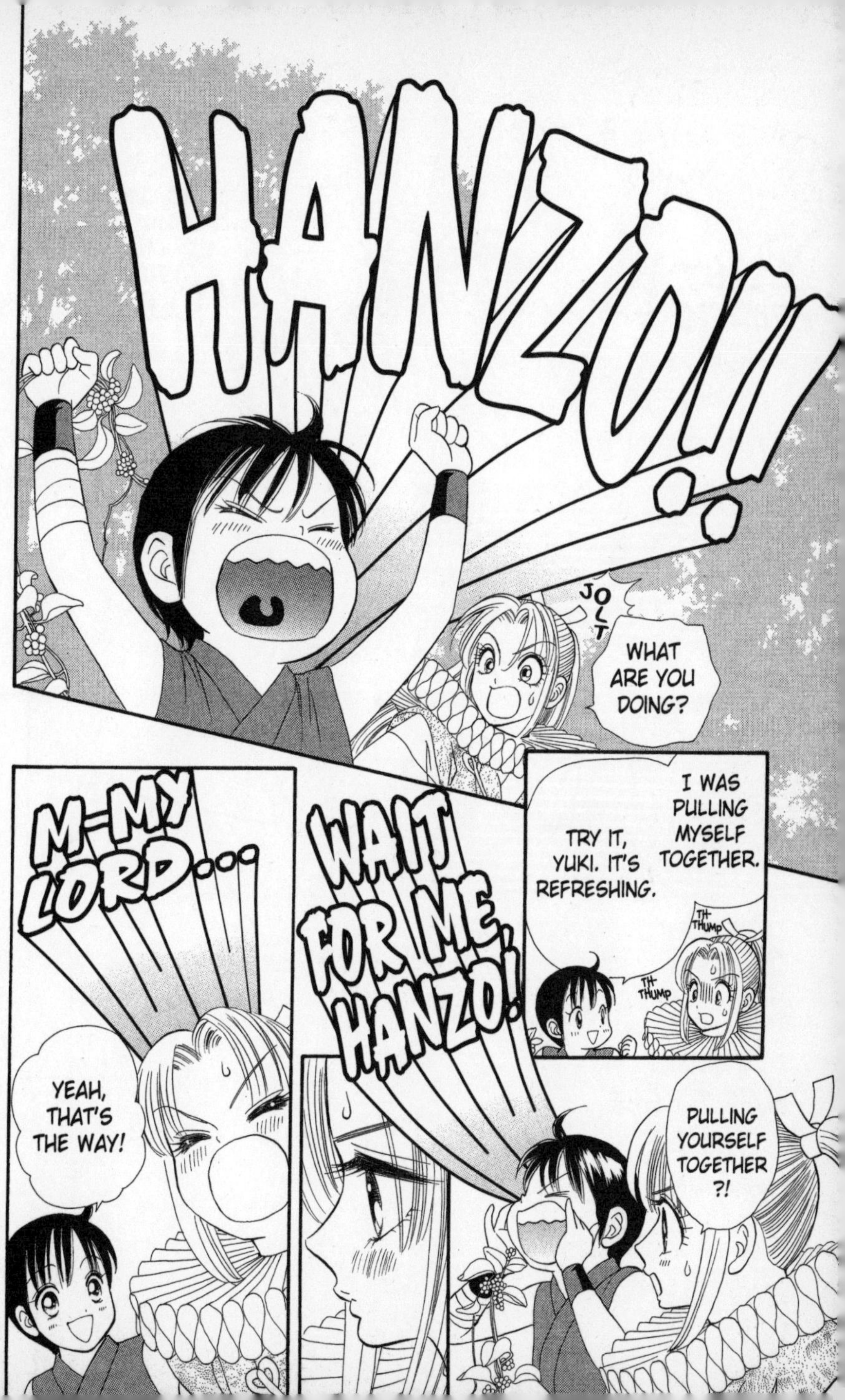
HANZO!!!
JOLT
WHAT ARE YOU DOING?
I WAS PULLING MYSELF TOGETHER.
TRY IT, YUKI. IT'S REFRESHING.
TH-THUMP
TH-THUMP
PULLING YOURSELF TOGETHER?!
WAIT FOR ME, HANZO!
M-MY LORD...
YEAH, THAT'S THE WAY!

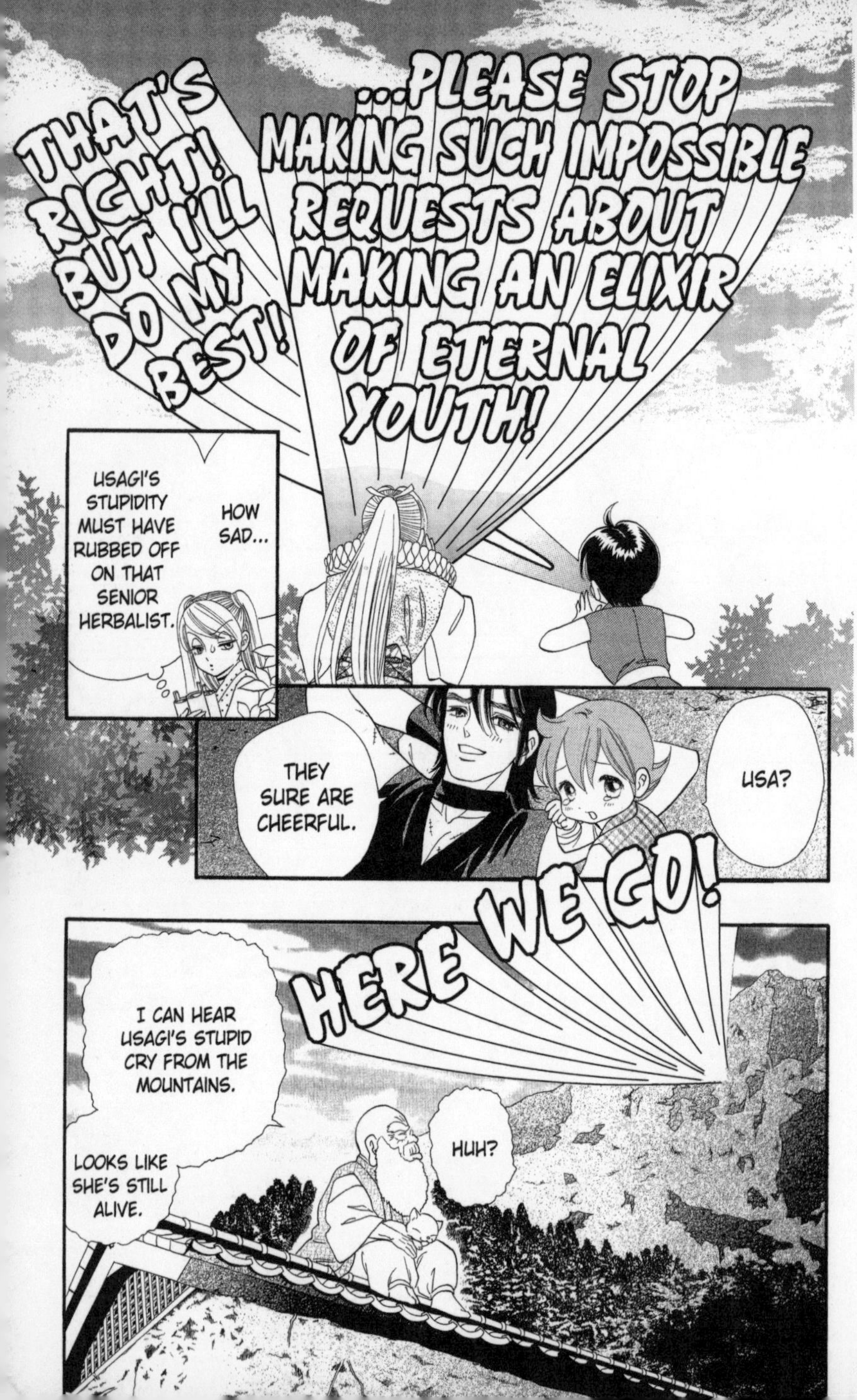
...PLEASE STOP MAKING SUCH IMPOSSIBLE REQUESTS ABOUT MAKING AN ELIXIR OF ETERNAL YOUTH!
THAT'S RIGHT! BUT I'LL DO MY BEST!
HOW SAD...
USAGI'S STUPIDITY MUST HAVE RUBBED OFF ON THAT SENIOR HERBALIST.
USA?
THEY SURE ARE CHEERFUL.
HERE WE GO!
I CAN HEAR USAGI'S STUPID CRY FROM THE MOUNTAINS.
HUH?
LOOKS LIKE SHE'S STILL ALIVE.

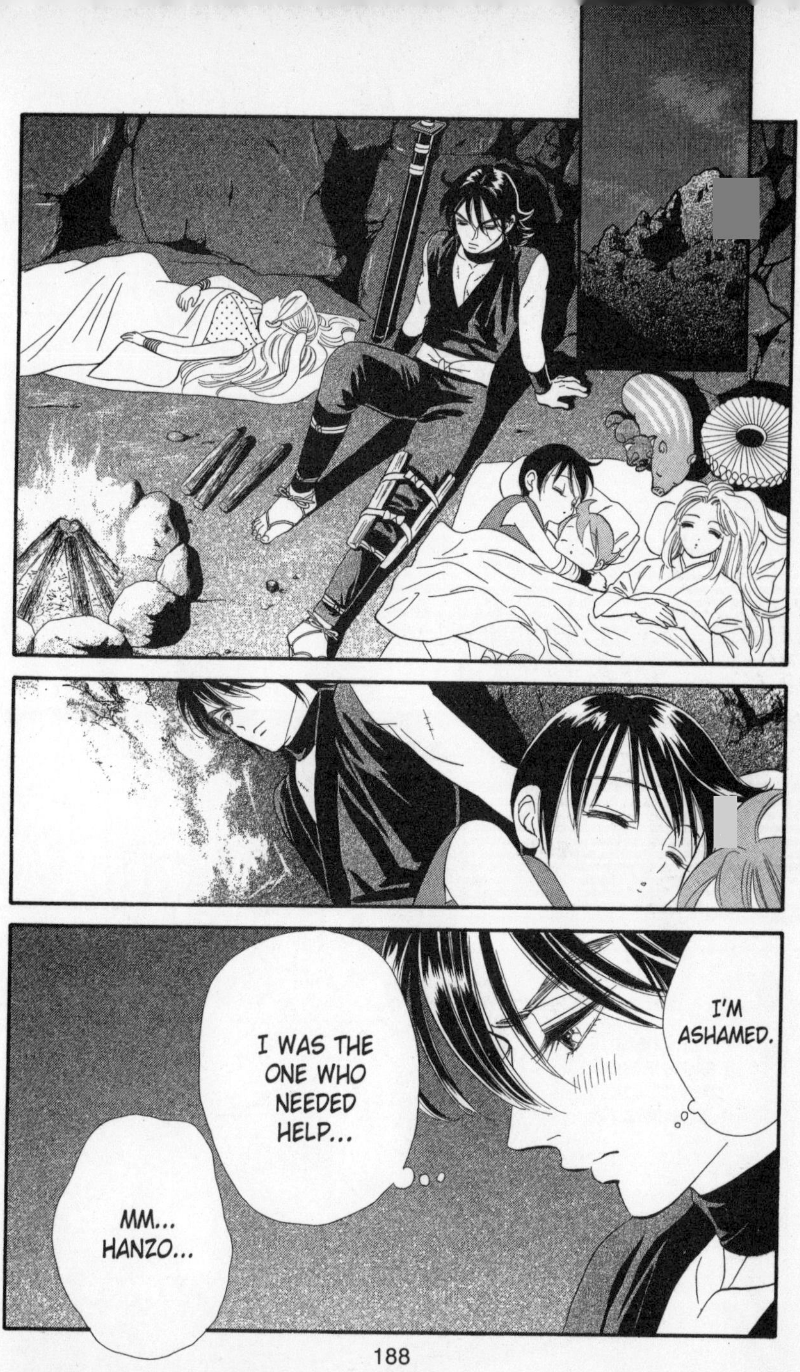
I'M ASHAMED.
I WAS THE ONE WHO NEEDED HELP...
MM... HANZO...

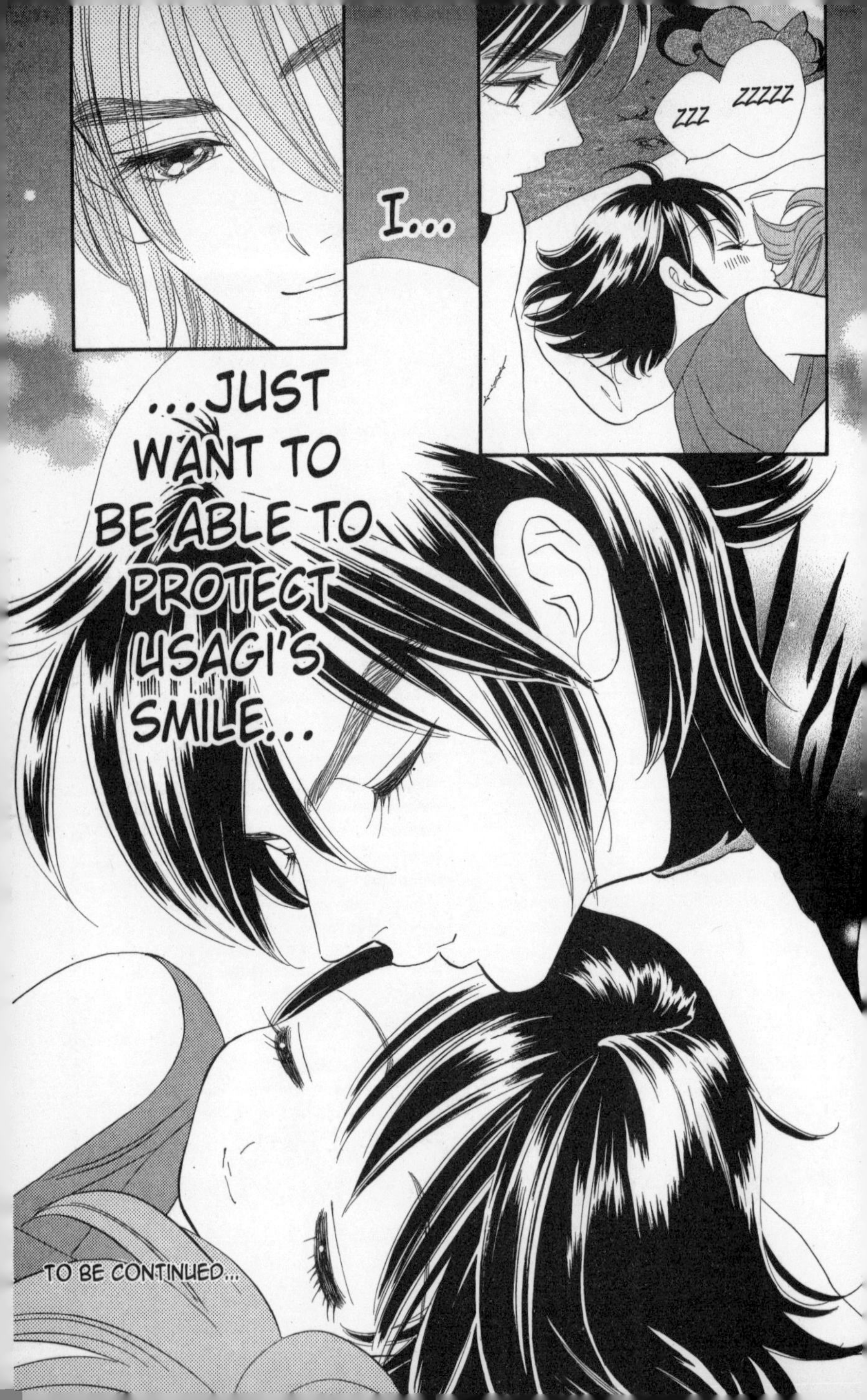
ZZZZZ
ZZZ
I...
...JUST WANT TO BE ABLE TO PROTECT USAGI'S SMILE...
TO BE CONTINUED...

The ways of the ninja are mysterious indeed, so here is a glossary of terms to help you navigate the intricacies of their world.

Page 2: **Shimo no Hanzo**
Shimo no means "the Lower," and in this case refers to Hanzo's geographic location rather than social status.

Page 2: **Iga**
Iga is a region on the island of Kyushu, and also the name of the famous ninja clan that originated there. Another area famous for its ninja is Koga, in the Shiga prefecture on Honshu. Many books claim that these two ninja clans were mortal enemies, but in reality inter-ninja relations were not as bad as stories paint them.

Page 2: **Kami no Hanzou**
The term *kami no* means "the Upper," and can refer to social status. However, since Hanzou is a member of a branch family, it is very unlikely that his status is higher than that of the head of the entire clan, Hanzo. The term *kami no* can also refer to geographic location in relation to an important city center, such as the capital. Hanzou is from Okazaki, which is closer to Edo than Hanzo's home in Segachi.

Page 3: **Kuwabara**
"Kuwabara kuwabara" is a phrase used nowadays by old people whenever something fearful or scary happens.

Page 7, panel 3: **Big earlobes**
There is a Japanese saying in which people with large earlobes are likely to get rich. This is because Fuku no Kami, the god of good luck and fortune, is depicted with large earlobes.

Page 11, panel 9: **Mokume Obake**
Mokume Obake is a name given to ghosts that rise up from wooden ceilings. When looking at the wood grain in darkness, faces may look like they are appearing from the wood. *Mokume Obake* literally means "Wood Grain Ghost."

Page 19, panel 2: **Irori**
An *irori* is a traditional Japanese fireplace inside the house.

Page 38, panel 7: **I...Ro...Ha...**
These are the first 3 syllables of the *Iroha-uta*, a song/poem that is written by using every hiragana character only once. It was often used in the old days to teach Japanese hiragana to children.

Page 39, panel 1: **Ninja dog**
A "ninja dog," or *ninken*, is a dog specially trained to help ninja.

Page 45, sidebar: **Iga-ryu**
Iga-ryu means "in the style of Iga."

Page 73, panel 4: A ninja's secret outing
The original Japanese text is a pun: *shinobi no oshinobi. Shinobi* is another way to say "ninja," and *oshinobi* is a word used to describe a "secret outing" of someone of high status.

Page 121, sidebar: Sasuke or Azumi
Sasuke and *Azumi* are manga series about ninja.

Page 129, panel 1: Fairy
This is a *zashiki-warashi*, or a Japanese fairy that brings good fortune to the family of the house where it is living.

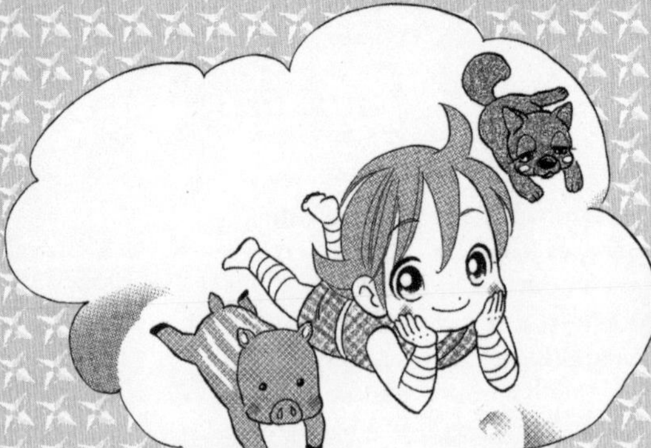

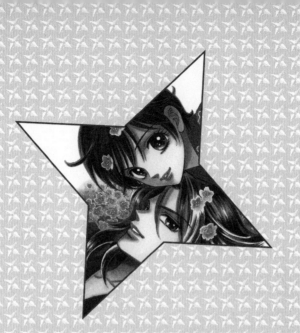

I have written up to volume 3, and the personality of each character has begun to stand out much more now. This is especially true of Hanzo, whom I never expected to change so much when I started this series. This must be the so-called "character development." I'm sure that these characters will keep growing and developing, so I will be very glad if you would all keep a close watch on them.

–Rinko Ueda

Rinko Ueda is from Nara prefecture. She enjoys listening to the radio, drama CDs, and Rakugo comedy performances. Her works include *Ryo*, a series based on the legend of Gojo Bridge, *Home*, a story about love crossing national boundaries, and *Tail of the Moon (Tsuki no Shippo)*, a romantic ninja comedy.

TAIL OF THE MOON

Vol. 3

The Shojo Beat Manga Edition

STORY & ART BY

RINKO UEDA

Translation & Adaptation/Tetsuichiro Miyaki
Touch-up Art & Lettering/Mark McMurray
Design/Izumi Hirayama
Editor/Nancy Thistlethwaite

Managing Editor/Megan Bates
Editorial Director/Elizabeth Kawasaki
VP & Editor in Chief/ Yumi Hoashi
Sr. Director of Acquisitions/Rika Inouye
Sr. VP of Marketing/Liza Coppola
Exec. VP of Sales & Marketing/John Easum
Publisher/Hyoe Narita

Printed in Canada

Published by VIZ Media, LLC
P.O. Box 77064
San Francisco, CA 94107

Shojo Beat Manga Edition
10 9 8 7 6 5 4 3 2 1
First printing, February 2007

store.viz.com

PARENTAL ADVISORY

TAIL OF THE MOON is rated T+ for Older Teen and is recommended for ages 16 and up. This volume contains brief nudity and ninja violence.

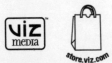

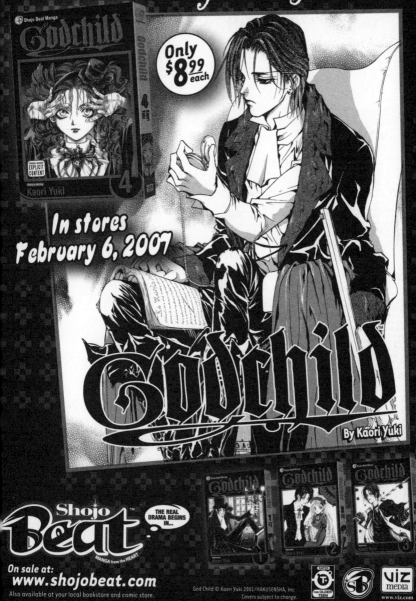

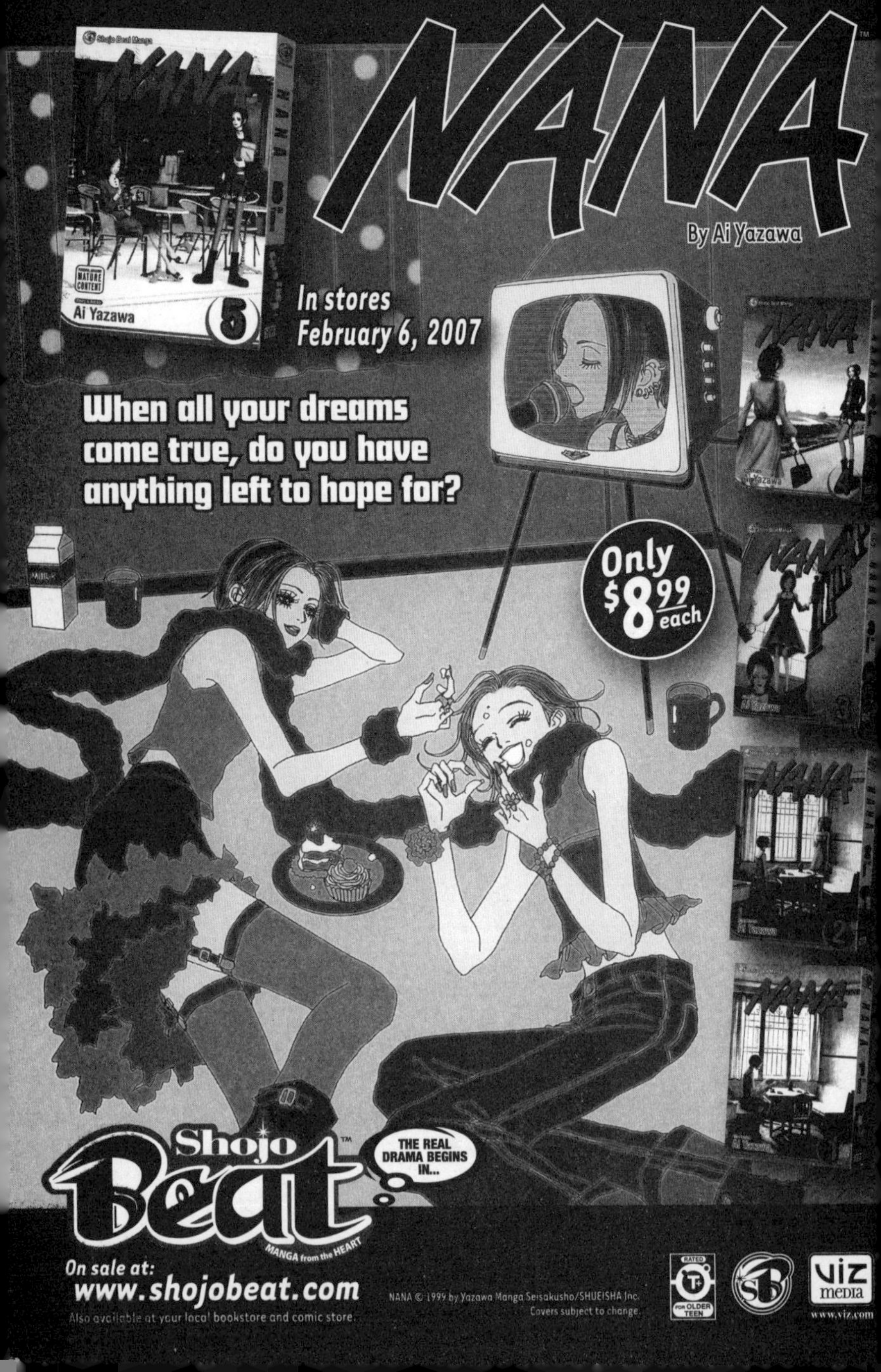
NANA™
By Ai Yazawa
In stores
February 6, 2007
When all your dreams come true, do you have anything left to hope for?
Only $8.99 each
Shojo Beat™
MANGA from the HEART
THE REAL DRAMA BEGINS IN...
On sale at:
www.shojobeat.com
Also available at your local bookstore and comic store.
NANA © 1999 by Yazawa Manga Seisakusho/SHUEISHA Inc.
Covers subject to change.
RATED T+ FOR OLDER TEEN
VIZ media
www.viz.com

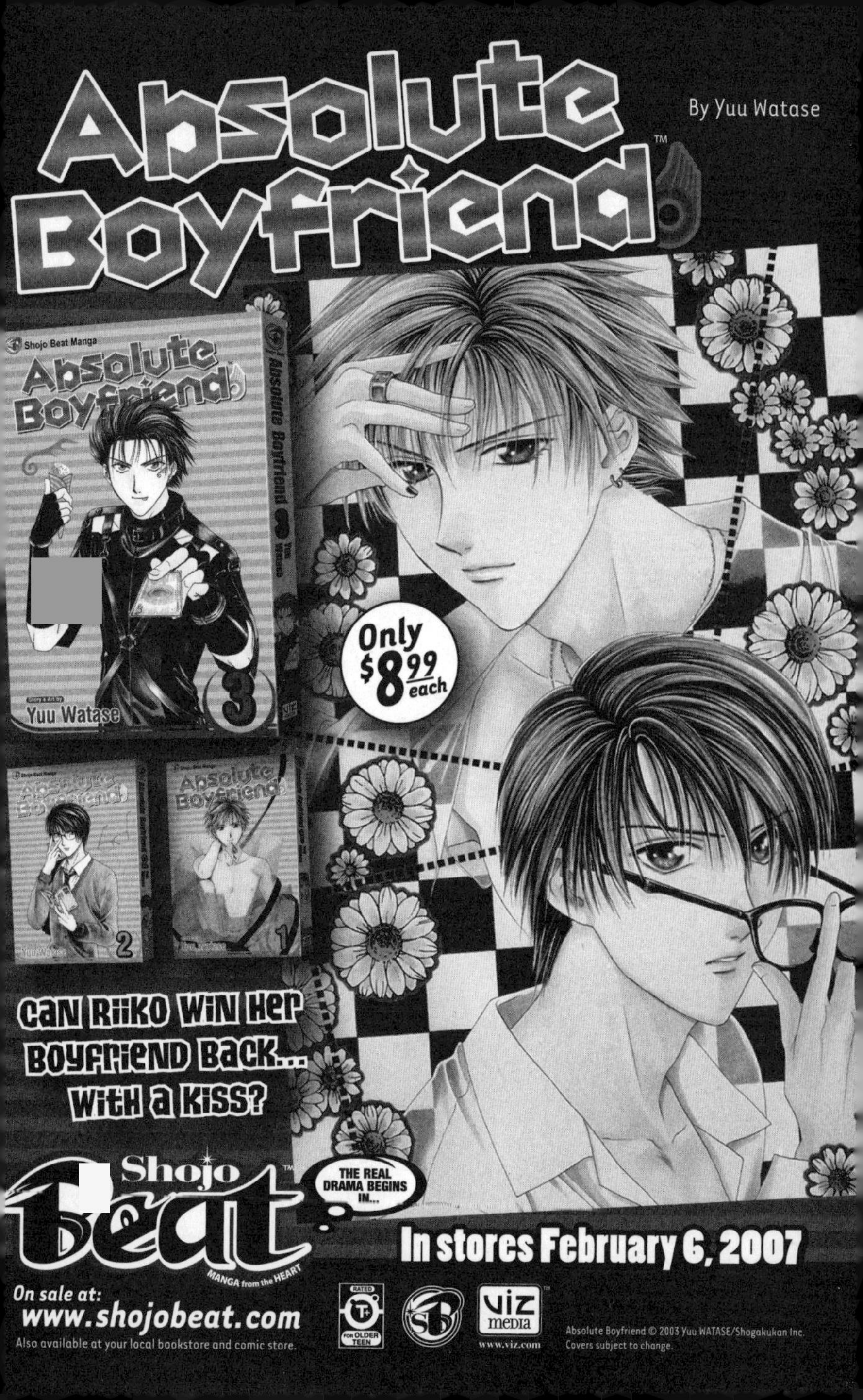
Absolute Boyfriend™
By Yuu Watase
Shojo Beat Manga
Absolute Boyfriend
Story & Art by
Yuu Watase
3
Absolute Boyfriend 2
Absolute Boyfriend 1
Only $8.99 each
Can Riiko win her boyfriend back... with a kiss?
Shojo Beat™
THE REAL DRAMA BEGINS IN...
MANGA from the HEART
In stores February 6, 2007
On sale at:
www.shojobeat.com
Also available at your local bookstore and comic store.
RATED T+ FOR OLDER TEEN
viz media
www.viz.com
Absolute Boyfriend © 2003 Yuu WATASE/Shogakukan Inc.
Covers subject to change.

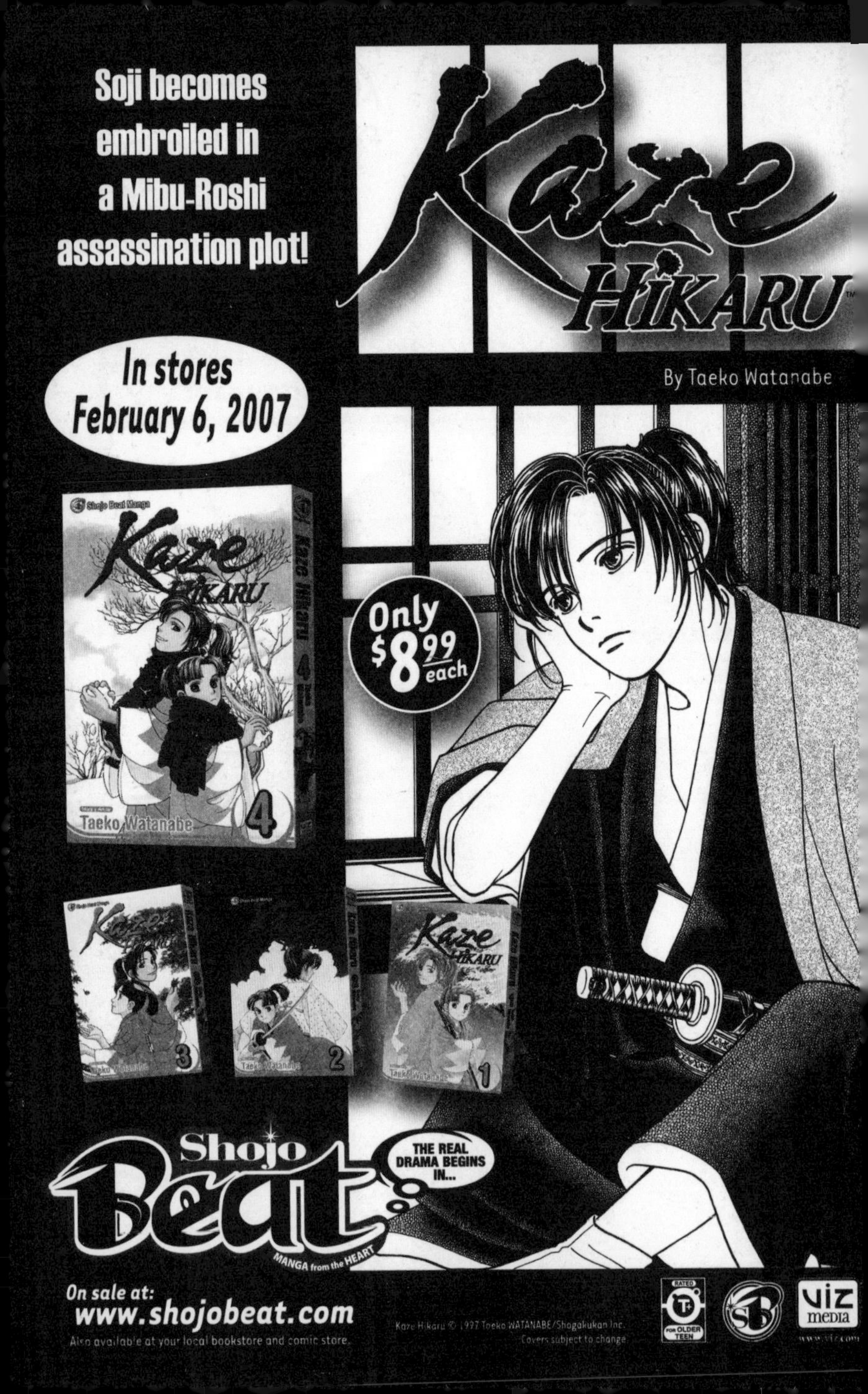
Soji becomes embroiled in a Mibu-Roshi assassination plot!
Kaze Hikaru™
By Taeko Watanabe
In stores February 6, 2007
Only $8.99 each
Shojo Beat
THE REAL DRAMA BEGINS IN...
MANGA from the HEART
On sale at:
www.shojobeat.com
Also available at your local bookstore and comic store.
Kaze Hikaru © 1997 Taeko WATANABE/Shogakukan Inc.
Covers subject to change.
RATED T+ FOR OLDER TEEN
viz media
www.viz.com

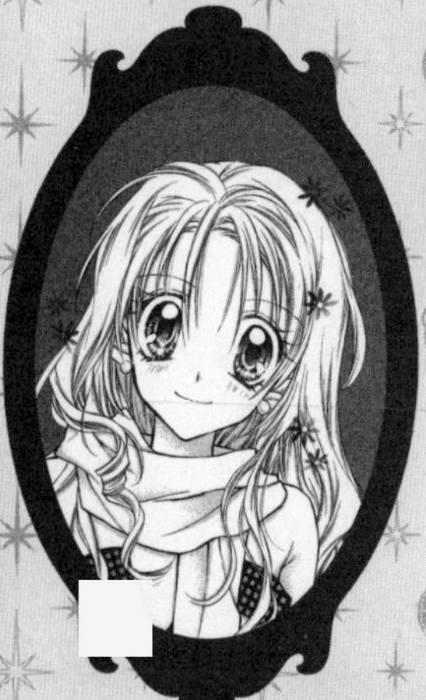

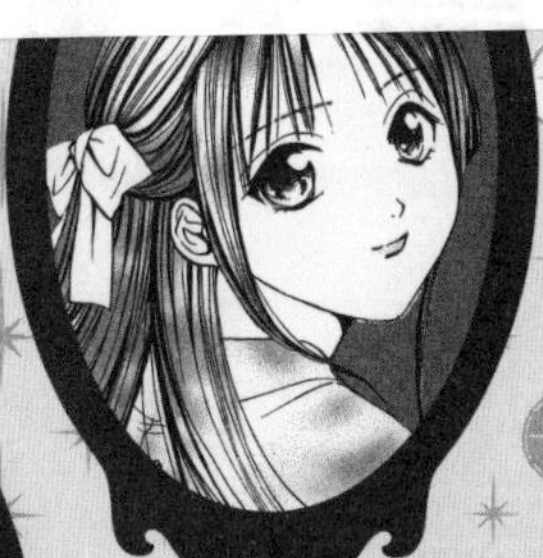

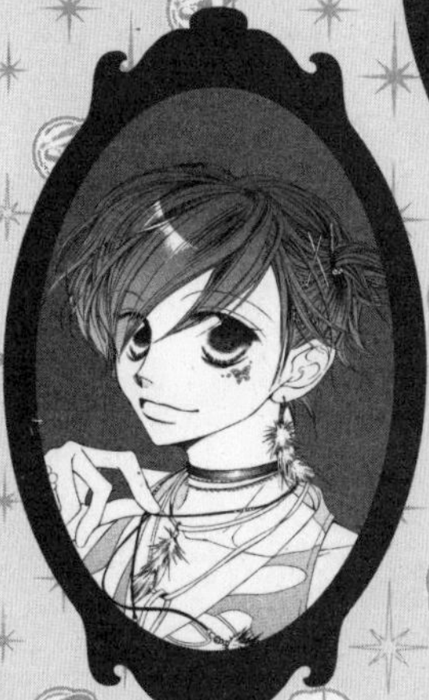